Gemma Hill was born in East Donegal. She was told that as a child, she never had her head out of a book. When the first of her three sons was seven, she returned to study at Ulster University and graduated with an honours degree in Social Sciences. Completing postgraduate study, she taught Psychology, Sociology and English at North West College Londonderry where she specialised in Adult Education and Special Needs. She lives in Strabane with her two Jack Russells and a Welsh Cocker Spaniel.

For my beloved husband, Fran, who believed in me.

Gemma Hill

THE TWINS' TWINS

*To Cousin Margret
Enjoy
Jill*

AUSTIN MACAULEY PUBLISHERS™
LONDON * CAMBRIDGE * NEW YORK * SHARJAH

Copyright © Gemma Hill 2023

The right of Gemma Hill to be identified as author of this work has been asserted by the author in accordance with sections 77 and 78 of the Copyright, Designs and Patents Act 1988.

All rights reserved. No part of this publication may be reproduced, stored in a retrieval system, or transmitted in any form or by any means, electronic, mechanical, photocopying, recording, or otherwise, without the prior permission of the publishers.

Any person who commits any unauthorised act in relation to this publication may be liable to criminal prosecution and civil claims for damages.

All of the events in this memoir are true to the best of author's memory. The views expressed in this memoir are solely those of the author.

A CIP catalogue record for this title is available from the British Library.

ISBN 9781398409767 (Paperback)
ISBN 9781398409774 (Hardback)
ISBN 9781398413511 (ePub e-book)

www.austinmacauley.com

First Published 2023
Austin Macauley Publishers Ltd®
1 Canada Square
Canary Wharf
London
E14 5AA

Simon Canning, who was my Sherpa when I climbed Muckish as part of the research for this book. And for Cathy, Evelyn and Big Tony who bore with me on the way down when my legs didn't want to go on. For The Scribblers Writing Group whose weekly short stories kept the writing juices flowing. But most of all for Austin Macauley Publishers who took a chance on my book in these uncertain times.

Table of Contents

Chapter One	13
Chapter Two	25
Chapter Three	34
Chapter Four	47
Chapter Five	54
Chapter Six	64
Chapter Seven	77
Chapter Eight	91
Chapter Nine	100
Chapter Ten	105
Chapter Eleven	113
Chapter Twelve	122
Chapter Thirteen	133
Chapter Fourteen	139
Chapter Fifteen	148
Chapter Sixteen	151
Chapter Seventeen	156
Chapter Eighteen	162
Chapter Nineteen	170
Chapter Twenty	175

Chapter Twenty-One	179
Chapter Twenty-Two	187
Chapter Twenty-Three	203
Chapter Twenty-Four	209
Chapter Twenty-Five	212
Chapter Twenty-Six	218
Chapter Twenty-Seven	224
Chapter Twenty-Eight	227
Chapter Twenty-Nine	231
Chapter Thirty	234
Chapter Thirty-One	241
Chapter Thirty-Two	247
Chapter Thirty-Three	250
Chapter Thirty-Four	256
Chapter Thirty-Five	261
Chapter Thirty-Six	271
Chapter Thirty-Seven	279
Chapter Thirty-Eight	285
Chapter Thirty-Nine	290
Chapter Forty	294
Chapter Forty-One	299
Chapter Forty-Two	305
Chapter Forty-Three	308
Chapter Forty-Four	310
Chapter Forty-Five	319
Chapter Forty-Six	326
Chapter Forty-Seven	332

Chapter Forty-Eight	338
Chapter Forty-Nine	348
Chapter Fifty	352
Chapter Fifty-One	356
Chapter Fifty-Two	364
Chapter Fifty-Three	368
Chapter Fifty-Four	372
Chapter Fifty-Five	377
Chapter Fifty-Six	382
Chapter Fifty-Seven	387
Chapter Fifty-Eight	392
Chapter Fifty-Nine	397
Chapter Sixty	401
Chapter Sixty-One	404
Chapter Sixty-Two	411
Chapter Sixty-Three	414
Chapter Sixty-Four	417
Chapter Sixty-Five	423
Chapter Sixty-Six	428
Chapter Sixty-Seven	434

Chapter One

Rayan's long fingers tensed on the computer keys as she caught Nathanial's familiar aroma of sand sea and aftershave. "What have you got there, babe?" Nathanial asked, leaning over her shoulder.

"Why are you *always* sneaking up behind me; checking out what I am doing?" she said, whirling around to face him.

"I wasn't sneaking up on you. You just didn't hear me come in."

The familiar feeling of insecurity made Rayan's voice strident. She'd never admit it but she *knew* that one night she'd get a call from Nat telling her he was leaving her for one of the beach babes he taught Pilates and Yoga to every day.

"You're late. And you're not wearing your thongs," she said caustically.

Nathanial looked down at his feet, bare and cool without his flip flops. His guts tightened. It was like walking on eggshells. He never knew if Rayan would be in a loving or a black mood when he got home. A word or a gesture could send her into a melancholy mood or a meltdown.

"Come here, babe," he said in a placating voice trying to gauge the level of her mood. "I didn't plan to be late. I stopped at the bottle-shop, like you asked. You OK?"

Rayan cast an irritated glance at the clock. "Bottle shop must have been busy."

"I had to make a stop at the vets on Market Place. That meant I hit the rush hour traffic on the Canning Highway. Sorry babe. I should have phoned," Nat said, working hard to keep his tone even.

Temporarily mollified, Rayan traced her finger over her name tattooed on his forearm. "How was work? You didn't check in midday."

"It was busy and hot—up in the 40s in the afternoon. I had a group of young women students from a theatre production dance team…" As soon as the words left his lips, Nathanial knew it had been a mistake to mention it. He waited, expecting the usual stinging remarks about the pleasures of his job.

Rayan refilled her wineglass. The image of well-toned long-limbed dancers' bodies, legs up to their armpits, arms stretched above their heads, every rib, every curve of their supple sensuous figures revealed to Nathanial, filled her mind.

She glanced at her own body. She'd never fit in with a group like that. And Nat knew it. Her lips curled. He was ribbing her; throwing their perfect bodies in her face.

She cast her eye over the beautiful limited-edition figurine of a dancing couple she had bought on impulse. *Stupid cow, you imagined it was you and Nathanial dancing, didn't you*, her inner voice sneered. A feeling of humiliation washed over making her hand shake. The wine sloshed in her glass. She had a strong desire to pick up the figurine and smash it over Nathanial's head.

"Why were you were at the vets?" she said, forcing her voice to come out normal. *No doubt something else for spoiled little Miss Biscuit*, she thought, scowling at the curly wheat-coloured teddy bear labradoodle Nat was cuddling.

"Some birdbrain tied a dog like Biscuit to a bench beside the beach and left it there to bake, poor little bugger. The vet said they get that all the time. Families get these 'designer' dogs and then abandon them when they grow out of their puppy cuteness," he said in disgust. "Just like they did with you," he murmured stroking the dog's ears.

Rayan turned away. "I hope you left it at the vets."

"I have it in the Ute," Nathanial admitted sheepishly.

Rayan spun around, almond eyes flashing. "You brought another dog home without *asking* me? Just like you did with her," she said pointing angrily at the small dog. "You can forget it. Cleaning up after one dog is enough—"

"I'll take it back tomorrow," Nat said resignedly. Breaking open the six-pack, he turned towards the lounge room switching on the television to the sports channel.

Rayan went back to the computer. "Some woman in Ireland is looking for a year house swap and a job as a beautician in Australia," she said over her shoulder.

Nat glanced across the open plan lounge to where Rayan sat in the dinette-kitchen. Her melancholy mood seemed to be lifting. "She must be mad or legging it from something," he joked. "Who would be crazy enough to want to live and work in a summer heat wave in Western Australia?"

Rayan hunched her shoulders. "I don't know. It might be nice to live someplace else for a change."

Nathanial savoured the cold beer and wondered if he dare raise the question of kiddies again. He drained his can. He'd wait until he'd showered and changed. By that time, Rayan might be in a less tetchy mood, he thought.

Infuriated Nat hadn't asked her to join him; Rayan listened to the sound of the water splashing into the shower tray. She closed her eyes and visualised it cascading over Nathanial's hard muscled tattooed torso and strong muscled legs. She sighed. There was a time when they'd showered together soaping each other into a frenzy of sex. "But all Nat can think about these days is making love when I'm ovulating, hoping I'll give him the kid he wants," she muttered. *Well, he can forget that idea. It's never going to happen*, she thought as Nathanial came back into the kitchen.

Standing in the middle of the dinette, water glistering off his bare chest, Nathanial smiled tentatively at Rayan. He wondered if he should mention the offer to work over east in Sydney. He'd wait until he decided if he was going to take it or not.

"You got news for me, babe?" he said. "You see the doc today?"

Rayan jerked upright. "I have a business to run. I don't have time to see doctors. Anyway, I know I'm not pregnant." She felt the black feeling of despair creep over her. Nat didn't seem to *understand* how important it was for her *not* to get pregnant. Tears gathered behind her eyelids. When she and Nathanial had gotten together six years ago, she had felt sure he was the One; the one that would *understand* that she *never ever* wanted to be a mother. "I've told you. I'm not getting pregnant."

Nathanial's disappointment was palpable. He was sure she'd get pregnant despite what she said. All was needed was a bit of covert planning on his part.

His toned upper body muscles rippled as he plucked a sleeveless vest from the stack of fresh laundry and worked it over his broad biceps. "You could at least go and see the doc…"

"What makes you think I'm pregnant?" Rayan said incredulously.

Nathanial shrugged. "I'm thirty-six. I want a kid, a son, before I'm too old. Is that so terrible?" He glanced surreptitiously at her. Now wasn't the time to mention she'd soon be menopausal and too old to give him a child.

Rayan's heart beat in trepidation against her ribs. What would make Nat think she might be pregnant this month? Quickly, she went into the laundry room where she'd hidden her birth control pills. "Nat is so obsessive about me getting pregnant I wouldn't trust him not to replace my birth control pills with something he bought in the health shop," she muttered. She gulped, relieved to find the blister package still intact.

Going back into the kitchen, she searched for a more secure hiding place. "Maybe I *should* go to the doctor and change to something more fool proof," she murmured. She could hear Nat opening and closing the drawers in the bedroom. "You going out again?" she asked suspiciously as he came back into the dinette.

Nat swallowed back his sharp retort. It was getting that he saw his mates less and less. "I thought I might see if some of the guys would take the little dog."

"Take it to the dog rescue place. They'll find it a home."

Nat shook his head. "They'll give it to some other family who'll only keep it for a short time—"

"I'll ask Sienna if she'd take it," Rayan offered.

Nat raised his eyebrows. "You mean, Sienna, your hairdresser assistant?"

Rayan nodded as she opened the fridge.

Nat snorted. "Sienna's an airhead. When is *she* going to have time for a dog? She works all day in the salon and parties at the weekend."

"You like her well enough when she's ogling you with her eighteen-year-old big baby eyes," Rayan snapped, slapping a chopping board onto the kitchen worktop as she began to tenderise steak with a mallet.

Taking a cold beer from the icebox, Nat trailed gloomily back into the lounge room. *It's useless arguing with her when she gets into one of her moods*, he thought, the familiar sense of unease starting to crawl about in his belly. He could hear cupboard doors being slammed and a chair hitting the kitchen floor. He turned up the sound on the television.

"Maybe you'd like to feed your steak dinner to that four-legged bitch in your Ute," Rayan's voice bawled. Nat felt himself tense. Rayan's mood wasn't lifting. She was spoiling for a fight. This was how it always started, he thought.

"My father was right. You're nothing but a beach bum looking for a good time with your beach babes. And drinking and womanising with your mates." Before Nat could answer, something hit him square on the back of his head.

"You'll not do it again," Rayan screeched manically, rushing into the lounge room.

"Do what?" Nat asked stunned.

"Sneak in on me, snooping on my private messaging on the Internet."

"Rayan, I wasn't snooping. I came in through the garage entrance to the kitchen. You didn't hear me because I was in my bare feet. Don't do this tonight again, please," Nat pleaded as she stood over him her face contorted. "You promised—"

"And I promised myself I would *never* have a baby but you don't listen, do you!" she screeched, hurling her wineglass at him.

Nathanial gasped as the heavy crystal hit the wall, showering him in shards of broken glass. Momentarily stunned by the pain in the back of his head and temporarily blinded by the red wine dripping in blobs down his face, Nat sat immobile in shocked disbelief.

Rayan had never physically struck him before. She lambasted him with her accusations, yelled and threw things at him, scratched and bit him but she'd never struck him with anything before.

Shocked to his core for a moment, the only thing he could see or hear was the sport's commentator's mouth moving and Rayan's raspy breathing as she lunged at him. Instinctively, his fingers reached for her black shoulder length hair. Grabbing her head, he forced her angular body to collapse on top of him.

"Let go of me," Rayan shrieked, trying to wrench his hands away from her scalp.

"Not until you calm down and stop beating on me," Nat panted.

Something caught him on the cheekbone, tearing the skin and sending a searing pain through his head. "Rayan, please stop," he pleaded. "This is madness." Ignoring his plea, Rayan raked her nails over his face and neck. Nathanial swore voraciously. Forcing her backwards, he thrust her down between the loose squishy cushions of the seating pinning her flailing arms to her side. Incensed, Rayan spat in his face.

Nathanial retched as the full force of her spittle caught him on the mouth. Enraged, he grabbed her by the throat and began to squeeze.

Without warning, the corner sofa units separated and they crashed backwards down the stone slab steps that separated the lounge room from the kitchen-dinette. With a sickening thud, Nathanial's head slammed off the high gloss Chinese tiles. The last thing he heard was Rayan screaming as he lost consciousness.

He came around to find her sobbing hysterically. "Look what you've made me do. It's your own fault. Creeping up on me; bringing that dog without asking me, coming home late…"

The room spun as he dragged himself to his feet. "Stay away from me, you fucking crazy bitch," he choked as Rayan made as if to help him. Holding his head, he staggered past her and into the lounge room.

"Nathanial! Look what you are doing!" Rayan gasped as blood dripped onto the oriental rugs.

"We can't have my blood on your precious things, can we," Nathanial said, his voice cracking. Staggering back to the kitchen, he leaned against the work island.

"I can't help it if I like beautiful things, can I," Rayan huffed, frantically mopping at the red stain spreading across the rug.

Nathanial felt a hysterical laugh rising in his throat. "You're something else. Do you know that, Rayan? You're a wildcat. Do you know that? You don't need nice things! You need to be fucking caged up in Perth Zoo," he moaned grabbing up a handful of kitchen towels to stem the blood that was dripping into his eyes and on to his sweatshirt.

"A troop of theatre dancers," Rayan mocked. "You think I don't know you flirt with those *babes*…swanning about in their little short shorts and leotards," she said scathingly.

Nathanial's face crumpled. "I don't flirt with the women who come to my classes. *They're my students*."

"Yeah, that's what you say. It never stopped my father," Rayan said. Her legs wobbled and she sank into the only chair in the lounge room standing upright. "It never stopped my father," she quivered.

After a while she rose, unlocked the screen door and stumbled out into the semi-dark patio. Her body shook involuntarily. Visions of the deathly pallor of Nathanial's face as he'd lay motionless, blood congealing on his temple rose before her. Her insides trembled like jelly. She had to stop whacking on Nathanial. Or one of these nights, she was going to do him serious injury…or kill him.

Overhead, the flashing light and the drone of the midnight plane from Perth to Sydney reminded her she had been looking at when Nathanial had sneaked up on her. She watched the fading lights of the plane and wondered again what it would be like to live someplace else—to have a different kind of lifestyle—to leave the person she was behind—take on a new identity. She gulped in self-pity. "I'll be forty soon and I have never been out of Australia, except to go to Bali in Indonesia with Nat—a busman's holiday for Australians," she muttered.

Coming back in, she watched as Nat searched amongst the trashed cushions for his keys. A heavy uneasy silence descended on the room.

"How am I going to show up for work tomorrow looking like this?" Nathanial finally choked out, jabbing his finger at his face.

Rayan looked dispassionately at him: His left eye was puffed up, the lid bleeding. Red welts ran like mangled railway tracks from his forehead to his chin. Blood seeped from a cut along his hairline.

"You force me to behave like I do. It's your own fault, Nat," she said unrepentant. "You should know not to say things…about the dancers. You're the one that is pressurising me into having a baby. We love each other. Why can't I be enough for you?"

Nathanial looked at her incredulously. "Call this love! I'll be lucky if I don't have concussion." Nat turned so she could see the lump ballooning behind his left ear where she'd hit him with the heavy dinner plate.

"What about me? I have to go to work too," Rayan retorted, her hands going to her head. She gasped as a clump of fine hair came away in her fist. Alarmed, she checked her reflection in the mirror. Under the bright kitchen lights, the skin of her scalp looked scalded and patchy as if she had alopecia. Her face collapsing, she whirled on Nathanial. "You worthless beach bum. You're no better than my father—a woman basher," she screamed, angry tears coursing down her cheeks. "You did that on purpose. You bastard! You know how delicate my hair is. How can I face my customers looking like this?"

Nathanial's eyes were riveted on the marks of his hands clearly visible around Rayan's throat. Fuck! He might have choked her to death. *If the corner sofa hadn't separated when it did, I might have kept on squeezing*; he thought his heart thudding in his chest. Next time he might not get the chance to stop—might not want to stop. The unbidden thought made him draw in his breath in shock. Shuddering, he turned away, feeling sick to his stomach.

It was over. He couldn't stay; couldn't trust not to choke her again when she attacked him. He'd pack a bag; come back for the dog later. He held out his hand. "Give me the keys to the condo. I'll sleep there tonight."

Rayan barely glanced at the holdall in Nathanial's hand. Where was he going to go? Both the house and the condo were hers. Her eyes travelled to his face. He'd threatened to leave many times. Something in the set of his stance told her this time was different.

"You've gone too far this time," Nat said as if to confirm what she was thinking.

"You'll sleep in the condo tonight; where will you sleep the nights after that? Will one of your beach *babes* or one of your *mates*—"

"I've been offered a short teaching contract at the Bondi Beach Summer School over east. I wasn't sure if I'd take it. But I can't take this anymore," Nat said his gaze sweeping the trashed room. "You need professional help."

Rayan recoiled. "*I need help!* It's you who needs the help. You need to believe me when I say I am never, ever, having a baby—yours or anybody else's."

His heart heavy, Nathanial clicked off the security alarm and moved to open the outer door.

Rayan pushed down the old feelings of abandonment that were never far away. "You're leaving? What about all your precious personalised bespoke gym stuff?" Rayan couldn't keep the sneer out of her voice.

"I'll be back for it as soon as I get a place to keep it."

He was really going, Rayan thought, swallowing past her feeling of panic. *I always knew he would leave. I won't beg him to stay*, she thought. She had been abandoned before. She could live on her own again, she told herself.

But no one loved her like Nathanial did. She knew that. She felt her resolve not to beg weaken. Trying not to look at him, she said in a small voice, "I promise it will never—"

"Don't say it!" Nat interjected. "It's what you always say. 'I'm not my father's daughter.' It's what you have been saying for years. You're sorry. You'll get help. You'll go to group therapy. It'll never happen again."

"I promise…"

Wearily, Nathanial's shoulders slumped, "If I stay, like all the other times, you'll get up tomorrow morning and act as if nothing happened. And you'll expect me to do the same." He wiped at his face. "It's over. The job over east will give us a breathing space…gets me away from that copper for a few months." He turned to face her. "The cops *believe* I'm a woman-basher. They pull me up for every stop sign. Every little thing they can think of. Some of these days, they'll get me for real. I need to get out of Perth."

"If you stay, I'll…admit it's me…"

"Who's going to believe you," Nat said a desolate note in his voice. "They look at you a member of the business community; the daughter of a 'respectable' family. And who am I? Perth's testosterone, steroid junkie beach bum! Who do you think they'll believe," he said, gathering up his bag. "I want a wife and kiddies," he said resignedly. "I was hoping you were going to tell me you were pregnant. We could have gone to Indonesia—had a Bali wedding in one of those temples you like so much—god knows I have asked you often enough."

Rayan gritted her teeth. Every year since they had been together, Nat had asked her to marry him. *He didn't get it*. She was *never* getting married. "If you loved me like you say you do, you wouldn't leave me." Rayan hated herself for resorting to what she thought of as a weak woman's emotional blackmail.

"Oh Rayan, what is there to love?" Nathanial said, wincing as he hoisted his bag on his shoulder. "A woman who lives her life by some bizarre promises she made when she was a teenager…"

A hammering on the door startled them both. Through the opaque glass, Rayan could see the dark outline of a uniform. "That bitch neighbour phoned the cops, again," she moaned.

Nat threw the holdall into the hall cupboard, sprinted for the shower room and locked the door. No way was he letting the coppers see him in this state—beaten and mauled by his woman. His reputation would be in the toilet. He heard the door getting another resounding rap. "Open up! Report of a disturbance," the voice stated.

Reluctantly, Rayan opened the door a crack. It was the same policeman as the other times.

PC Ben Watts took in her dishevelled appearance and the lurid choke marks standing out like welts on her windpipe. "Did your boyfriend do that?"

Rayan nodded.

"There, is he?" he demanded.

"He's not here."

"I'll come in, check," he said stepping forward.

"No! It's OK."

"You're covering for him."

Rayan could feel the sweat gathering on her upper lip. "I'm not, Officer Watts," she quivered.

The cop's lips tightened. "You should get those injuries checked out at Memorial Hospital," he said, reaching for his radio.

The blood roared in Rayan's ears. For a minute she thought she was going to faint. Going to the hospital would make it official. No, no, she couldn't do that.

And she couldn't let him into the house. He'd see Nathanial's bashed head and bloodstained clothes. He'd guess right away she was the violent one. She'd be arrested and charged. Her mother would never forgive her for disgracing her father's standing in the community, yet again.

Stiff with fear, Rayan wrapped her arms around her body and listened as PC Watts gave a running summary of her injuries to someone at the other end of the phone.

She caught the words—strangulation marks on throat, bruising on face and head… "Yip, needs check out by the medics…soon as a WPC is available…"

"I'm not going to hospital," she said defiantly stepping out onto the paved driveway to stand beside the policeman. "It looks worse than it is. I'm going to take a shower and go to bed," she said her voice cracking. "I have a business to see to in the morning," she said stoically.

Ben Watts gave her a perplexed look. "This is turning out to be a regular thing, Miss… Ritchie," he said consulting his sheet. "This is the—"

"Last time," Rayan said interrupted him. "I promise. You'll not need to come again."

Ben shook his head in pitying disbelief. *Why does she go on living with him?* he wondered. *She's a right good-looking Sheila—if you like the plain willowy kind. A bit too tall for a woman; wouldn't be bad-looking if she fixed herself up a bit*, he mused. In her mid-thirties or thereabout, he guessed, with a good little business going in the town centre with living quarters above it.

"Are you sure he's not in the house? The truth now," he said fixing her with a stern stare.

"He's not in the house."

"Is he in the condo above your shop? I could arrest him just as easily there."

Rayan shook her head vehemently. "No. My assistant, Sienna, stays there," she lied. "She opens the shop in the morning," she babbled, hoping it would keep him from checking it out.

"Did you read the literature I gave you last time?"

Rayan nodded, her teeth beginning to grind in frustration. Why couldn't he just *go away*! She'd glanced through the damn pamphlets he'd given her on women and domestic violence. She snorted. It didn't apply to her. But Nathanial had found them and now he was *convinced* she needed help.

"…I'll have him picked up," Ben Watts was saying, bringing her out of her reverie. "These gym junkies think they can get away with—"

"No, no," Rayan said hastily shivering in spite of the heat. "It's over. He's going to work over east."

Ben shifted and scrutinised her. Something wasn't kosher here. But he just couldn't put his finger on it. "Out east you say. Did he say where, exactly?"

Rayan shook her head.

Perturbed, the copper turned away and then turned back. "A few nights in the cells would soon cool his fist—"

"Thank you, officer," Rayan said stepping back into the porch and swiftly closing the door behind her.

She waited a while and then peeped through the slatted blinds. He was still there talking to her neighbour. She said something to him and he glanced in the direction of the garage.

"Bitch," Rayan spat. "She's telling him your car is still here," she said as Nathanial reappeared. "He's looking towards the house. I won't be able to stop him if he insists on coming in," she said her voice trembling.

Nathanial covered his face with his hands. "If he arrests and charges me with domestic violence, my licence will be revoked. I will never work again," he said despair creeping into his voice.

Sweat oozed out and pooled on Rayan's body. *If Nathanial loses his job, he will never forgive me,* she thought. *And it will prove to my father that he was right all along that Nathanial is a bum.*

"If I'm not in the house, he can't search it," she said. She hissed Biscuit's name. Shaking like a leaf, the dog crawled out on her belly from behind the broken seating.

Nathanial gathered her into his arms. "She's terrified of all the shouting and screaming," he said.

"Put her down," Rayan said sticking her feet into her walking shoes and reaching for a sweater. "She'll get over it." Hurriedly, she clipped the leash to the dog's diamante studded collar. "Just like me, she has all the trappings but no security," she muttered, flashing Nathanial a look.

Nathania checked the street outside. "He's gone." Silence filled the room as he retrieved his holdall and prepared to leave.

"Nat," Rayan said stretching out her hand, "don't go."

Nathanial took a step back, fear resonating with him.

"I'll...admit it—like I said."

Exhausted, Nat righted a kitchen chair. "Perth's testosterone, beach bum, isn't that what you just called me? What your father the bigwig college administrator calls me?"

Rayan's hand went involuntarily to the scar under her chin. It was what she'd gotten for defending Nat against her father six years before when she told him Nathanial was a better man than he would ever be.

Nat recoiled as she touched his arm. "You know I didn't mean it. Please Nat, don't leave me," she pleaded.

Nathanial stared at her. "The cops would never believe you. They'd probably say I got this from playing fast and loose with one of my students," he said pointing at his swollen face and his eye rapidly closing. He gathered up his bag. "I love you, Rayan. I have always loved you." He looked at her. "I want to marry you." Rayan stiffened. "What then? Be your *little woman* while you *position* all those 'babes' on…beach rugs!" Vehemently, she shook her head. "No Nat, I will not turn out like my mother. I will be no man's little woman," she said her voice deathly quiet. "I made myself that promise when I was sixteen. It's a promise I intend to keep."

Nathanial had heard enough. He'd take his chances with the cop, he thought stepping out into the shared garage area. Dribbling nervously, the dog tried to follow Nathanial. "I can't take you now, Bisky. I'll be back for you as soon as I come back from Sydney," Nat promised his voice thick with emotion.

"And what if she's not here," Rayan challenged, angry at herself for pleading with him to stay and being rejected.

Nat hesitated. "What do you mean?"

"What if I decide to take that Irish woman Imelda up on her life swap?"

Chapter Two

Imelda hadn't expected there'd be so many people. Excitement made her breathless as President Clinton, smiling enigmatically, stood to speak outside the Guildhall.

Huge crowds of men, woman and children were sandwiched elbow-to-elbow in front of the city's historical building swayed like a great colourful wave in greeting.

Imelda's eyes were drawn to a handsome dark-skinned man to the left of the President. His dark hair brushed back from a high forehead, ruffled in the light mid-day breeze as he scanned the faces of the crowd for any sign of trouble. She could imagine him in traditional ankle length Arab dress, his dark hair covered with a *guitar* and secured with the thick black rope band. For fleeting seconds his dark brown eyes rested on her.

Imelda's heart flipped. The crowds melted away; it was 1975 again. She was nineteen and madly, crazily in love with Ayman who was twenty-two and a third-year law student to her first year.

Ayman, the son of an American mother and a Muslim father—they met while studying at Queens University in Belfast. Almost twenty-one years ago now, she thought.

She closed her eyes. What if things had been different for her…for him, all those years ago? Life would have been so far removed from the life she had led…was living now. What would Ayman look like now in 1995?

Shrugging off her melancholy, she checked her watch and began to work her way to the back of the crowd and the Ferry Quay Gate entrances to Shipquay Street. Reaching it, she stood for a moment looking back. Wild ecstatic, cheering and catcalls rose to a crescendo as John Hume; a local politician welcomed the American President to Northern Ireland and Derry's walled city.

Leaving the plethora of flags, American, flags of the Irish Republic and the Union Jack dancing ecstatically in the November afternoon breeze, she quickened her step up the steep street leading to the War Memorial in the Diamond that represented the War Fallen and followed the street until she came to Walls Restaurant where she was to meet her sons.

A warm satisfying feeling of pride spread through her as she saw her twins, Isaac and Raphael come through the door. She stood up and waved, smoothing her leopard print dress down over her curvy figure. She'd worn a skinny ribbed vest under the plunging neckline today to save Isaac's blushes. "Don't know where he gets his demure, sensitive nature from," she murmured. "He definitely didn't get it from me. If you have it, why not flaunt it? That's what I say," she murmured, glancing down at her rose-gold coloured knee-length boots.

There are those who wouldn't agree with me, like the twins' granny, Norah, she mused, *but that's her problem. I've been a good mother to my boys. Now it's my turn for a bit of me time*, she thought.

Isaac, her firstborn, weaved his long jeaned legs between the tables. The cold Irish weather had done nothing to diminish his rich coffee complexion. Raphael, tall and handsome, second-born by five minutes, followed leisurely, casting his roving eye over a group of female diners. The mirror image of his twin, Imelda mused, except for the small birthmark below his left eye that disappeared into his high cheekbones when his tawny eyes smiled.

"Great to see you, Ma," Raphael said, now loping into the chair across from his brother, his curtain of mid-brown hair fanning his dark eyebrows "I hope you brought plenty of money. I'm busted." He laughed.

"Nothing new there then," his mother said giving him a playful slap on the sleeve of his khaki jacket.

"What'll it be, Ma A beer or a glass of wine?" Raphael asked unwinding his long legs from beneath the table and standing up.

Imelda considered. "Since I'm going to be paying for it, I might as well have a bottle of Prosecco with our meal," she smiled.

"You have to drive the forty miles home to Donegal, to Muckish," Isaac reminded her.

Imelda smiled indulgently at him, resisting the urge to reach across and push back the long fringe that flopped over his startling eyes. The thought crossed her mind that if Isaac had been born a girl, he would have looked sensational. She could imagine him made up and dressed in a figure-hugging dress and high heels. Quickly, she slammed her mind shut on the image.

"They do B&B here. So I booked in for the night. I thought we might have breakfast in the morning and then you two can take me on a tour of Derry's famous City Walls." Her face sobered. "It might be a while before we can spend some time together again."

Isaac's eyes darkened. "You're still thinking about that life swap in Australia?" he asked, fiddling with the cutlery.

"Isaac—elbows off the table," she said automatically. Then realising how absurd it was to reprimand a twenty-year-old grown man who would soon be a practicing lawyer, she apologised. "Sorry Isaac, old habits are hard to break."

Isaac stopped fiddling. "It's OK Mum; you have always been strict with Raffi and me."

"I have, haven't I? But it was only because I had to bring you up on my own."

"And you did a good job. It's your turn now to have a bit of fun," Raphael smiled "What about this house swap to Australia? Did you get any decent enquiries? Have you decided where you want to go: Sydney, Melbourne...?"

"Be careful, Mum," Isaac interjected throwing his twin a hard-eyed look. "The internet chatrooms are full of freaks."

"Imelda reached across and gently touched his long-tapered fingers clutching at the cutlery again." It OK. "I've only had a few emails—none that took my fancy." Relieved, Isaac let his hand rest in hers. Imelda smiled. "You don't have to worry about me, Isaac."

A petulant looked crossed her son's smooth lightly tanned features. "What will you live on for a whole year?"

Imelda felt a little of her happiness beginning to seep away. "I'll work—just like I've always done. Look, stop worrying. I'll be careful who I house swap with. After all, whoever it is will be living in my house and keeping an eye on you two."

"Pick somebody...who's up for a bit of a party...and curvy." Raphael laughed, his eyes wandering to the girls at a nearby table.

Imelda followed his gaze. "Forget it! There will be no more house parties after the last time, Raphael," she warned.

"Raffi, call me Raffi, Ma," he teased, as a girl walking past raked her eyes over him.

"I mean it, Raphael. The last party you had, the Guards—the police—were called."

She thought of her boss and her colleagues she worked with as a beauty therapist in the Body Beautiful Spa at the Shingle Beach Hotel in Donegal Town. *Crowd of bitches, can't wait to see the back of me, or me them*, she thought.

She was getting near the bottom of the deep glass now. Daintily, she tried to scrape out the remaining ice-cream with elegance. "I'm not leaving it," she chortled. "It's too delicious." Ignoring the looks from the other diners, she half-stood half-crunched and spooned the last dregs of the dessert into her mouth. With a sigh of pure satisfaction, sated, she sank back in her seat.

"Why do you want to go to the other side of the world, Mum? Is it…a mid-life crisis?" Isaac said quietly. Imelda sipped her prosecco.

"It is, in a way," she confessed. "You and Raphael are grown up now. I want to do something…before I'm too old."

Isaac heart plummeted to his feet. He had hoped this mad idea of a year's life swap was just a fanciful idea his mother would get over. An irrational sense of abandonment came over him. His Adam's apple bobbed up and down. *Apart from holidays and uni, I have never been away from her*, he thought. "So, you are really going to go, then?"

"You were three months old when I brought you and Raphael back from Belfast to live at your granny's house in Donegal," Imelda said as if she knew what was on his mind. She drew in a deep breath. "I have never had a real holiday since. This trip is like a present to me for my birthday."

Isaac swallowed the lump in his throat. "Forty is not old. You have a lot of years left to do things yet, Mum," he stammered. "Things you could do at home. You could return to study. I see plenty of mature students…" He let his words trail off. What could he say? *I don't want you to leave me? Oh, for God sake. You're a man, not a child*, he berated himself.

Imelda gulped at her drink. She knew she should pace herself but she drank it down anyway.

"Granny Norah didn't want us, did she? I remember that," Isaac said into the silence.

Imelda tightened her lips. "She was always more concerned what the neighbours and the Catholic Church might think."

"Just as well you didn't put us into one of those mother and baby homes run by the nuns in Belfast, isn't it," Isaac went on. "We might have been separated, sold off or adopted by rich American families."

Without answering, Imelda took another swallow of the wine. She had been very circumspect about what she told the twins about their beginnings. Or, her initial plans for their future. Her thoughts flew back to Ayman. She'd have to tell them soon, but not yet, she resolved—after they graduated. She didn't want anything distracting them from getting top grades—especially Isaac, she mused.

"I always did my best for you and Raphael," she said in a low voice. "It might not have been the life you deserved but I did my best. Now it's up to you both to build your own life…" *And it's time for me to reclaim the life I gave up for you before it's too late*, she thought draining the lasts few drops from the wine bottle.

Isaac raged inwardly at Raphael. He could have left his womanising to another night, he fumed. *He knows Mum always gets maudlin when she drinks. It's probably the only time we see her "soft" side*, he realised.

"Promise me you'll be a brilliant lawyer…get a job in a top-class law firm," Imelda said in a too loud voice. "Ireland is changing, the Celtic tiger… They're going to need smart-assed barristers. You might even be a judge in Dublin or Belfast one day, who knows."

Isaac felt his neck begin to redden. His mother's speech was becoming slurred. "I see a space at the bar," he said hurriedly signalling for their bill.

"Yeah, you could be a judge. You might even work…work for the government…." Imelda hiccupped climbing up on the circular barstool.

"What will it be, folks?"

Imelda gave the young barman an appreciative once over. "Are you on the drinks list?" she quipped.

The barman laughed and shook his head. "In that case, let me see," Imelda said focused on the array of bottles reflected in the huge glass mirror behind the bar.

"Maybe something…different…a soft non-alcoholic drink," Isaac offered, mentally crossing his fingers and hoping his mother would say she'd had enough.

"Make mine the same as whatever that girl over there is drinking," Imelda trilled, nodding at a girl at the end of the bar drinking something pink with slices of lemon floating in it.

"Good choice for a port city. One Pink Gin Cocktail coming up for the lady," the barman smiled, setting the cocktail glass in front of Imelda.

Isaac smiled, embarrassed. "Budweiser for me," he said.

"Yes, you could be a judge," Imelda said going back to her favourite subject.

"I haven't even graduated yet, Mum. It takes more than good grades to be a judge." He looked sideways at Imelda. "I have to pass the bar exam. It takes years... I'm not even sure I ever wanted to study Law... That was your idea," he said under his breath.

"What did you want to study?" Imelda said an edge creeping into her voice.

Isaac hesitated. "Well. We have acres of ground at the Manse. I could start up an upmarket Garden Centre," Isaac said tentatively. "I don't think I'm cut out to be a bigshot lawyer like you want me to be."

Imelda could feel the fuzzy feeling in her head that told her she'd had more than enough to drink. What the hell. She waved her glass in the air to get the barman's attention.

"Maybe you've had enough, Mum."

Imelda shrugged. *Maybe I have had enough. But I want to drink tonight*, she thought. Maybe if she drank enough, she'd have the courage to tell Isaac about his father and the dreams she'd given up for him and his twin.

"Mum, did you hear what I said? I don't think I'm cut out—"

"Don't be ridiculous. Of course, you're cut out to be a judge. Have you seen some of those old farts that reside in the Circuit Court in Dublin? "Imelda snorted. "Run *a garden centre*. That is one of Raphael's stupid ideas, isn't it? He's jealous. He has never been clever and smart like you," Imelda retorted.

"It's not Raphael's idea, it's mine."

"You are going to be a judge," Imelda insisted starting into her third cocktail.

"Politics...and law are Raffi's area," Isaac shouted about the laughing and the clinking of glasses. "He'd make a much better lawyer than me."

Imelda ignored hm. "I saw Bill Clinton today. Didn't you want to see him? He has a degree in law. Look where it has got him."

Isaac ordered a beer and vodka as a chaser.

"You don't want me to go to Australia? You're trying to blackmail me. Get me to say I'll stay at home and you will continue with your studies. Is that it?"

"No! It's just that...it's usually...the young who take a year out—who leave home and travel to the other side of the world," Isaac mumbled into his beer.

Feeling fuzzy and relaxed, Imelda, sitting on the barstool, ignored Isaac's huffy face and let her body sway to the sound of music coming from a man playing a guitar. She wished Isaac would lighten up and enjoy himself. Surreptitiously, she glanced at his sullen face. His full bottom lip stuck out like a child in a huff. *What he needs is to get laid. Loosen him up a bit*, she mused.

She looked down towards the end of the bar. The girl drinking the pink gin was still there. She nudged Isaac. He turned around and followed her pointing finger. "She's from our Ethics class at uni. A lot of the students come in here."

"Why don't you go up and buy her a drink—talk to her," Imelda urged. The girl looked their way and gave a small smile. Isaac's ears reddened. His mother's tight leopard print dress had ridden up over her knee but she didn't seem to notice.

"Mum, don't start that. I'm not Raphael. I don't pick up girls in bars."

"Maybe you should." A chuckle bubbled in her throat. "Derry is a port city. If your twin was a sailor, he'd have a girl in every port," she tittered waving her glass about. "Go on—talk to your friend from uni. She probably feels out of it sitting there all by herself." She gave him a nudge. "Go on! I see a seat at a table over there," she said climbing unsteadily down off the barstool.

Isaac groaned. "Mum, you haven't been in the city for a while. Girls sit at the bar on their own all the time."

"Go up, stand beside her as if you're waiting to order a drink and strike up a conversation with her," Imelda said mutinously. "Ask her what she's drinking."

"I know what she's drinking!"

"For God sake," she said exasperated, "you're going to be a lawyer. Do what lawyers do best, lie—pretend you don't know what she's drinking!—and get one for me when you're at it," Imelda ordered. She frowned as she watched Isaac drag himself towards the girl like a man going to his execution.

The thought returned to her that Isaac with those long eyelashes and startling eyes was too pretty to be a man. Was that his problem? She shook her head. He was just immature. Raphael was right; she mollycoddled him too much. Fending for himself the year she was in Australia would be good for him.

The next offer of a life swap she got, she was taking it before he talked her out of it.

Chapter Three

Rayan straightening from counting the towels piled up beside the wash basins as Sienna in white shorts and a tied sleeveless tee-shirt that showed off her long legs and tanned midriff breezed into the salon.

Rayan sensed a fresh glow and vitality about her. *She obviously has a new boyfriend*, Rayan thought grudgingly, her heart aching for Nathanial. She hadn't heard from him since the night they'd had the row and he'd walked out a month ago. It was the first time he had ever stayed away so long.

She raised a questioning eyebrow at the bulging bag slung diagonally across Sienna's reed-thin figure. "What **do** you have in that bag? It looks as if you have everything but the kitchen sink. Are you moving to a new place?"

Sienna's waist-long glossy curtain of chestnut hair fell forward concealing her face as she started for the back of the shop. "Oh, the bag, oh things—beach towels, sandals, my new bikini—you know, just things. Back in a mo.," she said evasively hurrying through the beaded curtain to the back of the shop to change.

Rayan's thoughts turned back to Nathanial. The Christmas holidays were over and the January summer heat was stifling despite the air conditioning. She wondered if it was as hot in Sydney and how Nat was coping with it.

"What are you doing?" Sienna asked coming back into the front of the salon and examining her eye makeup in the mirror above the hand basin.

"I'm taking an inventory of the stock."

"Constable Watts is here again," Sienna remarked giving her boss a look. "Wonder what he wants this time?"

Rayan's gut tightened in annoyance. PC Ben Watts had taken to dropping in regularly to have his hair trimmed. Or, on any other pretence he could think up. She knew he was really checking up on her.

"G'day, Rayan, any chance of a haircut if you're not too busy?" His eyes flicked around the salon as if he half expected to find Nathanial there. He touched his cap to Sienna.

"I'll do it. I'm between customers," Sienna offered flashing him a smile.

"Yeah? Kind of a slow day, is it?"

Sienna nodded.

"Why don't you nip out and bag me a sandwich from the Deli across the street?" PC Watts said.

Sienna pouted and looked at her boss. "Can I get you something when I'm out?" she asked, her eyes narrowing.

Rayan glanced at her assistant. Sienna was obviously reluctant to leave. *She's beginning to become suspicious of PC Watts' visits.* Rayan thought. She shook her head. "No. I'm fine," she said.

"You should eat more; you're too skinny," Ben said sternly. "Men like something to hold onto."

Rayan stared poker-faced at his reflection in the mirror. "What can I do for you today, Officer Watts?"

Ben cleared his throat. "The little woman—the other half—laid it straight on me this morning. Get that mop sheared before you come back in this house tonight, she said." Ben chuckled. "Secret of a happy marriage—never argue with the boss."

"How is your wife?" Rayan asked pretending interest.

"Yeah, she's pretty good. I and the little toerags keep her busy. Made a hell of a mess over Christmas—with the barbie and all—but she's a good little wife and mother. She had it licked back in shape in no time."

"Sounds just like a family Christmas should be," Rayan said a note of unhappiness creeping into her voice. She'd had a miserable Christmas with just her and the dog. Nathanial hadn't phoned or sent a present. She'd phoned her parents on Christmas day. Her mother had been offhand and short with her. Probably afraid I'd come over there and upset my *dear* father, she thought bitterly.

She tugged the elastic band holding the ponytail that lay against Ben Watts' thick neck. "How short do you want it?"

Ben took careful stock of his reflection in the bevelled edged mirror. "I reckon the tail can go." He grinned at his reflection. "Yip, the little woman is right," he said affirmatively. "I need a more conventional cut now that I'm no longer in charge of the Aborigines' communities. Leave enough at fill the Stetson," he chortled.

Rayan forced a smile at his joke.

"You hear about my promotion," he asked settling back in his chair. Relief washed over Rayan. Maybe he wasn't going to berate her today about not filing a complaint against Nathanial.

She shook her head. "No, I didn't."

PC Watts looked slightly miffed. "Don't you read the Cannington Post, girlie?"

Rayan felt her irritation mounting. "It's a while since I was a girl. I'll be forty on the 14th of February—Valentine's Day," she said gloomily.

PC Watts went on as if she hadn't spoken. "You are looking at the new designated liaison officer for the Man Up Domestic Violence Project that's being rolled out over Western Australia," Ben said importantly.

Rayan felt her knees begin to tremble in anger. So he is here to pressurise me into making a statement so he can arrest Nat, she thought dragging the comb roughly through his hair. "Congratulations," she said wishing there was some way she could wipe the self-satisfied smug smile off his face.

"Yep, the Police Force across WA intends to track down and bring Shelia abusers before the courts. But we can't do that unless *women report the abuser*," he said eyeballing her in the mirror.

Rayan swallowed past the lump forming in her throat. He reminded her of a dog with a bone. He was going to gnaw on her until she agreed to blame Nat for the fights. She wished Sienna would come back. Or a customer would come early for their appointment.

"Has he been back to the house since he bashed you up—or given you any more aggro?"

Rayan shook her head and busied herself with his hair. She could feel him scrutinising her. She shifted her position and swung the revolving chair sideways so he couldn't see her in the mirror.

"I hear he's running with the 'bike crowd' now."

Rayan's hands began to sweat. "Have you…been talking to Nathanial?"

Before he could answer, Sienna rushed back into the salon and proffered a packed sandwich at Ben.

"Good onya." He smiled.

"I hope they're what you wanted."

"No worries. They'll be dandy. What's happening at the weekend?" Ben asked casually. He reckoned he'd get more information of her than out of her boss.

"I'm going swimming at Scarborough Beach," Sienna volunteered. Rayan waited for her assistant to fill Ben in about her latest conquest. But for once, Sienna was unusually reticent about her love life.

"A group of us went surfing last weekend," she finally said, glancing at Rayan. She should tell her Nathanial was back from Sydney. She shrugged. She'd find out soon enough.

Rayan glanced at her assistant. It wasn't like Sienna to hold back, she thought. *She's usually bursting to tell anybody who will listen who she's slept with.*

"Yeah? Sounds like you had a good time," Ben commented encouragingly.

"We did. The sand on the beach was so hot we couldn't stay out of the water. I wore my new bikini top with my boardie's."

"No sharks in the water, then," Rayan said drily.

Sienna went into peals of helpless giggling as if Rayan had said something really funny. "Not unless you count guys."

Ben considered asking her if she'd run across her boss' boyfriend. *He's laying low out in the bush since he came back from Sydney. But I'll get the bugger*, the policeman thought doggedly.

His eyes fixed on Rayan's reflection as Sienna went off to see to a customer. "You didn't go to the hospital to get checked out," he said in a low voice.

Rayan had an overwhelming urge to nick Ben Watts big sticking out ears to shut him up. "It was my fault—"

"It's never the victim's fault, girlie," Ben said kindly.

Rayan's hands were slippery with sweat. Why couldn't he stop harassing her? "Look Officer Watts," she said fighting to control her rising anger, "I told you. It won't happen again." Annoyingly, she felt the tears pricking her eyelids. She blinked them away. Crying would only convince him she needed protecting from Nathanial "Please," she whispered hoarsely, "I just want to forget about it. I have my business to run. I can't afford any gossip."

Ben half turned in the chair. "If you thought his arrest wouldn't get in the papers, would you sign a complaint against him?"

Rayan startled when she heard Sienna's voice behind her. "Want me to finish off Officer Watts?" she said seeing the tell-tale signs of rage on her boss' face.

Rayan wondered how long she had been standing there and how much she had overheard. Fear gripped her. Sienna had a mouth like a leaking sieve. *It'll be all over town in no time*, she thought.

Her hand jerked.

PC Ben Watts let out a howl like a dingo caught in a trap. Horror-struck, Rayan watched droplets of blood fall onto the handle of the scissors.

"Oh my God, you've cut his ear," Sienna squealed going a pasty colour under her tan.

"It was an accident. I didn't mean to," Rayan stuttered. "Get the First Aid kit. It was an accident. It was an accident. I swear it was an accident," she stammered.

"Easy there, girlie," Ben admonished taking the scissors out of her trembling fingers. Then seeing the look of terror on her face, he relented… "No drama. I've had worse when the aboriginals have had a drink too many," he said examining his ear in the mirror.

"You've been attacked and fought off an aboriginal tribe single-handed!" Sienna said looked at him in wide-eyed awe.

"Not exactly," PC Watts admitted. Gripping the bleeding lobe between his thumb and finger he screwed up his face and squeezed. "Old aboriginal medicine trick," he said. "I knew their mumbo jumbo would come in useful someday," he said checking the weeping cut.

Sienna smothered a giggle. "It's only a nick, not a shark attack," she tittered.

PC Watts reddened and dug in his pocket for money.

"No, no. It's on the house," Rayan said shaking with pure panic. "Call in at the pharmacy and get it dressed properly," she babbled. "And if the blood stains don't come out with washing, send your uniform and shirt to have it professionally cleaned and tell them to send me the bill." She realised she was panting as if she just been running.

PC Watts picked up the cap of his uniform and turned to leave.

"I saw your poster for the Man Up thingy," Sienna said as she put away the First Aid box.

His cut ear seemingly forgotten, the cop beamed at Sienna. "You did? Yeah? Think the boyfriends and hubbies will man up, get educated about beating on their women?"

Sienna drew back her shoulders. "I wouldn't let a man beat on me," she declared, her gaze shifting to Rayan where she'd slumped into the seating area.

"Good onya. Smart girlie you got here," Ben smiled, nodding approvingly.

"Some women beat on their man," Sienna said.

PC Watts' antenna went up. "Yeah, you reckon guys get whacked too?"

Sienna, delighted she'd gotten Ben's attention, nodded. "Yeah, men who live with *angry women* get pummelled too. It's a control thingy," she said frowning.

Ben stroked his cut ear thoughtfully. He looked at her boss. Underneath Rayan's carefully applied makeup, he could still make out faint traces of finger marks on her throat. She'd cut her hair in a shorter style to disguise the bald patches but he could see where it had been pulled out by its roots.

He shook his head decisively. *I can't see the likes of that beach bum with his muscles, body art and shaved head letting a woman beat on him*, he thought as he looked at Rayan shaking in the chair. No! He's the abuser here, he mused. *I will get the bastard*, he promised himself.

He stuck a thumb in the loop of his trouser belt and moved closer to Rayan. "When he does it again—and he will—you know where to find me," he said softly.

"Yeah, I saw the *Man Up* poster on the back window of a Ute at a 'roo barbie," Sienna tittered as the policeman made for the door.

Ben stopped in his step. "Kangaroo steaks at a barbecue, you say? Hope the owner is a licenced holder and he killed them in a humane way?"

Sienna leaned on the brush she was about to use to sweep up Ben's hair and giggled. "I don't know. It was a great party. I had to keep telling my ride home to stop swigging the grog and lane hopping on the highway on his Harley on our way home."

"Yeah? You reckon? Drunk, was he?"

Sienna shrugged.

PC Watts gave a pretend laugh. "Girlie. You've just given me a list of law-breaking misdemeanour offenses to keep me and the boys down at the station busy for weeks."

Sienna's hand flew to her mouth.

Ben Watts winked. "No worries, girlie. I reckon by your description, everybody had a good time." He twirled his cap in his hands. "The guy who was driving the bike—get his driver's plates?"

Sienna shook her head. "He was just making sure I got home."

"Seeing him again this weekend?"

"Sienna, you have a customer waiting," Rayan said tersely. *Stupid little cow*, she thought as she watched Ben Watts stride out into the street as if he owned it. Angrily, she nodded to Sienna to follow her into the back of the shop "You have a big mouth, do you know that. He'll be back to get the name of the driver, you stupid little cow!"

Sienna gave her a sullen look. "At least I had fun," she said cattily. "I didn't tell him it was Nathanial who was driving, did I." Her eyes widened in shock and her hand flew to her mouth when she realised what she had said.

Rayan blinked, surprise showing on her face. "Nat was there! He's back from Sydney? He left you home!" She could hear her voice rising. "You are a little liar," Rayan sneered, closing the space between her and Sienna. "Nathanial is still in Sydney. If he was back, he'd come to see me and Biscuit. What's more," she said pushing her face right up to her assistant's, "he *never* eats kangaroo meat. He has too much respect for his national flag."

Sienna backed away, looking frightened. "What do you mean?"

"The Kangaroo is the emblem on *our* National Flag, you stupid little bimbo," Rayan said through gritted teeth.

Sienna lifted her chin defiantly. "He was there. I don't know if he ate—"

"Who was he with?" Rayan demanded, gripping Sienna by the arm.

Sienna's voice shook. "He was there with me."

Rayan thought she hadn't heard right. "What did you just say?"

"I was going to tell you…but PC Watts came in… I didn't think you'd want him to know where Nathanial was," Sienna said perceptively.

Rayan gave a derogatory laugh. "*You,* he was there with *you!*"

At the front of the salon, the customer coughed loudly. "The customer," Sienna quacked, freeing her arm and backing away from the rage in her boss' eyes.

Rayan shook as she opened the Esky and took out a cold drink. She held the door open for a while and let the cold air fan her. Sienna's words reverberated in her head. *He was there with me. But she's a stupid child! Nat's twice her age,* she thought in confusion. What could Nat possibly want with a girl half his age with a mouth like a leaky pan?

Visions of Sienna's pert bottom in a pair of short shorts, her bare thigh tight against Nathanial, and her breasts pressed into his back; sharing a beer as he left her home, made Rayan feel physically sick with jealousy.

She paced around the small back room of the salon waiting for Sienna to finish off the customer. Then she turned the key in the salon door.

"You're shacking up with Nathanial, aren't you, you little tramp? That's what the bag of clothes is all about. You're moving in with him!"

Sienna wound a strand of her long hair agitatedly around her fingers and sucked the ends. "No, I'm not, Rayan. I'm not," she wailed, her eyes welling up with tears. "He needed a place to stay when he came back from working at Bondi Beach. There was a spare room…one of the girls moved in with her boyfriend and Nathanial got her bed," Sienna babbled "The bag of clothes is his laundry."

"He has a *room* in the house you share?" Rayan said incredulously. "But it's all *young girls* who lived there. Why would Nat want to share a house with a bunch of empty-headed teenagers when he has a bed of his own with me?"

Sienna chewed on her hair. "Nathanial told me it was over between you. He told me he wasn't going back…"

Rayan glared at her, desperate to believe she was telling the truth. She didn't want to believe Nat would be so cruel, so insensitive as to *sleep* with her employee. She shook her head in disbelief. *What would Sienna know about keeping a sensuous man like Nathanial satisfied?* she thought.

"We share the house, that's all," Sienna huffed.

"That better be all you do or you'll be out of a job, you little tramp," Rayan said savagely. "Nathanial is **my** man. He has been my man for the past six years! He will always be mine. Do you understand?"

Sienna edged towards the door. "If you sack me, I will tell PC Watts you beat on Nathanial."

Rayan gasped in shock. How would she know that unless Nathanial had told her?

"Did Nathanial tell you that?"

Sienna nodded.

"Don't be ridiculous. Who is going to believe a man like Nat would let a woman beat on him?"

Sienna blinked uncertainly. "He told me you—"

"You tell Nathanial to come home to his own bed where he belongs. And keep your lying little mouth shut tight if you want to finish your apprenticeship," Rayan said unlocking the door and shoving Sienna out into the street.

Biscuit's ears went up and she raced to the door, turning round and round in excited circles. Rayan's heart leaped. The only person who got a welcome like that was her beloved Nathanial. "Hello my darling," Nathanial cooed, scooping the dog up in his arms and kissing the top of her head. She leaned her head against him like a child clinging to an absent parent. "I told you I'd be back for you, didn't I? Miss me, baby," Nat asked. For answer, the little dog rose up and put her front paws around his neck and licked his face. "I missed you too," Nat said his voice husky.

From her seat at the computer, Rayan gave him a hesitant smile. "There was a time when those words were for me," she said softly breathing in his familiar smell of sweat and sea spray.

"Hello, *babe*," Nathanial said satirically. "You might like to know that fat-assed bastard copper Ben Watts had me arrested. He's convinced I'm beating on you. You obviously gave him the wide-eyed hurt Sheila look."

Rayan's heart fluttered erratically in her chest. She wanted to get up, kneel before him and like Biscuit put her head in his lap and beg him to give her one more chance.

"Did he charge you?"

Nathanial sank wearily into his favourite chair, his sarcasm dissipating. "He tried to goad me into landing one on him so he could prove his point that I am a violent beach bum. When that didn't work, he got me for drinking and driving last weekend."

Rayan looked at him. He didn't look like the man who used to shave and shower every day and was particular about his appearance. He looked dishevelled and exhausted. A glow of satisfaction spread through her. He was missing his home comforts.

"You must be hungry. I'll make you something to eat," she said.

Nathanial laid his head against the squishy cushions of the sofa. It felt good. He let his tired body sink into the coolness of the soft leather. He had forgotten how comfortable it was to relax on after a day on the beach with the sun belting down.

"You're exhausted, Nat. Why don't you have a shower and a change of clothes?" Rayan offered… "While I cook—"

"*Can't stay*—meeting someone…some of the guys," he said quickly, glancing at her.

"That's OK. The steak will be ready as soon as you come out of the shower," Rayan said persuasively.

It sounds good, Nathanial thought. It had been a while since he'd had a long leisurely shower and a steak dinner. Sienna was no cook. And by the time the girls in the shared house showered and pampered themselves, there was hardly a trickle of water or shower soap left for him. He closed his eyes. A long leisurely shower sounded heavenly.

Rayan opened the Esky and sighed in relief when she located the sixteen-ounce steak at the back. Steak was Nat's favourite. Quickly, she plated it and put the microwave on high defrost. She knew exactly the way Nat liked it done.

She offered up a murmur or of thanks to her mother who had made her learn to cook properly, believing the way to a man's heart was through his stomach. Rayan smirked. She'd have been better honing her skills in the bedroom, she thought. Then, my father might have had fewer affairs with his students, she thought.

"You sure you don't mind me showering and changing? I just came for some more of my things…and to let you know I was back from over east."

It was two weeks since Sienna had let it slip about Nat taking her home from the barbecue. Rayan considered whether she'd tell Nat she knew he had been back for a while. She decided to let it pass.

"Biscuit and I are glad you're back," she asked lightly touching his arm.

Nathanial felt his body relax. Sienna had told him about the grilling Rayan had given her about sharing the house. He had been unsure of the kind of welcome he would receive but she seemed genuinely glad to see him.

"I've missed you both too," he said carefully.

Rayan leaned against the counter and listen to the familiar hum of the shower water coursing through the pipes. The sound excited her. Heat rose in her groin. She stood undecided for a moment. Would he reject her if she went to him? *What have I to lose*, she thought. *If I don't, he will walk out the door…back to that little bitch Sienna.*

Opening the showroom door, she stripped off the old housecoat she had taken to wearing since Nat left and stood naked in front of the shower cubicle. Nat's hand stilled on the sponge he was using to squeeze shower gel over his chest. Water ran in small soapy rivulets over his hard stomach and disappeared into his pubic hair.

"Can I come in?" she asked meekly. There was a beat of silence. Rayan's heart stilled. He was going to refuse her.

Nat pushed open the glass shower door. "I've missed showering with you, Rayan," he said choking up. "I've missed these babies too," he smiled soaping her breasts with his hands.

Rayan closed her eyes, trying not to visualise him showering with Sienna as his touch ignited a fire between her legs.

"It's good to have you back," Rayan smiled watching Nathanial tuck into the steak.

Nathanial put down his knife and fork. "It's good to be back but I'm not going to move back in…"

Rayan stilled. "You're still going to live in Sienna's place?" she said, the old jealousy surfacing.

Nathanial nodded. "We need to talk. I had time to think when I was over east. There need to be changes if we are ever to live together again."

Rayan felt her body slump and then stiffen. "What kind of changes?" she asked. But she already knew. Nat wanted her to 'get help' as he called it. Damn PC Watts and his stupid leaflets, she thought.

Nat focused on a mark on the wall where the faint wine stain from where Rayan had flung her wine glass at him was still visible. "You need to find a therapist to help with your anger issues before I come back," he said quietly. "I don't trust myself not to hit you back, even hurt you badly…the next time."

Taken aback, Rayan was at a loss for words. Nathanial had never physically fought back. She was shocked to hear him say he might hit her back in the future. She looked at him. There was a subtle difference in Nat; a detachment that hadn't been there before.

She straightened her spine. "I don't need a therapist. I promised it would never happen again and it won't."

Nathanial fed Biscuit the scraps of the steak. "I'm sorry, Rayan. I can't take that chance." He drew in a sharp breath, remembering the feeling of his hands choking the life out of Rayan and the compelling desire not to stop.

"You'll only come back to Biscuit and me if I'll do as you asked and get help for my…temper?"

"You can't change without help."

Rayan felt her joy at making love to him ebb away. He wasn't back to stay. He was back to make demands. If she didn't meet them, he'd leave her and go back to Sienna. She lifted her chin. "You need to change too, Nat. It's not all me. What about your insistence about having kids? You knew when we met I was never having kids."

"No more talk of babies or marrying in temples in Bali or anywhere else," Nat said reaching across the table and curling his fingers around hers. "I love you, Rayan. It'll be just you and me from now on, babe."

Rayan searched his face. "Are you sure, Nat?"

"Yeah, I'm sure."

"You'll not change your mind once I get help?" Nathanial shook his head.

"If I want to be with you then I can't have kids. I see that now. And I do want to be with you," he said quietly. "We'll have nice breaks away, you and me, like before." He hesitated. "A holiday in Bali before I have to go back out east would be nice," he said getting up and wrapping his arms around her.

"No talk of babies or marrying?" Rayan said warily.

"No more talk of babies or weddings; just you and me?"

"A holiday in Indonesia would be great but what about Biscuit? You hate leaving her in the boarding kennels."

"Yeah, I do hate to leave you with strangers," Nat said gathering the dog into his arms. "Remember, she's a rescue dog, a stray. I don't want her to feel she'd been abandoned again," he said. "A holiday in Bali is just a thought. It's OK if you don't want to go. But if you did want to go, maybe Sienna would keep Biscuit," he said an edge creeping into his voice.

Rayan raised her eyebrows. "I thought she was too irresponsible to have a dog."

"It would only be for a week. Maybe you could get her to stay in the condo while we're away and she could look after Biscuit and the business at the same time. What do you think?"

Rayan wrinkled her forehead. Sienna was still working at the salon but they were barely on speaking terms now. *She doubted she'd cooperate if she knew Nat was bedding me again*, Rayan mused.

She glanced surreptitiously at Nathanial. She wondered if he would tell her they had made love tonight. Or, would he go over there and make love to her too? Quickly, she slammed the door to her mind on that subject.

"It's getting late. I'll take the dog for a run in the park to do her business before I go," Nat said.

Rayan gathered up the plates and glasses and stacked them in the dishwasher. Maybe she could persuade Nathanial to stay the night.

Going into the bedroom, she stripped off in front of the full-length mirror and scrutinised her body. Her breasts were still high and firm. *I'm not carrying extra weight thanks to my tennis and boot scooting*, she thought. "Only my ass and my Mum's thick ankles let me down," she scowled. She did a half turn and scrutinised her bottom. *It's too big—out of proportion to the rest of me*, she thought. She wondered when Nathanial made love to her, did he compare her body with the willowy Sienna's or the unblemished bodies of the younger women he taught Pilates on the beach every day?

She took down her birth control pills and checked the dates on the packet. She'd have to go tomorrow and get the morning after Pill. She'd gotten careless about taking the Pill regularly when Nat and she were living apart. A feeling of guilt assailed her. Despite what Nat said, she *knew* he wanted a kid. Maybe being pregnant wouldn't be that big a deal, she thought. She shook her head resolutely. It wasn't going to happen. No way was she getting pregnant.

Slipping into the old housecoat, she went back into the dinette and clicked onto the holiday deals. There was a special offer package that appealed to her. The hotel was perfect and the price was right.

Memories of other holidays, of Nathanial making love to her on the warm secluded sandy beaches of Indonesia decided her. If they were going to Bali, they would need to go before the families and teenagers schoolie summer break. "No way do I want to spend three hours on a flight with crying babies and giggling adolescent girls, like Sienna," she mused.

"Look at this. It's perfect. But we need to go next week," she said as Nat came back in.

Nathanial leaned over her shoulder. "Looks good—hotel is central—has a pool and spa and leisure centre; book it."

Rayan hesitated. "What about our work and Sienna and the dog?"

"Ring her now. It'll be easier if you're not face-to-face and sparking off each other. Catch her on the hop—could work," Nat said letting his hand slip under her housecoat.

With a shiver of the old excitement, Rayan clicked on the holiday deal; it was like the crazy impulsive things they used to do when they first met.

Her exhilaration flagged as Sienna's phone rang and rang. "Little bitch, she's probably holding it in her hand watching my number flash up," Rayan muttered just as Sienna's breathy voice said "hello."

Chapter Four

Nathanial is gone for good. The words boomed in Rayan's head like claps of thunder. She crossed the darkened lounge room and glared at the blank windows of her nosy neighbour.

Bali had been staggeringly good. They'd basked in the sun on the loungers on the rooftop pool of their hotel. Fed each other copious amount of delicious ice cream; walked hand-in-hand through Poppies Street Markets soaking up the atmosphere; made love on the beach as the sun slid down behind the horizon. It had been pure bliss…until the flight home.

In the still of the night, despite being bone weary, she wouldn't sleep. Padding over to the computer she tapped the keys. The screensaver sprang into life showing a picture of Puncak Java, the volcanic mountain they had visited during their time in Indonesia. Choking up, she let her fingers trace its outline. How happy they had been that day. How she could have been so *stupid* to do what she did, she asked herself. "I need a drink," she said to Biscuit huddled in her basket.

Stepping out to the patio, she sank dejectedly into a wicker chair and gazed desolately at her potted plants shrivelled up from the relentless heat wave. "Don't waste water on plants," the weatherman was advising.

Rayan pressed the cool glass to her thumping forehead. In one moment of madness, she thought, I lost Nathanial's love and got rugby tackled to the floor of the plane like a suspected terrorist. Now, Ben Watts is focusing on *me*.

Overhead, the lights of the midnight flight bound for Melbourne winked like stars against a black sky. It reminded her of her lingering thought of the life swap. Ireland would be cool…and well out of PC Watts' jurisdiction. She moaned. *I'm fooling myself. You do that when you're forty*, she thought. She sipped at the wine. It tasted as bitter as her thoughts. She thought of all the things she had never done: She had never finished high school, never went to Europe like most Aussies did; never went to a dress up formal like other girls had. *She* had been too busy leaving home at sixteen, determined to show her father she was *somebody*. It had taken her twenty odd years; yes, she was a successful businesswoman but without Nathanial, she might as well live on the other side of the world. *It's too late to start taking risks now*, she berated herself.

Just the same, she surfed the net looking for the site. Her heart heavy as lead, she clicked on the chatroom link. Her heart leaped in her chest. The post was still there. This was crazy. What would she say? My boyfriend has left me? I need to get out of Perth before I'm arrested for assaulting an airline stewardess?

The computer bleeped. A message from Nat flashed up. Hope and then rage surged through her. PC Watts had talked him into signing the complaints form. She hit the delete button. He was pressing charges against her. "Cheating bastard, having sex with your eyes with that glammed up bitch," she muttered. *I'll show you what he can do with your abuse charges*, she thought. "I'm interested in your life swap." She punched the words out on the keyboard and hit the 'send' button.

Trailing into the bedroom, she slipped under the light duvet. The king-size bed felt cool but empty without Nathanial muscular body to fill it. She rolled over to Nat's side and pressed her face into his pillow breathing in the faint smell of his aftershave and body odour that still clung to the donner. She willed sleep to release her from the oppressive heat and her melancholic thoughts.

Outside the birds' morning chorus started up. She trailed back into the lounge and sat down at the computer again. There was another message in her inbox. Her heart flopped about in her chest. Maybe Nat had had second thoughts. He was going to work out east again; this time in Paradise Island. She still had Biscuit. He wouldn't leave without seeing the dog. "And when he does, I won't be too proud to plead with him to come back to me," she whispered to the silent room, her anger dissolving.

Her body slumped. It wasn't Nat. It was a response to her swap. There was a phone number to call. She backed away from the computer and topped up her wine; she tugged at her hair apprehension crawling about in her belly. She hadn't expected such a quick response. Wasn't there a time difference? She wouldn't phone. She'd ignore it. Delete it, she decided as she found her hand reaching for the phone.

She listened to the phone's incessant ringing. This was crazy, she thought, preparing to put down the phone.

"Yes."

Rayan let out her breath. The voice sounded cheery. It must be morning there, she thought. "I'm ringing about the year's life swap," she stammered out, her heart drumming against her ribs so hard it was making her breathless.

"Hold on. Wait there. Don't you go away," the female voice said.

Rayan could hear someone at the other end of the phone talking and laughing. "Thank you," she heard the woman say to someone. This is sheer madness, Rayan thought. I should just put the phone down. She was startled as the woman's voice came loud and clear across the line.

"Sorry for keeping you. My neighbour, Mac O Lochlainn, always seems to call when the phone rings," the woman joked. "Now, what did you say your name was? Where are you ringing from?"

"I'm Rayan… Rayan Ritchie and I'm ringing from Perth in Western Australia," she said, the words coming out in a rush.

"And they say the Irish talk fast. Slow down," she laughed.

Rayan had a sudden need to go to the bathroom. She slammed down the phone. "What the hell is happening to me? I'm turning into a jabbering incoherent fool," she moaned. But relieved, she moved away from the phone. She'd make an appointment to see her doctor. Get him to say she was menopausal and it was making her volatile she'd gone to him for the morning after pill and he had more or less said that anyway; telling her not to worry about becoming pregnant because at *her age* it was most unlikely she would conceive. She had been both insulted and relieved at the same time. She startled as the ringing of the phone broke into her thoughts.

"Are you the woman from Australia I was just talking to a while ago? Did you say your name was Rain? I think we got cut off."

"Yes, it's pronounced Ray-an."

"We get plenty of your namesakes here. Ireland is famous for its rain. That's why everything is so green," the woman quipped.

Rayan's felt her sense of loneliness deepened. The woman sounded happy. And she was obviously on friendly terms with her neighbours. Not like the bitch across the street who is always spying on me, she thought. She wondered if Ben Watts had asked her to keep her informed of her comings and goings. She carried the phone to the window. Her neighbour's house was in darkness. You're becoming paranoid, she told herself. After the doctor, she'd go and see PC Watts. She didn't want him coming into the salon to arrest her.

"What time is it over there?" she asked feeling foolish.

"What? Oh, the time? Mid-day, I suppose you'd call it lunch or brunch or something like that where you are. I don't bother too much about clocks or time. Ticking the minutes of your life away, especially when you are nearing forty, like me," she laughed. "What time is it with you?"

"Dawn is just breaking," Rayan said watching the red, orange glow beginning to dispel the semi darkness. "This was a mad idea. Sorry for wasting your time—"

"Wait! Don't hang up."

"No, really, I had a row with my boyfriend…partner. I've never been to Ireland. I just thought… I'm sorry. This was a big mistake," Rayan said desperate to get off the phone now.

There was a slight pause. "Don't you know there's no such thing as a mistake?"

Oh yes there is, Rayan thought. If I hadn't made the mistake of tipping my drink over a flight attendant and threatening to smash a beer glass in Nat's face, he'd still be with me and I wouldn't be phoning you, looking for a year away in Ireland.

"What's for you never passes you."

"What? What do you mean?" Rayan asked in confusion.

"Karma! You've heard of Karma? We're meant to be talking to each other," the woman said blithely. "By the way, my name is Imelda. Now, what do you want to know," she asked suddenly becoming very business-like.

The change of pace threw Rayan. "Know?" She hadn't thought that far ahead.

Imelda tapped the phone to make sure it was working as the silence lengthened. She'd had a few time wasters who had no real intention of swapping with her. This one sounded as if she didn't know what she wanted.

"Where are you in Ireland?" Rayan finally asked as if telling her would make her any the wiser of the geographical layout of a country she knew absolutely nothing about except what she saw on the news from time to time.

"I'm in Donegal, the most beautiful place in the world. I take it you want a life swap too?"

"Yes. No! If it's gone, I'll totally understand."

Imelda shrugged. "I've had a few emails. There's one from Brisbane or was it Sydney? I was thinking of accepting."

Relief washed over Rayan. She felt free to ask questions now. "Where would I live—if I decided to swap for a year with you? How would do you get about? Is there transport—buses, trains, in Ireland?" She jerked the phone away from her ear as Imelda gave a great big belly laugh.

"Oh, I have a horse and cart…and a pair of good stout walking shoes I can lend you. It's only five miles to Creeslough, the nearest village and twenty miles across the Border into Derry City; just a good stretch of the legs," she chortled down the phone.

Rayan frowned. She wondered if all Irish people were as impertinent as this woman. She let a chilly silence fall between them.

"I'm sorry. I'm joking. It's the Irish humour. Letterkenny town is literally on your doorstep and you can use my car while you are here. Or take the local bus—if you're not in a hurry," Imelda said. "You'll live in my house at the foot of the Muckish Mountain. You'd have the house to yourself. But you would have to look after my dog, Dizzy."

"Do you live in a cottage?" Rayan had a vague recollection of a picture postcard she'd seen once of an Irish cottage with roses growing around the door.

Imelda was beginning to tire of the conversation. "It is, in a way," she said evasively. "It's in the country and quite isolated." She was beginning to wonder would she ever get the right Aussie to swap with. It had to be soon. Isaac had starting to come home every weekend now. She felt he was putting pressure on her not to go. "I was planning to come to Australia around April—6 weeks from now or, sooner if that suits you."

This is crazy, Rayan thought. Why am I asking all these questions when I have no real intention of going there. What would I do with my business? I have spent the last twenty years building it up. Am I really considering going to the other side of the world because Nat left me or because he has been *sleeping* with fucking Sienna since he came back from Bondi Beach?

"Where would I live if I swapped lives with you?" Imelda asked.

"I have a house—and a condo—a smaller place—at my hairdressing in the town centre," Rayan said succinctly. She didn't want to give too much away. She didn't want a strange Irish woman landing on her doorstep on top of everything else.

"You *own* a hairdressing salon?"

Rayan caught the raised interest in Imelda's voice. "Yes, I-I've built it up from scratch—"

"I trained in Beauty and Hairdressing. I'll run it for you while I'm there," Imelda said an excited note creeping into her voice.

"I built the business up myself. It's like my baby. I'm not sure I'd trust a stranger to run it," Rayan blurted out tears choking her throat. *Shit! The woman will think I'm a real nutcase*, she thought.

She heard Imelda laugh. "I get that. I have things I have invested in since I was at university in the 70s. Like my house and my boys. So I know where you're coming from." A deep chortle crackled over the line. "At least you get a profit out of your investment," she said wryly. "I have twin boys I brought up—mostly single-handed. I work as a beauty therapist in the Health and Fitness Spa in the Shingle Beach Hotel in Donegal Town. Most of my earnings up to now have gone on educating them."

Rayan sighed with relief. Imelda had given her the perfect reason for not going to Ireland. "No, no, I couldn't have children in my house. I…don't ever want children in my life," she said to hammer home her point. "Hope you get a life swap soon. Sorry for wasting your time," she rushed on, getting ready to put down the phone.

Imelda sniggered. "My twins are hardly children. They're twenty-year-old second-year law students living away from home." She laughed. "They'll soon be having children of their own, especially Raphael if he doesn't learn to keep his pecker in his trousers," Imelda said dryly. "I'm not ready to be a granny yet. I'm planning on having a bit of fun and a life of my own before that happens."

Rayan fell silent. The last thing she needed was to be living on the other side of the world with a pair of testosterone-driven teenagers.

"Don't let the twins put you off," Imelda hurried on, sensing Rayan's reluctance. "They share a student flat in Derry City. They are rarely here, except for the few weeks in July and August. And even then I don't see much of them. They can stay in the student accommodation while I'm away," she assured her. She paused. "I hope you decide to come. I think I'd like you looking after my house," Imelda said persuasively. She hesitated. "Are you intending to work while you are here? I could ask my boss if she'd be interested in finding something for you. The hotel gets a lot of upmarket patrons. It's always looking for competent hairdressers, especially in peak season."

Rayan felt her interest peak. It was a good offer: a house and a job. Her business would still be kept open. Her customers had dwindled since the news of the incident. With a new hairdresser, the gossip would fade and die and her customers would come back to the salon. And by the time she got back from Ireland, PC Watts would be cooled down about her holding out on him and trying to put the blame for the violence on Nathanial. The plan, if you could call it a plan, was beginning to look promising.

Rayan sat down abruptly. "I might be interested in your life swap."

"Why don't we leave it for the time being? Think about it and get back to me. I have to go now; there's another call…get back to me," Imelda said hastily, noting how long she had been on this international call. "On second thoughts, I think I am going to accept the one in Sydney," she said reaching a decision. The way this woman was assing about, she'd be coming one day and changing her mind the next, she mused. And she didn't have time for that. If she didn't get away soon, Isaac would persuade her to stay until after his and Raphael's graduation. And I'll be another year older and nearer the menopause then, she thought.

Rayan felt the heat of the day beginning to close in on her. She'd have to get dressed and face down PC Watts. "I'll do it. I'll do the life swap with you for a year." The words seemed to leap out of her mouth of their own accord. She'd show Nathanial she *could* live without him. He wasn't the only one who could have a geographical move—a new beginning, she thought.

What about Biscuit, the dog? her inner voice mocked.

Chapter Five

Rayan checked her watch and swore under her breath. Where the hell was Imelda? She was supposed to be here half an hour ago. She glanced around the bar-restaurant of the hotel in Dubai where they had arranged to meet to exchange house keys and other stuff. Some Arabs, but most of the customers eating their midday meal were smartly dressed Westerners.

With the exception of a few stares, she was ignored. But she was beginning to feel conspicuous sitting by herself. Had Imelda come in and she hadn't recognised her? Maybe she'd changed her hair colour since this photograph was taken, she thought looking at the small photo. It looked like one of those photographs you took in a booth in fairgrounds, she thought glancing at it again.

Her head shot up in anticipation as the door opened again. She drew in a ragged frustrated breath. It wasn't her. She smoothed down the short-sleeved shirt over black capri pants and sat back in her seat trying to appear relaxed.

After a few seconds, she rummaged in her bag and took out the rambling letter Imelda had sent her about the job in the Shingle Beach Hotel. There was a footnote to it. *When you get to the bar, don't order a drink unless you know an expat who has a licence.* What the hell did that mean?

Two men in shorts and smart tee-shirts, their arms browned from the sun, were shown to the table next to hers. They cast a casual glance in her direction before focusing on a skinny Sienna-lookalike barmaid serving their drinks. Except, unlike that bitch Sienna, this one has a decent pair of boobs, Rayan thought with satisfaction. Obviously an expat or an expat's daughter, she mused.

Nat is definitely a breast man. What he's doing with that *underdeveloped child* I don't know, she thought. Unconsciously, she straightened her posture. She clamped down hard on her thoughts. Nat's love life is part of my past, she told herself firmly. I'm about to start a new life—at least for a year—if that woman ever gets here, she fumed.

Following the impromptu telephone call about the possible life swap, she had seesawed crazily between not going and the irrational perseverance to accept Imelda's offer. *After the airport police took me off the plane in handcuffs, I really had no other choice*, she thought. *And when word got around that I had attacked Ben Watts with a pair of scissors—despite it being an accident—I had no customers worth keeping the salon open for*, she thought dolefully staring into her coffee. She sighed deeply.

"The life swap is better than Ben Watts arresting me for what he calls perverting the course of justice and wasting police time," she murmured.

But even having flown for twelve hours and feeling irritated by bloody Imelda's lateness, something in Rayan prompted her to pick up her bag and disappear before Imelda arrived.

I could go back to Perth and plead with the police to give me a chance, she thought. She considered the possibility. But she knew in her heart that that was never going to be an option. Ben Watts' ego was bruised. He'd told her in clipped tones that she had 'deliberately' let him believe it had been Nathanial who was the abuser; made him look a fool in front of his colleagues. He even had hinting that she had attacked him with the scissors because she hated all men.

Her throat went dry. She wished she could have glass of wine.

"There was a message left for you," the Sienna-lookalike said, jolting Rayan back to the present. Rayan's heart rushed into her throat and a sense of doom washed over her like a huge black wave. Imelda wasn't coming. She would have to go back to Perth.

"A message?"

"I placed it under your napkin when I brought your coffee."

"Sorry, I hadn't noticed," Rayan said feeling flustered.

"Your coffee has gone cold. I will bring you a fresh pot," she offered.

"Could I have a glass of wine instead?" Rayan asked.

"I think that will be OK."

Rayan rolled the taste of the wine around on her tongue and cursed Imelda. Cautiously, she took another sip of her drink. If she had to take a flight back to Perth, she didn't want to appear drunk.

She shuddered. Her thoughts went back to the flight back from Bali. A small boy in the seat in front had stared unblinking at her through the gap between the seats. His direct gaze had made her feel nervous; like when her father used to fix his stare on her when she was young.

She took another sip of her wine and let her mind slip back to the last day of her and Nat's holiday. Nat's carefree mood had given way to preoccupation with his phone. Certain he was phoning Sienna, she had gotten upset. "You're phoning that bitch," she'd said.

"That bitch, as you call her, is running your business and babysitting my dog," Nat had retorted. "Of course, I'm going to phone her. And tell her what time I'll be back to pick up Biscuit."

She'd made a grab for his phone to read his messages.

"Oh, come on, babe, we've had a brilliant time. Don't let's spoil it," Nat said moving away. "Forget the phone. Let's have one more romp—enjoy the time we have left," he murmured stretching out his hand "Wow! I think the Indonesian sun worked wonders for these babes," he'd cooed, kissing the tip of each breast.

"Nat, we don't have time—our flight," she moaned as Nat's lips moved down her navel.

"We have time, babe. I can't turn up at the boarding gate with this bad boy," Nat moaned glancing down at his erection.

But as soon as the seatbelt sign was switched off, he was back on the phone to her again, Rayan sighed, separating the note from the napkin.

"Rayan," a woman's voice asked.

Rayan startled. She'd been so preoccupied thinking about the last time she'd been with Nat and the possibility of going back to Perth that she hadn't noticed the woman approaching her table.

"I'm Imelda. Sorry I'm late. Don't ask, it's a long story," she said rolling her eyes to the ceiling. "I see you got my note. You look very different from your picture," she went on sliding into the seat opposite.

"I had my hair cut," Rayan responded in a clipped tone. Momentarily, she thought about the photos Nat had taken in Bali. She hadn't been able to face having them developed. It hurt too much to see how happy they had been and the love in Nathanial's eyes.

"I'm just saying. You're different from the way I thought you'd look, that's all," Imelda said blithely looking at the stressed-looking black-haired woman wearing barely any makeup sitting opposite her.

Rayan looked pointedly at her watch.

"Imelda shrugged." I know I'm late but I met these two guys—shit, "I think that's them over there," she exclaimed.

Rayan looked where Imelda was looking. "I don't think so. They've been here a while," Rayan said coldly.

"No watch—remember? I don't do time," Imelda said slightly miffed.

What was I thinking leaving this scatter-brained person to run my business and look after my customers? Rayan moaned to herself. A small inner voice sneered. Why should you worry about your customers? They weren't long in taking their custom elsewhere when the news spread about your imminent arrest. She pulled her mind back as Imelda rose to her feet.

"What's that you're drinking?"

Rayan placed her hand over the lip of her glass. "I'm not having any more. Sit down, there is table service," she said sharply.

"Not having any more? Come on, you're on your holidays. And I have a temporary drinking licence," she chuckled. With a flourish, she held afloat a small square of paper.

Rayan gaped at her. "Where did you get that?"

"I got it off the two guys I met earlier. And as long as we are good little girls, drink in moderation inside the hotel and don't get tangled up with the police, we're safe enough." She winked. "Come on! You need to get in some training for Ireland," she joked. "What's your poison?"

Rayan looked at her in confusion.

"Never mind, that skinny thing with hair down to her butt will know what you're drinking," she laughed, signalling the waitress. "But first, I need the toilet. I took a taxi. The guy didn't appear to know where he was going. It took ages to get here," Imelda said, getting up again.

Rayan watched the Irish woman stride away from her. "My mother would probably say she was too loud, that a woman of certain age shouldn't wear such short skirts and a top that barely conceals her bare midriff, especially here," she murmured. She noticed the men at the tables were having trouble keeping their eyes on their food as Imelda passed, her halo of red hair bouncing off her shoulders like a golden beacon.

"Bring your drink with you," Imelda said coming back to the table. "The two guys over there have asked us to join them. They've offered to show us the hotspots in Dubai and dinner here later."

Rayan shook her head. "We have things to discuss before I catch my plane to Ireland. And there are things I need to tell you about my business, my house," she said coolly, opening her small backpack and withdrawing a bulky envelope.

"What is left to tell?" Imelda grumbled, looked perplexed. Rayan's emails had been long-winded and detailed.

"Well, is your friend interested in a bit of sightseeing?"

Imelda smiled up into the face of the man from the other table. "It sounds great. But apparently, we have things to talk about," she said indicating Rayan's stony face.

A disappointed look washed over the man's face. "We could take the traditional water taxi across Dubai Creek—best way to see the buildings and the architecture—even visits the spice markets: what do you say, sound good?"

"It was good of you to offer to show us the tourist spots in Dubai. I don't suppose I'll ever be here again," Imelda said wistfully.

"Glad to do it. I've been to Ireland. The folks there showed me a good time. It would have been nice to return the favour," he said regretfully. "Maybe we could meet up later, have a chat and a drink," he said. "Say, about eight, here, in the bar?"

"Yeah, why not, sounds good to me. My name is Imelda and this is Rayan," Imelda smiled.

The man proffered his hand. "Good to meet you. I'm Denis and my mate is Brian. Can we get you a drink before we leave?"

Automatically, Rayan began to refuse.

"That sounds a good idea," Imelda said cutting across her. "It looks as if it might be thirsty business," she chortled looking at the bulky envelope Rayan was still clutching in her hand. Imelda smiled at the man called Denis.

"See you at eight. Don't be late," Denis joked, fixing a cowboy hat on his head. "Some sassy female we met last night gave me this," he laughed "Be seeing yam," he smiled turning towards the door.

Rayan frowned. "They both look like married guys, if you ask me."

Imelda shrugged. "We're not having an affair with them. We're just having a bit of dinner and a few drinks with them."

Imelda scrutinised the Australian woman across from her. *My boys will be safe enough with her*, she thought. *She's hardly the type to set the world on fire with her wild parties*, she mused.

She wondered if she should mention Raphael's off-centre take on life. *She looks a bit harassed as it is. I don't want her scuttling back to Perth*, she thought. *She'll be grand*, she thought. *And Isaac is a pet. She'll mother him and he'll keep his twin in line*, she convinced herself, tinkering with her glass.

"Is there something you need to tell me?" Rayan asked perceptively.

"Well, it's something and nothing," Imelda admitted, turning the glass in her fingers. "Isaac and Raphael are identical twins but very different in nature. Raphael is woman-mad; bursting with testosterone," she smiled. "His twin is quiet and good-natured. And so far, is showing no real interest in woman. I'm hoping that will change," she said under her breath.

Rayan's heart plummeted. Apart from the children of friends, she knew nothing about teenage children. "You never mentioned any of this in your emails."

Imelda laughed and sipped her drink. "I've had a good stout bar fitted on the back of the bathroom door. Be sure to slide it into place when you're in the shower if Raphael's about," she joked.

Rayan was appalled. "But I thought they were away a university, that I'd have the house to myself?"

"You will—most of the time. But they will be home for part of the summer holidays. It'll not be a problem. They both have summer jobs."

Rayan's back stiffened.

Imelda laughed. "Will you stop panicking? Lighten up. I brought them up decent. They're good boys. You'll hardly know they are there. They're never in." She laughed. "You can have the craic with them."

Rayan startled. This was turning into a nightmare. "Craic? You mean drugs!" She gave Imelda a horrified look.

"Drugs? No! It means…having a laugh and a bit of fun," Imelda said, sobering. *Shit,* she thought, *it'll take more than a year in beautiful Donegal to thaw out this bloody woman. She's as tightly wound up as the spring on a broken clock.*

She dug deep in her bag and drew out a set of keys. "This one here is for the front door. The rest you can figure out when you get there. The boys will meet you at Belfast International Airport in Belfast and drive you across the Irish Border into Donegal. OK?"

"What about the job at the hotel—in the Spa?"

"Ah, yes, the job," Imelda murmured. *I wonder what the bitches that pass for therapists and beauty consultants will make of her,* she thought, looking at the less than fashionably dressed woman with short almost mannish hair that seemed to be growing out of her heads in tufts. She has good bone structure and with a bit of pummelling and exposure to the good country air coming off

Muckish, she could be whipped into a presentable shape, I suppose, she conceded.

But for a hairdresser, her hair is appalling; and from the look of her skin it's been a while since that face had a good face mask; and her nails! Not my problem, she thought as she prepared to leave. Quickly, she looked over Rayan's head. "I'm sure the job will be fine," she said evasively. "I'll read this on the ten-hour flight to Perth," she promised bagging the bulky envelope.

Rayan finished her drink and picked up her handbag. "We meet here again when the year is up and exchange house keys. That is the arrangement," she said faintly, trying to look confident.

Imelda nodded, keen to get away. "I'll email you—when I'm over the jet lag." One thing she wasn't going to do was spend her time listening to the whinging of this Aussie woman via emails. The twins would keep her up to speed about her house and Dizzy, the dog. "Safe journey to Ireland," she said.

Suddenly, Rayan felt very frightened. This was really happening. Imelda was about to walk out the door and board a plane for Perth, stay in her house. And run her business. What kind of madness had possessed her to agree to that! *She* had agreed to go and live in a country with a culture she knew nothing about and this woman expected her, at least in part, to be responsible for her teenage sons. She felt her stomach heave. The wine she'd drunk was making her feel like it had in the cabin of the aircraft that day on her way back from Bali. She felt herself sway against the table.

"If you're going to be sick, do it in the toilet," Imelda warned, one eye on the bar manager who was focusing on their table.

"I'm not going to be sick; I was just thinking about the row Nathanial and I had on my last flight," Rayan blurted out trying to get a grip on her emotions.

"Nathanial?"

"My boyfriend. My ex-partner of six years," she corrected.

"What happened?"

"I was arrested during the flight."

Imelda's eyes widened. Maybe she had been wrong about this woman. Filled with curiosity, she sat down again. "Tell me everything and leave nothing out," she said, signalling the waiter to bring them another drink.

Rayan's drink hit the back of her throat as she drank it down in one nervous gulp. "The cabin attendant was being *very* attentive to Nathanial and he was lapping up every moment of it. I warned her to leave him alone and when she ignored me, I threw my glass of wine over her and called her a jumped-up waitress," Rayan admitted.

"Holy shit," Imelda gasped. An image of a busty stewardess, wine dripping over her expertly made up face and pristine dress uniform, flashed into her mind's eye. What did she do?

"She went for the Flight Captain."

"What did your boyfriend say?"

Rayan thinned her lips. "He kept apologising; saying I wasn't well. I was menopausal—it was the heat and my age."

Imelda almost giggled. *I'm sure that soothed troubled waters*, she thought. "What did you do?"

Sweat broke out in Rayan as she recalled the scene that had unfolded. "I beat on Nathanial and shouted at him not to dare apologise for me to that jumped up waitress…" Rayan fell silent.

"Surely you didn't get arrested just for calling her a waitress," Imelda probed.

"I threatened to smash Nat's beer glass in his face."

Imelda sat in stunned silence. What had she done? She had agreed a year's house swap with a bloody violent drunk.

A sob escaped from Rayan. "That was when an Air Marshall who was on board, with the help of the crew, dragged me out of my seat and pinned me to the floor of the cabin. Nat says he is never coming back to me. I miss him so much." Rayan tried to hold back the tears that were streaming down her face. She'd cried copious amounts of tears, apologised profusely to the cabin staff and the pilot. But it was no use. Mortified, she'd walked head down, handcuffed to the Air Marshall and was handed over to airport security when they landed in Perth Airport.

"We better get out of here before they ask us to leave," Imelda said, seeing the bar manager threading his way between the diners. "Come on, we need to go to the ladies. You need to fix your makeup. And then you're going shopping at the gift shop."

Rayan felt a hysterical giggle rising in her throat. "Am I going to buy a souvenir from Dubai to take to Ireland with me?"

"They'll overlook your meltdown if you're spending money," Imelda said laconically.

"I'll come with you to meet the guys tonight," Rayan offered as Imelda helped her touch up her makeup and fix her hair in the plush upmarket Ladies.

Imelda shook her head. She needed time on her own to decide was she going back on the morning flight to Ireland and home or the night flight to Perth. "I've decided to go on one of the guided sightseeing tours. I don't know if I'll be back in time," she lied. She eyeballed Rayan in the mirror. "I don't think you should drink anymore. If you're drunk or hungover, the Airline may not let you on the flight. I think you should go to your room…"

Stung by the cheek of the Irish woman, Rayan retaliated, "Don't talk to me as if I was a child! I'm going out to see Dubai."

Imelda frowned. "You're in a strange city. And you've been drinking. You could be arrested if you go out on the street—"

"You know nothing about me and yet you're passing judgement on me," Rayan said coldly. "What do you know about me? Or the life I've lived? All you are interested in is ensuring I go through this swap with you so you can have one last fling before your precious boys make you a granny." She stopped to get her breath. "Well, I will never have to worry about that because I am never going to have children," she said agitation making her voice shrill.

Imelda looked at her. "You're right. I know nothing about you. And I don't want to know anything about you or your breakup with your—what's his name, Nathanial. I intend to have a ball in Perth—might even meet a man there, who knows."

"All I need to know is that you will take good care of my house and my dog. Don't go anywhere until I decide if I'm carrying on with this swap or not," she said as she picked up her bag and headed to Reception.

The bar manager was there. "Your friend is drunk. I do not allow women drun—"

Imelda tossed back her mop of fiery hair "She's not drunk. She's just come off a long-haul international flight. She's feeling unwell. You should take better care of the patrons of your establishment," she said her eyes flashing.

The male desk clerk smiled as the manager moved away. He arched his eyebrows slightly. "Your friend—I will send someone to her room to help her. How can I help you, madam?"

Imelda smiled. "Thank you. I don't think she is used to travelling alone. Now, what should I see while I am in your beautiful city?" she asked. "I have my drinks licence," she murmured seeing the question mirrored in the man's eyes.

"One ticket for the Big Bus sightseeing tour," he beamed. "You can get on and off as you wish. And in that way, see the new and old Dubai," he grinned. "I recommend," he said. "Pick up outside the door and you will be back in plenty of time to meet your gentlemen friends."

Imelda laughed. "You don't miss much, do you," she said, going out to wait for the Big Bus.

Chapter Six

Rayan peered out the window of the plane in astonishment. The fields and runways were covered in *snow*. The antenna crackled again and the smooth voice of the pilot announced there was up to three feet of snow on some parts of the airport. "The maintenance crews are working diligently to clear the runway of ice. We are just waiting for clearance to land," he intoned. "For those passengers travelling from Dubai and other Eastern destinations, the landscape of snow is a breathtakingly awesome sight from up here. However, take care when disembarking; the walkways and tarmac may be icy and slippery."

"Here we go," the woman beside Rayan moaned. White-knuckled, she gripped the side of her seat as they began their descent. "I've flown all over the world. My son was in the British Army but I still get nervous going up and coming down." She glanced at Rayan. "I can't believe you're so calm—it being your first international flight and everything," she babbled as the undercarriage bounced on the runway.

Rayan's stomach flipped over as the plane freewheels on the runway. The antenna crackled. "There is a severe weather warning in place for Northern Ireland. For those passengers travelling on by coach and car, take extra care on the roads. And for those passengers here for the St Patrick's Day celebrations in a few days' time enjoy your holiday and thank you for travelling with British Airways."

"That's easy for him to say. It won't be much of a holiday for me," the woman beside Rayan sighed, glancing at the man's diamond-set ring that glinted on her left index finger. She'd confided in Rayan that the ring had belonged to her son who had been shot while manning a checkpoint in South Armagh. "The Murder Triangle, they called it," the woman sighed, watching the heavy snowflakes floating past the small rectangular window. "It's the first anniversary of his death."

Rayan nodded vaguely. The Northern Ireland Troubles was something she knew nothing about. Bone-weary after her 26-hour flight, all she could think about was stretching her back out on a bed.

"I hope you don't get stuck in a snowdrift on your way to Donegal. How many miles did you say it was from Belfast?" the woman enquired.

Rayan looked worriedly out the window. "I'm not sure. About a hundred miles, I think." What if the roads were too icy to drive that distance? She wished now she had planned a stopover in Belfast. She waited for the seatbelt sign to be extinguished before freeing herself and rising to open the overhead locker.

"Bit of a change for you, this weather," her neighbouring passenger commented, eyeing what Rayan was wearing on her feet.

"It was in the high thirties the day I left Perth—nearing the end of our summer. But even in autumn, I can still wear these," Rayan admitted glancing down at her open-toed sandals. "Is the weather in March always as bad as this?" she shivered as the cold began to seep into her back and legs.

"March is usually blustery and wet. But I haven't seen snow like this for years—even in winter." She eyed Rayan's lightweight jacket. "I hope you have a good warm winter coat in that hand luggage."

Feeling like a child that been reprimanded, Rayan shook her head. Clothes hadn't been high on her list. Getting out of Perth had been her priority. Ben Watts was as dogmatic about having her charged as he had been about arresting Nathanial.

Along the aisle, overhead lockers stood open like huge pelicans waiting to catch fish. A man touched Rayan's hand as she struggled to release her hand luggage. Jauntily, he freed a huge straw sombrero and plonked it on his head. Despite her weariness and rapidly freezing feet, Rayan couldn't but help smiling at him.

"Don't think I'll have much use for this here, but what the hell," he said winking at her.

The passengers in front were moving along the narrow walkway between the seats. Somebody behind dug their hand luggage into Rayan's heel. Outside the window, she could see their luggage being loaded ready to be ferried across the white ground criss-crossed with tyre tracks. "It's snowing again," the man with the huge sombrero announced. "You far to travel?" he asked.

Rayan shivered in her light jacket and slacks. The numbness from her feet was beginning to creep up the backs of her legs. *I hope the twins have a rug and a flask of something hot in the car*, she thought. She wondered fleetingly if the twin, like their mother, were partial to a drink. She could do with one right now. She hadn't dared drink on the flight—just in case. I hope they got here, she fretted. If they didn't what would she do, she wondered. She searched for the woman from London who was travelling on to Armagh. She might know of a hotel. "I'm going to Donegal."

The man sucked his mouth into a round O as if she had said something that pained him. "Travelling over the Glen Shane Pass into the North West? Don't think it'll be the night, love."

Rayan gave him a cool look. "I was just saying," he grinned holding up his hands up as if to defend himself. "It's a mountain road. It'll be closed with the snow," he said smugly. "You're Australian. Wouldn't be used to weather like this," the man went on. "What part of Australia you from?" he asked. Rayon could feel his heavy breathing into the gap between her shoulder blades.

She turned and glared into the face beneath the ridiculous looking sombrero. "What's it to you?" she hissed.

His eyes widened and he took a step back, tramping on the toes of a small boy behind him. The child set up a loud wailing. "I was only asking—trying to be nice to our visitors, so I am. Keep your hair on, wee girl," he retorted.

"I am not 'wee', and it's been a while since I was a girl."

"Is that so? Well, in that case—sorry I spoke. Have a *wonderful* holiday," he said folding his arms across his chest. Rayan edged her way forward. Several passengers who had remained seated filled the space between her and the man.

She struggled her hand luggage over the raised step of the cabin doorway and out into the tarpaulin-covered walkway leading to the airport's main buildings and Arrivals. "Here," a voice said at her ear, "my number—in case you get stranded in the city in the snow."

Rayan snapped it from him and marched on as fast as her icy cold feet would allow. Unperturbed, he overtook her and strode out in front. Rayan noticed he now had the sombrero tied to his backpack and it flapped and bounced about like a huge colourful bird that had lost its radar and ended up in the wrong climate. A bit like me, she mused.

The heavy-duty plastic covering the walkway crackled and flapped about with the rising wind. Rayan's steps slowed. This was pure madness. There was no way she was going to be able to survive in a climate like this. She felt her legs tremble. She wanted to race back to the aircraft, climb back into her seat and stay there until they touched down in Perth again.

She stood frozen to the spot as passengers streamed past her. She shook involuntarily and looked down at her luggage. There was nothing in there to match this weather—except Nathanial's sports kit. It was all she had left of him. "And I wouldn't even have that if it hadn't been in the boot of my car the day he cleared out his stuff," she muttered. Teeth chattering, she made her way down the crowded walkway to the toilets. Snapping the lock on the door, she unzipped the bag and pulled Nat's sports zipped hoodie over her shaking body. At the bottom of the bag, she found his knee length soccer socks and an old pair of battered trainers she had planned to wear on the flight if her feet became swollen. Pulling on the socks, she yanked the laces from the first few eyeholes and pushed her ice-cold feet inside.

She edged the toilet door open and peered out. The chatty hand washing passengers who had been there when she'd struggled in were gone. Despite her black mood, she giggled when she saw her reflection in the long mirror. She hardly recognised the dishevelled, disgruntled image that stared back at her. "I look ridiculous." She grinned. The zipped hoodie that showed off Nat's man boobs and muscular body hung baggy on her long straight body. It sleeves stopping well above her wrist and its wide gapy waistband skimmed her midriff.

She smiled wryly at her reflection. "One look at me in this get-up will soon cool the ardour of the sombrero-tooting Belfast man," she mused stepping out in search of the carousel and her luggage.

Her suitcases with their distinctive Ferndale Dockers football logos Nat had plastered all over them on his trip to Sydney trundled towards her on the carousel. She scrambled the smallest one over the edge, too tired to worry about the curious looks her appearance was attracting. "I've got them," a man's voice said, hauling the rest of her cases onto a waiting trolley. She turned, expecting it to be the man from the flight. It was an airport attendant. "Keen Aussie football fan," he grinned, indicating the cases. "Hope you follow Aussie rules," he quipped.

"Not me—my boyfriend. Or rather, my ex-boyfriend," Rayan amended.

"Sorry to rush you along. But we are trying to get as many passengers through as possible. This snowstorm is about to close the airport down," he apologised. "Just follow the arrows and you should be OK," he smiled moving back.

"They can send people to the moon but they can't make wheels that go in a straight line," Rayan moaned as the baggage trolley nose-dived for the nearest passenger's legs. Too weary to be offended by the indignant looks cast her way, she wobbled through the entrance marked Visitor's Waiting Area.

The whiff of coffee from a nearly cafe area assailed her, making her feel nauseous. She searched the sea of faces for two men with identical features. There was no sign of anybody filling Imelda's description.

Every time the outer glass doors opened, a blast of cold air hit her. She could see people holding up placards with names scribbled in big letters. She craned her neck. The lettering was difficult to make out but she was fairly certain none of them were for her. Most of the card bearers had on thick padded parkas with the fur trimmed hood pulled well down over their faces. The snowflakes were rapidly turning the dark coloured parkas snow white making it difficult to distinguish one person from another. The twins might be amongst them.

Putting her rapidly ebbing strength behind it she trundled her trolley through the outer doors. Immediately, a blast of icy air took her breath away and she turned to go back in.

"Sorry love, security, you can't go back in that way."

Rayan startled and looked down to where a young soldier was crouched low his rifle cradled in gloved hands. She backed away and tripped over the trailing laces of her trainers. "Need help, love?" a man wearing a navy weather coat with a badge that said 'Security' on it asked looking slightly bemused at the odd get-up she was wearing. "Somebody meet you, love?"

Rayan nodded. "Yes, identical twins—two young men that look like each other," Rayan stuttered through chattering teeth.

The security guy gave a questioning smile. "Right. Do you know their names?"

A few minutes of confusion passed as she searched for the twins' names. "I did have it on a piece of paper their mother gave me…"

"What's your name, love?" the security man asked. She looks harmless enough, he thought. But in view of Clinton's visit to Northern Ireland…

"Found it. Their names are Raphael and Isaac Wright," Rayan panted.

The two-way radio crackled as the man relayed the information to someone inside. "Aye, right-right-do that," he said. "They're putting it out over the antenna," he said just as he spotted two gangly young fellas join the end of the queue.

"What did you say your name was again?" he asked.

"I didn't but its Rayan Ritchie."

The security man smiled faintly. Strange name, he mused. "You got a picture of these twins," he enquired.

Rayan shook her head.

"Those two over there," he said indicating the men. "Could it be them?" The placard holders were thinning out but the two young men with parkas obscuring their faces against the falling snow were still there.

Rayan looked balefully at the security man. "Can't be many twins named Isaac and Raphael. Imelda must have been on something when she named them," she said through chattering teeth.

"Wait here."

The security man walked purposely towards the two men. Rayan breathed a sigh of relief when all three began to walk back towards her. "Definitely twins—mirror image—and one's called Isaac and one's called Raphael," the security man quipped handing them back their driver's licences. Too cold to even thank him, Rayan pushed her luggage towards the twins. "Take care—roads like a bottle," the man called after them.

It's like driving on glass, Rayan thought shivering. She willed herself not to stare at the road ahead. In the beam of the car's headlights the road surface glittered and sparkled like cut diamonds. She looked out at the bright moon that illuminated the stark outline of the trees and the strange sight of smoke puffing from the chimney stacks of houses covered in patchy snow. It looked like a scene from a movie set.

She couldn't be sure which of the twins was driving. Coming out of the airport carpark there had been an argument about who was going to drive to Donegal. Raphael had insisted he would drive. Isaac insisted he would because Raphael only had a learner's licence while he had a full licence.

"You drive like an old biddy," Raphael scoffed his twin. "It'll take hours to get home. That's why we were late picking you up," he said over his shoulder to Rayan. "Isaac was driving like a snail."

"We were late because you stopped at that pub," Isaac argued back.

"I'm driving," Raphael insisted moving the seat back to allow for his long legs.

Rayan felt her heart lurch as the car slithered on the ice.

69

"Don't drive too fast in this snowstorm," Rayan mumbled. Raphael caught her eye in the rear-view mirror and gave her a baby face pout.

"How was your flight?" Isaac asked politely.

"It was twenty-six hours long," Rayan lamented. "And I had a four-hour wait at Heathrow for my flight to Belfast."

Raphael shifted in the driver's seat. "A lot quicker than when the Brits transported people to Queensland in New South Wales for stealing a loaf of bread."

"They were thieves and criminals," Isaac said.

"You call stealing food to feed your family a crime worth being sent to the other side of the world and a life of hard labour!"

"I had an overnight stop in Dubai," Rayan said hastily. "Your mum and I had dinner together. She gave me a set of keys. Do you have keys to the house?"

"Don't need them, Mum's always there," Isaac said.

Rayan studied the twins. From the back, the outline of their heads looked the same but Raphael has a much stronger jawline, she mused. Even sitting down, both twins' heads were well above the level of the windows. *Imelda isn't that tall. Must have taken the height from their father*, she thought.

The snow-capped hedgerows seemed to be just outside the car windows. Blearily, she checked the mileage hand on the dash. They had been driving for a while but it didn't seem to have moved. Her eyes grew heavy. She woke with a jolt as the car wheels spun out of control. They had turned off the main road onto a winding mountain road. The snow lay in drifts. The moon, bright as a lamp, illuminated the vast expansion of ground. Rayan felt a prickle of panic. "Where are you taking me? Is this the way to Donegal?" she asked, her voice quaking with fear.

"Just a shortcut to the top of the Glen Shane Pass," Isaac reassured sensing her unease. She looked out at the snow banked up on both sides of the road and shivered. They hadn't passed a house or seen another vehicle since they'd turned off the main highway. The car engine struggled and coughed hoarsely as they climbed steadily. If they had a breakdown here, they'd be frozen to death before anybody found them, Rayan thought.

"Here we are," Raphael said cresting a hill and changing down into first gear.

Rayan's heart began to pound. Her thoughts rushed back to the covert way Imelda had half-jokingly half-seriously explained away Raphael's womanising ways. "Why are we stopping?"

"Pub over there," Raphael said sliding out of the driver's seat. Pulling open the passenger door, he reached in a hand to help her out.

Stiff with cold and fatigue, Rayan fumbled to the edge of the seat and peered out. A faint rectangle of light briefly illuminated the snow in the front of an otherwise dark building. She could see deep rutted tracks in the snow as if a vehicle with heavy tyres, possibly a tractor had driver up to or past where they were parked. She shrank back into the seat. "How far are we from Donegal?" she quivered.

Raphael stamped his feet on the ground to keep them warm. "We're about hour and a bit from home—fifty miles or so. We'll get something to eat in here. They do a good pint of Guinness or a strong Irish Coffer. Come on. I'm freezing my ba…feet off out here," he scowled. He was quite close to her now and Rayan could smell the pungent but not unpleasant smell of his aftershave.

"I'm only going in if you promise not to drink." In the bright moonlight, she saw Raphael raise his dark eyebrows.

"Isaac can drive down the other side of the mountain. If that's to your pleasing," he joked, giving her a playful nudge and tucking her arm into the crook of his elbow. "Mind your step—cow dung under the snow." He looked down at Rayan's feet encased in her old trainers and Nat's damp bulging football socks. "You'll fit right in here. It's mostly farmers and old-timers who drink here." He smiled. "Better keep a good grip on you. Some old farmer will think his prayers for a wife have been answered," he chortled stepping her into the rectangle of light.

"Well, as I live and breathe, if it isn't Mr Romance himself," the big breasted girl behind the bar chortled. "Must be something special to bring you out from Derry City in the middle of a snowstorm," she smiled. Coming from behind the bar, she kissed Raphael full on the mouth.

"Daughter," an old man chided her. "Give the critters hot whiskies. Can't ye see they're near frozen," he reprimanded. The girl gave him a sulky look but did as she was told. "Come and sit by the fire and heat yourself, me dear," the old man said patting the worn padded seat beside him. Rayan found herself sitting before a blazing fire that was rushing headlong up the chimney. Its heat warmed her stiff cold legs and feet. Despite her feeling of foreboding, she let her back relax into the comfort of the seat.

She glanced about her. The bar seemed to have a warren of small rooms running off it. The one they were in wasn't much bigger that an old fashioned 'best room' with a bar at one end. Through an open door she could see people huddled around another fire in a similar sized room. As she watched, a gust of wind blew down the chimney sending a cloud of smoke over the drinkers. The glow of lamps set their faces in shadow and gave the rest of the room a dark sinister look. It was obvious some kind of meeting was taking place.

The old man followed her gaze. "Shut the outside door, Daughter," he said to the barmaid. "They'll be no more stragglers out the night. See to the lads down the bottom room and bring this wee lass another good strong drink and a bite of something to carry her over the Donegal Hills," he smiled.

"Right ye are, Dada," the barmaid said swinging her ample hips as she marched across and pushed a thick bar into place on the pub door.

The sound of the stout bar sliding into place made Rayan feel frightened. "You're closing up for the night. We should be going," she began, starting to rise...

"Sit where ye are. The night's young," Manus said knocking his pipe on the black iron side of the fire surround. "Tell me, what brings you to these parts?" She was saved from answering as Raphael placing a heaped plate of thick chicken sandwiches between them.

"We just picked her up from Belfast Airport," he explained catching the gist of Manus' question.

"Oh, Aye?" Manus said refilling his pipe.

"Eat up, I made these with my own fair hands," Raphael joked. It was obvious that Raphael was no stranger here. Munching the sandwiches, Rayan followed the upward spiral of the old man's pipe. It mixed with the blow back smoke from the fire circling the low ceiling above their heads. Her eyes steadied on a raised platform. She wondered did it hold a bed. Was it where Raphael bedded the barmaid?

"And what part of the world did ye say ye came from?" Manus asked.

"I'm Australian. But my grandfather was a Pom."

"Is that so? Your granda was a Brit?"

Rayan nodded as she munched on the sandwich.

"Ach well, since you're a visitor, we'll not hold that against ye," Manus said dryly.

Raphael gave her a small almost imperceptible wink and quickly turned the conversation to Isaac who had said little up to then. "Drives slower than our Ma," he joked with Manus. "My belly thought my throat was cut. I was so hungry for a bit of grub," he laughed.

Manus eyed the silent Isaac. Rayan noticed the old man didn't display the open face to him he extended to Raphael. "You didn't persuade him yet, then," he said turning back to Raphael.

A clock above their heads struck the hour. In the room across from them the meeting began to break up. Men with flat caps and heavy booted feet huddled into donkey jackets and an overcoat drifted out of what Rayan supposed was a side door, in ones and twos.

"Farmers and dwellers from the border farms," Isaac said in an undertone to her.

"Community alert meeting?" Rayan murmured.

"Yeah," Isaac lied.

"We should go too," Rayan said getting to her feet. She swayed a little. Embarrassed, she apologised. "Your bourbon is very strong."

"It's poteen," Isaac murmured.

"Poteen?"

"Illegal whiskey made in the mountains," Manus chuckled.

"Illegal bootleg," Rayan gasped.

"Divil the harm it'll do ye, woman. Give you a good sleep your first night in Ireland," Manus said nonplussed. "Sit down, m'dear. It's long 'til mornin'". Something in his voice told her he would broach no argument.

In the other room a woman started to sing. Soon, everybody in the small pub was singing, clapping, keeping time with their feet. Caught up in the music, it was a while before Rayan realised that Raphael was missing and that the girl was no longer serving behind the bar. Sure enough, the low ceiling above them gave a little shiver and the springs of a bed would be faintly heard.

Rayan glanced at the old man. Apparently unperturbed, he tapped in time to the singing with his foot.

Rayan arched her eyebrows and raised her eyes towards the low ceiling and the creak of the bedsprings. "We need to go," she mouthed at Isaac.

Isaac smiled and shrugged. "That's my brother; woman mad. But he'll work the better at the shovelling of the snow around the Manse after he's been with her," he murmured.

"Do you always stick up for him?"

Isaac studied his feet. "We've been sticking up for each other since we were born."

"Time to hit the road," Raphael said reappearing and grinning at them like a happy pup. "See you, Manus," he said grasping the old pipe smoker's hand.

"Aye, you will. Keep the flag flying," Manus said waving his pipe. His eyes slid past them to focus on his daughter as the drinkers in the other room gave her a rousing cheer. "Don't be long till you're back. Might need you if a pimple rises," he said eyeing the girl's flushed face.

"You can depend on me," Raphael laughed.

"If ah can't, you'll know about it," Manus said a steely look his sharp eyes.

The old man had been right. The strong illegal mountain whiskey made Rayan sleep. She woke as the car shuddered to a stop beside a hut with the sign that declared "Army Police Checkpoint". She gasped as a blackened face appeared and a voice demanded to see Isaac's driving licence. "Where you coming from, mate?" the soldier asked with a show of friendliness.

"Belfast Airport," Raphael snarled before Isaac had a chance to answer.

The soldier flashed his torch full on Raphael's face. "Wait here," he ordered.

Rayan's heart thudded. Armed police wearing flap jackets and armed with what looked like machine guns were checking out the car. "What are they doing? Why have they stopped us?" she breathed nervously into Isaac's ear.

"It's just a routine checkpoint. You'll soon get used to them," Isaac soothed.

"We'll soon be crossing the border into the Irish Republic," Raphael smirked. "We chased the Brits out of there in 1922. And it'll not be much longer until we get rid of these shower of bastards out of Ireland altogether," Raphael spat through gritted teeth.

Isaac turned a furious face to his twin. "Don't you say another word. Rayan has had a long flight. She doesn't need to spend the rest of the night in Strand Road Police Station," he hissed just as the soldier returned.

"Step out of the vehicle," he ordered. Isaac threw a mutinous look at Raphael.

Rayan's knees knocked together and her whole body began to shake. The soldier indicated they should go into the green galvanised search area.

"Names and address," a bored looking younger soldier said.

Isaac and Raphael started talking at the same time.

"One at a fucking time and talk fucking slowly," the soldier bawled. He turned and smirked at another soldier. "I can't make out a fucking word these paddies say, can you, mate?"

Rayan felt Raphael stiffen. After a few attempts at misspelling the twins' names and some snide remarks and crude jokes about them being twins, it was Rayan's turn.

"Name?"

"Rayan Ritchie," she said shakily.

The soldier pulled down his brow. "You trying to take the piss?" he snarled.

Rayan looked at him in confusion. "No. Why would I?"

"No fucking Irish women is called Raining!"

"She's Australian," Isaac put in quickly.

"And her grandfather was a Brit, just like you," Raphael scoffed.

"You finished that paperwork yet?" The soldier who had stopped the car roared over to the young rookie. "Get a move on. I have a fucking carload of drunks here who swear they're coming from an Alcoholic Anonymous meeting," he bawled. "Hurry the fuck up."

"It's not spelt like rain. It's spelt Rayan," Rayan pointed out.

"You are taking the fucking piss, missus."

"I'm not. I'll show you. It's on my passport."

Another, more senior, soldier moved in beside Rayan. He eyeballed the younger soldier. "That's enough fucking swearing out of you, mate," he growled.

"I have it here somewhere," Rayan said searching frantically in her bag.

Raphael jerked her arm. "Don't give them bastards your passport."

"Step back," a heavyset policeman in body armour ordered, poking Raphael with the butt of his gun.

"Right, move these showers out," the first soldier yelled at the rookie.

"But, sir, I haven't finished taking all their det—"

"You 'ave now, mate," Raphael smirked imitating his cockney accent and drawing Rayan back into the car.

What kind of a country have I come to where its border is guarded by heavily armed police officers and the British Army? Rayan thought shaking from head to foot.

"We'll be home very soon now," Isaac smiled meeting Rayan's terrified eyes. He looked away and then sought out her gaze again. "But you have to admit, you do have a very unusual first name."

"My parents are unusual too," Rayan muttered.

The only sounds in the car was the swish, swish of the window wipers and Raphael making little snorting, gurgling noises in his sleep.

"You have different kinds of names too—biblical names. Is your mother religious?"

Isaac laughed. "My granny Norah is."

Rayan nodded vaguely. She was too tired and stiff from travelling to listen to a story.

"We're here," Raphael's sleep voice said from the gloom of the passenger seat. "Beautiful Muckish Mountain," he yawned. Stepping out of the car, he spread his arms wide and bowing, paid homage to the snow-covered peaks of the mountain behind the house.

My new home for a year, Rayan thought, her heart sinking as she took in the isolated two-storey house.

Chapter Seven

The beautiful bouquet of bright yellow daffodils and wild daisies seem to light up the whole kitchen. Rayan's heart soared. Nathanial had sent her flowers. She cradled the cellophane-wrapped flowers and stroked the bright coloured ribbon tied in an expansive bow.

Above her head a floorboard creaked. The twins had arrived the Friday before for the Easter uni break. They were always out with their friends. She pressed her face into the flowers. Loneliness and homesickness jabbed at her like a physical ache like it had every day since she had arrived in mid-March. She wondered if Nat was as lonely and miserable in Sydney as she was in Ireland.

"Another sunny day; that makes three in a row," Raphael yawned, trailing into the kitchen. "I brought you a present," he said, nodding to a wicker basket brimming over with beauty products. "All Irish made," he yawned, absently scratching his groin. Rayan stared as he stood barefooted wearing a crumpled tee shirt and shorts. *I'm sure he's not wearing any underwear*, she thought.

"Students don't have money to spend on expensive presents," she said.

"Win it at the rifle range. There was a fundraiser for the local hospital. If you don't want it, leave it for Ma. She'll use it when she gets back," he said with a shrug.

"You're a member of a gun club? You must be a good shot."

Raphael laughed. "Yeah, I'm a fair good shot. Do I belong to a gun club? I suppose that's one way of putting it. See you have an admirer already," he smiled nodding at the flowers.

"Nathanial, my boyfriend, always sends me flowers at Easter time..." She let her voice trail off. She had said it as if she and Nat were still together.

Raphael whistled. "It must have cost a packet to send them through Intra-Florist. He must be missing you," Raphael said stretching. His tee-shirt rode up revealing his tanned belly. "Mac O Lochlainn, the old fella that does the bus tours, might be calling for me. Give me a shout if he does," Raphael yawned heading for the stairs. Rayan noticed when he crinkled his eyes, the small birthmark in the folds of the skin in his cheek disappeared. It was the only way she could tell him and his twin apart.

She spooned tea into the teapot. It was one of the things she liked about living in Imelda house—the taste of real tea. That and the thick unsliced bread, she thought. Plucking a knife with a serrated edge from the wooden block on the black veined granite worktop, she sliced the bread. She wondered idly if one of Imelda's former boyfriends had been a chef. The cooker was a gleaming combination of electric plates and gas rings. A top of the range chrome food mixer stood on the worktop ready for use. It was obvious no money had been spared.

Imelda's whole house—an old Manse—had taken her completely by surprise. From the front with its real stain glassed windows in the porch and its original bay seats, it looked like a well-maintained, if a bit dated, two-storey houses with small arched attic windows overlooking the gardens. But inside, it was very different—state of the art.

It's like its owner, full of contradictions, Rayan thought. Carrying her tea, she went into the sunroom off the kitchen and sank into one of the deep buttoned cream wicker chairs and gazed out of the floor to ceiling double glass doors that opened out into a paved patio area.

Raphael turned on the stairs and went back into the kitchen.

"Rayan," he said hesitantly, "I think Isaac is missing Ma. Could you, maybe, cook dinner for him—or something?"

Rayan stared at him. *I'm not his mother*, she thought.

Carrying her cup, she sat it down on the gleaming kitchen island beside the flowers breathing in the scent of the daffodils. Was Nathanial missing her? Maybe she had been wrong about him and Sienna. Should she email him? Afraid to allow herself to hope, she pulled on an old pair of boots she'd found in the back of the hall closet. Walking on Muckish always helped her think more clearly.

Right on cue, making a sound somewhere between a yawn and a sneeze, Dizzy the half Irish wolfhound, half god knows what, sniffed, stretched from the comfort of the leather kitchen sofa and got ready to go with her. Perplexed, Rayan looked at him. Compared to little Biscuit, he was the size of a small donkey. It was costing her a fortune to feed him. "Not today—no walking—more like pulling the arm out of its socket," she said.

Ignoring her, the dog shook his shaggy wheaten coloured coat and began pawing at the back door. "You are untrained and wilful," she berated him.

Stepping into the yard, she saw the B&B sign swaying in the wind on the corner of the outer porch. Imelda, it seemed, sporadically offered bed and breakfast for hill walkers. "Another one of the *little* things *dear Imelda* forgot to mention," she muttered. She'd have to get it removed before somebody asked to stay.

She startled as the rooster let out a sharp screech, warning her she was too near the chickens in the yard. Rayan brandished the black stout hawthorn stick she carried when she went walking. The rooster stuck out its red flaming beak and planted its webbed feet firmly in the dirt. Dizzy backed away. He gave Rayan a baleful look as if to say "See what you've done now. You've antagonised him."

"Some help you are—you're a great big chicken," she reproached him. "One of these days, you'll be gnawing on *his* bones and I'll be enjoying a nice dinner of curried rooster," she promised pulling up the zipper on her Barber jacket against the wind. She snuggled into the fur-lined wax jacket. *It's the one thing I have spent any real money on since I left Perth*, she mused. Except for my beautiful handcrafted Aran sweater, according to the shop owner, knit in an ancient Gaelic stitch.

She wondered what Sienna would make of her if she could see now. Most of the time she wore Isaac's jogging bottoms and his baggy sweaters she shrugged. Apart from going to her part-time job in the Spa at the Shingle Beach Hotel five miles away, she rarely went out.

She took the shortcut across the two fields below the house to the foot of the mountain. The boots made sucking noises as she threaded her way through the marshy ground. It's better than driving along that narrow winding mountain road in Imelda's jeep. If I met another car, I'd have to pull into the edge of the bog to let it pass. "That's another thing," she said to the dog, "your mistress didn't tell me I'd have to drive her four-wheel drive on these bendy roads."

She cringed in embarrassment, remembering Imelda's chortle when she'd asked how she would get about. Her idea of Ireland was what she saw in old films and postcards—Pony traps bumping over rutted roads and quaint little white-washed thatched cottages perched on the side of a hill where twelve children had been reared. She'd been surprised, shocked even, when she'd seen the beautiful substantial two-storey houses standing in extensive grounds; their gardens landscaped to within an inch of their live and upmarket car with their 1995 registrations parked in the driveways.

She was panting and breathless by the time she reached Muckish Gap in the foothills of the mountain. She stopped to draw breath, craning her neck to get a glimpse of the huge iron cross that dominated the mountain's summit. This morning the mountain wore a veil of mist.

"This is a lot harder than going boot scooting or playing tennis," she panted as she left the greenery of the bogs below and climbed higher. Raphael had told her this path was the easiest way up—that only experienced climbers climbed the face of the mountain on the other side where the old disused glass mines used to be. "I'll take you up when you get fitter," he promised.

The wind whistled around her, making her eyes water. She felt the boggy ground suck greedily at her boots as she stepped off the path to avoid some fallen rocks. Sweating now, she unzipped her jacket. Perching on a boulder, she looked back. The mist was lifting, revealing the fields and lakes below spread out before her like a gold and green quilt.

Imelda had been truthful about one thing, she thought. The view was panoramic.

Her feet slithered in the too big boots but she pressed on. She had a goal. Each morning she climbed a little higher. "Before summer comes, I will climb to the summit."

She called the dog. "That's far enough for today," she said. Dizzy ignored her like he did most of the time. Loose gravel skidded under his feet as he plunged into the spongy heather in pursuit of a mountain sheep. Rayan laughed. "Not your kind, Dizzy. You need to be a bit quicker on your feet to catch it," she said as the dog bounded back to the path. Watching him racing ahead of her Rayan wondered how nervous little Biscuit was getting on living in a strange city apartment over east.

A thought jumped into her head. When I email Nat to thank him for the flowers, I should ask him to come to Ireland.

Crossing back over the field the cows moved towards her as if of one accord. The dog cowed behind his ears flat to his head. Then he shot across the fields making for the gap in the hedge and the road beyond. Rayan quickened her step wondering if the bull was amongst the cows. She wasn't sure if she could tell what a bull was and what a cow was.

She walked faster; the wild rushes springing back against her legs. *I'm fitter*; she realised as she clamouring over the top bar of the gate of the field and dropped onto the grass verge of the road leading to the Manse. The thought pleased her and she was smiling as she went into the kitchen.

"Did you see Mac's tour bus on the road?" Raphael asked. Dressed in khaki bottoms and a tight body-hugging jumper that showed off his tattooed forearm, he stood beside the kitchen island shovelling breakfast cereal into his mouth.

Rayan shook her head. "I came across the field. Maybe he went without you," she said glancing at the clock on the wall.

"Don't think so…who is going to entertain all those flush tourists from the cruise ship that's docked in Derry City if I'm not there," he mumbled, his lips closing around the spoon.

I bet he's a great kisser. The thought jumped so unexpectedly into Rayan's mind that the glass of water she was drinking rattled against her teeth.

"Think I hear him now," Raphael said flashing her grin as he made for the door. Turning away, Rayan swilled the glass under the running water. She had the oddest feeling that Raphael had guessed what she was thinking. Her nipples hardened. Oh, for fuck sake. You could be his mother. Living in the middle of a bog at the foot of a mountain is making you fanciful. Get a life, she berated herself. She sighed. How I wish I could, she thought.

The few brief emails she had had from Imelda said she was having a great time enjoying the heat and going to the beach every weekend. She was even talking about taking a trip to Bali with all the new Australians friends she'd made. A stray thought crossed Rayan's mind. How had Nathanial known where to send the flowers?

She heard Raphael's feet on the gravel outside. "Mac says why you don't come with us on the tour," he said poking his head around the door.

Rayan stared into the small mirror perched on the windowsill. Bright pink scorch patches shone on her cheeks from the mountain air. Her hair stood up in wisps from the wind. The girls at the Spa had warned her that when she went out in public, she was a walking advertisement for the business.

"I have things to do."

"Come on. It's going to be a cracker of a day. There's going to be dinner and dancing. You've always said you'd like to visit Glenveagh Castle. Come on, now's your chance."

Rayan hesitated. She was tempted; it would be a good opportunity to see more of Donegal and something to talk about when she went to work. *Nathanial and Sienna are not moping about. They'll be out partying or making love,* her inner voice taunted her.

"Right, I'll just tell Mac you're coming," Raphael said reading the decision in her eyes.

"Wait! I have nothing to wear. And who will look about the dog?"

"I'll take care of the dog," Isaac's voice said coming into the kitchen.

"I didn't bring any decent things to wear."

"Mum has a wardrobe full of clothes she buys and never wears," Isaac said sulkily. Rayan noticed there was a quiver to his lip when he mentioned his mother.

"I can't raid her wardrobe—"

"What she doesn't know can't hurt her," Raphael said. "Hurry up. Mac's in a good mood. Don't keep him waiting."

Rayan tried matching up the few skirts and tops she'd flung into her suitcase in her rush to get away. She had wanted to be gone before Nathanial left for Sydney. That way it would look like *she* had left him. "I look frumpy and old," she moaned staring into the mirror. Disgusted, she stripped off again and sat down on the edge of the bed. Tears pricked behind her eyelids. She gritted her teeth. Why was it that these days she was always ready to cry?

"Ready?" Isaac's head appeared around the jamb of the door. He withdrew quickly when he saw her sitting in her bra and knickers.

"Sorry, Raphael wants to know if you're ready," he said from the landing.

"I have nothing suitable to wear."

"Wear something of Mum's."

"I can't wear your mother's clothes."

"She's probably using yours," Isaac said sullenly. In truth, he knew his mother wouldn't be seen dead in the kind of clothes Rayan wore. They were more like what his granny Norah wore.

Rayan opened the sturdy antique wardrobe that looked as if it had been in the house since it was built and stood staring at the array of bright clothes; many of them still had their labels still attached. Imelda obviously didn't stint when she went shopping, she thought, her eyes widening at the prices. In desperation she pulled out the plainest thing she could find; a red woollen long-sleeved wrap-over dress. Pulling it down over her hips she sighed in despair. She was a good head and shoulder taller than Imelda. The dress was way too short.

Isaac came back into the room. "Mum bought that in a sale. She never liked it. She said she'd give it to granny Norah; except they haven't spoken to each other for years." His face reddened when he realised what he had said. He backed out again, leaving the door open behind him.

Rayan could hear talking below her window. She glanced out. The bus driver was checking his watch and gesturing to Raphael. She moved to the mirror again.

"I can't wear this. It's supposed to be ankle length. Look at it. It's halfway up my calf," she muttered mutinously, staring at her reflection in the dressing table mirror.

"You have the legs to wear it as a maxi dress," Raphael said admiringly from the half open bedroom door. He grinned. "You'll need something warm to wear over it. In Ireland we get all four seasons in one day. What about that Aran knitted jacket thing you bought in Letterkenny? It looks great on you," he grinned. "I'll just tell Mac you're coming," he said letting his eyes travel over her. "Here, put on some of this stuff," he said thrusting the basket of beauty product at her. "The American women looking for their Irish roots are going to be green with envy when they get a load of you," he quipped.

"I'm not wearing it. It shows off my mother's fat ankles," she wailed but Raphael was already out the door and down the stairs.

Flushed with agitation, Rayan slashed eyeliner across her lids, pursed her lips together to even out the lipstick her boss Vivian at the Spa insisted she wear. Raking a comb through her short hair, she surveyed her scalp. "At least the hair has grown back and the new growth covers the bald patches," she muttered.

"It's better looking on you than it was on Mum," Isaac said sourly as she self-consciously walked down the stairs. "You and Raffi have a good day. Dizzy and me…we'll be fine here."

The bus was empty except for the driver. "Your man, Raphael, has them out taking photographs of Muckish," Mac O Lochlainn grinned. "That young fella could charm the snakes out of their baskets."

"Sorry for keeping you. I hope it doesn't disrupt your schedule."

He gave her an appreciative look. "It was worth the wait, darlin." He eyed the material of the dress stretched across her breasts. He got out of the driver's seat and came to stand beside her. "The Donegal air is doin' you the world o'good," he grinned. Rayan looked at him. Was he what Sienna called 'hitting" on her or just being friendly? Sometimes, she didn't get the Irish sense of humour.'

"Take the seat across from me. That way I can keep me eye on you." Mac winked as he climbed back into the driver's seat. This time she was definitely sure he was hitting on her. A small quiver of pleasure washed over her. It had been a while since she'd seen that look of admiration in a man's eye; even in Nathanial's she realised with a start.

A babble of voices rose as the tourists trickled back on to the bus. "Beautiful country—glorious view of the mountain dressed in purple heather," a smiling woman said beaming at Mac.

"You can't beat the old country for nature's beauty. Be sure to tell all your friends back in the States," Mac smiled.

Raphael plucked the mike from its bed in the dashboard and tested it for sound. "We are just leaving the Derryveagh mountain range," he pointed out in guide mode now. "I hope everybody got plenty of photographs. But before we leave Muckish Mountain, I am going to ask our driver, Mac, to make a short unscheduled stop at the Bridge of Sorrows." He glanced at Mac. "You OK with that, driver?"

Mac nodded his assent.

"Have we any Americans or Canadians with us today?" Raphael enquired with a smile. Rayan noticed that half the tourists were nodding vigorously.

"Is there anyone on the tour who has ancestors from Donegal?" There was a general murmur of assent.

"My great grandfather came from Falcarragh," the woman who had been admiring the bloom on the mountains said proudly.

Raphael beamed at her. "That's just a short distance from where we are now. When did he leave Ireland and immigrate to America?"

"In 1800," she said filling up with tears.

"He would have had to cross this bridge—The Bridge of Sorrows—to walk to the Docks in Derry City to board a ship to America. So the story I am going to tell you about this little stone bridge will be very personal to you," Raphael said moving down to sit beside her.

Rayan's gaze fixated on Raphael. His face had lost its grin and a serious look clouded his eyes. "During the Famine time in the 1846–48, the people of west Donegal, Falcarragh and surrounding villages, sons and daughters had to emigrate to America, Canada and even England and Scotland to find work to feed their starving families…"

A woman at the back of the bus spoke up, "My great-great grandfather was from north Donegal. That is one of the reasons I came on this tour today. To see for myself what it was like. But there's no poverty here," she said indignantly. They have bigger, better houses than we have in Canada," she snorted.

Raphael's jaw firmed.

Mac threw him a warning look.

"You're not wrong. Despite the Troubles in the North—which started in the late 1960s—the Celtic Tiger has made Ireland rich," Raphael said fixing a smile on his face. "But back in the famine times it was a very different story. There were no railways. Only horse and carts or a carriage and horses if you were gentry," he pointed out struggling to keep his voice on an even keel. "Families walked, all day sometime, with their son or daughter to the end of this bridge. Once their children crossed the bridge on their way to catch a ship at the Port of Derry—where you docked this morning—they knew they would never see them again." His voice quivered and died away.

"I've read about it, they held a wake—shed tears because they knew they would never see each other again in this lifetime," the woman beside Raphael said sadly. "Is that why it was named the Bridge of Sorrows?" she asked.

Raphael nodded as Mac shifted the bus into gear and manoeuvred the bus off the stone bridge. "Next stop the smallest pub in Ireland," he shouted above the hum of the engine.

A man and women across from Rayan snorted into their guidebook. "There's one in every tour we've been on," the man sneered.

Raphael sat down for a minute beside Rayan. "I didn't know you were so knowledgeably about the mountain ranges and what happened here hundreds of years ago," she murmured.

Raphael shrugged.

"Why aren't you studying history instead of law? You obviously have a flair for history," Rayan continued.

Raphael looked out at the passing countryside. He didn't answer for a minute as Mac negotiated a narrow strip of road. "Ma wanted Isaac to be a solicitor. So I did it too. It was what Ma wanted," he finally said.

"Do you always do what Imelda wants?"

Raphael gave a wry smile. "Yeah, I suppose we do," he said a surprised note in his voice. "Anyway, I'd rather live history…and help make more rather than learn it from books," he said.

Rayan was acutely aware of the smell of his aftershave and the heat of his thigh next to hers. She looked the other way as Mac slowed down to let the tourist take pictures of a man spading turf in a bog. He turned and winked at her. Hurriedly, she pulled at the dress so her knees weren't showing.

"Leave it," Raphael smiled covering her hand with his.

"The driver…he's staring at my knees every chance he gets," Rayan protested.

"Take it as a compliment. You have great legs. Don't know why you've kept them hidden under those ugly bottoms you insist on wearing, belonging to Isaac."

Rayan pulled her hand away. She didn't know whether to be angry at him or be pleased that he'd noticed. Nathanial never commented on her legs. But then, he was a breast man, she thought.

Raphael turned down country singer Daniel O Donnell singing 'Cutting the Corn in Creeslough today' playing on the bus' music deck and reached for the mic again.

"Best Guinness and Irish whiskey—as well as tea, coffee, homemade soda bread and plenty to eat, served in this little pub we're just coming to now," he said with an impish smile.

"Be sure to spend plenty—the Irish economy will love you for it," Mac laughed reversing the tour coach neatly into a parking space close to the pub door. "We'll be ready to go again in about an hour. Just be careful—don't wander too far. The bog land looks safe but it's full of holes further in," he warned everybody as they got off in twos and threes.

"Far too much crammed into this day tour. Why did you waste time parking the bus like that when our time is so limited here," the Canadian woman grumbled.

Mac tipped back his cap to her. "Good point, me darlin," he chuckled good-naturedly. "Always see better goin' in than coming out of the pub," he joked.

Rayan hurried inside, leaving the tourists taking photographs of the little cottages nestling in the shelter of the mountain. "Haven't the heart to tell them that most of them are holiday cottages owned by foreign tourists now," Raphael said. "Most of them stand empty except for the occasional visit from their owners every few years. That's how Ma came to get the Manse."

"Yeah," Rayan said not interested in how Imelda had come to be living there.

It took a minute for her eyes to adjust to the gloomy interior of the pub. It was tiny for a public house. The bar looked as if it had been a farmhouse kitchen in its day. Except now its walls were dressed in large mirrors in brown frames advertising Guinness and Irish whiskey. Scrubbed tables on wrought iron trestle feet littered with glasses surrounded by wooden stools were jammed close together. A bench to one side was weighted down with cycling helmets. Their owners gathered round its edge jabbering in broken English to a young woman stoking up the fire with turf.

"Mind the steps," Raphael advised grabbing her elbow as the small bar opened onto a much larger room. Long trestle tables laden down with food dominated its centre. Rayan recognised some of the people from the coach who had joined the long queue of people moving slowly towards it. Her belly rumbles and she remembered that in the rush out she hadn't any breakfast.

She scanned the pub for a toilet. Her thoughts slipped back to her doctor's comment in Perth about the menopause. She wondered if going to the toilet oftener was one of the symptoms. "Keep me a plate; I'll be back," she instructed Raphael.

"You need to be quick or this lot will have scoffed everything. Here, I have a better idea. We'll eat in style. I know the chef," Raphael said. "Go on, powder your nose—or whatever," he laughed giving her a friendly pat on the bottom. *What's the betting the chef's a woman?* Rayan thought.

The heat hit her in the face like a forest fire as they pushed open swinging doors into the kitchen. A small army of staff scuttled to and fro laden down with mouth-watering looking platters of food. A plump woman in chef's whites was stirring something in a pot on a huge cooker. "Maddie!" Raphael shouted a big cheesy smile creasing his face. The woman looked up with a perplexed frown preparing to challenge whoever was calling her by her name when they should've been addressing her as chef. Rayan noticed she was older than the barmaid Raphael had bedded on their way back from the airport.

"Raphael," she said sounding pleased. "What brings you out this way?"

"Cruise ship docked in Derry City and Mac O Lochlainn was short of a guide for showing the visitors Donegal. So I pulled him out of a tight spot. What are mates for," he laughed reaching across and giving her a lingering kiss.

A young waitress tittered then quickly moved away as the chef fixed her eyes on her. Raphael peered into the pot the chef had been stirring. "Any chance of a bit of grub for a poor starving student," he grinned. "Oh, by the way, this is Rayan. She's Australian," he said as if that explained why she was standing in the chef's kitchen.

Maddie drew her eyes away from Raphael and focused on Rayan. Seeing nothing to cause her any concern, she smiled. "You're welcome to Ireland. How are you finding it?" she said cordially wiping the sheen off her forehead with her forearm. "Missing the sun I'd say," she went on taking in Rayan's tall figure in the calf-length outfit. *No competition there*, she decided. Raphael likes something he can grab onto at night. Something with a bit of meat on their bones, like me, she thought. All the Aussie has going for her are her boobs. No worries there.

But still, you never know, she thought switching her focus back to Raphael. She glanced surreptitiously at Rayan again. Unlucky in love from the cut of her drooping mouth, she thought. "You with the cruise ship?" she asked to cover up her interest.

"She's doing a year's life swap with my Ma," Raphael explained before Rayan got a chance to speak.

Maddie's eyes narrowed. "Are you the Australian who's working at the Shingle Beach Spa?"

Rayan nodded, surprised. Seeing the expression on her face, the chef laughed. "News of people leaving a hot climate like yours to come and live in the wind and rain in Donegal spreads like bush fire travel in your country," she laughed.

"What about that grub before Mac comes looking for me," Raphael coaxed putting his arms around the chef's waist.

"Not in front of the staff," Maddie said pretending to scowl at him. "You know where the wedding garden is at the back?"

Raphael nodded.

"A table is set up for a bridal couple but they had a change of heart. Use that—I'll get somebody to bring you something as soon as I get a free minute." She hesitated. "Will you be back this way any time soon?" she said a hopeful note creeping into her voice.

Raphael shifted, putting the width of a broad work table between them. "Exams…from now to end June," he said giving a mock sigh.

Maddie felt her cheeks grow redder. "A nice batch of French champagne—just waiting to be savoured," she offered a plaintive note in her voice.

Raphael leaned towards her." What are the chances of you coming down and spending a night at the Manse? Bring a case of it with you. With Ma away, we could have a great wee party—just you and me. You wouldn't mind that, would you, Rayan?" he coaxed pretending to beg like a puppy.

Rayan bristled. Was he asking this woman to come and sleep with him at the Manse? A frisson of jealousy mixed with anger at his arrogance stirred in her.

The chef went back to stirring the pot. *Young cur*, she thought. *Comes here when it suits him. Then expects me to go and make love to him with that sour-faced Aussie listening to our every move*. She stirred the liquid in the pot faster. *I wish I hadn't mentioned it. It sounds as if I'm begging*, she fumed as the sauce she was stirring too vigorously started to curdle. But all she said was, "I'll let you know."

Mac waved them over as they passed out through the bar again. "Maddie is getting us a bite to eat. We'll be as quick as we can," Raphael shouted into Mac's ear above the rising din. Mac pointed in the direction of the dining area. The tourists from Mac's coach had taken over the now empty buffet table and the grumpy Canadian man and his wife who had complained about not having enough time on the tour to see everything were ensconced at the table, in full throttle belting out their version of Danny Boy accompanied by a fiddler and an accordion player. "Don't be in any hurry," Mac chortled. "It's going to be a while before we get this lot shifted."

"What about your schedule?" Rayan asked her eyes widening. Raphael pulled her closer to him as Mac turned to put his arm around her.

"What?" He shouted putting his hand behind his ear.

"What about your time schedule."

"Wait 'til I tell ye, darlin', it's them that's paying. When they're ready, I'm ready. And isn't the customer always right," he laughed. "Slainte," he chuckled raising his pint in salute.

"Yeah, especially if they're buying the Guinness," Raphael laughed.

A waiter was hovering beside their table as they ducked under the wedding bower decked out with hearts and roses. His eyebrows shot up as he took in their casual dress. Then he shrugged and uncorked the bottle of champagne that had been cooling in the rose-decked ice bucket. "You married," he beamed. "Congratulations."

Rayan guessed he must be Polish. "No. Not married, just…friends," she said emphatically.

The waiter looked confused. "Not married—just friends," he repeated.

Raphael laughed and held out his cut glass goblet for a refill. "Yes, we got married today. But don't tell the chef. At least not until she feeds us," he quipped.

"Stop it," Rayan scolded.

The waiter winked catching on to the joke. "No married—just friends—having…domestic tiff," he laughed as Rayan kicked Raphael under the table.

"I'll have a green salad and salmon," Rayan said.

"And I'll have steak and more steak with all the trimmings and more of that champagne. After all, it's not every day a man gets married," Raphael chortled.

The thicket hedge in the small wedding garden seemed to muffle the sound of the singing or maybe it's the wine, Rayan thought as she topped up her glass again. She hadn't been drinking since the night she had partied with the two guys she'd met in the hotel in Dubai. Her recollection of the night was hazy. But she did remember Denis, who was from New Zealand, undressing her.

"Have you ever been married?" "Raphael suddenly asked her."

She shook her head. "No, and I never will." There was a beat of silence. Rayan could hear new-born lambs bleating in the field behind them. "I have been asked," she said. "My boyfriend of six years asked me just before I came to Ireland. I refused him—for the sixth time."

Raphael raised his dark eyebrows and divided the dregs of the second bottle of champagne between them. "Good for you," he said raising his glass to her.

"Has Imelda—your mother ever been married?"

"No. Isaac and I have had a *long* succession of 'uncles'."

"Who was your father?" Rayan asked the wine making her tactless.

Rising abruptly, Raphael drained his glass. "That is the million-dollar question, isn't it," he said all the laughter gone from his face. "Come on, Mac will be looking to get on," he said striding out in front of her.

Chapter Eight

Rayan woke with a start. She'd been dreaming Nathanial was making love to her except when she looked at him, it was Raphael. Heart thumping like a drum, she lay feeling hungover and exhausted from the tour the day before.
It had been never-ending. Mac had skilfully manhandled the coach along narrow cliff top roads in search of round towers and ancient burial grounds; where one tiny jerk on the steering could send them all plunging to their deaths on the empty beaches below. The landscape had literally taken her breath away with its wild beauty but she'd kept a constant vigil on the sheer drop of the cliff face, worrying how much the driver had had to drink.

Outside the bedroom window, a lone bird opened its throat and welcomed the birth of a new day. Others joined in. Dragging herself out of bed she banged on the window hoping to shut down the dawn chorus that sounded like a full-blown orchestra in her throbbing head. She should have stopped at the champagne.

There was the sound of footsteps on the gravel below the bedroom window. Rayan shrank back. She didn't want to speak with the twins. She intended to stay in her room all day with a blackout on her eyes. Had someone come in or gone out? She listened. The house was silent. The only thing she could hear was the loud ticking off the clock at the top of the landing.

When she'd gotten in last night, a note propped up against the kettle from Isaac saying Dizzy had been fed and not to let her wander outside because there were new-born lambs in the far field. A scribbled postscript added not to wait up. He'd late back. She hadn't heard him come in. She wondered where Raphael had stayed last night. "It definitely wasn't in the student halls, studying," she muttered. She fidgeted about. She needed something for her pounding headache.

Dizzy was in her usual place on the sofa. Her tail beat a welcoming rat-a tat against the black leather. "Stop making that racket," she hissed.

Filling a glass under the cold tap grateful for the ice-cold water that came off the mountain streams she drank it down greedily. Soaking a cloth, she held it to her throbbing temple and leaned her back against the kitchen island.

Dizzy's eyes followed her every move. Satisfied she wasn't going walking, the dog rolled on to his back into a perfect yoga position, paws sticking up in the air, head lolling, pink tongue sticking out the side of its mouth.

Rayan wondered who the step on the gravel had been. Then she noticed the bread and fresh cream fingers on the kitchen windowsill. It had only been the woman from the mobile shop.

Plucking two tablets from the First Aid box, she washed them down with another tumbler of water. It had rained during the night and the green ivy leaves clinging to the wall opposite the patio dripped shiny moisture. She opened the glass door of the sunroom and stepped out. Shivering, she tightened the belt on the man's thick dressing gown she'd found hanging behind Imelda's bedroom door.

Beyond the trellis that separated the patio from the back of the Manse she heard the rooster making his clucking sounds. Sensing her presence, he gave a blood curling screech. "What is it with that bloody bird," she rasped holding her head. Bending down, she picked up a handful of loose stones from the pebbled edge of the patio and flung them over the fence. The flurry of feathers and his high-pitched squawking told her the pebbles had found their mark. Satisfied, she went back in.

In the stillness of the early morning she heard the loose boards on the stairs creak. Isaac plodded into the kitchen. She stepped back into the sunroom, hoping he'd get what he wanted and go back to bed.

"You're up early. Good day out with Raffi yesterday?" he asked.

"I didn't think it would last so long," Rayan mumbled. "It was early evening before the tour reached The Point Hotel," she said tiredly. "And then the eating and dancing…for hours."

"Cup of tea?" he offered casting a glance at her. Without waiting for an answer, he plugged in the kettle. Rayan pressed her fingers to her temple. The rattling of the cups sounded like clashes of thunder.

"I bet that crowd from the cruise tucked into the mulled wine and full on dinner," Isaac grinned.

Rayan groaned. "They did. Then they strolled around the manicured lit gardens as if they were ancestors of some ancient Irish lord," she muttered gulping at the mug of tea he passed over to her. She looked at him. He was definitely more animated this morning. Like Sienna after a good night out with her latest conquest. She wondered if he'd had a date the night before.

"Did Raffi come home?"

"He went back to Derry with Mac."

"Yeah, Easter...busy time of the year for his *friends,*" Isaac sniggered. She glanced at him. There was an undertone in his response she didn't quite understand.

Rayan felt herself unwinding as the headache tablets began to work. The sky's fading streaky dawn colours slipped away and a weak sun filtered across the glass domed sunroom roof teasing out the rustic stone of the Manse wall that made up one side of the patio.

"Who lived here before Imelda?" she asked remembered Raphael's remark about the house.

Isaac yawned. "I think it had a few owners. It belonged to a church minister at one time. He was promoted to bishop and moved," he said. "It lay empty for a while and then an American businessman bought it. He was going to turn it into a secluded getaway for his business cronies. It was him who spent the big bucks and added on all this," he explained, the wave of his arm taking in the new kitchen patio and sunroom.

"How did Imelda come to live here?"

"Mum got a job at the hotel. We lived in granny's house then," Isaac said looking out to the small orchard of apple and pear trees. "The American owner threw lavish parties. Mum worked at them serving drinks. Long story short, right," he yawned. "The American got bored with it all. The house lay empty for a long time. Campers and hill walkers started to use it as a free place to kip down in. Mum began to bring us here at weekends and school holidays to get away from granny Norah. Her and Mum were always shouting at each other so one day Mum packed all our things and brought us here to live."

"She rented it from the American owners?"

"Not exactly...we lived unofficially in a few of the rooms...and then Mum started fixing the place up so we could live here permanently."

"What about the American owner? Does he know Imelda has been squatting in his house for...eighteen years?"

Isaac fidgeted with his cup. "Mum's never let on...as far as I know."

Rayan looked at him incredulously. "He doesn't know Imelda is living here?"

Isaac was silent. Too late she remembered he didn't like criticism of his mother. "Mum has saved it from being vandalised," he said standing up. "She keeps all the repairs done—"

"By keeping paying guests—hill walkers and German tourists, if that sign outside is anything to go by," Rayan pointed out. "I bet she doesn't even have public liability insurance, does she?"

Isaac hunched his long back. "She set out the vegetable garden. Set up a small market business. I helped her," he said under his breath. "Granny Norah didn't want us."

"What if the owner decides to come back? What then? Imelda will be homeless and so will you and your brother! And I'll be trespassing!"

Isaac rounded on her. "She needed a home for Raffi and me. That's all she thought about. That's all she ever thinks about," he said stoically.

Rayan looked at the set of his jaw. She'd offended him. "She might have told me the house didn't belong to her before she decided on a year's life swap." The shrilling of the phone startled them both.

"You expecting a call?" Isaac asked.

Rayan moaned. "It's probably bloody Vivian." She and Vivian had taken an instant dislike to each other.

"We need someone front of shop," Vivian Cleary's clipped tones snapped out. Rayan ground her teeth into her bottom lip. She wanted to scream down the phone she was a hairdresser; a paid-up member of the Chambers of Commerce—not a bloody receptionist.

"I feel unwell. I can't come in today," she said. She could feel the chill coming down the line. "Forget I called. You can't work on Reception yet, can you?" Vivian's syrupy voice said. "Not until you have work done," she said mockingly.

The sight of Rayan's skin and short hair and fuddy duddy clothes had sent Vivian into a state the first day Rayan had shown up at the spa. "That look may be in fashion in Australia," she'd said, curling her lip, "but our clientele expects our female staff to look like *feminine woman*. The vintage look is not the image we want to put out there," she smirked taking in Rayan's squared-necked top over trousers and open-toed scandals. "Our clientele relax in an environment where they feel young and chic—new millennium, not 1960s," she'd finished haughtily.

Rayan's temper had gone from nought to one hundred in seconds. Imelda had made no mention of her bitch boss. Hands on hips Rayan had pivoted a full 360 degrees until she was eyeball to eyeball with her new boss. "In Western Australia, painted mannequins don't pass for people," she had retorted glaring at Vivian. Damn cheek of her, she'd fumed. Thirty-something with breasts like pancakes, non-existent hips and a sour face made up like the painting of the Mona Lisa. How dare she insult me like that, Rayan had seethed.

She'd fought down the urge yet again to tell Vivian where to stuff her job. "I'm not needed, then?"

"We do have a senior ladies seminar booked in. I will pencil you in for that," she said cattily, clicking off.

"I have to go to work," Rayan said angrily.

"I'll drive you," Isaac offered. "It's tricky driving on the mountain roads in the mist if you're not familiar with the sharp bends and potholes. You shouldn't drive Mum's jeep when you're hungover."

"It would be just terrible if I damaged your mother Imelda's precious car."

Rayan looked at him mutely. I'm spiralling back into my old angry ways, she thought staring at the hurt in Isaac's eyes. Raphael hadn't spoken to her since she'd insensitively asked who their father was. Back on the bus, he'd acted as if she had tricked him into disclosing something private. The giddy happy moments they'd shared sipping the champagne vanished as like the snow that had covered the roads on her first night in Ireland. Now, she had offended Isaac too.

She placed her hand on his arm. "I'm sorry, Isaac. I didn't mean to be so blunt—Australians can be like that. Why don't I make it up to you by buying you a nice meal at the hotel?"

Isaac drew in a breath. "It's OK. I have revision to do." He hesitated. "A home-cooked meal would be nice," he said in a rush.

"You're on. And I'll be glad of the lift if the offer is still there. But first I'll freshen up the water in the flowers before I go," she said.

A small smiled played around the corner of Isaac's mouth. "They're beautiful. Mum will be furious she missed seeing her bouquet."

Rayan looked quizzically at him.

"The flowers—they're from her latest conquest. I found his business card tucked inside the wrapping."

Rayan sipped the wine she'd bought in Creeslough on her way back from the Shingle Beach hotel. She needed it. Vivian had been a real bitch, finding fault with her at every turn. When she got back to the Manse, Raphael still hadn't come back. Was he still in a strop with her? It was obvious Raphael had no idea *who* his father was. What you shouldn't have asked, she told herself. It's hardly Isaac's and Raphael's fault if Imelda slept around and got pregnant with twins, she mused. You know how so-called home truths hurt *you*.

Knowing her parentage had *been* her problem. Her father the college Administrator. He reminded her at every opportunity how her behaviour reflected on his reputation. Pity he doesn't look at his own behaviour, she thought.

She could clearly recall as she grew up, her father's belittling snide remarks, when he had an audience at one of his legendary dinner parties or barbecues, "This is my beautiful wife, Dawn," he'd smiled playing the devoted husband. "And this is my little plain Jane—I mean Rayan, my daughter," he'd chortled.

As she'd gotten older, she'd hurt him back. "He's not really my father. He adopted me from one of those institutions who looked after aboriginal mixed-race unwanted children," she'd tell a shocked guest in pretend confidence.

She startled out of her reverie. Dizzy's wet nose nudged against her palms. "What possessed Imelda to get such a big brute of a dog like you?" she muttered.

"She rescued him from Donegal rehoming Centre," Isaac said coming into the kitchen. He laughed as the dog stood up and looked expectantly into his face, his tail wagging furiously. "I'll take him for a walk before he breaks the door down," he said slipping the walking harness over the dog's bulky body. "We have campers on the edge of the field beside the orchard," Isaac said, the wind blowing through the open door rattling the pot lids on the cooker.

Rayan stilled. "Did you see them?"

"Dizzy was sniffing about yesterday and I saw a bald spot where a fire has been lit. There were empty takeaway cartons and empty beer cans. Don't worry. It'll be Easter Bank Holiday revellers," he soothed seeing the anxiety in Rayan's face.

"Do you think we should check it out? What would Imelda do?"

"She'd invite them to dinner."

Rayan eyes rounded. "She'd invite strangers to *stay* in the house!" Her mind flashed to the B&B sign she could clearly hear creaking in the wind.

Isaac nodded. "She used to take in all kinds of people until the local Garda—the police—warned her not to do it anymore; too dangerous now with the Troubles just across the Border in Derry. They advised her to get a good dog—scare people off."

Rayan snorted.

"I know," Isaac laughed. "You're afraid of your own shadow, you big lump, but you look the part," he joked rubbing Dizzy's ears. "You see what I mean about Mum saving this old house…"

"Yes. I'm sorry about this morning…" Rayan waved aside Isaac's protests. "How Imelda lives her life is none of my business. I hope this nice meal will make up for what I said."

Isaac blushed. He had the strongest urge to kiss her. He couldn't stop staring at her full lips. What the hell was going on? He had never felt like this with any of the college girls who had tried chatting him up. "After I walk Dizzy, I'll chase the chickens down off the trees and close them in for the night in case the fox is prowling around," he mumbled, acutely aware of Rayan's nearness.

She chuckled. "I hope the fox gets the rooster. Don't be long. I'm ready to plate the dinner." She turned away. "Raphael will be home soon and then you both can go and check the chickens and the prowlers," she said trying to quell her fear as she looked out of the kitchen window at the solid black blanket of inky darkness. It had been a real shock to realise there were no street lights or no neighbours for miles.

"Why don't we have it in the other room? We can lock up the back of the house. I'll light the fire…if you like."

Rayan felt frightened at the idea of somebody close to the house. Raphael had told her there was a lover's lane behind the house. Courting couples parked up there. But he had also impressed on her that if she heard cars on the road at night, she was to draw the blinds and keep the light low and not answer the door. "Did you hear any cars?" she asked tentatively.

Isaac shook his head. "It's nothing. I'll walk the dog later on. Let's have our dinner."

He's such a child compared to his twin, Rayan thought. But she was glad he was here and she wasn't alone in the house tonight. On impulse she leaned over and traced the outline of his face with her index fingers. He is such a pretty boy, she thought. "Lighting the fire sounds a good idea," she said softly.

All thoughts of prowlers left Isaac as he went back to thinking about kissing Rayan. Don't be stupid and brainless. She's as old as mum, he reminded himself as he put a match to the fire and unfolded the small card table and set it up between the winged armchairs in front of the fire in the dining room. He rummaged in the oak sideboard for the cutlery his mother used for special occasions. What was so special about this occasion, he couldn't say. He just *felt* it was.

Raphael wouldn't worry about age if he had a woman like Rayan that liked him. He kisses women all the time. If kissing got him good grades, he'd be coming out top of the heap, he thought.

"But I'm not Raphael," he muttered, going back to search for wine glasses. He gave the glasses a cursory wipe. He was sure Rayan liked him. He was *certain* she liked him more than Raphael. Euphoria like a flash of lightning surged through him. She liked him better. "But maybe not in that way," he moaned.

He closed his eyes and visualised how her body had looked, womanly and curvy, when he'd walked in on her yesterday when she'd been trying on Imelda's clothes.

Flustered, he looked down at the wineglass he was clutching in his fist. Should he put on the table lamps or the main lights? He startled. Rayan was calling him to come and help her carry in the food. He gave the glasses another cursory shine, hoping Raphael wouldn't come to monopolise the dinner.

Rayan was totally thrown with the change that had come over Isaac. He seemed to have changed—grown up. Sitting across from him with the lamplight shading the room with its subtle glow and the light of the fire playing on his features she was struck again by the uncanny resemblance he and Raphael shared. She could be sharing a dinner with his twin. And yet, they are so different. Isaac has none of his brother's arrogance, she mused.

The conversation ebbed and flowed easily between them. For the first time in a long time Rayan felt her anxiety and homesickness dissipate. Even the fact that the flowers had been for Imelda and not from Nathanial for her didn't bother her tonight.

Much as I hate to give Imelda credit, Rayan mused, she has brought her boys up with gentlemanly ways, she thought, watching Isaac skilfully uncork the second bottle of wine and refill her glass.

"How did you come to run your own business?" he asked.

Rayan's hands stilled. "It was the only way I could get away from my father and earn enough money to support myself," she said surprising herself with her honesty. "What about you? You're studying law?"

Isaac looked down at his dinner plate. "Mum's choice, not mine."

"What would you have liked to do?"

"Market Gardening, I think."

"Then do it. Tell Imelda you're changing courses. Students do it all the time."

Isaac smiled at her. "Mum planned to be a barrister before she got pregnant with Raffi and me. I did try to tell her law wasn't for me but she has her mind set on me being a judge."

Rayan's head felt a bit woozy from the wine. She gave a giggle. "A judge? I'm sorry. I'm not laughing at you…it's the wine," she chortled, feeling lightheaded.

Isaac proffered the bottle again.

Rayan held her hand over her glass and then relented. "Just a little—I don't think drink and I make very good companions," she tittered.

"It's OK. I think my being a judge is a daft idea too," Isaac admitted. Moving the table aside he stoked up the fire trying to think of ways he could keep his mind off Rayan's lips. "Right, here's the deal," he joked to cover his confusion. "I'll tell the first joke and you have to better it with another."

At some stage Rayan's awareness of their age difference fell away. Isaac was good company. She felt young again. Even more amazing, she hadn't thought about Nat or Sienna all night! Maybe this life swap thing would work out for her after all, she thought.

"Thank you. I had a lovely time," she smiled as they cleared away the dishes.

"You're welcome." Buffeted by the wine Isaac kissed her. "I think you have beautiful lips," he blurted out.

"And I think you need to go to bed. You have uni in the morning," Rayan chuckled, kissing him back as she pushed him in the direction of the stairs.

"One for the road," Isaac teased. Before she could object, he cupped her face in his hands and ran his tongue around her lips.

Rayan's groin tightened. Oh god, how I missed Nathanial's hands roaming over my body, she thought. But Isaac… Isaac was only a boy!

She put her hands on his chest and gently pushed him away. "Goodnight Isaac," she said her voice coming out all quivery. "See you when you get your summer holidays in June."

Chapter Nine

From her lounger on the startling white sands of Scarborough Beach, hardly daring to believe she was actually in Western Australia and drinking in the beauty of the Indian Ocean and the surfers, Imelda watched the lithe figures of a group of young women stretch and manipulate their bodies into yoga positions she would never ever get into. Or out of if she was foolish enough to try them, she thought ruefully.

Pushing her sunglasses onto to her hair, her gaze fixated on the yoga class instructor. Five nine tall, she guessed, with the physique of a body builder, which got every woman on the white sand's attention.

Nathanial, Rayan's ex, was back from Sydney. And boy, he's something else, she thought.

Listening to Rayan ranting on about him, she hadn't known what to expect. But not this handsome Mr Universe type guy! Jesus! He was *amazing* to look at. Like something you'd see in the movies, Imelda thought in awe.

Overhead, peachy coloured clouds scuttled across the sky and dipped to meet the horizon. Their orange hue reflecting off the white capped waves transformed the clear waters of the Indian Ocean into a dramatic backdrop of liquid fire.

Its beauty was just another day at the office for Nathanial. Standing absolutely ram rod tall like a dancer, he rested his left leg on his inner right thigh and raised his hands in prayer form to create an arched heart shape above his head as he went into the final tree pose.

The setting sun behind him painted his body into a perfect silhouette.

Imelda sat transfixed.

The light breeze, Sienna called the 'Ferndale Doctor', held its breath as the group and Nathanial held their pose.

Like a bronzed work of art, Imelda said, suddenly palpating.

"That will be all for today. See you tomorrow," she heard Nathanial say.

There was a murmur of thanks as the students drifted in twos and threes off the beach and climbed the wide sweeping stone terraced amphitheatre steps towards the restaurants and bars that lined the long wide street that made up the Scarborough resort.

Imelda lingered, soaking up the beauty of the magnificent sunset. Then, she gathered up her things. She needed to get back and get ready. Sienna had invited her to join her and Nathanial in a community barbecue tonight.

As she tossed scented bath oil into the bathtub, she remembered she'd neglected to mention to Rayan that she had given Sienna her job back. And 'promoted' her so she could take responsibility for opening the salon on the days they hadn't many appointments. "Hell, I didn't come twelve thousand miles to the other side of the world to be stuck listening to old biddies murmuring their life's secrets as if they were in the confessional and asking me did I ever see any faeries in Ireland. I intend to soak up every blink of Aussie sun and return to those bitches at the spa with a tan they would kill for," she chortled, dipping a toe into the bubbly frothy bath water.

Sienna was no pushover, she mused as she breathed in the aroma of the scented candles and placed her wine glass within easy reach. She'd haggled until Imelda had agreed to reinstate her hairdressing apprenticeship and let her and Nathanial live in the condo.

Imelda stilled as she disrobed. She hadn't been happy about that. It didn't seem *right*. Nathanial was old enough to be Sienna's father. Seeing them together as a couple had been almost as big a shock as imagining plain jane Rayan and body beautiful Nathanial together as a couple—and for six years, she mused as she soaked in the luxurious bubbles.

Sienna loved to chatter—especially about her conquests...and about Rayan, Imelda mused as she stretched out one well-toned leg and watched the bubbles sparkle like a rainbow. Not that she believed half of what Sienna told her. Nathanial didn't seem the type to let women abuse him... Still?

A woman wronged—whatever her age—venomous as the snakes in the long grass she'd been warned to watch out for here, she mused. And Sienna definitely *felt* wronged because Rayan had sacked her in a fit of jealous rage.

She's definitely out for revenge, Imelda mused. She's talking of opening up a hair and beauty place of her own in direct competition with Rayan as soon as she qualified. And by the set of her she just might do it. She's not as empty headed as she likes people to think, she mused, savouring the wine.

Towelling herself dry and liberally splashing on sun aftercare, Sienna's vindictive vendetta against Rayan gave Imelda an idea. She could train her in beauty therapy work—hair and face makeovers; simple head massages…. Add a bit of class—expand the type of boring clientele the salon currently attracted—earn a bit of extra cash while she was here.

She considered the idea as she got ready. It could work. It wouldn't eat into the profits that much if she employed casual staff like the young school drop outs that had come in enquiring about job sharing so they could take turns looking after their baby.

The young fella had reminded her of Raphael bursting with testosterone. She hoped *he* was keeping his pecker in his trousers or at least using a condom. No way was she ready to be a granny yet—not by a long chalk, she thought as she heard Nathanial's car pull into the driveway.

She'd not rush out to meet him. She'd let him use his house key; offer him a drink. See where it went from there…

She shrugged. Where was the harm? If you wanted something go for it, had always been her strategy. She wanted Nathanial. Not for long—just while she was here. She wasn't looking a serious relationship; just a guy, like Nathanial, to take her out, show her a good time. After twenty years of bringing up my boys I deserve it and I am dammed well going to get it, she resolved. Anyway, she could tell Sienna was already getting bored with him

She checked her tan in the mirror. After three months in Perth, despite arriving at the tail end of the summer, beginning of autumn even, she had already lost her pale ice cream Irish skin look. Now her skin was beginning to have a soft Mediterranean glow to it.

Going into the lounge room she arranged herself on the sofas and crossed her legs in what men had often told her was an easy-on-the-eye chic style. She smiled. It was how she liked to think of herself. She knew she looked good in the new pale orange shift dress with the swirly tails she bought when she went shopping with Sienna. The dress went well with her sandy coloured hair that had shades of gold in it now from the Aussie sunshine.

She'd worn the new two-piece bikini she'd bought, underneath—just in case the barbecue turned into a beach party. She thought it was a bit *riskier,* for her age, but what the hell, when in Rome and all that—she smirked as Nathanial gave a light tap on the door before stepping in.

"Nice ass," Imelda murmured as he took the seat opposite her.

"Thanks," Nathanial said laughing, used to woman commenting on his body parts.

"Sorry. I do think you have a nice ass. I thought so when I was watching you taking your class on the beach today. But I didn't intend to say it out loud," Imelda lied. "Too much Aussie sun," she quipped.

"No worries. I've had much worse than that said to me. You should have joined us. Didn't you feel cold sitting out there on the beach today?"

Imelda shook her head. "It was amazing. I loved watching the students. All that dedication and energy… And what about that sunset—amazing."

Nathanial grinned. "Yeah, this lot are keen. Probably want to pack in as much beach work as they can. Its late autumn now—soon be June—the start of winter. Don't you feel the weather getting cooler, especially in the evenings?" He paused. "Now that I'm here, I should show you how to set the air con to winter setting," he offered.

Imelda laughed. "Your weather temperature in autumn is like our best sunny summer days in Ireland."

"Yeah? I've never been to Europe."

"No? Maybe you will soon."

"We should go," Nathanial said beginning to feel uncomfortable in the familiar surroundings. Despite knowing full well Rayan was living in this woman's house on the other side of the world, he felt her presence in the room. He noticed the Oriental rug was back to its pristine condition. Rayan had had it specialist cleaned.

A little shiver travelled down his spine. He could just imagine the hot throbbing rage his being alone in *her* house, amongst her things, with another woman, would arouse in Rayan.

His eyes were drawn to Biscuit's empty basket. She hadn't liked Sydney. And Sienna had been useless at taking care of her, he thought. He glanced surreptitiously at Imelda wondering if she was fond of dogs. How he would love to see little Bisky in her own basket instead of cooped up in the condo with Sienna yelling at the poor little mutt every turnaround.

He looked out through the window. The leaves on next door's tree had been a lush green when Rayan had gone away. Now they were a yellow gold tinged with red. Time was passing. The seasons were changing. Everything was changing. Despite all that had happened he missed her. Sienna was hard work!

Always pouting and preening—never happy. He looked longingly at the kitchen-dinette. And she can't cook for squat, he thought.

"Where did you say Sienna was? I thought she was coming…"

"She changed her mind and went shopping at the Mall with her friends instead."

"Did she? I thought it was her idea to go to the barbecue?"

Nathanial stood up. "It was—that's Sienna for you, as unpredictable as the Aussie weather."

Imelda stood too. This close she could smell the salty smell of sea spray off him. Turning to pick up her bag, she almost found herself in his arms. "Do you really want to go to this community get-together? I could cook us a dinner here…"

Chapter Ten

Rayan watched surreptitiously as two guests stopped at the hotel staff notice board and kissed. Her gaze wandered past them. Her photo and details had been added to the staff profiles, finally.

The photographer had taken Rayan's photograph three times before Vivian had consented to have it posted on the board. "Do you like it?" Sue, one of the beauticians, asked, stopping to chat to Rayan who was (again) manning the Spa's appointment desk.

Rayan shrugged. "Vivian had to go and spoil it by commenting that it would 'do' as it was only a head and shoulders shot."

"Yeah, she can be a mean bitch. But you have to agree she did write you up a good spiel. She even upgraded you to 'masseur'." Rayan was saved from answering as the young couple arm in arm sauntered across the foyer and stopped at the desk. "We want to book… Everything—sauna, massages—the works," the man laughed.

"Certainly sir, and have you decided which staff member you'd like for your treatments?"

The young woman cast a coy look at the man. "We want to have the massages together."

Rayan glanced at the matching gold wedding rings gleaming on their third finger. She raised her eyebrows and glanced at Sue.

"I'm sure that can be arranged. I'll just book you in for Vivian, our head masseur," Sue said edging Rayan aside. The guests glanced back at the staffing board.

"We want you," they said in unison looking at Rayan.

Sue stiffened.

"You're Australian, like us," the man said as he playfully stroked his bride's hair.

Rayan smiled. "Yes I am."

She guessed he was in his late twenties; younger than Nathanial but older than Isaac and Raphael. She jerked her mind back to their room details. Ever since Isaac had kissed her, she seemed to have become fixated on people's ages.

"Enjoy your stay at the Shingle Beach Hotel. And I will see you tomorrow morning for your first joint appointment," Rayan said giving the couple a smile.

Sue checked the appointments on the computer. "Vivian is not going to be too pleased. She likes to get the young hip-swingers."

Rayan gave her a puzzled look.

"There's a perks order in the Salon. The management get first bookings of the hotel guests, the permanent staffs get the regular customers and part-time and temporary staff gets what's left."

Rayan drew her newly waxed eyebrows into a frown. "They asked specifically for me. What was I supposed to do? Refuse to take them?"

"I like your new look," Sue said changing the subject. "The facials and the regular hair styling has worked…makes you look much younger. Your hair will be nice when it grows down into a short bob cut."

Rayan carefully felt her hair.

"You have great cheekbones," Sue went on, "with the right shade of foundation and eye makeup, you could look fantastic."

Rayan felt flustered. Sue could be tricky. She never knew if she was paying her a compliment or making fun of her.

"Have you had lunch yet?"

Rayan shook her head.

"I was hoping you'd come and eat with me at that new fish restaurant in town."

Rayan shook her head. "Too upmarket for a temporary masseur like me," she said coolly.

"Freebie lunch for the hotel staff and some of our guests courtesy of the new restaurant owner and an opportunity for the hotel to poach some of their patrons for some pampering here," Sue pointed out.

"Sounds lovely, but I'll pass," Rayan said. Then she had second thoughts. It was Friday. The weekend stretched long and lonely in front of her. "Yes, maybe I will," she said. Turning, she saw an oddly pleased look filter across Sue's face.

"Great, I'll go and get one of the others to cover here while we're out," she said.

Rayan watched Sue sashay across the expansion of glossy flooring and disappear into the back of the salon. She drew her brows together and frowned. Then remembered it was a habit she was trying to break she relaxed her face. She couldn't make up her mind about Sue. She and Vivian were partners, joined at the hip. Sue always took charge when Vivian was away, like today. She wondered if Sue was on an information gathering exercise. "She'll get no juicy bits of my life to pick over," she murmured as she stole a quick look in the mirror opposite at her new appearance.

As they waited to be shown to a table, Sue noticed the young newlyweds "Nice piece of ass, isn't she? Wonder if her tan fades in winter. Says he met her in Melbourne," Sue murmured into Rayan's ear. "Don't look so shocked. I saw you checking out her new husband," Sue chuckled.

"She's very beautiful. I'd guess she's part Aboriginal," Rayan said.

Sue's eyes widened. "I thought her skin tone looked a bit like yours."

"You think I look aboriginal?"

"Well, not your hair obviously; sorry I didn't mean to be personal," Sue said flummoxed as the waiter showed them to a table.

Watching Sue pick at her food Rayan wondered if what the staff whispered behind Sue's back was true. She was Vivian's partner in life as well as business. Gina, a student on a week's work placement from the local college, had bluntly asked Vivian, "You two an item, then?"

"All you need concern yourself with is the *report* I will be writing up for your tutor," Vivian had said icily.

"You clocking his bodywork," Sue smiled giving the couple a small wave.

Rayan studied the menu. "Nathanial, my...ex-boyfriend was into body art. Our guest reminded me a bit of him that's all."

Sue smirked.

"I did have a life before Ireland," Rayan snapped. She let her finger slide aimlessly down the list of fish dishes.

"What about a glass of wine to go with our meal..."

Rayan shook her head. "I'm on the late roster."

"The girls at the Spa don't know what to make of you," Sue said ignoring Rayan's remarks and giving the wine order to the hovering waiter. "Go on, give me a bit of dirt to dish up during the coffee breaks," she coaxed.

Rayan smiled grimly. So, I was right. Her fishing expedition is about me. She steeled herself for the inquisition that was sure to follow. She'd been working in the Spa long enough to know the staff loved to gossip.

"There's nothing to tell. I started my first hairdressing business in my teens. Worked hard long hours; built up my clientele and now I'm taking a year out. Enjoying the perks of a single woman," she said smiling sweetly.

Sue snorted. "You're hiding something. Why would you swap wall to wall sunshine every day for this rain?" she argued.

Rayan looked into the far distance. "You can get too much of a good thing sometimes," she said as the waiter put the bottle of wine in an ice bucket in the centre of the white tablecloth. "Sorry to disappoint. But there is no unrequited love. No love affair to run away from. No dirt to ditch."

"Seems a bit odd," was all Sue said. "Vivian and Imelda didn't get on either. We didn't believe her when she said she was looking on the Internet for someone to swap with her for a year," Sue stated watching Rayan closely.

Rayan sipped the wine. There was no way she was about to spill her guts to Sue. She might as well put it in the Donegal Chronicle. "Why didn't they get on?"

Sue carefully carved her fish into small sections and then cut them into smaller pieces again. "Imelda was….is…too flighty and too 'live in the moment' for Vivian…" She hesitated and forked a tiny piece of fish through glossy red lips. "Besides, men who came in for massages always asked for her just like that couple asked for you. Vivian suspected she slept with the wealthier ones," she confided.

"She brought twin boys up without much family support," Rayan protested trying to ignore the thought that she had had similar feelings about Imelda.

Sue's fork stopped halfway to her mouth leaving a miniscule piece of fish dangling precariously in mid-air. "You like Imelda," she said in surprise.

Rayan cursed herself for falling into the trap. "I don't really know her. But I can see she has brought Isaac and Raphael up decent."

Sue waited until the waiter had removed their plates and proffered the dessert menu. "Have you had a visit from the Garda yet—the Irish police…?"

"I know who the Gardaí are. Why would I get a visit from them?" Her mind raced. Had the dog got out and attacked the new lambs? Had she been caught speeding on the main highway into Letterkenny? Sweat coated her palms making her fish knife slip onto the floor. What if she got into bother with the authorities?

What if the Irish police had charged her with a crime? They'd be sure to contact Perth and PC Watts would be able to tell them she had come to Ireland to avoid an assault charge.

"Is killing sheep a criminal offense in this country?" she asked as the waiter retrieved her knife and gave her another.

"What? What are you babbling about?" A light dawned in Sue's eyes. "You think that's why the Garda might want to search Imelda's house?"

Rayan's mouth fell open. "Search the Manse? Why would the police do that?"

Sue moved impatiently in her seat. "Mac O Lochlainn stopped at the hotel with a busload of tourists. He was badmouthing the Northern Ireland police and saying more young men like Raphael Wright were needed to carry on the fight for freedom in the North. There was shooting and rioting at Easter time in the Bogside in Derry City and Raphael was arrested."

Rayan's drink splattered over the new top she had spent last week's earning on. "Raphael wouldn't be involved in anything illegal," she said trying to curb her rising anxiety.

"It's true," Sue insisted.

"It has nothing to do with me or Imelda's house. He lived in a student flat near the university. He or Isaac haven't been back to the Manse since Easter…" She let her voice fade away remembering the night she'd made dinner for Isaac. There had been campers in the field next to the orchard. Had they been hiding guns used in the rioting? She choked on the bass. Should she contact Imelda?

Sue raised her eyes to the ceiling. "It has *everything* to do with you! You are living in Imelda's house. What if the Garda search the house or grounds and find…paramilitary stuff! You could be arrested."

Rayan gulped down her wine.

"I keep forgetting—you don't understand about the Troubles in the North," Sue said in exasperation. "Good enough for Imelda if they did find something in that house. Living there rent free." She looked at Rayan. "You do know you are renting a house that doesn't belong to Imelda. Right?"

Rayan was glad she had found out before Sue sprung it on her.

"Blowing and boasting about 'her twins'; how well they're doing at school and then uni. Nobody else's kids could match them," Sue sneered.

"And this is what you brought me to an expensive seafood restaurant in the middle of the day to tell me? You could have told me this over a cup of coffee any day of the week." Grounding her teeth together Rayan began to gather up her bag.

"No! No, that's not what I wanted to talk to you about," Sue said hurriedly. "I have a problem…with Vivian…"

Rayan inhaled. "Me too in case you haven't noticed!"

"She knows I fancy you."

Rayan stared at her. The idea was so preposterous she started to laugh. She swung her bag on her shoulder. "You can tell her from me I'm not looking for *love*," she said succinctly.

A look flitted across Sue's face. She's right, Rayan realised, and she didn't bring me here to tell me about what's going on with Raphael or about Imelda living rent free. She brought me here to make Vivian jealous.

Rayan gripped the handle of the bag. What did you say when a woman used you to make her female partner jealous?

She moistened her lips. "Look, Sue, I like you…but not like *that*. And I know you don't like me in that way either."

"You don't have a very high opinion of yourself," Sue murmured.

"Look, whatever your and Vivian's problem is, I don't want to know. I can do without Vivian making my life any more awkward than she has already."

"Sit down. You're drawing attention to yourself."

"Can I be of any assistance," the waiter asked edging over to their table.

"Thank you. We're fine," Rayan said sitting down.

She pushed the creamy dessert she had ordered to one side. "It's easy to have poise and confidence when you have parents like yours Sue, who travel a round trip of two hundred miles from Dublin to Donegal to spent time with you; or when, like you were, a former beauty queen and finalist in the Rose of Tralee beauty international pageant," Rayan's voice tapered off. "Try being brought up by parent's who wished you'd never been born. Add in tall for a girl and a face like mine and then tell me about your self-esteem," she said stiffly.

Sue looked taken aback for a moment. "Looking like I do is a facade, a front," she said. "When I was young, I looked like the round towers the visitors are so keen to photograph in Ireland."

Rayan gave her a disbelieving look. Sue started to rummage in her oversized bag. "It's true. I'll show you," she said pushing a photograph across the table.

Smoothing out the crumbled picture, Rayan saw a group of young girls in gym slip uniforms and knee socks flanked by nuns in black and white habits.

"I'm the fat child on the end with legs like tree trunks," Sue said tapping the picture with a manicured nail.

The girl on the end of the second row was staring into the camera an unhappy expression in her eyes "I hated getting my photograph taken and I hated my frizzy hair. I looked like a red-headed gollywog," Sue said candidly.

"Did you get teased and bullied about your...size," Rayan asked.

"I did and about my hair." Just for a moment the look of the self-assured, confident beautician slipped and Rayan saw her own childhood hurts mirrored in Sue's eyes.

"Coffee?" the waiter asked.

"Yes."

"No."

Both Sue and Rayan said together. The waiter hovered.

"I told the others were having a business lunch—have a coffee," Sue pleaded.

"Vivian could never love the person in that photograph," Sue murmured stirring sugar into her coffee. Rayan opened her mouth to remind her she never took sugar and then clamped it shut. "She really is only in love with the image I bring to the Spa," Sue murmured.

Lost for an answer, Rayan stirred sugar into her own coffee. "But you—you could love the real me," Sue said tears jumping into her eyes.

Rayan shook her head vehemently. "Sue, I'm sorry if I've given the wrong impression. I lived with my partner, Nathanial for six years. I have never...fancied...felt love for a woman. Not even my own mother." She stopped, shocked at the revelation.

Sue wiped the corner of her eyes with a tissue. "So you came to Ireland to get over a broken heart." She smiled. "I knew you were running away from something or someone," she gulped.

Fear rushed through Rayan. The last thing she wanted was Sue or the rest of the Spa staff nosing about in her business. "I came to Ireland because I'm forty this year." She paused. "I was afraid I was taking the menopause and that life was passing me by," she rushed on.

Sue took out a small mirrored compact and reapplied her eye shadow. "I'm forty this year too. But I'm not telling anybody," She said looking around fearfully someone had overheard her. "I want to have a baby before I have the menopause. But Vivian..."

Rayan held up her hands. She didn't want to hear Vivian and Sue's problems. "Please don't tell me. I really don't want to know."

Sue looked beseechingly at her. "Wouldn't you like a family before all your eggs shrivel up?"

"No, I would not!" Rayan's hands shook as she signed the chit with the Shingle Beach Hotels details.

"In a roundabout way I'm flattered you fancy me," Rayan said touching Sue's arm. "It's been a while since somebody has really wanted me, for me," she said thinking about Nathanial's obsession with making love to her so she'd get pregnant.

She glanced at Sue's face as she wriggled into the small bucket seat of her sports car.

"I like your car."

"Thank you. Present from Vivian for my birthday. It came with my own allotted parking space in front of the hotel," Sue said petulantly. She was silent as they edged out into the stream of traffic. "No room for a buggy," she said a catch in her voice.

Rayan reached across and touched her hand. "I never really had a best friend. Just girls at school whose parents asked me to stay over hoping my father could get their daughters into the college. I could really do with a good friend. Couldn't we just be friends?"

Sue's lower lip trembled. "I never want to go back and be that fat girl in the photograph again but I want Vivian to see me; the real me and not the beauty queen she like to parade at business dinners," she said her voice wobbling.

A silence fell between them. "You're off reception for good as from right now," Sue said as they came in the rotating doors of the hotel.

"What about Vivian?"

"It's time Vivian got to know the real me," Sue said quietly. "I should have a say in our relationship and the running of this business too, don't you think?"

Rayan shrugged. *I have enough bother trying to stop myself thinking about Isaac's kiss*, she thought.

Chapter Eleven

The hens scattered, squawking loudly as Raphael rammed on the brakes and slid the car to a stop inches from the back door of the Manse. Relieved to have arrived safely, Isaac unbuckled his seatbelt and unwound his long legs.

Raphael threw open the driver's door and breathed in the fresh mountain air. "Derry City may have history in its stones and wall to wall women but it has nothing on you Muckish," he breathed, giving the mountain his customary salute. "It's great to be home. No more studying until September," he yelled cupping his hands over his mouth and roaring out the words.

"We're not quite finish yet. It's only the end of May," Isaac pointed out.

"Come on bro; let's see what kind of mood our Aussie renter is in before we fill the fridge with drink," Raphael joked throwing a careless arm around Isaac's shoulder. "Hey-hey, Dizzy," he chortled as the dog launched himself at them. "Yeah, that's it, plant one right there," he laughed as the dog's long tongue tickled his earlobe. "You're a better kisser than any women I know. Well, maybe not as good as sassy Maddie chef," he chortled throwing back his head and laughing uproariously.

"Have you asked Maddie to the end of term party?" Isaac asked opening the back door.

"Are you mad, wee bro, couldn't do that she'd put a bigger damper on it than Ma," Raphael looked around the empty kitchen. He sighed. "This is when I miss Ma the most," he said a serious expression coming over his face.

"You should be glad she's on the other side of the world. Otherwise they'd be no party," Isaac grinned. "Remember what she said that day in the Walled City bar in Derry? If you caused another disturbance of the peace it'll be her, the house owner who gets into trouble."

Raphael pouted. "Would you give over? Ma has nothing to worry about. It'll be a great party. It's just," he gestured around the kitchen, "look at the *clean* and tidy this place is! If Ma was here, there'd be a bottle of wine open on the worktop and the place would be steamed up with Ma cooking something nice for us coming back." He marched over and threw open the fridge. "See, empty, except for bloody rabbit food and health shit. Ugh," he said, taking the lid off a container and smelling it.

"Rayan doesn't cook. Well, not often anyway," Isaac amended thinking about the night they had shared the mouth-watering chicken—and the kiss. The kiss! It was all he could think about. He didn't understand his feelings for Rayan. He had never felt like this about any of the women Raphael or his mother had fixed him up with. There was just something about Rayan. It was weird.

"Shit! I knew there was some reason I always asked Maddie to the parties. She brings a load of grub," Raphael said slapping the kitchen island worktop. "Everybody is bringing their own booze. But what am I going to do about grub— for later—in the wee hours of the morning," Raphael complained.

"It's going to be an all-nighter?"

"And all of the weekend," Raphael laughed.

"You better warn Rayan. She's not used to noisy raucous Irish get-togethers," Isaac warned. "You know how things can get out of hand when the students have a skinful…"

Raphael slapped the worktop again. "I know now why I didn't ask Maddie chef. Kate from the Top of the Hill Bar is coming. And if I don't show her a good time, I'll have her Da Manus to contend with." He paused. "Fuck it!" We need food and plenty of it. "I'll ask Maddie anyway?"

Isaac opened the double doors of the sunroom onto the patio. "French champagne Maddie?"

"Spot on, bro, just in case, she's takes the hump and doesn't come; you ask Rayan if she'd cook up a curry or something that will go round. She'll do it for you. She fancies you, bro," Raphael laughed play boxing his twin.

Isaac swallowed. His skin tingled thinking about the closeness of Rayan's body and the taste of her as his tongue had traced the soft pillowed curve of her lips. Colour suffused his neck. It was all he could think about. He could feel his penis harden just thinking about it.

"How many are coming to this party."

Raphael grinned. "I stuck a notice up on the students' community notice board." He paused and looked sideways at Isaac. "There will be a few…from the gun club."

"What gun club? Who would let you join a gun club," Isaac chuckled.

"That's what Rayan calls the IRA volunteers."

"Oh, right," his twin said his stomach tightening.

"You should volunteer bro. This peace thing is getting a bit shitty."

"If Maddie doesn't come, you could always ask the mobile chippy to come back this way when he's finished outside Hole in the Wall in town," Isaac said tactfully changing the subject.

Raphael swore irately. "With Ma away who's going to pay. Come on, Dizzy and I need a walk on the mountain," Raphael muttered snapping on the dog's harness, "you coming with us?"

His twin shook his head. "I'll wait for Rayan."

"Mention the party and get her to agree to cook for it."

Isaac snorted.

Raphael smirked. "I'm telling you, bro, she fancies you. She'll do it for you."

Isaac stretched out on the wicker lounger in the sunroom and let a long slow breath escape from his lungs. He was glad to be home; glad most of his exams were over at least for this year. His lecturers had told him if he kept up his grades, he'd graduate top of his class—above Raphael—well above Raphael. A sense of triumph washed over him.

Raffi hadn't done well at all. Not at all. He was lucky to get enough assignment grades to scrape back for his third year. Would Mum be disappointed? She doesn't expect him to graduate with colours flying anyway, he mused. "But Imelda always, *always* kept the pressure on me," he muttered irritation tempering his good humour. Now, she's not even here to shower praise on *me* for working my ass off to please her, he thought resentment souring his mood.

The very first thing he'd done when he'd gotten confirmation of his grades had been to email her. Indignation flared in him. It had taken her *two whole days* to respond. Two days! Then it had been a brief message to say, well done to *both* of them. No real acknowledgement of the effort it had taken on his part to get top marks. She'd gone on to say sorry for not getting back sooner but she was busy running the salon. She'd gotten a new trainee and upgraded Sienna, the one that was there before. The rest had been a blow by blow account of the wall-to-wall sunshine, barbecues on white sandy beaches and the magical beauty of the sun setting on the Indian Ocean.

The outside door slammed. Rayan was home. He watched covertly as she slipped out of her jacket and kicked off her high heels. Fuck, he wanted her. His reward for working so dammed hard at a subject he had little appetite for.

Glancing through the open door Rayan gave him an awkward smile, unsure if it was him or his twin. "Summer holidays here already?" she commented slipping into the seat opposite him. She checked for the distinguishing birth mark. It was the only way she could tell them apart.

Isaac nodded, moving the cushion so it obscured his swelling penis. For a minute he was lost for words. "Last weekend in May—Bank Holiday break—but we will soon be breaking for the summer."

Rayan felt her breath quicken. Was there a promise in those words?

"The assignment work is handed in and the exams are nearing an end," Isaac stuttered thrown by her closeness. It was a lot easier when he imagined undressing her lying in his bed in the student flat.

"Good grades?"

"Top grades," he said triumphantly. For a moment she ceased to be the woman he had slept with, no, had wild unimaginable sex with every night since she had kissed him the night they had the intimate cosy dinner in front of the fire. Just for a second he wanted her to be Imelda. He wanted her to jump up wave her arms about and dance around in delight at his news.

"Raphael home too?" Rayan asked rubbing the tension out of the back of her neck she stretched her arms above her head. Jealousy ate at Isaac. Why was she asking about his twin, for god sake?

"Yeah," he mumbled, the rise of her breasts creating more heat in his groin. "Love your new image…and…hairstyle," he blurted out.

Rayan looked down the length of her body and wriggled her bare toes. She was about to blow the compliment away when she remembered Sue's remark that she should rethink her view of herself. "Thank you. A bit more toning needed yet," she smiled.

"I think you look fantastic. Working at the Spa is…helping?" Isaac blustered to cover the heat that was radiating through his body. He wondered if this was what they called falling head-over-heels in love.

"It's much better working there now that I am friends with Sue. I hope you and your brother don't mind but I've been inviting some of the girls from work for a walk on the mountain and a light supper some Saturday nights."

Isaac thought about his absent mother. "Sure. Why not; Imelda likes a bit of…company. I'm sure she's using your house to entertain," he said tersely.

Rayan raised her eyebrow at the veiled criticism of his mother but all she said was, "Raphael walking the dog on the mountain?"

Isaac nodded and moved slightly towards her. He wanted to say he didn't want to talk about his brother. He had other things on his mind now that they were alone together but the words stuck in his throat.

Rayan gave him a slow smile. It hadn't been her imagination because she was missing Nathanial. Looking at her with those big puppy dog eyes, Isaac was definitely giving her the come-on.

"If you want, I'll help you move your stuff into the double room Imelda used for the hill walkers. It will give us more privacy," she said reaching out for him.

Isaac startled. "But I've always…what will Raffi say?"

Ryan stiffened. The snivelling petulant little boy lost look was back on his face. *Had* she read the signals wrong?

"It's just—I've always slept with Raffi…we're twins," Isaac's voice petered off.

Rayan looked at him incredulously. "It was just… I thought you wanted—never mind. Obviously, I was mistaken," she snapped flouncing out of the sunroom. Who's acting like a child now, she berated herself. I thought it was *me* he wanted to sleep with—not continue sleeping in the top bunk in his brother's room. She wanted to ball her fists and scream at him. *Nathanial has rejected me and now you have too.*

"You moved into the other room and got Rayan to agree to a Friday night—all weekend party. How did you soften her up…?" Raphael's mouth fell into a gape as Isaac's neck and face blazed bright red.

His eyes widened and he cursed softly. "You scored with her in the hill walkers' room when I was out with the dog!" he said an incredulous note of something approaching respect and admiration in his voice. He threw back his head and laughter uproariously. "You got laid—at last!" he shouted jumping up and making for the fridge. "This calls for a celebration. My wee brother finally got laid!" Raphael chortled gleefully tossing his twin a can of Budweiser. "Did she…? Wait! Don't tell me. Let me see the evidence for myself," he chortled. In one swift movement closed the space between them and yanked up Isaac's shirt.

Isaac shook him off. "Get off me!"

"Just checking if she clawed the back off you—see the length of those nails she has?" Raphael chuckled shaking his head in disbelief. "I'd say you got lucky, bro; she's pining for that boyfriend she left in Perth."

"What boyfriend?"

Raphael helped himself to another beer. "She keeps a picture inside her Aussie driver's licence of a muscled looking guy; all white teeth, tattoos and big biceps…"

"How do you know what she has in her driver's licence?"

Raphael sniggered. "You jealous, wee brother? Think I might—"

"Fuck off, Raffi. You have a mind like a sewer when it comes to women. How do you know—"

"What's in her bag?" Raphael interjected. "Threw a quick check just to make sure she is who she says she is…for Ma's sake," he added hastily.

Isaac levelled him with a scornful look. "You mean you were checking her out so you could tell your so-called 'friends' from Derry she's not a plant by the Brits and it's safe for them to come to the party. Got contacts, have they? Going to help you get off that rioting charge—"

"Shut your mouth!" Raphael hand tightened on his beer. "You blab to her or Ma about me being arrested after the Easter Commemoration parade…?"

Isaac studied the markings on the beer can. "No, I did not. I'm no tout. But when Mum sees your grades, she's going to know you're spending your time on things other than your uni work."

"You shut your mouth and keep it shut when the boys from the Bogside come tonight," Raphael warned.

"Mum needs to be told. If you're charged with stoning the Brits, it'll be in the papers," Isaac pointed out.

Raphael smirked. "Ma's not interested in reading papers in Australia. She's having a ball, literally. She's dating Rayan's ex-partner," Raphael said his voice full of disdain.

Isaac drew his lips into a straight line. "You mean the guy in the photograph?"

Raphael threw his eyes up to the ceiling. "How should I know? She just said…he was Rayan's ex."

"Mum never mentioned anything to me about having a new boyfriend."

Raphael slopped the beer around in the can. "She wouldn't, would she? You'd get all protective and jealous…like you always do."

"I don't! That last guy—the one who sent her the flowers at Easter—he wasn't treating her right…?"

"Yeah? What about the one before that? You hate to share her—even with *me*."

Isaac whirled around. "You and her are just like each other, you know that. More concerned what goes on between your legs than in your head." Coming into the kitchen, Rayan looked from one to the other as the two brothers glared at each other. She had no idea how to settle a fight between brothers or siblings for that matter.

"When is this party and how many are you expecting to come to it?" she asked moving around the drink in the fridge to make room for the freshly cooked pieces of salmon the chef at the hotel had given her in exchange for a pedicure.

"I hear the postman. Better get him before Dizzy bites the arse off him again," Raphael said.

Rayan studied Isaac's stormy face. "What wrong? Did your twin object to you moving out of his room?"

"We had an argument about the party," Isaac mumbled.

"Maybe you should phone your Mum. Check if it's OK."

"I already talked to Ma," Raphael said coming back in from collecting the post. "She'll not mind. She's a bit of a party animal herself," Raphael smiled.

Rayan gave him a wry smile. "She'll not party much in my house. It's a built-up residential area," she said with a touch of pride. "Besides, the neighbours love to phone the cops if there are late night goings-on." Abruptly, she turned away. The homesickness had subsided but even to think about Nathanial made her heart ache. She'd sent him an email. He'd ignored it.

"I'm going over to the hotel. I can send Imelda a message about the party from there."

Raphael bristled. "And let all them bitches know my business!"

"I *am* responsible for your mother's house and property," Rayan said turning to face him. *Except it's not hers, is it? It's an American's*, she thought.

"Why don't you use the computer here?"

"I've tried but it has a security password. I'll be going that way, anyway. I'm collecting Sue. We're going shopping."

"I know the computer password. I'll unlock it and send a message to Ma," Raphael said slamming out of the kitchen in search of the Windows 95 computer they'd bought Imelda for Christmas.

Rayan smiled at Isaac. His lovemaking had been naïve and inexperienced. But what he lacked in knowledge he'd made up for in staying power. Her shin tingled. She shifted her body so that it rubbed against his thigh. Making love had made her hungry for the sex she used to have with Nathanial. A sense of longing for him rushed over her. She ripped her mind away. Isaac might not be as accomplish a lover as Nathanial but he was here and Nat was fucking Sienna....

"Don't go out tonight. Be here when I get back," she murmured.

Isaac slipped his hand under her loose shirt. His breath quickened. She wasn't wearing a bra. He had an immediate erection.

Rayan cast a surreptitious glance in the direction of the stairs. "What about your twin?"

"It'll take a while for Raphael to figure out Mum's password."

Rayan examined her body in the full-length mirror inside the wardrobe door in Imelda's bedroom. Pouting her lips and lengthening her spine she posed the way Sue had shown her. Walking on Muckish and using the gym at the spa was definitely helping her body become curvier. A girlish giggle rose in her chest. "The mountain air is doin' ye the world of good, girlie," she spluttered imitating Mac O Lochlainn stock in trade remark every time he called at the house... Randy old devil, she thought but she was smiling as she came downstairs into the kitchen to pick up her car keys.

Raphael whistled appreciatively. "They're going to love you at the party," he said following her out beer in hand he lounged against the wall of the Manse. Rayan felt his eyes on her as she leaned back to adjust the driver's seat. Flustered, she let the engine stall. *Unlike his twin, he has nothing to learn about woman. He's a fully-fledged womaniser*; she thought a frisson of excitement shooting through her.

"Buy something to wear to the party next weekend," he smiled, sauntering over to the car and sticking his head in the open window.

Rayan could feel his breath hot on her cheek. "Imelda agreed it was OK to have this party, then?"

Raphael smiled into her eyes. "I left a message. She'll get back to me," he said smoothly. "Drive easy on the back roads. Buy something that shows off your...assets," he murmured his eyes trailing leisurely down her bare legs. Rayan felt the heat rise on her cheeks.

"Got your driver's licence?" he asked easing his face out of the window.

Rayan lingered, checking her bag even though she knew she had it. "Yes, I have it."

"You'll need it for the Brits checkpoint on the Derry-Donegal border."

Rayan chortled. "They have checked my name so many times now it just pops up on their computer search straight away," she joked.

Raphael's eyes darkened. "Just let me know if them bastards gives you any hassle."

Rayan wondered at the venom dripping off his voice. Old history between England and Ireland still strong, she thought. "No, they don't say anything. Just snigger at the idea of my name being Rayan—like rain." She shrugged. "They're just kids…"

"Yeah, fuckin' child soldiers picked off the streets of England. Give them a uniform and they think they can give orders to the Irish," Raphael growled.

Rayan gunned the engine. "Sue will be wondering what's keeping me."

"Drive safe. You'll be alright in the Maiden City. Ceasefire is still on," he stated as she began to move the car forward. She braked.

"Ceasefire?"

Raphael waved her on. "Never mind, I'll explain later. See you when you get back. Take the shortcut over the mountain road I showed you on the map. It'll save you a few miles," he shouted as the car shot forward.

As she drove off, she looked in the rear-view mirror. Isaac was framed in the doorway, a petulant look on his face. Had he wanted to tell her something? Probably telling me to mind Imelda's damn car in Derry, she thought. Rolling up the window again she checked her lipstick in the wing mirror. "After just three short months in Ireland, I'm beginning not to recognise my own reflection," she murmured, pleased with how she looked. Maybe she would take Raphael's advice and buy something…different from what she usually wore.

Chapter Twelve

"I enjoyed today; nothing like a bit of retail therapy to cheer you up," Sue chortled, as Rayan dropped her back at the hotel. "Enjoy the party. You will look fabulous in that outfit," Sue said leaning over and giving Rayan a hug before getting out. She stood for a minute and waved.

Waving back Rayan accelerated and tuned in to Friday night Radio FM. After a while she turned off the main road and took the back road Raphael said would save her fifteen minutes on her hour's journey home.

A farmer drawing home a load of turf from the bog drew in to let her pass. Rayan gave him thumbs up and a yelled thank you as she whizzed past him. She couldn't wait to get back, have a shower and pamper herself before slipping into the drop-dead gorgeous designer dress and accessories she'd bought in Vanessa's designer dress shop in Derry the week before.

She gave her imagination free rein. She had a vision of herself the centre of a group of admirers, like she was the most popular and stunning woman there. She imagined Raphael's eyes out in stalks when he saw her in the dress; and Isaac showing her off like beautiful sparkling arm decoration; proud to show the assembled student he was with a real woman.

She'd never attended her graduation for her Diploma in Beauty at the University of Perth. She'd never been asked to partner anybody for the end of College formals. I've never ever really dressed up for anything in my life, she thought. "Well, for this end of academic year party I will," she murmured. "It'll be my coming of age—even if I'm forty and not twenty-one. Ugly duckling finally a swan," she laughed turning up the music and singing along.

She slowed as she crossed the humped back Bridge of Tears. Fleetingly she recalled Raphael explaining to the tourist about Ireland during the Famine time. She glanced in her rear mirror at the road she had just travelled. She'd clocked the miles the people had had to walk to get to the port in Derry from West Donegal during the Famine in the 1840s. She had driven the sixty odd miles in little over an hour. "But it took the emigrants days upon days," she mused. Resolutely, she closed off her mind to such sad times. Tonight was a night to party and be happy.

She could hear the music and see the startled look on the cows' sombre faces as they hugged the hedge of the field along the last double bend in the lane before the Manse. "Just as well our nearest neighbours are a good few kilometres away," she mused. Gathering up her bags, she stood wide eyed for a minute listening to the ear-splitting noise. Every door and window in the house seemed to have music pulsating out of them.

The house was heaving with people inside and out. "Shit, did Raphael have to ask the whole frigging student body," she gasped. The smell of barbecued food wafted in the air. Just as well, she thought, looking down at the Sainsbury's bags of crisps, nibbles and dips she'd bought. No way was it going to go anywhere near satisfying this mob.

"Hi. Good to see you again," a woman yielding a spatula in one hand and a large glass of something red in the other called out to her. Rayan looked at her blankly.

"Maddie—chef…smallest pub in Ireland," she said shouting to be heard above the din.

"Oh, right. Where's Raphael?" Rayan shouted back.

The chef hunched her shoulders. "…think I saw either him or his twin go that way." She waved the spatula she was turning burgers with in the direction of the orchard. "Want a hotdog or a burger?"

Rayan shook her head.

"Glass of French champagne?"

"Champagne," Rayan indicated, excitement mounting. "It's my first real party," she shouted. "This ugly duckling is turning into a graceful swan," she giggled as the champagne bubble went up her nose. "I'm off to get into my new dress. It cost me a packet."

The chef laughed. "Here, before you go, let me top that up for you," she said refilling Rayan's glass. "Come back when I get this lot fed and we'll really celebrate Irish style," she chortled waving her glass in the air.

Rayan threaded her way around the side of the Manse. She could see musicians propped against the trees in the orchard strumming guitars and roaring out the words of a song.

"Have you seen Isaac?" she shouted into a girl's ear.

"Who?"

"Isaac."

"Don't know any Isaac," she shouted back. Rayan stared at her.

"The party…was posted up in the Student's Halls…at the uni," the girl said very slowly as if Rayan didn't understand.

Rayan elbowed her way into the house. The kitchen and sunroom were groaning at the seams with young chic looking women and skinny, lanky tee-shirted men clutching beer bottles in their fists. She scanned for the twins. Not finding them she headed for the stairs. If Raphael was anywhere, he'd be in bed with some "chick" as he called them.

"Hey, are you Isaac's mother," a girl slurred moving her feet out of the way to let Rayan pass.

Rayan threw her a contemptuous glance. "No, I most certainly am not," she said.

"Here, don't you be thinking you're goin' to be jumping the queue for the bedrooms," another girl hiccupped making as if to pull Rayan down to the step below her. Rayan shook off her grasping fingers and forced her way up the stairs over a mangle of feet and legs.

The pulsing, throbbing beat of the music vibrated through the floorboard. Her eyes scanned the landing. Couples in all stages of undress and drunkenness were clamped together kissing and fondling each other, apparently oblivious to the other people there.

"If Raphael has a woman in my room, I will kill him," she fumed pushing forward to her bedroom door.

"Here you, are you blind or drunk or both? See that notice? It says, *Out of bounds*," a voice boomed as Rayan was yanked roughly backwards. "It is *out of bounds*," a beefy man with a bald head shouted, rapping out the words with his fist on the bedroom door.

"What? Don't be ridiculous! I *live* here. Well, I'm rent…" She stopped. Why was she explaining to this goon? He was trespassing in *her* house. "Get out of my way," she ordered making to push past him.

The bouncer folded his thick arms across his muscled aps and pointed his gaze somewhere above Rayan's head. "Oh, fuck off. I have enough to do with this crowd of bollocks without you starting," he said exasperated. "Drink your wine and come back later when it's your turn, missus," he snarled.

Rayan stiffened. How dare he talk to her like that? "I will not. *I live here.* You let me into my bedroom or get out of this house or I will have you thrown out, you…you gym junkie," she bawled.

The bouncer gawked at her. "You threatening me! Nobody, but nobody is to get into this fucking bedroom tonight," the man growled.

Rayan's good mood evaporated and ice-cold rage consumed her. "I *LIVE* here, you big goon. This is my bedroom. I have to do is get in there to get DRESSED for the party," she screeched.

"If you're not waiting year turn, you're goin' to the back of the queue." Grasping her arm in a grip of iron the bouncer forced her backwards towards the stairs.

Rayan screamed. Losing her balance, she stumbled backwards spilling her wine over the girl she'd seen earlier.

"You Isaac's mother," the girl repeated smiling drunkenly.

Too angry to apologise to a boy she had nearly knocked down the stairs, Rayan ignored the question.

What was she going to do? There has to be some way to get past that bastard, she fumed. Raphael or Isaac had obviously posted him to keep the students from using her bedroom. "You Isaac's mother," the drunken girl repeated. Rayan felt like lifting her hand and wiping the stupid grin off her stupid face.

A thought struck her. Maybe if the bouncer thought she was the twins' mother he'd let her in. "Yes, yes, I am Isaac's and Raphael's mother," she yelled into the girl's ear.

The girl leaned in to Rayan. "Please to meet you. I'm Raphael's girlfriend," she slurred. "He talks about you all the time," she said with a foolish grin.

"Come with me and tell that gorilla at the top of the stairs who I am," she ordered, hauling the girl to her feet and pushing her in front of her up the stairs. "Stop that," she ordered as the inebriated girl introduced her to other guests. She knew. "Go on, tell him who I am," she ordered thrusting the girl in front of the bouncer.

"She's Raphael's and…and…what's his name—the other guy's mother—her son is my boyfriend," the student hiccupped smiling foolishly at the bouncer.

"She is? What's her name then," the bouncer grinned playing with her.

The girl giggled. "How should I know? I just met her."

Stupid little cow, Rayan thought pulling her aside. "I'm Imelda, Raphael and Isaac's mother. And this is my bedroom," she said in an icy cold tone.

Smirking, the bouncer let his gaze trickle from her head to her feet. "Oh right." he said as if he was happy with her lie. He'd met Imelda in the Walled City Bar, before she gone to Australia. She was a good looker; that fiery red hair and that body… If it hadn't been for Isaac interfering in his plans that night he'd have had her. "You think I came up the River Foyle in a bubble?" He let his eyes rake over Rayan again.

Rayan felt as if he had undressed her.

"OK. I'm not Imelda," she admitted. "But my clothes for the party *are* in that bedroom. I need to get in there to get ready. When you were told to keep people out, it didn't include *me*," she yelled at him.

The bouncer folded his thick arms across his belly and rolled on the balls of his feet. "I have my orders, *nobody,* but *nobody* is to get into that bedroom the fuckin' night. But I could be *persuaded*…if you were a bit more *accommodating*," he smirked. Rayan had had enough. She lounged at him.

"Mad oul fuckin' Aussie bitch," the man said through gritted teeth thrusting her off him.

"You bastard! You knew who I was along…"

"G'day, mate, pegged you first time," he smirked.

Rayan felt red hot rage boiling up in her.

"First slap is free. I hit back after that," the bouncer warned registering the rage on her face.

"You're one of those *volunteers* from Raphael's supposed gun club," she roared scratching wildly at his bare biceps. "Get out of my house—Imelda's house—before I phone the cops—Garda," she screamed. Suddenly, the door to hill walkers' room flew open.

"Isaac," Rayan gasped. "This buffoon will not let me into my bedroom."

"Calm down. Calm down. I'll sort it. Where's your Irish hospitality? Get our Australian visitor a drink," Raphael hiccupped drunkenly.

Infuriated, Rayan rounded on him. "I will not calm down. And I had a drink but it got spilled when this buffoon pushed me…" She broke off at the idiotic grin that spread across his face. "You're drunk, Isaac," she said in disgust. "When I agreed to let Raphael have this party, I didn't expect him to ask the whole fucking student body. Where is he? Get Raphael. Or I'm calling the cops," she screeched.

A sudden hush fell over the drinkers.

"Mad oul bitch. You better get her sorted." The bouncer glowered at Raphael. "She goin' to call the Guards." His face darkened. "Is that the plan? Get me out here to the sticks—get me arrested or knocked off—nice an' handy for dumping a body in the mountain," he snarled.

"Get Raphael," Rayan shrieked.

"Shut up your mouth. He's there beside you," the bouncer roared into her face.

"This is Isaac," Rayan spat at him her freshly painted nails extended like a cat's claws.

"It's getting to something when a *woman* doesn't know the difference in the men she's sharing a house with," he mocked.

Rayan's eyes narrowed. What did he mean? "Which of the twins are you," she asked feeling foolish.

"I'm the one you haven't slept with yet in the hill walker's bed," Raphael chortled. "But tonight's your lucky night," he shouted attempting to pulled her into the bedroom. Wrenching free Rayan lurched in the direction of her bedroom throwing the bouncer a look that said if you dare to stop me *I will kill you on the spot*. Raphael followed her in to a chorus of catcalling and cheering.

Incensed, Rayan rounded on him. "I take it that…buffoon is from your 'gun club'," she roared at him. "This party was for *students*. And don't think I don't know what your 'gun club' is now because I do. I may not know much about Irish History but I have heard about the bombing and shooting and the Troubles," she stopped to catch her breath. "I didn't think you'd be *so stupid* as to bring the likes of men like *him* into your mother's home!" she raged.

Raphael swayed unsteadily. "Look, look. Calm down. Calm down. Everything is going to be OK. I was…asked as a favour if they could come…"

Rayan stopped yelling. "You mean there's more than him here?"

"It's just a wee night out for them in Donegal. They're my brothers-in arms," he grinned spreading out his hands. "You have to ask your friends to your party. That's how it works, Rayan," he grinned. "There's only him and…a few others. The rest are students."

Rayan flung her bag at his chest. "How can you bring bombers into your mother's house, you're despicable," she said through gritted teeth.

"You're a real wee firecracker when you're roused," Raphael laughed, focusing on her heaving breasts. He took a step towards her. "I saw the marks you left on Isaac's back…"

Rayan shoved him away.

"It's all right. I'm glad he finally got laid," he chuckled.

"Get out of my room. I'm phoning your mother. I think she should know that it's open season in her house tonight, don't you? And if your 'mates' from your *gun club* are still here when I've done that, *I am phoning the Garda.*"

Suddenly sober, Raphael straightened. He couldn't let her do that. He was already in enough trouble with the boss and the big boys in Derry. "You don't want to do that, Rayan," he threatened. "Look," he said, softening his tone, "all they want is a few free beers and a bit of a party." And a safe passage back across the border into Northern Ireland, he thought, beginning to sweat. Otherwise, *he'd* be the one buried in a shallow grave on the mountain. He looked at Rayan. "You're taking this far too serious. Loosen up—get dressed up—have the craic with the students. Enjoy yourself."

Hating him with every fibre of her being, Rayan looked him in the eye. "That was exactly what I had planned to do," she said her voice dripping disdain. "They've been here before, haven't they," she said in a deadly quiet voice, remembering the night Isaac had said somebody was in the field beside the orchard.

Raphael took a step towards her again. "I promise this will be the one and only time they'll be in the house," he said distractedly swept back his hair heavy curtain fringe revealing the small birthmark on the edge of his left cheek. "You know nothing about…the politics…about the fight for a thirty-two county Ireland."

Rayan shuddered. *What madness possessed me to come to this war-torn country*, she thought dismally. "Shut up! Shut up! Go away. I'm not interested," she muttered, retrieving her bag. "I'm phoning your mother and then the cops."

Raphael leaned his long back against the wardrobe door. "You sure you want to do that?" he said in a low voice.

"Yes. I'm sure. Why wouldn't I?"

"If the Guards raid the house, the Derry men may not be the only persons to be arrested."

Rayan stilled. "What do you mean?"

"Ever been deported?"

It was on the tip of Rayan's tongue to tell him she'd never been anywhere to be deported from, except Bali, and she wouldn't be going back there again any time soon. "No, I have not!" Her palms started to sweat. "Why would I be deported from Ireland?"

"You might be if I reported you."

"You'd report me for doing what? Having sex with your brother! He's twenty years old, for god's sake. He should have lost his virginity years ago," she snorted.

A smile played about the corners of Raphael's mouth. "He's infatuated with you. Why do you think I got him to ask you about the party?"

Rayan's hands tightened into fists. Raphael was playing cat and mouse with her. "Get out of my room. I need to get dressed."

"What if I tell the Guards you skipped bail in Perth?"

The handbag slipped from Rayan's fingers and clattered on to the floor scattering its contents. In one fluid movement that belied his drunken state, Raphael bent and picked up her phone.

Immobilised with shock, Rayan stared at him. "How did you find out?" she quaked.

"Brendie had you checked out."

"Brendie?"

"Guy outside the bedroom door."

Raphael fingered her dress, still in its designer bag. "Pity. It would have looked great on you. But Cinderella ain't going to the ball, at least not tonight; or making any phone calls to the Guards," he said pocketing the mobile phone. "I'm ordering Brendie that you're not to be let out of this room until the party is over and him and the other volunteer are safely back across the border."

Rayan looked at him as if he was mad. "You listen to me, Raphael Wright," she said in an ominously quiet voice. "I'm going to the party. And you are not going to stop me! I have been preparing for it all week; spend my money on the dress...and accessories." She threw herself at him. She had been able to cow Nathanial. She could bully this *child,* not even out of education yet.

"You're staying in this room." Raphael panted wrestling her on to her back on the bed. For the beat of a few seconds, lying on top of her, he savoured the firmness of her breasts pushing against his chest, felt his blood quickening before he rolled off her.

"You bastard..."

"Look, Rayan, I know you're disappointed. But I *promise you* there will be other parties where you can wear your dress. You're in Ireland. *Everything* here turns into a party," he said trying to turn it into a joke.

Rayan wilted into the pillow. "Not for me. As soon as the Irish police find out about me, I will be deported."

Raphael smirked. "I'll make a bargain with you, Rayan. You're skipping bail in Perth will be our secret, providing no phone calls to the Garda."

"I can get dressed and go to the party?"

Raphael shook his head.

Rayan looked at him with such loathing that Raphael felt his stomach chill. "Isaac is twice the man you'll ever be. Fighting for a *cause*, sheltering killers, bombers, doesn't make you a man." She heard him draw in his breath.

"When you phone Ma tomorrow, be sure to tell her you practically raped her wee boy. See how long you get staying in Ireland then. See you when the party's over," Raphael said savagely, slamming the door behind him.

Rayan hurled her new high pumps at the bedroom door. "I hate you, Raphael Wright," she screeched. "I will get you back, you bastard."

Defiantly, she got off the bed and cleansed her face. She was going to the party. Raphael was not going to hold her prisoner. She'd put on her new makeup; pencilled in her eyeliner. Isaac was bound to come looking for her.

There was a knock and Maddie stepped into the room laden down with a tray of food and two bottles of champagne. "Did I nearly get caught in the crossfire?" She laughed looking at the array of things Rayan had thrown at the door.

"Is that buffoon Brendie still out there?"

Maddie grinned. "He's a big lad, isn't he? Did you see those muscles?" she said admiringly. "Yeah, he's still there. The students are round him like bees round honey." She popped the cork on the bottle of champagne. "I did promise you a celebration, didn't I? You know what they say," she giggled, "if the mountain can't come to Muhammad he must come to the mountain."

Rayan looked at her. "Raphael sent you, didn't he?"

Maddie gave her a sheepish look. "He's very drunk. He overreacts…sometimes."

Rayan looked at the big-breasted woman. Tonight, dressed in a brightly patterned blouse tucked into her chef's bottoms, she looked like a squishy cushion tied in the middle. "Raff doesn't want me to be at the party either. He has to babysit Kate—business, you know," Maddie sighed.

"You mean the barmaid from the Top of the Hill pub," Rayan said remembering the night she had arrived in Ireland and the creaking of the loft bed as Raphael had bedded Kate.

"Business—is that what cheating with another woman is called now," she said under her breath. She wondered if Maddie believed her own lies. Her eyes wandered to her dress shimmering in the rays of the setting sun casting its glow over the room. Fuck Raphael. She had bought it to wear to the party and she was damn well going to wear it.

"We're safer in here," Maddie said following her gaze. "It's like a madhouse out there. C'mon, we are going to have our own party. You can try the dress on. It looks amazing. I'll see you get to wear it at another party where there are more grown-ups and fewer drunken assed children," she chortled.

Rayan wasn't convinced. "I want to go to this one," she said mutinously.

"And you will, you will. C'mon drink up; plenty of time to dress up for the party; it's going to be a weekender."

"Raphael has told the bouncer not to let me out."

Maddie's face registered shock. He hadn't told her *that* when he'd coaxed her to come up and keep Rayan company. *Looks like we are both babysitting tonight, Raffi,* she mused mentally lifting her glass to him. She smiled. They'd have their own party later. The quicker she got this Aussie woman into a drunken stupor and into bed, the quicker she could get back to Raphael.

She smiled at Rayan. "Drink up. The bouncer can't stand out there all night," she soothed. "The way he's slobbering over the female students, he's bound to get laid soon," she giggled.

Rayan snorted. "He propositioned me."

Maddie looked at her enviously. She wished it had been her. *If somebody like Brendie fancied me, maybe Raphael might pay more attention to me*, she thought. She gave herself a mental shake. She was wasting time. "Come on; drink up. This stuff is too good to waste on drunken teenagers. Here's to a real party—you and me," she toasted raising her brimming glass.

"Do you have a phone?"

"Never leave home without it," Maddie said slapping the pocket of her chef's chequered bottoms.

"Can I use it?"

"Sure thing," Maddie began beginning to fish it out of her trouser pocket. "Who did you want to phone?"

"I'm going to phone the Garda and then Imelda—"

"Shit! The battery's dead," Maddie, said hastily shoving the phone back into her pocket. "Drink up. Isn't there a time difference between Donegal and Perth? We'll phone Imelda later."

"Yes, eight hours."

Maddie checked her watch. "It's after midnight in Perth. Don't think Imelda would thank you for waking her—especially if she's in bed with some handsome man," Maddie chortled. "Drink up. We'll give her a phone later," she soothed, refilling Rayan's glass.

Woozily, Rayan opened one eye. The room tilted and swayed. She closed it again. After a while moving cautiously, she groped for the bedside light. "No light. Moonlight is more romantic."

Her heart leaped. Isaac had come to take her to the party. "Isaac," she breathed into the darkness. She felt him unzip her bra. She struggled against his fumbling. "I'm glad you're here, Isaac. I'm dressed and ready for the party."

"The party's over."

Had she been to the party? She had a vague recollection of her trying on her new party dress and sashaying across the room; Maddie clapping—images and flashes of the two of them trying on all the clothes in Imelda's wardrobe and falling about on the bed, laughing; Maddie, lining up small glasses of different colours and then a shouted countdown to see who finished their drink first.

She started to giggle but it ended in a whimper. "Isaac," she garbled, "Raphael made Maddie and me stay in the bedroom and drink champagne." It sounded so absurd she started to laugh. Then she started to cry. The taste of her salty tears filled her mouth choking her.

"Shush…. Don't cry, someone will hear."

Through the haze of drink, she felt fingers tracing their way down her ribcage and over her belly. She sank back into the bed and wrapped her legs around Isaac's back. Isaac's lovemaking feels *different* tonight, she thought, closing her eyes and smiling in the darkness.

Chapter Thirteen

Rayan felt bone weary. She wanted to go home, crawl into bed and let Isaac give her a foot massage. She ushered out her last client of the day and went in search of Sue.

"Have you seen Isaac?"

"I saw him a while ago going out to caddy for a group of woman tennis players."

"I'm beat," Rayan sighed slipping into a seat beside the empty treatment bed.

Sue wiped down the surfaces and tidied up the bottles and jars of creams and lotions in readiness for the next morning, she glanced in concern at Rayan's bowed shoulders. Her glow and enthusiasm seemed to have dwindled away. "Did you make that doctor's appointment?" she asked.

Rayan shook her head. "I'm trying out that new alternative treatment Vivian told me to use. She says it's brilliant for mood swings."

Sue frowned. What was Vivian playing at? Those were just samples some sales rep left. She didn't think Vivian had even tried it. She scowled. Vivian was a real mean bitch where Rayan was concerned.

Rayan fanned her face. "I swear it's nearly as hot here as it was it the end of the summer in March when I left Perth."

"Hottest July we've had in Ireland for years. You brought the Aussie weather with you," Sue quipped just as Vivian pushed open the cubicle door.

"I have a message for you," she said brusquely to Rayan.

Hope flared bright as a beacon in Rayan. Her heart leaped. Nathanial had sent her a message to ask her to come back to him?

Vivian smiled maliciously. "You look awful," she said appraising Rayan.

Rayan ignored the jibe. "What's the message?"

"Isaac says go home. Don't wait for him."

Disillusionment made Rayan's voice sharp. "Why is that?"

Vivian smoothed down her designer bespoke tunic top over her well cut tailored bottoms and checked her pristine appearance in the mirror. Dissatisfied with what she saw, she frowned, picked up a bottle and gave the silver streaked hair at the front of her head a short blast.

She turned back to Rayan. "I've partnered him off for tennis with the daughter of one of our regular guests. Pretty little thing," she added. She waited expectantly for Rayan's barbed response.

Rayan held her counsel, too exhausted to go another round of mind games with her manager.

"I'm so glad you asked me to give Isaac a summer job. The young female guests *love* him."

Bitch, she's deliberately goading me, Rayan thought. *She knows about me and Isaac.*

She looked at Vivian' stick body and carefully applied makeup. Beneath all that muck, she's just a plain mean ugly self-doubting woman, she realised.

Her glance shifted to Sue. Vivian doesn't deserve someone like her, she thought. It would serve bitch Vivian right if somebody came along and loved Sue for who she really is. Despite wearing the regulation spa shift, her hair highlighted in vibrant blond streaks and secured at the nape of her neck with a rubber band; her make-up shiny from the heat of the steamer, she's still very beautiful, Rayan thought.

She summoned up a smile for Vivian. "Thanks for taking Isaac." A blush crept unheeded up her cleavage. Ever since the end of term party, sex with Isaac was a bit of a rollercoaster. One night he'd be eager and loving, bringing her to a climax; the next he'd indulge in great sex that lasted longer and was hotter than she'd had with Nathanial. His latest fantasy was making love by moonlight. Her mind's eye filled with the image of his erect penis silhouetted in the shadowy light as he stalked naked to her bed.

She wrenched her mind back to Sue and Vivian.

"…Especially around women," Sue was saying. Rayan looked at her in confusion.

"Isaac? He's gaining more and more confidence around women. Imelda will be delighted. She was always telling him he should take more interest in girls. Not that she'd think anybody around here is going to good enough for him," Sue chuckled.

Vivian placed a possessive hand on Sue's arm. "The Cool Tub is free tonight. The good weather has taken the guests to the beach."

Sue raised her eyebrow and glanced at Rayan. "What do you think?"

"No staff—just the two of us," Vivian said tersely.

Sue shook her head emphatically. "No! Not tonight."

Vivian looked astounded. "Why not? It's been ages since we had any time alone to ourselves."

"Rayan and I have other plans," Sue said sulkily shaking Vivian's hand off her arm.

"Cancel them. The hotel is booked solid. The summer will be over before we get another chance—"

"I'll see you back at the staff apartment," Sue huffed.

"Sue…"

"Vivian, *I said* I'd see you back at the flat. OK!"

The smell of scented candles and the aroma of body oils hung heavily in the silence that descended like a heavy fog. Pivoting on her heel, Vivian threw Rayan a vicious glower and strode out the door.

"What plans? Did we have something planned?"

Sue shook her head and finished cleaning up. "Vivian assumes I'll drop everything and fall in with her plans. As if I had no life of my own," she blurted out. "She wouldn't even consider spending time with me if it hadn't been for the cancellations," she said indignantly. "It's the Spa, first, last and always. I come a very poor second." She turned away and leaned against the work counter.

A deep weary sigh escaped from Rayan. "I wish you wouldn't do that."

"Do what?"

"Use me to make Vivian jealous."

Sue blushed. "I don't."

"You do." Rayan gave her friend a half smile. "You do," she repeated.

Sue reached up and tugged the elastic band from her hair. "Who else am I going to use? The rest of the staff is scared to even go out for a drink with me in case she cuts their hours." She stood up and shook out her long curly locks. Her hair expanded like a halo around her head and shoulders. "Vivian knows you don't give a toss about your hours. You don't need the money and she knows it."

Rayan stretched her aching back and sighed. "So, instead of my hours being slashed I can look forward to another week of crappy appointments," she said resignedly.

"Come on, Rayan! Don't cave in now when I have her on the back foot," Sue protested. She stopped when she caught the sheen of tears in Rayan's almond-shaped eyes.

Looking at her now, with the coral blusher she was wearing lifting and lightening her sallow complexion and her black mascara making her eyelashes appear longer and thicker, it was hard to believe Rayan was the same woman who had walked into the Spa four months before; a dowdy middle aged woman dressed in what looked like 1980s clothes. She looks thirty something rather than forty plus now, she thought. Tonight she looked exhausted.

"Why don't we take the cancellation?"

Rayan shook her head. "No way. I'm going home."

"Come on," Sue coaxed.

Rayan leaned her aching body against the wall of the cubicle. It would be blissful to submerge her body in the cool scented pool and let the water sooth her aching bones.

"What if Vivian decided to…join us?"

Sue shook her head. "She'll not. She's trying to sweeten me up…about something we've been arguing about for a while."

Rayan still looked doubtful. "She'll be jealous of you and me sharing the tub? I don't care about the hours she pays me for but I would miss you and the others' company if she sacked me—banned me from the hotel."

Sue gave her a half-smile. "She's shit jealous of you but she's not stupid. Where is she going to get a hairdresser as experienced as you at short notice during one of the busiest seasons of the year? You heard her, the hotel is booked solid. Come here, your mascara is beginning to smudge," Sue said passing Rayan a tissue.

"You sure Vivian won't come in? I'm too god dammed bushed to go another round with her tonight."

"Forget Vivian. I have a present for you," Sue said. "Vivian will, as my granny in Cork used to say, 'cool in the water she het in'." Sue chuckled at the pun as she watched Rayan unwrap the new towelling robe.

Tears choked Rayan as she stroked the satin lapels of the robe. Getting up, she wrapped her arms around Sue's curvy figure. "Thank you. It's beautiful. The nicest present anybody has even given to me."

"I saw it in Brown Thomas' in Grafton Street the last day I was in Dublin and I immediately thought of you. It's your colour," Sue said gently wiping away a black blob of mascara off Rayan's cheek. "Come on, enough blubbering...time to pamper ourselves for a change."

Sue trailed her hand in the lavender scented water and watched Rayan's body relax and unwind; eyes closed, head thrown back, her feet making little splashing noises as she moved her toes Rayan floated gently. She could have any man, Sue thought. *Why did she choose a childlike Isaac as her lover?* she wondered.

She hadn't believed it when gossip started about Rayan's dating a boy half her age. Shock waves had shot through her when she learned it was Imelda's son. Jesus! Imelda will declare war on her, she thought. Everybody at the Spa, including her, assumed it was Raphael. Sly nods and winks abounded. His reputation as a womaniser was legendary. There were very few women in the locality he hadn't bedded—young, single or married. Women were drawn to him like bees to nectar, she thought. When she'd learned it was Isaac, she didn't believe it. It was the talk of the staff room for weeks when Rayan wasn't there. What does she see in him, she wondered.

You could ask yourself the same question, about Vivian, her conscience sneered; you and her are like winter and summer. She's cold and frosty; you're vibrant and sunny—both of you want very different things. Vivian's energies go into growing the business; you want to 'grow' your family. "Can you really decide who you fall in love with," she said under her breath. Her parents hadn't believed it when she'd told them she was in love with Vivian, a woman, and ten years older than her. They'd told her to wait. It was a phase. It would pass. She'd miss not having children. Sue gulped. They had been right about the latter. How was she ever going to persuade Vivian they should look for a male sperm donor before her eggs were useless? When she hears about Rayan and me giving each other a scented water massage it might help to change her mind, she thought.

They had been partners for seven years. She'd be forty next birthday and Vivian who would never admit it, was nearing fifty.

"Her eggs are already like shrivelled prunes," Sue muttered. Vivian couldn't care less. She doesn't want a child, she thought despondently watching Rayan step out of the tub and rub herself dry.

When they reached the Manse, Dizzy ran to greet the car barking madly. "Did you leave the dog out?" Sue said as she drew to a stop.

"Raphael must be home," Rayan said her relaxed feeling beginning to dissipate.

"Have you...been talking to him since the student party?"

Rayan nodded. She'd confided some of the details to Sue. "He comes and walks on Muckish. He's usually gone before I get back from work." She glanced towards the house. "I can barely bear to look at him now."

"Should I come in…wait…make sure everything is alright?"

Rayan leaned over and kissed her. "Thank you for the beautiful wrap and the massage in the tub. I don't know what I'd do if I didn't have you as my friend," she murmured. "Go home. Vivian will be wondering where you are."

"If Isaac doesn't bring the jeep back tonight, ring me. I'll pick you up in the morning," Sue said softly cradling Rayan's face in her hands and returning the kiss.

As she drove out the gate Sue watched Rayan's retreating back in the rear mirror. "I would like to be more than your friend, if you'd let me," she murmured.

Chapter Fourteen

"Two women kissing—that's gross," Raphael said.

Rayan pushed past him in the kitchen doorway. "Why are you here? Imelda agreed you were not to be here." She could hardly bear to speak to him. "Here to plan that party you promised me before you persuaded that chef person to get me stinking drunk," she said icily.

She had woken up the morning after the party to the smell of cooking. Her stomach had heaved into her throat. Downstairs, the party was still going strong. Maddie was cooking dishing up a full Irish breakfast of bacon, sausage, eggs, beans and fried bread to the remaining party guests. The very look of it made Rayan feel ill. How did Maddie do it? She had drunk as much champagne last night as I did, Rayan thought—not to mention the shots.

There was no sign of Raphael or the bouncer. Maddie raised her eyebrows and smiled. "You look kind of green about the gills," she chuckled handing Rayan a mug of tea and two aspirin. "Swallow these. You'll feel better. You really tied one on last night. You beat these young ones hands down," she said admiringly.

"I doubt that very much," Rayan rasped out. Her throat felt as dry as the reservoir in Perth after a particularly dry season. She put a hand to her head. It felt as if it was trying to jump out of her skull.

"Where is Raphael?"

Maddie busied herself at the cooker. "He's away to take Kate home," she said her face losing its smile. She seemed to consider, then she yanked her phone out of her chef's trouser pocket. "Here," she said, unsmiling, proffering the phone at Rayan. "It's fully charged. You wanted to phone Imelda," she said a malicious look coming in her eyes.

Rayan snapped her mind back to the present. "*Get out*. And leave your key."

"Remember? I live here. It's my home," Raphael said.

"Correction—your mother lives here. I have swapped with her for a year. So, technically I live here. Give me your house key," Rayan demanded holding out her hand. "This house is not your home; it's just a place to bed your women."

Raphael looked at her, startled. How did she know he had Maddie here? He shrugged mentally. He had to bring her to make up for neglecting her the night of the party. He might need her again.

"Sorry, I should have let you know I was bringing Maddie. I'll let you know next time. But Mac is the reason I'm here tonight. He wants me to do the flight of the Earls Tour with him in the morning. A luxury cruise liner docked at Greencastle tonight. I'll be away when you get up in the morning." He looked past her. "Where's that wee brother of mine? I hear he's a hit with oul Vivian and those rich chicks at the Shingle Beach Hotel."

"He's working late."

"What about a bite to eat?"

Rayan flung him a dirty look. "Do I look like your mother or Maddie?"

"Ach, come on, you still can't be angry at me for that night of the party. That was months ago."

"Goodnight. Be gone when I get up in the morning," she said acidly, marching up the stairs.

She wished she had a key to Imelda's bedroom door. The lovely relaxed feeling she had following the massage evaporated. Wearily she plucked the big oversized man's dressing gown from behind the bedroom door and dragging it on she lay down on top of the bed fully clothed.

She turned her head and looked at the large tote bag Sue had given her to put her new wrap in. Rising, she pulled it out of the bag and took it back to bed with her. It felt slightly damp and smelled of the lavender and rose petals Sue had liberally scented the water with. *She is such a generous, open-hearted woman*, she thought hugging the wrap to her. For the second time that day, she thought a person like Sue was wasted on the likes of Vivian.

Vivian is an all-time bitch, she thought thinking back to her derogatory remarks and derisory glance when she's come in and found her and Sue talking together; jealous, insecure nobody that's what she is. I bet she's from some hovel in the ground...

There was a tapping on the door. "Can I come in?" Raphael's voice floated in through the keyhole.

Rayan clenched her teeth. Asshole. He was a real chancer. There was a sliver of silence. Then the door knob rattled but didn't turn. There was another silence. "Rayan. Can I come in? I need to tell you something."

"Go away. Isaac will be home soon," Rayan shouted trying to still the quiver in her voice.

"I need to talk to you."

"I don't need to talk to you," Rayan muttered in a low voice. Every muscle tensed, she lay listening. She sighed in relief at the sound of Raphael's feet clattering downstairs. With a bit of luck, he'd go walking on the foothills, like he usually did when he came home. She listened. She thought she heard him whistle for the dog. But she couldn't be sure. Sometimes a soft wind sighed through the apple trees in the orchard making a soft whistling sound.

Too wound up to relax she got out of bed and stood looking out of the window at the sun setting behind the trees. It looks so picturesque like the flicker of a candle winking through the leafy branches. Cautiously, she opened the door a crack. The old house was silent. The only noise she could hear from the kitchen was the humming of the refrigerator.

She'd tiptoed to the bathroom across the landing to clean her teeth, cream off her makeup and get ready for bed. She smiled. Sue kept encouraging her to follow a strict beauty routine morning and night of cleansing, toning and moisturising. She had to agree it was working. Her skin looked healthy, less sallow.

She stepped out onto the landing and froze when the old floorboards creaked beneath her. "Fastest teeth cleaning ever," she breathed as she stuck the toothbrush back into its holder and splashed cold water on her face.

"Come downstairs. I want to talk to you," Raphael's voice said from the doorway.

Rayan froze. She hadn't heard him creep up the stairs. "Not tonight. I'm bushed," she said praying Isaac would be home soon.

"I *need* to talk to you," Raphael insisted. "There's a crisis. I've made a cup of tea, come down, Rayan, please."

"Ireland's answer to every situation," Raphael muttered, wondering what the crisis was this time.

"Glass of wine—think there's a bottle somewhere…?"

"No thanks. I'm off wine. You can get too much of a good thing," she said caustically. "What's the crisis?"

Raphael squirmed and moved his mug of tea from one hand to the other. He's edgy, she thought.

"I want to apologise. I was very drunk the night of the party. If I did...or said anything...inappropriate..." He pushed the floppy curtain of hair back from his face with his left hand. (Isaac is right-handed, Rayan thought fleetingly.) "If I did, I'm sorry. The truth is, I remember very little about the party. I had a skinfold. Everybody brought bags of drink. It was all put into Ma's mixing bowl—everybody drank too much," he admitted ruefully, standing up and stuffed his hands into the pockets of his jeans.

Rayan crossed her arms over the thick dressing gown. "Oh really! That's your excuse for your appalling behaviour. You're telling me you don't remember giving that baboon Brendie orders keeping me a prisoner in Imelda's room?"

Raphael let out an audible sigh. "I do remember that," he said shamefaced. "But as I remember, it was your own fault." He held up his hands as Rayan leaped from her chair. "Wait, Rayan. There's something else I need to tell you."

He licked his lips. How could he say he had a vague recollection of being in bed with her; or was that just in his imagination—wishful thinking on his part? He turned away so she couldn't see the self-loathing on his face. Yeah, a wild night of free booze and free love. He grimaced. He'd had sex with a bunch of women that night. After a while, the faces blurred and all he remembered was the feel of their bodies... Had Rayan been one of them? He couldn't be sure.

"You don't remember leaving that *gorilla* on sentry duty all night outside my bedroom door?"

Turning back, Raphael spread his hands. "I told him early in the evening to make sure that *nobody* got into your room. I was sure you must be back and be already in there getting ready for the party. Once it all kicked off... I forgot about it."

Rayan bared her teeth. "He certainly knows how to follow orders. I suppose that's his *military training*."

Raphael let the jibe pass. "I'm sorry Rayan. I know. I fucked up, big time. He didn't know who you were. I'm sorry. What else can I say?"

Rayan leaped from her chair. "He knew who I was alright. And don't you toss away sending Maddie to get me so sodden drunk I wouldn't be able to phone your mother! You kept me prisoner..."

Raphael smirked. "Ach, don't be so melodramatic. You weren't a prisoner! You were drinking champagne with Maddie, enjoying the craic."

"You kept me a virtual prisoner in my own bedroom."

"My mother's bedroom…"

Red hot sparks like firecrackers flashed in Rayan's eyes. "While I am living in this house, it's my bedroom." She gave him a scathing look. She had phoned Imelda and told her about her son's inexcusable behaviours. Imelda had obviously demanded Raphael apologise to her. *Probably afraid her year's swap will come to a sudden end when I land back in Perth and evict her from my house and my business*, Rayan seethed. *And I'd do it if Nathanial shows the slightest interest me again*, she thought.

"And what kind of 'fairy-tale' did you spin Imelda?"

Raphael shifted. "I told her we had a party. I told her you got drunk on champagne. And were going around telling the guests it was your 'coming of age' party and that you were Isaac and my mother and that you had a go at Brendie…"

Rayan drew in a long shuddering breath. "You know I only did that so that buffoon would let me into my… Imelda's room."

Raphael looked at her surreptitiously and cleared his throat. "Ma wasn't exactly pleased. She said it seemed to be a habit of yours; drinking too much and then losing your head and attacking people."

Heat suffused Rayan's face and neck. Imelda had obviously told him about her tossing the wine over the flight attendant. She'd remember that to her, she thought savagely.

"I explained to Ma that Maddie, the chef from the Smallest Pub, made you something nice to eat and kept you company until you sobered up."

Rayan looked at him incredulously. She couldn't believe what she was hearing. He had turned the whole thing around.

"And how did you explain away your non-student *friends* from the *gun club*! How did you explain that to your gullible mother?"

Raphael crossed his arms across his chest. "I told her Isaac had brought them not realising who they were." He felt a frisson of guilt at dropping his twin in it with his mother. But he knew Imelda wasn't going to let her favourite son be questioned by the Guards. He moved closer and leaned on the table. "Have the Guards been snooping around?"

Rayan eyeballed him. So that was his crisis. That's what he wanted to talk to her about. He wanted to know if she had told the cops anything. Imelda had obviously not told him *she* had a contact in the local Guards. A few days after the party they had come and conducted a cursory search of the grounds. At the house owner's request, the cop said, doffing his peaked cap at her.

Rayan smirked. Imelda was nobody's fool. Her father had been a Garda sergeant. No way were Imelda's sons going to be seen to be involved in anything outwards to do with trouble in the North. Imelda had seen to that.

From the look on Rayan's face, Raphael guessed something had happened. The knot of apprehension in his stomach tightened.

"Big Brendie was taken in for questioning."

"Why should that concern me?" Rayan snorted. But she couldn't hide the feeling of satisfaction it gave her to know she'd get her revenge on him. So, the description she'd given the cop about him and his tattoos on his arms had been good enough to identify him. She had also mentioned there was some kind of 'activity' in the fields behind the house around Easter time. The Garda had seemed pretty interested in that bit of news. But she wasn't about to tell Raphael any of that. Let him stew. He had it coming, she thought.

"I'm going to bed. You can tell Imelda her *boy is a liar and a womaniser.* But I think she knows that already," Rayan sneered. "But like the good wee boy he is, he listened to his mammy and apologised," she sneered. "Maybe you should apologise to Maddie too."

Raphael looked surprised. "Apologise to Maddie? Why would I do that?"

Rayan stonewalled him with a look. "You're despicable. You brought her to a party; made her work like a dog and then shagged Kate and half the student body in front of her."

Raphael had the grace to look mortified.

She was sorely tempted to kick him when he was down by telling him Maddie had gladly given her the phone the following morning to make the calls. But it would mean dropping Maddie in it. She satisfied herself by casting him a derisory look. "I wouldn't be a bit surprise if there is a glut of twins born in Donegal and Derry in 1996," she spat at him.

Raphael shrugged. "Girls are not as naive as my Ma was in the 70s. Women don't get pregnant in the 90s unless they want to." He smiled complacently. "I doubt if any more bastard twins, like Isaac and me, will be born from my night of lovemaking," he mocked. Disgusted at his language, Rayan turned to go to bed. "There's something else I need to talk to you about."

"I'm done talking to you, Raphael. Leave your key. If you don't, I'll have a locksmith change the locks."

Raphael ground his teeth. "I know that bitch Sue…your *friend* told you about me and the court case for rioting. Did you tell Ma?"

So that was it. He was worried she'd tell Imelda. It hadn't occurred to her but she'd definitely be letting dear Imelda know the true fucking nature of her darling son now.

"I got off." Raphael ran his hand through his floppy hair. It would have been better for him if he hadn't. At least it would have given him some creditability. He would have rather faced his mother's wrath about him being in the IRA than what was happening now. He was in up shit creek without a paddle.

"Good for you. Your future career as a solicitor is safe for another while," Rayan said her voice dripping sarcasm.

If only that was all, Raphael thought. Big Brendie had been charged. Somebody had to have given information and the RA believed it was him. Raphael shivered. Old Manus had gotten wind of the melee between him and Rayan and her threat to phone the Guards.

Bastards, he swore silently. There was a time when the Brits, the cops in the North and the Garda in the south, mistrusted each other; now they're sucking up to each other, sharing information—working hand in glove with each other.

He shivered as if someone had just walked over his grave. There were whispers within the organisation he wasn't to be trusted. He was being watched. He was sure of it. He looked warily at Rayan. She hadn't phoned that night had she? He shook his head. No. Maddie had done a good job of getting Rayan drunk and keeping her mouth shut about it. But still…somebody had touted to the Brits. Unbidden, his thoughts went to his twin. Isaac knew. He shook his head. No way! Isaac was no tout. There had to be another explanation.

Rayan headed for the stairs. "Did you tell the Guards…anything about who was at the party?" Raphael asked.

"I am not interested in the politics of this country. Goodnight," she said. Raphael thought he saw her shiver. So, she had said something? Sweat broke out all over Raphael's body. This was bad, very, very bad; for him…and for Rayan.

One thing he knew, he didn't want his mother finding out about his involvement with the IRA from Rayan. He needed something to stop her telling. "I know about you and Isaac," he said.

Rayan drew in her breath. She wondered when he'd get around to challenging her about her and his twin's sex life. "I know you do. You accused me of *raping* him. You'd have me deported for taking his virginity. You tried to drag me into the hill walker's room to have sex with me. Then you followed me into your mother's bedroom to the cheers and catcalls of your drunken friends."

Raphael brushed his fingers through his hair. Fuck! He was never drinking again. Cold sweat broke out on him. Vague images flashed in his head. Had he he'd slept with Rayan? Isaac will *never* forgive me, if I did, he thought. He had no conscious about sleeping with other guy's girlfriends but not his twin's. No, he would do that to his twin.

"Did I…did you…did we sleep together?"

Rayan threw him a contemptuous look. "*No, we did not.*"

Raphael waited until his heartbeat settle down before he trusted himself to speak. "I'm sorry I said those things. I didn't mean them." He hesitated. "Isaac had never been with a woman…in that way…until you. Ma was worried he might be like, you know, your friend Sue and that dyke of a girlfriend of her—except with men. At least that's one thing she doesn't have to worry about anymore."

"Glad I could be of help," Rayan said derisively.

"Raphael sucked in his bottom lip." You have to admit, Rayan, he's half your age…

"You think I'm an old woman, trying to relive my youth by having a younger boyfriend."

Raphael shrugged. "I don't know what you think. But Ma has big plans for Isaac. I don't think it includes a woman old enough to be his mother. She wouldn't like to think you were taking advantage of an inexperienced boy," he said grimly. "But she doesn't need to know—not yet."

Rayan couldn't believe what she was hearing. "*You* won't tell Imelda about Isaac and me if *I* don't tell her you're up to your neck with the paramilitaries in Derry?"

Raphael shrugged. "That's it. And you mustn't tell Isaac…about me trying to get you into bed the night of the party."

Rayan's eyes bored into Raphael's. She clamped her teeth over her bottom lip. She wanted to fly at him. Dig her long nails into his self-righteous face and tear out his eyeballs. Hands shaking, she grasped the back of the kitchen chair until her knuckles turned puce. Her palpable anger sent a warning loud and clear. *Back off, you bastard, or I will rip out your eyeballs.* Raphael moved back putting the kitchen island between them.

Rayan looked at him cold steel in her eyes. "How can you and Isaac look so alike but be so different?" she said.

Raphael placed his palms upwards in a placating manner. "We might not be as different as you think, Rayan. After all we are *identical twins*—born from the one egg—same genes. It took Isaac longer than me to find women. Now that he has, like me, he has found he likes women, a lot," he said carefully.

Rayan's face twisted. What did he mean? *Isaac liked women a lot*? She remembered a drunken girl saying she was Isaac's girlfriend but she had assumed she had meant she was Raphael's girlfriend. And Isaac did seem to be working late quite a few evenings lately…

Rayan gave Raphael any icy stare. "You may be twins but Isaac is *nothing* like you. All you are is a lying scheming womaniser. Isaac is not like that. He may *like* stupid drunk girls but I'm his woman," she spat, lunging at him.

Chapter Fifteen

Coming into the kitchen, Isaac stopped dead when he saw the blood. "Where's Rayan? It's all over the hotel she was assaulted and taken to hospital."

"She's a lunatic. She went at me like a wild thing…"

Isaac swallowed hard. "You assaulted her!"

"No!" Raphael pushed his hands through his hair. "No! She flew at me and tripped on that long man robe thing she wears and banged her head off the edge of the worktop."

Isaac edged around the dried blood. "Is she alright? Have you phoned the hospital?" He asked feeling bad he hadn't come home with Rayan after work as planned.

He'd partnered Shawnee on the tennis court. She'd asked him into the bar for a drink after the doubles match. It had gone on for a bit. It had felt good to be in the company of a younger woman for a change. Rayan's constant need to be with him and know where he was at all times was beginning to overwhelm him.

"Rayan didn't seem in a bad mood when I saw her at work," he said splashing milk over a bowl of cereal.

"What? You think I did or said something to set her off. You hear her yelling at Dizzy. You know she has a short fuse." Raphael shuddered involuntarily and pushed the dog away from where he was sniffing at the congealed blood.

"She didn't just go for you. You must have said something." The spoon stopped halfway to Isaac's mouth. Raphael had made a move on Rayan and she'd went for him. He scanned his twin's face and body. There were no signs of any scratches or bruises on him.

Raphael stared his twin stuffing his face. Yeah; he scoffed to himself, whoever he was 'partnering paid off in spades. He seemed pretty chilled out and not overly concerned about Rayan, he thought.

He felt Isaac's eyes scrutinising him. "I didn't say a thing, bro," he lied. "I was here when that woman Sue left Rayan home from work. She gave me the cold shoulder treatment and went to bed. But not before she demanded my key to *my* home. She's still mad at me about the party. I tried to apologise but she was having none of it."

Isaac jiggled the keys of his mother's jeep lying on the table. "It did turn into a fiasco," he said bluntly. "Mum was spitting mad when she heard."

"Yeah, I know. She had a go at me over the phone and laid down the law in a long email. *And*, wait for this, I'm not to be here on my own or bring Maddie chef back to the house while she's in Perth. That's what I get for letting off a bit of steam after studying hard all year while she's away lying sunning herself in Australia."

Isaac's dark eyebrows arched. Worked hard at touring the country with Mac O Lochlainn, carry messages and doing worse for the Derry paramilitaries, more like, he thought.

"As usual, I get the blame. Wild child—that's me," Raphael went on dolefully. "You asked some of your friends too and put the notice of the party on the student notice board in big black lettering…"

"You told me to do."

"Yeah, well, I thought come June most of the student's into partying would have gone home. I didn't want the party to be a flop, did I?"

Isaac snorted. "Yeah, you have your reputation to think about for next year."

"Yeah, Maddie's barbecuing went down a bomb," Raphael preened, missing the sarcastic jibe.

Isaac stood up and stretched his long back just as the phone rang. "Rayan is being kept in overnight," he said replacing the receiver as he rummaged in the fridge for something else to eat. "Vivian asked me to partner Shawnee again tomorrow. How did you get Rayan to hospital?" he asked picking up the keys of his mother's jeep.

Raphael's stomach began to judder. The image of Rayan's slack body slumped against the foot of the kitchen island; her head at a funny angle filled his mind with horror. He had been sure she was dead. Stories he'd heard of fights where a person fell and hit the back of their head and died had raced through his mind.

He'd backed away from her. His mind completely swamped in panic. "I just stood there. It seemed like a long time but maybe it was only minutes," he said his words barely audible. "The mountain rescue guys took her—they were practising dummy rescue missions on Muckish. I'd seen them when I was walking the dog earlier."

Shaking, he leaned his head in his hands. He had been afraid to leave Rayan and afraid not to go for help. In the end, he'd pounded across the cow field praying prayers his granny Norah had taught him in his pre-school days. By the time he had reached the mountain rescue training team he was hyperventilating and incoherent; his words falling out of his mouth over each other. "Their paramedics worked with her and then phoned the hospital to say they were bringing her in," he said hoarsely.

"Well, as long as she's OK," Isaac said moving towards the door.

"I'm going in to see about Rayan. And so are you. She is your girlfriend."

Isaac fiddled with change in his pockets. "You go. She doesn't know the difference in us. Sue's here," he said as a car swung into the yard.

Raphael moved into the shadow of the sunroom. "Go and tell her about Rayan; she'll ask me a bunch of questions."

He watched Sue put her hand to her mouth in shock as Isaac related the news.

"Did she seem…overly concerned to you?" he asked as Isaac came back into the kitchen.

"She's upset. Says she'll phone the hospital as soon as she gets to the hotel. And she'll collect Rayan in the morning and bring her home."

Raphael curled his lips. "She fancies Rayan. They were kissing."

Isaac smirked. "Kissing? You sure Rayan didn't hit you a whack on the head with something," Isaac chortled. "It's Sue and Vivian who are partners, not Sue and Rayan." He gave his twin an enigmatic smile. "I can guarantee you Rayan is not like those two. I should know bro."

Raphael stilled. "I'll take your word for it, Isaac," he mumbled crossing his fingers Rayan hadn't been one of the women he had bedded the night of the party.

Chapter Sixteen

"Miss Ritchie, Rayan, how do you feel? You've had a nasty knock on the head. I'm Dr Crawley. Look at me," he commanded. "Can you follow my pen?"

Rayan pushed his hand away and struggled to get off the trolley. "I'm going home. My job...it's the busy season..."

The doctor straightened. "Your job is going to have to wait. You gave yourself quite a whack when you fell. I'm sending you for a CT scan."

"My medical insurance doesn't cover hospital treatment," Rayan snapped.

Dr Crawley raised his eyebrows. "We'll worry about the hospital coffers when we know you're OK," he assured her.

Rayan startled awake. She couldn't think where she was. Then she remembered the fight with Raphael, the CT scan and the whistling porter who'd parked her along the wall and abandoned her there. She raised her shoulders. Immediately a searing pain shot up her neck into her head. She was in a corridor that seemed to link to the main Accident and Emergency area of the hospital.

A cold draught stole up under the light blanket that was covering her. She shivered. "I'm cold," she said as yet another nurse asked her name. The nurse smiled. "You're Australian. My brother has just emigrated there. You're cold—missing the heat. I'll get an extra blanket."

She seemed to have been on the trolley forever. Every time the door opened at the end of the corridor, she was sure it would be Isaac. She moaned as a jagged bolt of pain shot through her neck and head. Another nurse moved into her line of vision. "Miss Ritchie?" she asked checking the name on the chart clipped at the end of the bed.

"Yes."

"We have a bed for you."

Rayan twisted around. "I don't need a bed. I'm going home!"

"Doctor would like you stay in overnight for observation," the nurse said settling her back on the pillows. Tears of frustration threatened to seep from behind Rayan's eyelashes. She swiped them away. Her chest felt as tight as a drum and her neck and head throbbed. Where the hell was Isaac! She wanted to go home.

"The place is heaving. Where's she going?" a porter asked.

"Temporary bed—post ops ward."

Rayan's bed jarred against the leg of another bed as it was manoeuvred into place. "Tight as a duck's arse," the porter joked.

"I want to go home. Isaac will be worried. And Dizzy might get out and attack the lambs," Rayan moaned.

A nurse leaned over her. "It's OK. Your sons have been contacted to say you're being admitted."

"I don't have sons."

Unperturbed, the nurse smiled. Patients with head trauma often became confused. "Try and rest," she soothed. "Buzz if you need anything."

"Contact my friend Sue for me?"

"I've just come on duty. I'll do it as soon as I get a chance."

"Thanks for nothing," Rayan said ungraciously.

She woke and called out. She'd been dreaming she was in a strange place where she didn't understand the language people spoke.

"Shush, you'll wake the rest of the patients," a nurse said softly.

"My scan, what did it show?"

The nurse straightened the crumpled bed and turned down the bed lamp. "Doctor will be around in the morning."

Agitated, Rayan clutched at her. "Did you get Sue?"

The nurse put her finger to her lips. "We have very sick patients just back from theatre. You must be quiet."

"Sue is supposed to be picking me up for work in the morning," Rayan insisted. "And my head feels like it's going to burst."

"I'll bring you something for the pain," the nurse said, tiptoeing out of the ward.

Rayan lay facing the un-curtained window wondering why Isaac hadn't come. She clenched her fists imagining the lies Raphael would spin him about how she came to be the hospital.

She felt around for the buzzer. It had slipped off the bed and was dangling just out of her reach. She pushed back the bedclothes. There was a loud clatter as she fell against the locker knocking over the water jug.

"Don't get out of bed again. Do you hear me?" the nurse hissed as buzzers shattered the quiet of the ward.

"I'm going home," Rayan said petulantly.

"You have concussion," the nurse said putting up the cot sides on the bed.

"I'm discharging myself," Rayan retorted loudly. Punching a hollow in the pillow, she gingerly lowered her throbbing head into it.

The swish of curtains being drawn back and the rattle of bedpans woke her. "Morning," a woman smiled stopping beside her bed. "You allowed breakfast, love?" she asked. "There's no notice. I'll just leave you some bacon, egg and a slice of toast," she said putting the plate down on the trolley at the end of the bed.

Rayan nodded filling up at the woman's kindness. "You'll feel better after a cup of tea," she smiled.

The bacon made Rayan feel nauseous. She gagged and pushed the tray away.

"How far along you are, love?" The woman in the next bed asked.

"I hate the Irish," Rayan muttered. "Complete strangers address you as 'Love' and 'dear'." She knew it was a form of colloquial speech but it made her teeth grind. She sank back on the pillows. "How far along am I…what?"

"How far along…how long until your baby's due?" the woman said tucking into her breakfast. At the sight of the fat pork sausage sliding into the woman's mouth, Rayan gagged again. Panic assailed her. She rattled on the bed sides calling out for the nurse.

"Stop that racket. All you have to do is press the buzzer," an irritable orderly snapped, flicking a sick tray under Rayan's nose. "Always one isn't there, just as the breakfast is being given out," she grumbled.

"Maybe if you had a bun in the oven and were in a foreign country far from your own, you mightn't be so chirpy in the morning, either." Rayan heard the woman in the next bed say.

Rayan's head pounded like a jackhammer. "I'm not pregnant," she ground out. "I have concussion."

She jerked away as the doctor probed the lump on the back of her head. "That's some whopper you have there," he said. "How did you get it? Do you have any headaches or nausea?"

White-knuckled, Rayan gripped the bedclothes. "Why do people in Ireland answer one question by asking another?" she spat out.

The doctor smiled good-humouredly. "You've noticed that too, have you," he said lifting her chin and checking her pupils.

"What did my scan show?" Rayan gasped cold sweat breaking out all over her body from the pain in her neck.

"Your CT scan shows you have a closed head injury and mild concussion." Rayan was startled.

"Your brain was shaken by the impact of hitting the worktop," he explained. "You'll have a headache for a day or two or slightly longer. If your headaches last longer than a week, go and see your own doctor."

Dr Crawley sat down on the corner of the bed. "You had a very restless night; you requested something for a severe headache and you were vomiting this morning." The doctor indicated to the nurse she should pull the curtains around Rayan's bed. "Does the smell of food often make you sick in the morning?"

Rayan stared at him.

"Is there a possibility you might be pregnant? CT scans are generally not harmful to a foetus as long as—"

Despite the throbbing in her skull, Rayan cut across him shaking her head emphatically. "I am absolutely certain I am not pregnant."

"Good. But I would like to do an ultrasound of the abdomen just to be sure," he added handing Rayan's chart to the nurse.

"You are not. I'm discharging myself; even if it means climbing over the bars on this bed and going home in my nightdress," Rayan said her eyes shooting sparks at him.

A faint smile flickered at the corners of the doctor's mouth. "This is not sunny Australia, *Rayan*," he said emphasising her name. "You'll not get far in the rain in your hospital paper gown," he said sardonically. "It's your choice."

"I am *not* pregnant. I am not! I never want to be pregnant. I never want to give birth; or be a mother. I can't be pregnant," she said beginning to shake uncontrollably.

"Have the ultrasound scan. It will set your mind at ease…"

Rayan fell back against the iron head of the hospital bed barely noticing the pain. She had always been so careful. She'd even gotten condoms for Isaac. She couldn't be pregnant! She balled her fists. "I was forty on my last birthday. My own doctor in Perth said I am too old. It was very unlikely I'd get pregnant at *my age*," she spat. "I am in early menopause." The realisation made her voice shrill. "Do you get anything right in this fucking place?"

"Please don't use abusive language to me or my staff," the doctor said crisply.

Rayan shot him a look of pure malice. "Don't talk bullshit, then. I'm not pregnant."

The doctor rubbed his hand over his face. His bleeper sounded. It was a bad start to what was turning out to be a busy morning. He checked his message and put the bleeper back in his breast pocket. "Look, what about a nice bed bath and a change of nightdress to freshen you up before your sons come to visit you."

"What is he talking about?" Rayan asked turning to the nurse. "I do not have sons!"

The doctor flipped over his notes. "Raphael came in with you in the emergency ambulance when you were admitted."

"He is Imelda Wright's son. *She* is the woman I have exchanged houses with for a year. *She* is in Perth living in *my* house and running my business. And I am in Donegal in *her* house. Is that clear enough for you, doctor!"

The doctor had heard enough. "If we discharge you, will there be somebody to pick you up—take care of you for a few days?"

Rayan's heart leaped into her throat. Finally, she was being discharged. "Isaac, my boyfriend, will be there for me," she babbled. She let out a long slow breath. "Doctor, if I was pregnant—which I know I am not—who should I see about an abortion?"

The doctor clicked his tongue in disapproval. Plenty of women were emphatic they didn't want children but once the child was born… "Abortion is not permitted in the Republic of Ireland, Miss Ritchie."

Chapter Seventeen

The silence lengthened as Sue eased the car around the potholes. "Sorry," she apologised as the front wheel skimmed another one. The jolt of pain that shot through her hardly registered in Rayan's brain. Her hands gripped the red leather seat she stared unseeing at green fields and the cows grazing contentedly. It couldn't be true! She couldn't be pregnant!

Sue glanced surreptitiously at Rayan. She had never seen her look so...she searched her mind for words to describe the devastating change in her. She looks shell shocked; as if the strength of character she always exhumed was crumbling from the inside, Sue thought. Reaching across she curled her fingers around the Rayan's hand. "We'll be home soon," she said soothingly. As they passed the road to Muckish Gap and the Bridge of Sorrows Sue could see some tourists preparing to climb the mountain. "Beautiful day for it," she murmured.

"Drop me at the end of the lane..."

"Jesus! Rayan Ritchie, I will not. I'm taking you straight to the Manse and then straight up the stairs to Imelda's bed." She laughed self-consciously. "You know what I mean." Rayan didn't give her usual spirited response.

"I need a walk and some of fresh air. I need to be alone; get my head around..."

"Not today," Sue said resolutely. "You'd be found halfway up that bloody mountain with that brainless donkey of a dog sitting beside you with a stupid look on its face," she scolded parking as near to the door of the Manse as she could.

Rayan hesitated on the threshold of the kitchen. Images crowded in of Raphael struggling with her. Their heated row seemed so unimportant now. "If you'll not stay with Vivian and me, stay at the hotel," Sue pleaded following her in. "You need looking after for a few days."

"I'll be fine," Rayan murmured sinking into a cushioned chair in the sunroom. She leaned her head back and let her body slump into its comfortable depths. She *was* pregnant. It was all she could think about. There must be some mistake. It had to be the start of the menopause. She needed a pregnancy testing kit. Only when she saw the blue line with her own eyes would she believe it.

Sue stalked around the kitchen. Her summer flip flops making a slapping sound on the tiles. "Nice welcome home," she fumed. "Where the friggin' hell are the mirror image twins? Did they even visit you in hospital? Why aren't they here to take care of you?"

"They had to go into Derry to the university—something about a study schedule." She felt her gut tighten. She was glad Isaac wasn't here. She might blurt out the results of the scan. She didn't want to tell anybody until she had the arrangements for an abortion.

"Not a decision to be made in a state of shock," the doctor said giving her a solemn look. "You should talk it over with the father. Perhaps have some counselling before you decide."

"I need to register with a doctor," she said as Sue filled the kettle. "For a follow up to the hospital treatment," she added quickly.

"Good idea. A proper MOT will do no harm," Sue asserted. "The staff at the Spa are under a private health scheme. I'm sure you could be too. Cuppa?" She asked holding the teapot afloat. Rayan gave her a wry smile. The teapot looked incongruous in Sue's manicured hand with its French polished tapered talons. It looked as much out of place as if she was holding a pick axe. "No. I'm going to feed Dizzy and then I'm going to lie down."

Sue caught the shudder that passed through Rayan as she skirted around the edge of the marble work island. She was sure Rayan hadn't told her the truth about what had happened. She remembered the silhouette of Raphael lurking in the shadow of the doorway, watching them last night when she'd brought Rayan home. She put down the teapot. "He attacked you, didn't he?"

"What? Who?"

"Raphael. He assaulted—"

"No! I tripped and hit my head."

"You might be a great hairdresser but you're a lousy liar." Sue's voice was even but rising anger made it tremble. "I wish I'd come in with you. I'd soon have told him where to go to cool his ardour."

Sweat broke out over Rayan's body. She needed Sue to go. If Raphael came home and Sue confronted him with what she thought had happened, he would tell her what had really happened. "Please Sue; I don't want to talk about it, not today."

Sue drew a packet of cigarettes out of her oversized crocodile bag and without asking lit one and shoved it in Rayan direction. "I am not leaving here until you tell me what really happened."

Rayan dragged on the cigarette. How do you tell someone you barely know that you're not always in control of yourself? She couldn't do it. She valued their friendship too much to lose it. "Vivian will be wondering…she'll be getting into a flap. You should go."

"Like testosterone on legs, that one," Sue snorted. "He tried it on and you told him to feck off. That's what happened, isn't it?"

"He did try it on the night of the party," Rayan admitted.

Are you going to let Raphael take the rap like you did with Nathanial, Rayan's conscience sneered. Tell the truth and shame the devil, her father's mantra boomed in her head.

Rayan took a deep breath. "It was cold when I came in so I put on the big dressing gown and I tripped," she finished lamely.

Sue trailed restlessly around the kitchen. "It's OK, Rayan," she soothed stroking her arm as she passed. "I know you like to be in control. But you can't be in control of every situation. You can tell me. I'm your friend. The wee shit tried it on. Didn't he?"

Rayan leaned on the mottled surface of the worktop. Her breath making little clouds on the cold marble "I'd tell you if he did. I told you about the party, didn't I?"

Sue was staring at the huge American style fridge. Jesus! Imelda really knows how to live in style, she thought. Wonder which of her boyfriends forked out for that?

Rayan's heart fluttered in her chest like a caged bird. An image of her flaying her nails down Raphael's forearms as he tried to hold her off while he had her jammed against the fridge, came back to her.

"Bollocks!" Sue scowled. "He threw a wobblier—threw the rattle out of the pram because he didn't get what Isaac got—sex with you. Those two have always shared everything. Why wouldn't they share their women?"

Rayan wished with all her heart that Sue would go. Her voice was beginning to grate on her nerves.

If only I had stayed upstairs instead of coming down to the kitchen and venting my anger on Raphael, she thought filling the dog's dish with water. *If only I hadn't lost my temper*. She swiped at the pool of sweat trickling down the back of her neck. If only she hadn't told the Irish police about Big Brendie. Raphael wouldn't have gotten his own back by telling her about Isaac.

"Sue. I need to take the dog out," she said.

She watched the dog, delighted to be free, romp through the orchard scattering loose earth beneath his big feet as he went. Sue came to stand beside her. "The woman that runs that re-homing centre saw Imelda coming," she joked watching the dog clamour up on a stump of an old tree and leap into the air trying to catch the low flying birds. "Never saw an animal so brainless. He and Imelda are a good match," Sue laughed.

"I had a dog in Perth. Or, at least Nat had." She was surprised to realise she missed little Biscuit. I wonder how she is coping living with Sienna, she thought. Suddenly, she felt utterly fatigued. She needed to be alone to think. "Vivian will be wondering where you are. You should go," she repeated.

"Something is wrong. And I am not going from here until you tell me what it is. Anyway, Vivian is still mad you and me and the massage in the tub. I don't want to go home to listen to her jealous ranting."

Defeated, Rayan turned her face away from Sue. She didn't want to see the look of revulsion in her friend's eyes when she learned what she was really like. "It's my fault I smashed my head against that," she said flicking her hand in the direction of the marble work island. "I attacked Raphael," she said shuddering uncontrollably. Behind her she heard Sue's chair scrape on the floor. "Before you go, you might as well know it all. I left Australia and came to live in Ireland because I was going to be charged with beating on my ex-partner. The police in Perth are probably looking for me." She drew in a deep breath. "I'm not the person you think I am. I have…anger issues."

Sue's mouth fell into a gape. She'd seen the picture Rayan carried in her wallet. He didn't look the type to be beaten up by a woman. And not for one nanosecond could she see Raphael… No. She had been right all along. Something was very wrong, very wrong. For a fleeting moment, Sue wondered if Rayan had ever suffered from a delusional illness. Or was it the effect of the whack on her head?

Watching the familiar look of disbelief spread across Sue's face, Rayan clamped her fingers in her hair.

Sue closed the gap between them and gently extracted Rayan's hands. "Don't; don't pull at your hair. You'll have a bald patch tomorrow."

Rayan tried desperately to gain control of her emotions. "It wouldn't be the first time," she quaked.

"I don't understand. Why would you beat up your partner?" Sue asked breaking the silence.

Rayan gulped back tears. "He was pressurising me into getting pregnant; always berating me—go to the doctor—go to the doctor. I had to keep finding new places to hide the Pill. I didn't trust him not to replace them with something else."

Sue drew in her breath. She'd give anything to be pregnant. Vivian didn't want children cluttering up her life. "You lived with Nathanial for six years. He expected that at some stage you would give him a child? What's wrong with that?" she said almost belligerently, her anger at Raphael forgotten momentarily.

Rayan felt hysteria rising in her. What would Nathanial say when he discovered a kid half his age got her pregnant?

"I told him when we met I wasn't never, ever going to have a kid. He thought I would change my mind." Rayan twisted her hands together. "He deserved all he got. He's living with my eighteen-year-old assistant Sienna now. Let her have a kid for him."

Sue moved back, shocked at the sound of venom in Rayan's voice.

Holy shit! Vivian was going to have a stroke or a heart attack. An abusive forty-year-old runaway working in *her* salon and wanted by the police on the other side of the world! She drew air deep into her lungs. Fuck you, Vivian, she thought. It's called retribution. It would. Serve her bloody right if Immigrations or the international police force came looking for Rayan. The papers would have a field day. Vivian was always saying publicity was good for business. Not this time, not this time, Sue thought maliciously. Vivian's precious Spa would be in the headlines for all the wrong reasons.

She pushed her and Vivian's problems to the back of her mind. "I don't know what happened between you and your ex-partner…maybe he deserved it. I don't know about jumping bail." She tried to gather her thoughts. "I don't know what to say or what to tell you, Rayan about that. But what I do know is this," she held up her hand when Rayan moved to speak. "Raphael was up for it last night. Sneaking about, spying on us, playing surveillance game or whatever he thought he was doing," she sneered. "I don't believe you would go at him for nothing."

Rayan clutched at her hair again. "You don't know me. You don't know me at all. But you're right. He accused me of raping his twin. Said he'd tell Imelda about me and Isaac—said Imelda had big plans for his twin. And they didn't include a woman twice his age with baggage…" The words fell like stones from Rayan's mouth.

Sue gaped at her. "He actually used the word *rape*? Oh my God!" she fanned her face with her hands. "I need a drink. Imelda must have some wine about here somewhere," she stuttered. Withdrawing her hand from the back of the saucepan cupboard, she held up a bottle of Chardonnay. "Not a great year," she mumbled checking the label. "But then this is turning out not to be a great year," she growled as she filled two tumblers to overflowing.

Dizzy whined plaintively and pawed at the back door. *He will scrape the glass*, Rayan thought absently. She recalled how anxious Nat's little dog got when the air was filled with tensions after one of her and Nat's rows.

"Shut up, dog," Sue said edgily. "You're getting on my bloody nerves."

The dog emitted a guttural growl deep in his throat and came and sat beside Rayan. She stroked his big head. "If Raphael reports me to the cops, I could be deported," she croaked out.

"You won't be deported for having sex with Isaac. He's almost twenty-one, for god sake! He's an adult… Oh you mean about…the other thing…the Perth Police." The word absconding rose to the surface of Sue's mind. She gulped at the wine. Rayan had just given Vivian the perfect excuse to get rid of her.

Dizzy shivered against Rayan's legs and growled deep in his throat again. Sue jumped to her feet. "That bloody dog's whining and growling is doing my head in."

"He knows there's something wrong."

Sue stomped into the sunroom. "Come in here and close that mutt out there." Rayan rose and took a doggy bone from the cupboard and coaxed the dog onto the small kitchen sofa.

She searched for her handbag and swilled down more painkillers. "I'm not supposed to drink alcohol…when I'm…taking painkillers," she faltered as Sue topped up her glass of wine for her.

Sue toyed with her second tumbler of wine. What a mess, she thought. Without Rayan around to make Vivian jealous, she'd never get her to agree to a sperm donor. She'd never have a child, be a mother.

Chapter Eighteen

"I'm off to the 15th August Band festival in Derry. Don't suppose you'd bury the hatchet and come with me?" Raphael said on impulse, looking at Rayan's tense body.

The look of venom Rayan threw him left no doubt where she'd like to bury the hatchet. It was *months* since she'd hit her head on the marble slab of the kitchen island. How long was she going to keep up this vendetta against him? He watched her surreptitiously. There was something *changed* about her. She was stick thin and obsessed with climbing Muckish.

"Weather's bad out there," he commented. "There was a high wind and it's been lashing rain all night. Muckish will be treacherous today," he commented as Rayan reached for her parka.

In sunlit summer days, being on Muckish was like being in another universe. The blue of the sky and the purple heather and green foliage of the mountain seem to merge and become one. But when the heavy rain came down like today and the mist obscured the designated paths it could be a death trap.

"Rayan! Did you hear me? Some of the paths will be blocked—loose boulders swept down with the—"

"What's it to you?" Rayan injected tersely.

A car horn blasted. "That's my lift," Raphael said. He hesitated. "If you wait, I'll take you up the Minors Trail," he offered.

Rayan blanked him and headed for the door.

"Did you put my and Isaac's mobile numbers into that new phone of yours, you've been up Muckish often enough now to know the dangers. Or is that what you want—to put yourself in harm's way," he called after her. He gritted his teeth. Fuck. She was one pig-headed woman.

"Go to your festival. I'm going walking around the lake," she conceded.

"Take the dog," he ordered. "Fuck! All of a sudden I'm her minder," he grunted jumping into the car and slammed the door shut with a resounding bang.

Something was definitely not right with Rayan. A part of him told him he should stay but what would be the point? She couldn't stand the sight of him. He drew his phone out of his pocket. He'd ring Isaac; tell him to go home and check on her.

He listened to Isaac's phone ringing out. He gritted his teeth. It wasn't the weather to be on the tennis courts. Where the hell was Isaac? He left a message. Pocketing his phone, he realised it had been weeks since he had had a face-to-face conversation with his twin. There was a time when they'd told each other everything—almost knew what each other were thinking. Were he and Isaac growing apart? The thought startled him.

Sleet lashed Rayan's face and mixed in with the tears that coursed down her cheeks. She pummelled on her stomach. This *thing* inside her was sucking the life out of her. Images rose up in her of insects, devouring and I crawling about in her insides. And I'm no nearer to getting rid of it, she thought turning back in the direction of the Manse.

Dizzy shook his huge head, sending a spray of water over the clean kitchen. Pawing his rug off the sofa he rolled on it to dry his back. Rayan hardly noticed. Hanging her dripping parka behind the kitchen door, in desperation, she wondered if she should phone Imelda; tell her. And say what? Your twenty-year-old son has gotten your forty-year-old renter pregnant.

Rayan scattered the loose tea leaves into the china teapot with its spray of red roses. The kind of roses I imagined growing around Imelda's cottage door, she mused. She cringed. How wrong could you be? About as wrong as thinking a geographical move eleven thousand miles would solve your problems, her inner voice sneered.

An ironic smirk spread across her face. She should go home and have an abortion in Perth. She wanted to see that stupid old doctor's face when she gave him the news. "Senile old bollocks; it's his fault I'm in this predicament I'm in," she snorted. Telling her it was unlikely she'd get pregnant; lulling her into a false sense of security.

She should phone Imelda. Tell her to evacuate her house and business because she was coming back. Her stomach turned over. She'd be arrested. Her name would be in the local papers. Her parents would read all about her running away to Ireland. The tea in the cup slopped over the side as she began to shake.

What a mess. She couldn't do it. She couldn't face them. She could hear her mother hissing, "You have disgraced your father yet again." She could imagine the loathing for her in Nathanial's eyes. To him it would be a kind of betrayal when she was adamant she would never ever have his child.

She had to find a way to fix it herself. It was no good asking Sue. She'd tried the local doctors to be told that it was against the law to even give her information on a termination.

Rayan pushed the cold mug of tea into the microwave to reheat. Birth control wasn't freely available in the Republic of Ireland.

What about Imelda? Surely at some stage she had need of someone who could help her get rid of it. It's all about who you *know,* she thought. That seemed to be the way problems got resolved in Ireland.

She picked up the phone extension in the sunroom and dialled. She could hear the familiar ringtone of her home phone. Her eye caught the time on the clock she kept on Australian time, on the coffee table. It was one am in the morning in Perth.

As if on cue, car wheels crunched on the gravel outside. "It's me," a voice called as she let the phone fall into its cradle. "You OK?" Isaac asked registering her red rimmed eyes and the stormy look on Rayan's face. He silently cursed Raphael for phoning him and insisting he come home and check on her. "She is your *girlfriend,*" his twin had shouted down the phone. "The least you can do is check if she is safe."

"If you are so concerned about her you stay at home, you mind her. She's all yours, bro," he'd shot back. He'd throw a quick check on her and go again to Shawnee.

Rayan caught the whiff of drink off his breath as he leaned in to kiss her. "Hotel serving alcohol on the tennis courts now?" she said sarcastically.

Isaac's jaw tightened. He was sick of Rayan's ball and chain attitude. As soon as he was back living in the student flat in Derry, he was dumping her. "Shawnee's family are staying at the hotel for the weekend. Her father asked me to join them for dinner. We had a few drinks, OK?" And I was having a bloody good time, he thought resentfully. Shawnee hadn't put out yet. She let him do some heavy petting. His blood quickening, he cleared his throat. "I have to go back. I'm on Reception later—it's one of those holy holidays days—staff off."

Rayan smirked. "You're getting to be as good a liar as Raphael." She smiled sardonically. "The truth is you can't wait to get back to your little girlfriend, can you?"

Isaac gave a shrug. Why deny it. Life was a blast. His mother going to Australia had been a good thing. I have my own life now, he though. He was having his cake and eating it, as his granny Norah would say. Rayan at home waiting in bed every night and Shawnee at the hotel during the day.

"Who was that on the phone?" he asked.

"I was phoning your mother. I didn't get her. Maybe she's in bed…asleep."

Isaac ducked his head and smirked. Yeah, probably with *your* boyfriend, he mused. He was surprised to find he was no longer jealous of his mother's boyfriends.

With sickening clarity, Rayan suddenly saw her and Isaac's relationship from Raphael's point of view. Isaac was little more than an adolescent boy sowing his wild seeds. She was a woman teetering on the brink of middle age. She had been living in fantasy land with him while she waited for Nathanial to come back to her. It was over. She could read it in his eyes. He was walking away from her as Nathanial had. Revenge strong and wilful rose up in her. He wasn't getting away free and easy. "Wait there," she said.

Coming back into the sunroom, she thrust something at him. "You'll need these unless you plan to get Shawnee pregnant too," she spat handing him a packet of condoms.

Isaac's face blanched. "Pregnant? What do you mean, pregnant?"

"I'm pregnant."

Isaac gaped at her in shocked disbelief. "You can't be! You're on the Pill."

"I'm three months pregnant."

"Is it mine?"

Rayan looked at him incredulously. "Of course, it's yours! Who else's could it be?"

Isaac backed towards the door, a look of horror on his face.

Rayan listened as the sound of him smashing the jeep's gears in his panic to get away. She picked up the phone again. She dialled Sue's private number. She could hear a discreet tinkle on the other end. "How the hell do they expect to hear that," she muttered about to put the phone down when Vivian answered.

"Hello."

The sound of Vivian's clipped tones threw Rayan for a second. If she asked for Sue straight away, she risked Vivian slamming down the phone. She remembered Sue had said she might be eligible to join the Spa's medical insurance scheme. "I'm glad I caught you," she said forcing a note of normality into her voice. "I have to register with a doctor. Sue thought I could sign in under the staff medical insurance," she said as calmly as she could manage.

"Sue said that?"

As soon as Vivian uttered Sue's name, Rayan knew something was wrong. "Is Sue there?"

Vivian snapped her mouth closed. She had nearly blurted out *she* thought Sue might be with Rayan. Obviously she wasn't. Relief washed over her.

"You are not working at the hotel…"

"I'm coming back next week—"

Vivian cut across her. "I have had to get another hairdresser in while you have been off."

"Why would you do that? You knew I was coming back just as soon as I could."

"You *are* considered *casual* labour," Vivian said coolly.

Bitch, Rayan thought. "I will make a doctor's appointment and be back at work next week," Rayan said stoically. I don't give fiddle about the work, but I miss seeing Sue, she thought. "Is Sue there? I'd like to speak to her," she said praying Vivian wouldn't slam the phone down on her. There was a beat of silence.

"Sue had a few days leave coming. She's gone to Dublin to stay with friends."

Rayan raised her eyebrows. She was guessing they had another row about the sperm donor and Sue had walked out. A wave of loneliness washed over her. I wish she had come to me, she thought. I could do with her company.

"What doctor's practice do you recommend I register with?" Rayan asked coldly.

"For a fit for work certificate, Dr Cronin is fine." There was a significant pause before Vivian spoke again, "For something more confidential, register with a doctor in Northern Ireland. You might have more success there."

Rayan's gasp was audible. "How did you find out?"

Vivian sighed in exasperation. "You let a whole ward know when you yelled it out in hospital."

Rayan's heart began boom boom in her chest. The way the rumour machine worked here, the whole of Donegal must know by now.

"Didn't you know abortion and terminations are illegal here unless the mother or baby's life is in danger?"

Rayan was silent. "I never even suspected I was pregnant. I don't know how it happened. I was so careful," she said almost inaudibly.

Vivian drew in a deep breath. "It happens. I had my first termination in England when I was eighteen."

Shocked at Vivian's revelation, Rayan stood gaping at the phone. There was silence for a minute at Vivian's end. "Are you sure it's what *you* want, Rayan?" she asked. "Do what is right for you. That way you'll have no regrets, later."

"Did you ever regret it?" Rayan asked when she could find her voice.

There was immediacy to Vivian answer. "No. I never regretted it. It was the right thing for me. My life is about me…and now Sue of course." She paused. "It was before I met Sue. She doesn't know anything about that part of my life and that's the way I want it to stay. She is feeling…very maternal at the moment. It will pass," she said brusquely. "Does Imelda know?"

"No. I'm going to phone her," Rayan choked out.

"Don't bother."

"I can't get an abortion here. I'll have to go home."

There was another lengthy pause. When Vivian spoke again, Rayan could hear the compassion in her voice. "Get yourself a GP in Derry. You'll find them listed in Yellow Pages," she said putting down the phone already regretting letting down her guard. She had allowed her distress at Sue's leaving to reveal a secret that not even her own family was privy to. I must be mad, she thought, confiding in Rayan Ritchie of all people.

The doctor cast Rayan a bland professional look. Why the hell had this imperious woman, wound as tight as a broken clock, been added to his patients' lists?

Rayan returned his stare. "The questions on this form are bizarre. This one, do you ever have suicidal thoughts? Everybody has irrational thoughts."

Beside her Isaac sat shuffling his feet like a schoolboy in the headmaster's study. Rayan threw him a cold stare that told him to stop fidgeting. She had to blackmail him into coming by threatening she'd tell Shawnee about her pregnancy.

"The questions are a way of assessing your state of mind. Tell me, Miss Ritchie, have you ever had thoughts of injuring or killing yourself—suicidal thoughts?" he asked bluntly.

Rayan thought of her excessive exercise regime. Getting rid of *this thing* had really taken over her mind. It was all she thought about day or night. She couldn't rest. She couldn't sleep. She had cut off all social ties with Sue and the other girls at the Spa. She avoided Raphael and Isaac as much as she could; locking herself in her room when they were at home. She had even begun to starve herself in the hope the *thing* would die from lack of nourishment.

Isaac jerked forward and was sick in the doctor's wastepaper basket. Ever since the nurse at the anti-natal clinic had insisted he check out the image of the foetus on the monitoring screen, he had been plagued with doubt. He wasn't convinced it was his. She doesn't look pregnant; he thought a sullen look settling on his features. If anything, she looks like the anorexic girls he saw at uni; all hollow cheeks and bony. He glared at Rayan. How the fuck did she even *get* pregnant? His throat felt bone-dry. He needed a drink. When he was drinking, he didn't think about what his mother and Raphael would say when they found out. He felt the comforting feel of the quarter bottle of vodka he had in the pocket of his zipped jacket nestle against hip bone. He considered downing its contents where he sat. Fuck Rayan. Her being up the spout was her problem.

Shawnee and her family were devout Catholics. If it was found out he was helping Rayan get an abortion….

This was the last doctor's visit he was coming to with Rayan, he thought resolutely. He'd been to the antenatal clinic and sat amongst all those swelling bellies. He'd been to the counselling sessions. He was fucked if he was coming anymore.

The doctor wrinkled his nose as the stench of vomit and stale drink wafted up his nostrils. He scrutinised the potential father. He was significantly younger than the mother, he noted. All baby-faced and the image of the clean-living boy he had no doubt his mother believed him to be. He supposed he should be grateful the boy was here at all. Most of the pregnant women he saw looking for terminations were half this woman's age and whoever got them in that condition was long gone before they reached his desk.

"Have you considered having the child and placing it for adoption? There are couples out there who would be more than willing…"

Rayan shook her head emphatically. "I am never giving birth."

The doctor turned to Isaac. "Have you discussed this with your family…?"

Isaac fidgeted. "No." He stuffed his hands in his pockets and spouted out what Vivian had told him to say. "I'm a student. I don't have a job. It's not the right time for me to be a father."

The doctor sighed. "Is there ever a right time?"

Rayan handed him back the completed questionnaire. "We have been through all this with the counsellor," she said testily.

The doctor's eyes scanned the form. There was nothing on it that indicated the patient would suffer any psychiatric or long-term psychological effects if she continued with the pregnancy.

He checked the midwife's report. It was early days and the sonogram wasn't very clear but as far as could see the foetus showed no signs of abnormalities or stress. This patient didn't meet the criteria for a medical termination in Northern Ireland.

He turned to face Raven. "There is very strict criterion for a termination," he said briskly. "And I'm afraid you don't meet it."

Rayan couldn't believe what she was hearing. She leaped to her feet. "It's my body. I have the right to do what I want with my body!" He was her last chance. Desperation made her vocal. "I am not interested in your moralistic, religious claptraps. I am not Irish Catholic. I am an Australian citizen. I have a right—"

"Sit down," the doctor ordered, "or I will have you removed," he said stonily. He rubbed his chin. There were other things to consider. She *was* an older woman. There was always the possibility of genetic conditions such as Down syndrome and Spins Bifida. He checked the gestational period—twelve weeks. He drew a notepad towards him, scribbled something on it and held it out to Rayan.

Chapter Nineteen

The sun rose lazily over the Derryveagh mountain range. Rayan paused briefly at the whitewashed holy shrine at Muckish Gap before heading north across the boggy ground, through a space in the rocks and on to a mountain track.

She noticed on the lower slopes some of the banks of peat were already harvested standing ready to be transported home for winter fuel. That means *hours* behind slow moving tractors on the road into Letterkenny, she mused.

She climbed for a while following the walkers' path. Where the path narrowed, she kept close to the rock face. She stopped when the wooden cross on top of the mountain came into view on the distant plateau. More familiar with the mountain tracks now, she veered to her right hoping she wouldn't meet any climbers descending. As the path became steeper and stonier, she began to pant but she pressed on.

Her stomach rumbled. She wished now she had taken some breakfast before she left. But she had been afraid it would give her morning sickness. She was pregnant. It was so mind boggling preposterous she simply couldn't get her head around it. She felt like a kangaroo had punched her in the gut. No way was she having it. One way or another she was having an abortion. She climbed Muckish every chance she got in the hope the excessive, strenuous exercises would bring on a miscarriage.

The calves of her legs began to ache but she climbed on. This was the highest she had ever climbed. Preoccupied with her thoughts she hardly noticed she was within a short climb of the summit. The sound of her blood pounding in her ears panting with the exertion of the climb, she resorted to crawling on her hands and knees up the grassy knoll that bordered the plateau and flopped exhausted on the fringe of grass.

Her success at having reached the summit momentarily thrilled her. But the rush of exhilaration she had expected to experience was dulled by the weight of the worry inside her head. Reaching the summit of Muckish was well down her lists of priorities now. *As soon as the clinic in London can take me, I will be booking my flight*, she thought.

She shaded her eyes and looked across the expansion of boulders and stones that peppered the flat plateau. The rocks jostled with each other. None of them seemed to be the same dimension or shape. Some were huge boulders; others the size of construction blocks. It looked much as she thought the surface of the moon might look, deadly jagged and dangerous.

She steadied her gait and began to pick her way towards a cairn to her right. Losing her footing she stumbled and fell backward on to the jagged rocks. She felt the shock of the fall reverberate through her body and up both side of her skull. She lay where she fell. Would the fall be enough to bring on a miscarriage? She hoped so.

Struggling to her feet she pivoted slowly and focused on the large wooden cross she had seen from below. It stood erect on a cairn of boulders against the outline of the iron grey sky. A pre historical burial place Mac O Lochlainn had told her. A shudder ran through her as if cold fingers had touched her. By the time she had picked her way amongst the boulders to the foot of the cross, the weak midday sun was obscured behind the clouds plunging parts of the mountain into deep shades of black like deep dark chasms. She felt the power leave her legs as she inched her way up to the top of the cairn. It had been a stupid climb to attempt so soon after her concussion.

Below her, she could see the bog pitted with water filled gullies and dotted with expansive areas of peats. She could see a beach and glints of sparkle where the sun caught the water. She knew at any other time she would have found the view breathtakingly beautiful. But today she didn't see the panoramic magnificence of the landscape, her mind was too preoccupied.

Her thoughts went to Nathanial. She still held out hope she and Nathanial would get back together again when all this was all over. He'd forgive her, say he still loved her. He would love this, she thought. He'd to come to Ireland, stay at the Manse with her. She'd show him the magnificence of the mountain—take him on Mac O Lochlainn's tour bus—show him Donegal. All she had to do was get to England, have the abortion and get back without him or Imelda knowing.

Picking her way down the cairn she wondered how Sue would take the news of her pregnancy and planned abortion. She knew instinctively Sue would be shocked beyond words. Sue believed that having a baby was a *given* in a relationship—even one like hers and Vivian's. Having a baby was a blessing. Not an abhorrence as it is to me, she thought.

A gust of wind flapped the hood of her parka against the back of her neck. She gave an ironic smile. The parka had been a Mother's Day present to her from Imelda's twins when she'd first arrived. "To save you from the March winds," Raphael had said as Isaac had proffered the bulky parcel.

Glad to have it now, she tightened its toggles as the wind gathering strength whipped under the coat filling it out like an inflated balloon; giving the impression she was already heavily pregnant.

Sick to her heart at the prospect, Rayan began to negotiate her way carefully across to the other side of the plateau; to fall here, alone on the mountain, would be, life threatening, she knew. Raphael had warned her that however awe-struck she was with the mountain and its views, rising winds and sudden mist thick as a blanket could leave her disorientated very quickly. She looked at the sky. Heavy rain clouds were scuttling in her direction.

She sighed in relief when a guide and a group of climbers with backpacks and stout sticks made their way towards her. The guide gave her a friendly wave as he steered his group towards several smaller cairns and a trig pillar.

A familiar figure detached itself from the group and came towards her. Rayan cursed under her breath and tried to pull the hood of the parka down over her forehead hoping he wouldn't recognise her.

"Rayan? I thought it was you. Saw you struggling over the boulders—what the bloody hell are you doing? You shouldn't be climbing to the summit so soon after your…accident," Raphael said an aggrieved note in his voice. "You're supposed to be rest—"

"You're supposed to be in Derry," Rayan shot back as she stumbled around, struggling to keep her balance on the rough terrain.

Hearing Raphael's voice, Dizzy bounded over the rough ground, his long tongue lolling to one side of the mouth, his tail wagging wildly. Rayan teetered backwards. Swearing, Raphael reached out his hand and steadied her. "What are you trying to do, kill yourself! That latrine is like a lance. It will cut you to the bone. I have better things to be doing than taking you to hospital again," he said tersely.

He must have come up the mountain from the other side where the old disused glass making mines are, Rayan thought. She might go down that way. It was the route the seasoned climbers favoured. "What are *you* doing up here?" She knew it was a stupid question. He was a regular walker on the mountain.

"There was a phone call for you from the hospital. They need to speak with you as soon as possible—thought it might be important," he shrugged.

Hope rose up in Rayan like a flag skimming up a flagpole. Her inside clenched. Had Dr Crawley arranged to arrange a termination after all!

Raphael watched the other climbers moving on. Should he offer to walk down the mountain with Rayan? She was barely able to look at him without loathing these days.

"Want me to walk bac—"

"I made my way up here. I can make my way back," Rayan said icily.

Raphael shrugged. "Just asking—no need to bite my head off. See ya, Dizzy," he said. "No, stay," he ordered when the dog made to follow him.

On the other trail, the raised voice of the guide carried on the wind as he pointed out the Blue stack Mountains to the east, and Falcarragh and Dunfanghy to the west.

Rayan walked as fast as she dared down to the lower slopes and past the gurgling streams that littered the mountains. Her footing slipped. It was trickier going down than coming up. Frustrated, she slowed her pace. At this rate she'd never be in time to catch Dr Crawley at the hospital before he left for the day. Despite his initial reaction to her information for an abortion, maybe he had come through for her, after all.

She drew in a rasping breath She could feel a stitch in her side; hear the breath coming in short gasps in her throat. Misjudging her step, she felt the loose screed near the foot of the mountain slither under her. With a supreme effort she stopped herself from falling on her mouth and nose. Dragging herself up from her knees she moved forward and fell down again. Sick at the delay, she resorted to sliding down on her backside. She had to get back; return that phone call. If she didn't the chance of an abortion not come again.

Finally, she was at the mossy bog land that separated the mountain from the road. She could feel where the slimy mud had soaked into her Parka and bottoms. She didn't care. All that matter was getting back to the Manse and making that phone call. She looked behind her. There was no sign of the other climbers. She didn't want Raphael listening to her conversation on the house phone.

She regretted she hadn't spent the money on a mobile phone then she could phone in the privacy of her bedroom. It probably wouldn't work when she got back to Perth. She could have left it for mother earth Imelda. "There hasn't been a phone call or an email from her since I dared to point out a few home truths about Raphael," she muttered. She started down the road, hoping Mac O Lochlainn might come along and offer her a lift. *He's never about when he's needed*, she thought.

Bile rose in her throat as she put down the house phone. Her precarious rush down the mountain had been for nothing. "All the hospital wanted was the fucking details of my private health insurance," she said bitterly to the empty kitchen and the panting dog. "Dr Crawley, you're a sanctimonious bastard," she yelled ripping off her sodden parka and dripping bottoms and flinging them into the middle of the kitchen floor.

Chapter Twenty

Isaac dropped his bulging backpack to the ground. Rayan raised her eyebrows and stilled her hand from going to the mound of her swelling stomach. She'd hoped by now she'd have been to the London clinic and back but there had been some sort of glitch. The clinic had informed her she'd cancelled her appointment. Now she was waiting on another date to go.

She caught her reflection in the high polished chrome of the toaster. She looked a mess. Her skin was spotty—her body lumpy.

"Moving out of the hill walkers' room?"

Isaac gave her a sheepish smile. "I'm staying with friends at the hotel for a few days before I head back to uni—"

"Let me guess—Shawnee's daddy is paying?"

Isaac's guts tightened. Rayan was going to make a scene.

Isaac turned away from her and picked up a carton of orange juice from the marble worktop. Tipping back his head, he drank deeply. Rayan tried not to grit her teeth. It was like trying to have a conversation with an adolescent. "Ours was just a teenage thing for you," she said. "Did you ever care about me?" She knew it was stupid but she wanted him say all those times he made love to her in his mother's bed, he had had feelings for her.

Moving over beside him, she lightly stroked his arm. Refilling his glass, Isaac moved away. Reaching into the fridge, he picked up a leg of cooked chicken. Averting his eyes, he stripped the skin from the drumstick and sunk his teeth in it. "You'll be going back to Australia soon. I still like you. Just not in that way anymore," he said wiping his mouth with the back of his hand. "Shawnee's father is hinting he might be able to get me into a reputable firm in Dublin to do my practice year." His voice trailed off. He glanced at her swollen abdomen. "The clinic in London gave you another date?"

"Why do your practice year in law when what you really want is to set up your own garden centre here?" Rayan said ignoring his remark. "I could talk about it to Imelda, if you want. You've always said you're only studying law because Imelda wanted you to."

Isaac looked at her suspiciously. "You'd do that—get Mum to let me open my own garden centre after I cancelled your appointment with the clinic in England?"

A ball of rage gathered inside Rayan. *So it was him, the little shit*, she thought incredulously. *After all the difficultly I had setting it up. And I had blamed his brother.* She wanted to pummel him to a pulp where he stood. She clamped down hard on her anger. She couldn't lose control.

She breathed hard and let her anger out in a slow controlled puff. "It was you? I thought it was Raphael." Her hand went involuntarily to her bulging stomach. The waiting for it to be over was dragging her down more and more. "Was I just a substitute mother figure?" she asked forcing a calmness she didn't feel.

Isaac's face went beet red. "I would never think the things about *my mother* that I used to think about you."

Rayan watched the crimson blush stain his tanned face and neck. She felt her control slipping away. "You and your twin are more alike than I thought," she said.

Isaac's eyes widened, and then narrowed. Had she found out about him and Raphael's game?

"What do you mean?"

Strange, Rayan thought. *I never noticed before how watchful his eyes are as if he had something to hide.* She felt her skin began to crawl. Something in the way he was looking at her made her feel dirty.

"He likes older women too, like Maddie from the Smallest Pub."

Isaac guffawed. "Surely you know Raffi well enough by now to know he likes anything in a skirt." He chuckled. *Maybe I'm getting more like him in that way*, he realised.

Rayan forced a smile on her face. "All that tennis over the summer has turned you into a very sexy man. We had some great times in bed, didn't we? I miss how you used to make me feel." She saw Isaac's body tense; saw the bulge rise under his Levi's. He wanted her. She was big as a house in her second trimester and he wanted her. He had that same look the first day she had made love to him in the hill walkers' bedroom.

Almost immediately, he was on her. Rayan felt his engorged penis slip inside her. She gasped out as he thrust deeper and deeper. Sweat glistened on him as he climaxed. He rolled off her and almost instantly straddled her again.

Rayan smirked. Obviously, the judge's little daughter was a good catholic girl. She wasn't putting it out for him.

Smart-assed bastard, she thought. He shrugged me off like an afterthought. She'd take pleasure in letting Shawnee know about the purpose of their little trip to England as soon as she was back. Reaching down, she cradled his balls in her hand. Isaac gasped with pleasure and flopped on to his back. He stretched, letting her stroke him. "Shawnee and I are together. But not like this," he moaned. "I don't see why you and I can't have our times together. I missed making love to you." He gasped as she brought him to a climax.

"Have you told—Shawnee—about the abortion?" she asked with pretend concern. It had the desired effect. Isaac's penis deflated like the air leaving a balloon.

Isaac shuddered. If Shawnee ever found out, she'd drop him like she'd been scalded. Her family were devout Catholics. She was already banging away at him for not going to Mass on Sunday. "You'd like to have a son that would look like you, wouldn't you? A little Isaac with big dark eyes." Rayan couldn't resist goading him.

"Yeah, in ten years' time," Isaac retorted pulling on his jeans "Only stupid no-hopers are fathers at my age," he muttered zipping the fly... "You're not thinking of having it now?"

"You cancelled the appointment. It could be too late now."

Isaac's face blanched. "You can't have it. You're the same age as Mum—too old to have a baby," he said fear making his petulant lips tremble.

The very thought that he might have to face up to his responsibility has sent the little bastard into a spin, she mocked. But the threat that she just might give birth was a thing to use until it was time for the next appointment. *Let's see the judge finding a place for him after that*, she sneered to herself.

A cold feeling was sweeping through her.

"Didn't your mother ever tell you that little boys who put their little soldier into little girls' pee pees and give them a baby must be punished? Over my knee young man," she commanded. "It's time you had a sound spanking to teach you manners."

Isaac felt the heat in his groin. He had time before he had to meet Shawnee. Unzipping his fly, he dropped his pants.

Rayan's eyes fell on Imelda's gilded hairbrush on the bedside table. She looked down at Isaac sprawled across her. She felt repulsed, rejected and used all at the same time. She thought about the promise she had made to herself as a teenager that no man would demean her.

She leaned close to Isaac's ear. "You have been a very naughty boy. You deserve a really good whipping!" she shouted as the hairbrush made its first contact.

Chapter Twenty-One

Raphael rolled down the windows of the four-wheel drive and followed the twisting dirt road that lead to the temporary car park. The road narrowed as they drove.

On either side, rustic, purple heather fanned out over bog land. Above it, wearing a cap of milky fog Muckish towered above her rugged blue grey rock face glinting in the morning light. Stones skidded beneath the car's wheels as they reached the car park. Several cars were parked there already.

Raphael scrutinised the few car spaces left. The best ones had been taken. He leaned his elbows on the steering wheel and pursued his lips. In front of him was a tricky left bend. To the right a steep drop into bog land. "We could chance driving a bit further—another half mile. It's tricky. Less walking when we come down again," he said turning to Rayan.

Rayan didn't answer. Raphael had offered to take her up the minors' trail. Her hand went involuntary to her spreading abdomen. She wondered if she was up to it. Taking her silence as consent to drive nearer to their starting point, Raphael put the jeep into 4-wheel drive and navigated the bend. "Don't worry, all four wheels are engaged now," he chuckled. But he was relieved when he reached the second parking place literally hewn out of the bog. There was one other car there. "We have company," Raphael smiled, pulling in behind the first car and cutting the engine. "Ready?"

Rayan nodded. Stepping out of the car on to the rough path she pushed her arms through the straps of her backpack. Pocketing his keys securely, Raphael leaned forward and straightened the strap where it had become twisted just beyond her shoulder. "There, that's you ready," he said. "There are steps over here—erected by the miners who used to work the glass mine," he said, Rayan looked to where a rail had been erected and steps hewed out of the rock face.

Soon they were on the screed path that seems to consist of boulders and stones tumbled down the mountain by the wind and rain. For some reason, a shudder passed through Rayan.

Head bent, watching her step, she started up the steep slope. Raphael grinned. "Eager to find this magical waterfall old Mac is always telling the tourist about, are you?" For answer, Rayan looked for the red arrows painted on large concrete slabs showing the starting point and the steps that lead up the rock face. Climbing in silence they zigzagged their way in the direction of the plateau.

Elated at being given his freedom, Dizzy shot on in front in search of mountain fowl. Raphael stopped to give Rayan a breather. Below a small lake glistened reflecting the green of a nearby field. "Why is there a green field amongst all the heather?" Rayan asked sitting down on a jutting out boulder.

"Probably cultivated for mountain sheep feed," Raphael explained. Searching in his pockets, he produced a bag of jelly babies. "Here, keeps the mouth from drying out when you are navigating the trickier bits," he joked popping a handful into his mouth.

Surreptitiously, he watched Rayan. Isaac was talking a lot of drunken dribble, he thought. She doesn't look pregnant, he thought, looking at her lean her body into the rock to keep her balance as they started their ascent again.

"What did the hospital want that day they phoned?" he asked.

Rayan averted her face. "An address to send the bill to." Rayan pushed on as silence fell between them again. "Thank you for bringing me up the Miners Path. It's much tougher than climbing from the Muckish Gap side. I don't think I could have made it on my own," Rayan's voice said behind him.

An unreasonable sense of pleasure washed over Raphael at the unexpected thanks. "Ach, not a problem," he said aiming for nonchalance. "I thought the dog could do with a good run." He hesitated. "Isaac told me you registered with a doctor in Derry. What's wrong with the Letterkenny ones?"

Rayan stumbled on a loose rock. She wondered what else had Isaac told him. "I needed to get a doctor's certificate to say I'm OK to go back to work in the Spa," she lied. She scrunched up her face making light of it. "You know how fussy Vivian is. All the 't's have to be crossed…"

Raphael laughed. "Glad to hear that's all it is," he said. She seemed more forgiving towards me these days, he thought. Did the doctor give her something for her black moods? *She* was calmer but Isaac was hitting the bottle! What's all that about? He shrugged. The summer was over. Soon it'll be time to go back to uni, he mused. He smirked. That will mean, miss rich chick Shawnee the judge's little indulged daughter will be returning to her posh private school in Dublin. That's what's probably wrong with Isaac, he concluded. He's going to miss her and not just for the tennis, he sniggered.

Isaac can be a bollocks sometimes, he mused, stopping to glance back at Rayan. He dropped *her* like a hot brick as soon as little miss money bags let him into her knickers. He supposed he should be glad Rayan was getting her come-upping—after touting on Brendie—but somehow it irked him that Isaac treated her like shit.

His mind went to Maddie, the chef from the Smallest Pub. You have no right to judge your twin. Look how you treat Maddie, he berated himself. *She* hadn't forgiven him for his womanising the night of the party. He had arranged to go over there today but had decided to take Rayan up Muckish before it got too treacherous to climb.

"See what I mean, this route up Muckish is more suited to seasoned hill walkers and climbers," he pointed out seeing a guide and a straggly line of what looked like a group of foreign tourists making their way down the mountain. Raphael frowned. If they were turning back it meant the weather was closing in. "I don't think we'll get to the summit. We'll go as far as the old mines? I have a flask in my backpack."

Rayan was glad of the excuse to turn back but she didn't want it to be so obvious.

"Right then? Just as far as the old mine but no further. Agreed?"

Rayan nodded. They climbed steadily until they reached the old glass mine. Gratefully, Rayan unhooked her backpack and shed her coat to cool down.

"Put your Parka back on. Your body temperature can fall down very quickly at this altitude," Raphael warned. "Anyway, we can't stay too long. I think there's a storm moving in this direction."

Rayan passed him a thick ham sandwich. They sat almost companionably side by side munching on the thick slices of bread.

Raphael laughed. "If old Mac could see us now, having a picnic so close to the magical waterfall," he scoffed glancing around at the rusting relics of machinery strewn around, "he'd be pea green with envy."

"Doesn't he come up this far anymore? He talks a lot about the magical properties of the waterfall."

Raphael drank in the sheer splendour of the fall of the rock face and the shadows and gullies below. "Na, Mac's too old—too much history lies beneath its beauty," he said almost to himself. "We should go. The sky is beginning to close in on us." He smiled. "But first I must heed the call of nature," he said moving off in the direction of a rock further back.

Rayan watched him go and realised she was enjoying his company—no Isaac—just the two of them. Quickly, she rose to her feet pushing the thought away. One of the Wright twins was enough for her. She was packed and ready when Raphael reappeared.

"Right. Let's go. Watch your step," Raphael warned. "It's more difficult in parts on the ways down, stay close to the face of the rocks and sit on your ass and go down that way if you need to," he advised, starting off.

They were making steady progress until they came to a blockage on the path. Raphael stopped and looked around him. "We must have strayed from the main path," he frowned. "We'll go this way," he said, grasping her hand and helped her climb over the dislodged rocks and on to another path. "The heavy rain we had earlier in the month must have caused a landslide. We'll have to go down a slightly longer route. Watch your footing," he warned as she lost her balance and slipped sideways.

"I don't see any of the red arrows that guide us down," Rayan said, her words coming out stiff and formal. Below her she could see a gaping gully filled with slimy green water.

"Wouldn't want to fall in there," Raphael chuckled following her gaze. "You'd come out looking like that the green giant they have in one of those children television programmes. Here, hold onto me."

Rayan felt the firmness of Raphael's secure grip. It made her think of Nathanial and the first time she had felt his hand holding hers.

He had been her instructor at the mix gender gym. There was no mistaken his interest in her as he'd shown her the most efficient way to get the best out of her session. The next day he booked an appointment at the salon to have his hair cut.

She let her fingers find his card in the zipped pocket of her Parka. She hadn't heard from him since she'd come to Ireland. Then out of the blue he sent her a postcard of Sydney's Bondi Beach. True, a lot of his tiny scribble was him complaining about Sienna not taking good care of the dog. It didn't matter. He had made contact with her again. Was it a sign he was tiring of Sienna? It gave her hope.

Her thoughts turned to Isaac. Her heart hardened. She hadn't seen him since the night she wacked him with Imelda's hairbrush. He had used her. She glanced at Raphael. He looked so much like his twin and yet she was beginning to sense that despite his blasé facade underneath he was kinder, more caring person. Why had she not seen it before? Had the incident at the party blinded her to his positive side?

Raphael's voice jerked her back to the mountain. "We need to hurry. The mist is falling down fast and I can feel rain in the air."

Rayan lifted her head. He was right. The lakes below were barely visible now.

"Keep close to me and the rock face. Don't step off the path, whatever you do," Raphael's tone had a ring of fear in it.

Rayan stumbled along in Raphael's wake, suddenly acutely aware of the danger of the mountain.

"Who was the postcard from that came the other day?" Raphael asked to keep Rayan's mind off their foggy descent.

Intend on avoiding a rutted stump on the narrow winding path, Rayan didn't speak for a minute. "It was from Nat." She could hear the pleasure in her voice. "I was thinking...after my short holiday in London, I might go back to Perth and try to get our relationship back again."

A stirring Raphael didn't want to acknowledge crawled around his belly. *I'm jealous*, he thought in astonishment. "You need to ask Ma, she might not be ready to come back here yet," he said wondering if Imelda was still bedding Rayan's boyfriend.

Rayan shrugged. Imelda had been in Perth for six months. If she wanted to stay for another six months, she'd have to find alternative accommodation. As soon as she got back, she was evicting Imelda from her house and giving sly little Sienna the sack again.

Raphael stopped and lifted his face to the mist. "An Mhuais," he murmured breathing out the words into the mist as if they were sacred. Too close behind him, Rayan bumped into him before she could stop herself.

"What? What did you say? Why have you stopped?"

Raphael reached back and steadied her. "An Mhuais, the Irish name for Muckish," he said holding her gloved hands longer than was necessary. Rayan frowned. She wasn't interested in what the mountain was called in Gaelic. All she wanted was to get safely off it. "Did you know it is also called the 'Pig's back' because of its flat top?" Raphael went on.

"Move on. We don't want to get stuck up here," Rayan said.

"Yeah, you're right. If we stumbled into one of the ravines, we'll never be found again."

Abruptly, Rayon's feet lost the will to move. She lost her balance and teetered precariously near the edge. Paralysed with fear, she stood frozen to the spot. Just when she'd gotten an appointment for an abortion and there was a chance she might get Nathanial back, she was going to die on the Muckish.

She felt Raphael beside her. "I don't want to be fodder for the wild fowl like the bodies the IRA bury on the mountain." She quaked out in the premature gathering gloom. She heard the sharp intake of Raphael's breath. "Touts," he said. "People who give information to the cops end up in a bog hole."

"I'm sorry…about Big Brendie…" she mumbled. She felt him squeeze her arm. A rock dislodged and tumbled down, down, the sound echoing back as it bounced.

Raphael loosened his grip and took the lead. "What's done is done. We need to move. It would please the bastards no end if I fell into a hole and was never found," he said righting himself again. "Save them the bother of wasting a bullet on me," he growled.

The path narrowed. Rayan's feet groped almost instinctively for the step down. Terror filled her; sure she would fall into the abyss below.

"Plant your feet firmly; try to walk side step. That way if you slide you won't go forwards," Raphael advised, his voice carrying back to her in the gloom.

Rayan trembled. She couldn't be sure if it was from the loss of the feeling of security and the warmth of being close to Raphael's body had given her or the cloying mist that was making it difficult to breathe. Slowly picking their way a baby step at a time, they could hear the drone of the Mountain Rescue helicopter hovering low further along the range of mountains. "Probably an inexperienced holiday climber—tough finding anyone in this mist," Raphael said worriedly.

Rayan was dead beat. Exhaustion washed over her in waves. She cursed her stupidity for insisting she'd climb the toughest part of the mountain. It's the same erroneously mind-set that has got me into bother all my life, she thought. Her legs wobbled precariously; her breath fanning out as she clung at the rock face.

"Where's the dog?" Rayan gasped. She hadn't heard Dizzy bark for a while. If she lost Imelda's dog, she'd never be forgiven.

"Don't worry about him. He's as sure-footed as the mountain goats. He'll be home before us," Raphael assured her. "You nearly took a tumble there," he said his back rigid to the wall of rock as he waited for her to catch up with him.

Sobs wrenched Rayan's body. "I'm going to die on this mountain," she rasped. "I'll never see Nathanial again."

Raphael didn't blame her for being scared. He was too. He had never seen it so bad. "Nobody's going to die. You're doing well. We're nearly down," he lied. They still had a way to go and the mist was almost impenetrable now.

Rayan forced her body to move one foot after the other. Her thoughts turned to her parents. It would have been better if I never had been born. I spoiled their lives. The pain of rejection she carried around with her felt like a physical weight in her chest. She was glad she'd never put that on a child. "You can't make someone who doesn't want to love you, love you," she shouted out.

Raphael stopped. "Did you say something? I heard you yell out?"

"I was thinking about my father and mother," she said choking back tears. "If I fell down a ravine, they'll play the stricken parent but they won't grieve my loss."

Raphael ignored her words. If Rayan took a meltdown here, they'd both perish. "We're nearly down now. You're doing brilliant." He gripped her gloved hand tightly. "Now, the mountain has one last challenge for us—the loose slippery screed—"

"I can't go any further," Rayan sobbed slumping against him.

Raphael shoved her upright. "You told me you were a survivor—all that talks about you starting your own business at sixteen? Now you're going to let a mountain beat you?"

"I can't do it."

"I'll wait for you on the other side of the blogland," Raphael bawled.

"You bastard," Rayan roared at his retreating back. "I hate you. I hate Ireland. I hate Donegal. Most of all, I hate this fucking Muckish Mountain," she shrieked sinking on to a boulder. "I give up. I give up," she screamed manically.

After a while, she could no longer hear the stumbling sound of Raphael's boots on the loose boulders. The lower slopes of the mountain were deadly silent except for the eerie sighing of the wild rushes. She could feel the bog water sucking at her. Fear propelled her to her feet. Sliding and falling, she made it to the foothills. She could feel the sharp edges of the stones cut into her gloved hands as she crawled over the screed, shouting abuse at Raphael for abandoning her.

Raphael crossed the short path through the bogland and waited in the shadow of the steps that lead to the road where the car was parked. It was pitch dark now. He watched the outline of Rayan's painfully slow progress as she floundered about in the marshy boggy ground. As he watched, he thought about what he had heard her shout out while they were on the mountain. "You can't force someone to love you." She'd bawled out.

His thoughts swung to his mother. Imelda loved him. "But I could never make her love me as much as she loves Isaac," he thought as Rayan, mad as a bull, stumbled out of the darkness towards him.

Chapter Twenty-Two

Rayan's hand trembled slightly as she waited for Imelda to pick up. She'd finalised her second set of travel arrangements for her trip to England. Isaac had vehemently refused to go with her. "You're coming with me. Or, I'll be telling Shawnee the real reason for my trip," she'd warned him. She sighed. She didn't want to waste time thinking about him. He did enough of that himself.

A sense of euphoria swept over her at being in contact with Nathanial again. She'd posted him a postcard of Donegal Bay, thanked him for his postcard of Sydney, enquired after little Biscuit and scribbled a cheerful message on the back describing the beautiful old Manse with its orchard and grounds literally nestled at the foot of the mountain careful to create the feeling that she was well and happy.

To her absolute delight, he'd emailed her as soon as he'd gotten it. Now it was a regular thing. They'd leave little goodnight message for each other. She told him about achieving her goal and reaching the summit of Muckish. She told him about the friendship that had blossomed between her and Sue. And about climbing the miners' trail with Imelda's son as her guide and the terrifying experience of coming down in the fog.

She scrutinised her words, making sure there was no mention of her pregnancy. According to her emails, Ireland was wonderful. She was glad she had made the decision to come. It felt as if the feeling they had for each other when they met were there again.

She smirked. It felt good to be cheating with Nat behind that trollop Sienna's back.

Nathanial hinted about a month's holiday to Europe. She posted a reply saying there was loads of room at the Manse—explained Imelda used to keep hill walkers. He could stay as her unpaying guest.

She was careful not to pressure him or show any expectation she anticipated he would share her bed. That would come later.

But he seemed to be cooling to the idea of the trip. She shrugged. It didn't matter. She had decided as soon as she was back from London, she was going home to surprise him. Now she had to tell Imelda she was cutting her year in Australia short.

"Hello," Imelda's voice said. "Is that you, Rayan?"

Rayan forced down her exasperation. Who the hell else was she receiving international calls from? "Yes, it is. I'm coming home early," she said without preamble.

Imelda chortled. "You *are*, I hope, pulling my leg?"

Like an air balloon losing altitude, Rayan's upbeat feeling took a nose dive. Imelda was going to be awkward. She took a deep calming breath.

"I *do* live there, you know." A wistful tremor shook her voice. "Can't wait to get back to see *Nat* and the dog." She gave a short laugh. "I can't believe I miss Biscuit."

There was a fraction of silence. "We have a year's contract."

Rayan wanted to shout, it's not worth the paper it's written on but she resolutely held her tongue. Having a catfight with Imelda would get her nowhere.

"I'm sorry, Imelda. If you plan to stay in Perth, you need to start looking for somewhere to stay. Perhaps there might be a bed in Sienna's house. I'm coming home. My money is getting low."

Paying extra for the late termination and her and Isaac's travel arrangement and their stayover in London for several nights had made a hole in her money.

"Are my boys there?"

"Isaac and Raphael?"

Rayan heard Imelda draw in a breath. "Of course, Isaac and Raffi—who else could I possibly—"

"They're not here." Rayan swallowed a titter. She couldn't very well tell Imelda Isaac was staying well away from her since the night she had lost the plot and whacked him with Imelda's ornate hairbrush.

"Tell them to phone me. I haven't heard from them in ages."

Rayan's stomach flipped over. The last thing she needed right now was Isaac letting slip about her plans. No doubt he had already blabbered it out to Raphael.

She pulled her mind back to the Imelda's voice protesting about their contract. "I'm going to England…for a short holiday. As soon as I come back, I will be coming home to Perth."

"Not enough for you to see on the Emerald Isle," Imelda said dryly.

Rayan tensed. "I've always wanted to see the sights of London."

"It's November. Not a lot to see in London in the winter. When did you decide that?"

Rayan's plan to be business-like and calm was ebbing away. "I didn't spend all that money on my ticket to stay in one place. I want to see as much as I can while I'm here," she retorted a fraction too quickly.

There was a beat of silence. "Same here—I'm planning on making the most of a real Aussie summer. I won't be coming back to Donegal until late February," Imelda said coolly.

"I'll be home as soon as I can make the arrangement."

Imelda held the phone tightly. She looked around Rayan's nice comfortable home. No way was she moving out to share; at least not to the very last second; especially now that Nathanial was a frequent bed partner. She'd needed some time frame so that she'd have him safely out of the way and the bed changed before Rayan showed up.

"How long do you think that's going to be?"

Rayan did a hasty calculation. She was booked into the clinic for the following Friday—a week from today. She planned to stay in a hotel near Heathrow over the weekend. She didn't want to risk travelling in case she started to bleed heavily. She'd allow herself two weeks to recover and two more to be looking her best when she saw Nat. She wanted to travel before the Christmas rush started—just in case she was feeling…fragile. Nathanial could pick her up at Perth airport. She considered. Maybe she should stop off in Dubai and get Nathanial to meet her there for a few days—have like a reunion before she got back to Perth and Ben Watts' interrogation.

"I will be taking over the running of my own business before Christmas."

There was another silence. "I'm still staying. It will be strange though," Imelda sighed, "with the temperatures in the high 30s and a barbecue on the beach on Christmas Day instead of a turkey dinner with a big turf fire roaring up the chimney in the dining room." She paused. All of a sudden, she was homesick. "How is my house? No more trouble…from anybody after Raffi's party?"

"Your house is fine." Rayan wondered if she should tell her the police had searched the grounds. She shrugged. She could find that out when she came home.

"Ireland is magical at Christmas and the New Year—loads of parties going on. I thought you'd want to be there since Nathanial might be there," Imelda said.

Rayan almost dropped the phone. "Nathanial told you he was coming to Ireland for Christmas?"

Imelda flinched. Shit. She hadn't intended to say that.

An intense stab of jealousy shot through Rayan. Nathanial had told *Imelda*? Why would he do that unless…?

Quickly, Imelda began to furiously backpedal to cover her slip. "Oh, he must have mentioned it while I was styling his hair."

A wave of homesickness washed over her for the twins, her own house and her dog Dizzy. All the Irish people she'd met in Perth told her Christmas time for them wasn't the same away from home. Maybe Rayan was right. She'd had almost eight months in Australia. Maybe cutting it short wasn't such a crazy idea. She could always come again. Maybe try Sydney and the east coast next time. There was nothing stopping her now. The boys were doing fine without her. Even Isaac, it seemed, she thought smiling wryly.

"Yeah, I'll see about changing my travel arrangements too," she said slowly.

Rayan's mouth went dry. An image of Imelda arriving off the next plane and disrupting her plans set alarm bells ringing in her head.

"No—wait! We need to talk about this. Maybe I only think I want to cut my trip short. You're right; Christmas in Ireland will be great—very different—and it'll be good for you to finish off your trip with Christmas on the beach," Rayan babbled.

"What you mean, *you think*. Either you are coming back early or you are not. Now make up your mind," Imelda said losing patience with Rayan's arsing about. "Make up your bloody mind."

"I need to find out if Nat is coming to Ireland or not for Christmas, before I decide. Is he…bringing Sienna with him?"

Imelda sniggered. Sienna had dumped Nathanial when she found out he was sleeping with her. Yeah, she'd miss the Aussie summer but on the other hand, she'd have the pleasure of showing off Nathanial to Vivian and the bitches at the Spa. She'd love to be a fly on the wall when Rayan arrived back in Australia only to find her ex-partner was in Ireland and staying at the Manse with her.

"I am going to the travel agency tomorrow to change my departure date," Imelda said succulently.

Imelda rose up like a spectre before Rayan. What the hell had she been thinking! She should have waited until after her appointment in London before contacting Imelda.

"When are you coming back?" she bleated down the phone at Imelda.

"Go and have your holiday in London. I'll see you when I get home. The house is still there, isn't it," Imelda said on a light-hearted note.

"I think you need to know something. Before you come back," Rayan said mulishly, angered at Imelda's jokey mood. It would be easier to deal with Imelda's rejoinder over the phone than face-to-face, she thought. And by the time she'd spent twenty-six hours in the air she'd have calmed down, she reasoned.

The serious note in Rayan's tone sent a shiver up Imelda's back. She straightened a feeling of apprehension stealing over her. If Raphael had done something stupid, again, she'd kill him! It had taken all her powers of persuasions and some old knowledge about the local duty Sergeant's *extra martial activities* to convince him it was nothing more than high spirited student exuberance and thumbing their noses at authority having known paramilitaries at her sons' end of academic year party. She had thanked him profusely assuring him she would absolutely deal with it and he could be absolutely sure it would never happen again.

A feeling of agitation crawled about in her belly. It couldn't be that serious, could it? Raphael would have let her know if something had happened to Isaac. Her thoughts flew to her neighbour, Mac O Lochlainn. It was no secret he was anti-British. Had he got Isaac involved in something in the North? Don't be stupid, she berated herself, trying to focus on what Rayan was saying, Isaac has no time for politics. It was Raphael. Her breathing settled. There! That was it. Raphael probably made a pass at Rayan or slipped in for a quick grope when she was showering. She let out a sigh of relief. "I did warn you about Raphael's womanising ways," she said defensively, interrupting Rayan.

"It's Isaac," Rayan quaked down the phone. As if on cue, she felt movement in her stomach.

"Isaac?" Imelda gave a gravelly laugh. "What has he done? Put his little summer tennis partner up the pole?"

"No. I don't think so," Rayan said crossing her fingers hoping Isaac had used the condoms she'd flung at him.

Imelda laughed. "I didn't think so. Those rich chicks know how to take care of themselves. Not like in my day," she sighed.

Rayan gulped in air. Imelda had given her the perfect opening. "What if, he did get Shawnee pregnant?"

"Shawnee? Is that her name? Her father's a judge, I hear. He might be able to help Isaac get started on his career," Imelda mused.

"What if he did get her pregnant?" Rayan persisted.

"I'm too young to be a granny. Haven't got the shoes for it," Imelda quipped. "Anyway, I'm pretty sure if she was *with child*," she pointed out, a cynical note creeping into her voice, "her father's friends in the medical profession would pull him out of a hole, if you see what I mean," she said.

Rayan drew in a careful breath. "You mean, arrange a…termination? Isn't that illegal in the Republic of Ireland?"

Imelda guffawed. "Of course it is. But if you have money and connections…?"

Obviously something I don't have, Rayan thought bitterly. Otherwise I wouldn't have to trek all the way across the Irish Sea to England. I could have had it done here and come home and recovered in my own bed; not alone in a strange city in some hotel room.

She slid gracelessly onto the tiled floor, resting her aching back against the heat of the range. She needed to tell Imelda the truth. Get on with it then, her inner voiced sneered.

"Anyway, Isaac is not that way inclined," Imelda went on, in a more conspiratorial tone. "I'm beginning to think he might have a foot in the Vivian and Sue camp." She paused. "What do you think?"

Heat sufficed Rayan like a tidal wave. She looked down at her swollen abdomen. A fit of hysterical giggling started in the pit of her stomach and gathering speed shot into her throat and out her mouth. Helpless to speak, she held the phone away from her.

"I don't think you have any worries in that direction," she spluttered thinking of Isaac's engorged penis thrusting deep inside her.

"That's a relief."

Rayan held the phone away from her ear as Imelda began to extolling Isaac's virtues. "Now, if it was his twin…that would be a horse of a different colour as old Mac O Lochlainn would say," Imelda chortled.

"If he did get her pregnant…would you…let him take her to England for a termination if she couldn't get it here?"

Imelda startled. Her breath left her. Rayan's words immediately winging her back to her student days when she had found out she was pregnant. Abortion wasn't that freely talked about in the 1970s but if you knew the right people, it could be arranged.

She gave a startled intake of breath. A rush of problems shot through Imelda's head like the rush hour train going through Perth railway station. "Jesus, Rayan. Is Shawnee—or whatever her name is, pregnant—up the duff? Are you and Isaac taking her to England without her parents' permission?" There was a significant increase in the volume of Imelda's voice. "What age is she?" Blood began to pound in her ears. Isaac could end up before the courts if she was underage. And even if she wasn't, he could end up in front of a judge, possibly Shawnee's father or friends of her father. He'd end up in prison. "I'm coming home. Isaac needs me."

Rayan felt herself slipping into a complete meltdown. Her appointment with the clinic would have to be brought forward. She looked down at her belly. She had come this far; she wasn't going to let Imelda or anybody else stop her now. She kicked out at the nearest chair. It fell with a clatter. "Cut the fucking umbilical cord, Imelda, he'll soon be twenty-one—key of the door and all that crap," she roared down the phone.

Sweating profusely, she struggled to her feet and began to pace trailing the phone cord after her. "You stay where you are and look after my business," she snarled down the phone. "You have no idea how many years…and the long hours…? You stay there as we agreed until I get there," she raged.

There was a stunned silence from the other end. Jesus! What a crazy bitch, Imelda thought. "Your business is fine but your name is shit here," she said already packing inside her head. There were several flights a day from Perth but some of them weren't directly to Heathrow. It didn't matter. She had to get home.

Rayan stopped pacing. "What do you mean, my name is shit?"

"A copper has been in a few times getting his hair cut—something about…domestic violence…?"

"He's a liar."

Imelda stared at the phone incredulously. She hadn't believed it herself. But listening to Rayan's denial, she knew instinctively there was truth in it. *Nathanial*, with his muscled, toned body, letting Rayan beat on him! Wow! Who would have believed it?

"You sure he's a liar, Rayan?"

Rayan stiffened. There it was. That veiled innuendo. Nathanial had been telling Imelda things—personal things, she thought angrily. He had no right; no right at all to share their private things.

She spilled her fury all over Imelda. "Yes, Isaac and I are going to London."

There was silence from Imelda's end. "I haven't been there since…before the boys were born. I'll fly into Heathrow and meet you and Isaac there."

Rayan's nerves felt as stretched as the phone cord. Visions of Imelda causing a scene at the clinic filled her with horror. "There's no point in asking Raphael to go… Under the circumstances…"

"Isaac! Bloody Isaac! Why is it always *him* you concern yourself with? Raphael is a far more decent human being," Rayan heard herself shout.

Imelda emitted a gasp. "You bitch! What are you suggesting? I make a difference in my boys?" Imelda's anger sizzled. That bitch! Implying I favour one of my boys over the other. "Fuck you and your business. I will have you know I have worked my guts out to make sure my boys, both my boys, had the best education, the best of everything I could give them," she said furiously. "I do not treat them different. How dare you."

Rayan's hand on the phone was slick with sweat and her heart was beating against her ribs like the wings of a trapped bird. She could feel Imelda's anger humming down the telephone line. Yeah, real mother earth material, you are, she sniggered. Worked your guts out—more like worked your ass off, she thought. Slept with any man with money and connections so that your *boys* and you could stand head and shoulders above the locals. *No wonder your precious twins have no moral compass*, she thought.

I wonder what you'll say when you discover Isaac is on the verge of leaving his prestigious law degree and is fraternising with the drunks on Derry's Walls instead of studying and Raphael has been keeping company with the IRA in the Bogside, she was tempted to screech down the phone. But if she did, Imelda would be on the first plane out today.

"How long have you been sleeping with Nathanial?" she shot at Imelda, glaring at the rising moon of her stomach.

There was a terse stillness at the other end of the line. "*Your* ex-partner," Imelda said disparagingly, "sleeps with whoever rolls under him!" To Imelda's immense satisfaction, Rayan gasped. "I am minding his dog for him," she lied.

"Why isn't Biscuit staying with Sienna?"

"She piddled all over Sienna's bed. She's a bitch just like you, isn't she?" Imelda said cuddling her face into the dog's silky fur.

Rayan gripped the phone tighter. "What did you just call me?"

"What? Not you! The dog—she's a bitch, just like Sienna. Oh, and here's something you should know before you come back, she's pregnant."

Rayan felt the room tilt. Sienna was *pregnant*. Nathanial was going to be a father.

Rayan pulled her travel bag towards her and checked she had everything she needed. She'd just taken what she would need. When she came back, she'd be packing for to go home to Perth. Minus her pregnancy, she'd take her chance with Ben Watts.

Tired from her sleepless nights when as soon as she lay down to rest, the *thing* started kicking as if it was exercising. She waited impatiently for Isaac to arrive. She heard the sound of feet on the loose gravel in the yard. She sighed with relief. She hadn't been sure he'd even bother to turn up.

She took a deep steadying breath. The journey to have the termination was finally here. She needed to keep calm. It would soon be all over. Involuntarily, her hand strayed to her stomach. A few days from now she could get on with her life and this would be all like a terrible nightmare. It would never be spoken of again, she promised herself.

She forced her swollen feet into court shoes. Her ankles mooned over the top of the shoes making her legs fat and unsightly. Never mind, she thought. Once I am on the flight, I'll be OK. And the clinic was sending someone to meet her at Heathrow.

"Ready?" Isaac said dourly.

"I'm ready." She caught the whiff of drink and body odour. She shrugged. Another few days and he'd be a part of her life she'd be putting behind her.

"I'll wait for you in the jeep," Isaac mumbled bending to pick up her overnight bag.

"Leave it. I have some more things to put in," she said sharper than she had intended. "Sorry Isaac," she apologised. She glanced at his stony face. "Where did you tell Raphael you were going for the weekend?"

"I didn't. He's away to collect Mum from the airport."

Rayan's heart leaped up into her throat. She hadn't heard from Imelda since they'd had the conversation about cutting their swap year short. Imelda had been emphatic she was coming home. But since she hadn't heard anything, Rayan had assumed Imelda had changed her mind and was staying to enjoy the heat of the Australian summer, after all. The news that she was on her way home so soon galvanised her into action. "What time is her flight due in?" she asked forcing the words out through stiff lips.

Isaac shrugged. "I don't know. I haven't really spoken to Raffi in a while." It wasn't strictly the truth. He had been hungover the last conversation he'd had with his twin. Raphael had made him promise he'd straighten himself out. Cut back on the vodka now that the new study year was underway.

He startled as another car pulled into the yard; its engine throbbing as if it had been driven over the pot-holed mountain road at speed.

Rayan stiffened. She really didn't need Sue's recriminations today of all days; she was nervous enough already.

Sue exchanged a baleful look with Isaac in the doorway. "Oh, Mummy's little helper is here," she said sarcastically.

"Please Sue, not today," Rayan sighed. It had been going on for weeks. Sue swung between berating her to cajoling her to change her mind. Over the last few days she had resorted to sending Rayan information on her emails about Irish women who had gone to England for abortions and regret it.

"Please don't, Sue. Nothing you can say…."

"I came to give you these."

Rayan drew back. Her heart thudded in her chest. Surely Sue hadn't brought *baby things*?

"It's moisturiser, lip balm, underwear and a few other things you might need."

Rayan felt the tears pricking the back of her eyes. She thought about all the little personal gifts Sue had given her over the eight months she had known her. Not to mention her beautiful wrap she had carefully put away in tissue ready to pack into her case when she came back from England.

She tried hard not to see the desperate mute plea in Sue's eyes. "Thanks Sue. You've been a good friend—best friend. The only real friend I've ever had." Rayan fell silent, shocked to see that her usually immaculately dressed friend looked dishevelled; her face naked of makeup.

She reached out and touched Sue's arm. "I'm glad you and Vivian are back together again," she said quietly. "You going away changed her; made her realise how much she loves you and what a wonderful person you are."

Sue gave her a look of pure bleakness. "Did you know, Vivian and I applied to be adopters and were turned down," she said her voice trembling.

Rayan pulled her coat around her to hide the obvious movement of life in her belly. "I'm sorry. I really am." Relief washed over her when she heard Isaac's feet crunching impatiently outside the back door. "I have to go. Will I see you when I get back, Sue?" Will you still be my friend, her eyes silently asked.

Sue jerked and clamped her bag to her chest. "You'll regret it, Rayan! You will," she insisted as Rayan opened her mouth to protest. "It's too late to go through with it now. Look at the size of you. You're as big as…as Muckish," Sue said bursting into tears.

Rayan looked down. It was true. Her belly suddenly seemed to have ballooned out. It was beginning to look like the shape of a dome. She put her arms awkwardly around Sue. "You and Vivian…you have each other, maybe the authorities will have a change of heart."

Sue pulled away. "They're nothing but a crowd of altar-hugging shower of bastards; kow-towing to the Church and the politicians."

"It's time we were going," Isaac said his voice sounding forced and loud.

Rayan gripped Sue's hands as she turned away. "I'm sorry, really sorry I can't see it your way; I really am. But Vivian would never accept…anything…from me anyway. She has never liked me from the first day I arriv—"

Hope leapt in Sue's eyes. "I'll leave Vivian. I will," she cried desperate to convince Rayan. "I know you'd want your baby to be loved after your own experience." Sue was babbling now the words tumbling over each other. "It wouldn't be as if the baby was a foundling like years ago when they were just abandoned on the steps of the church; or given to the nuns to make work slaves of—"

"Sue! Sue. Stop it, it can't be—"

Sue crushed Rayan to her. "We could rear it together! Think about it? We get on really well together…"

Rayan began to pant. Anxiety was making her breathless. "You don't get it, do you? I am not having this baby. I am never giving birth."

Sue drew back as if Rayan had punched her. "Neither am I. Neither am I ever going to be a mother. You could change that, Rayan," she said urgently. "All you have to do is give birth and I will do the rest. I'll be a good mother. You'll never regret it, never. Please, Rayan," she begged.

Stony-faced Isaac shoved Sue's car keys into her hands. The last thing he needed was bloody Sue convincing Rayan to give birth.

After Sue left, Rayan stuffed the things Sue had given her into her case. She checked her handbag again. The money to pay for the 'service' was zipped securely in along with her passport. She heaved a sigh of relief. She was ready to go.

"Don't forget to take the plane tickets and the address and telephone number of the clinic with you," Isaac growled.

"I'll not forget. They're on the notice board," Rayan snapped rattled at the look of sheer desperation that had been on Sue's tear-ravaged face. It shook her to the core to see Sue like that. Sue was always so *strong* and ready to face down anything. Sick at having brought her friend to the point of literally begging to give her the unborn child, distraught, Rayan scrabbled through the notice board in the kitchen with its coupons and clippings of special offers and bits of paper with numbers on them Imelda had left for her.

Her heart leaped into her throat. "The plane tickets—they're not here!"

Isaac cursed under his breath. Rayan was flapping about the kitchen like one of the agitated seagulls you'd see on the walkway along the River Foyle. Fuck. How had he gotten himself embroiled in all this? The hundred-mile drive to Belfast and the flight to Heathrow were going to be one long fucking nerve-racking dry journey.

He ran his tongue of his parched lips. He had promised Raphael he would cut down on the booze. Raffi didn't understand. The drink was the only thing keeping him sane. It took him away from all this; away from the confused look in his tutors' eyes. He wasn't top of the heap anymore; but the lower his grades got and the more negative the feedback from his student advisor became the more he needed to drink.

He needed a drink to get through this thing with Rayan. Once it was over, he'd stop drinking. He'd already had a humdinger of a row with Shawnee about not being there for her. Jesus! It was only for a couple of day. She didn't own him! Well, actually, she does a small voice inside him jeered, since 'Daddy' is paying for your weekend keep at the Shingle Beach.

"Calm down, they have to be here," Isaac said jerking his thoughts back.

"Calm down! I can't calm down. Without the tickets there is no point in going to the airport," she wailed feeling sick. Terror gripped her like a vice. She felt as if she was hyperventilating—dizzy and breathless.

"Here, let me look. You check the bag."

Rayan spilled the contents of her handbag on the table; neither the tickets nor the other details pertaining to her appointment or the clinic were there. She opened her travel bag and flung everything on the tiles and shook the empty bag upside down.

She tried to think. She had planned to put the details of the clinic and her plane ticket in her handbag last night but in her anxiety about what she might need and the thought of Nathanial and Sienna had distracted her. She looked around. She must have had the tickets in her hand and left them down somewhere. She shook her head. No! She had never taken them off the notice board.

A chill passed over her. She drew back her lip. "Sue took them."

"Sue? Sue wouldn't take the tickets."

"She would—she did. That was her reason for being here this morning. The lying scheming bitch, pretending to be my friend, bringing me a present!"

Isaac watched perplexed as Rayan frantically searched through the scattered contents of her handbag yet again and through the clothes from her overnight bag; now strewn across the kitchen floor. It was obvious the tickets weren't there but she still kept searching. Pity stirred in him at the state she was in, her belly pushing out through her coat.

Why had he listened to Raphael and that old fart Mac Lochlainn spurting his religious bollocks? Between them they had sent him on a guilt trip that ended with his ringing up and cancelling Rayan's earlier appointment. If he had left things are all this would be done and dusted.

He glanced surreptitiously at his watch. They were never going to make the flight now. "Maybe you should prepone it to another day," he blurted out.

Rayan's eyes narrowed into slits. "I can't miss a second appointment. Look at me! *Look at me! I'm twenty-eight weeks pregnant.* If I don't get it done now…" Her words dried up, too awful to think of the consequences.

She paced like a caged tigress. "Sue took the tickets to keep me from going to London," Rayan screeched into Isaac's face. "Maybe you and the Judge's little daughter would like to adopt it. Or maybe Imelda will get the old pram she had for you and your brother out of the attic and play mother earth for a second time," she yelled kicking at the kitchen bin. "Because, believe me, I am not going to be around to *mother* it!"

Dizzy slunk down off the small kitchen settee and tried to get his bulky body under the kitchen table.

Isaac backed away. He wasn't staying around for Rayan to thrash him again. No way. He was out of here.

"You keep looking for the tickets. I will go to the Spa. If Sue has the tickets, I will get them off her and come straight back here. It's foggy. Maybe the flight will be delayed. Or, we can get a later one," he said clutching at straws. Panic assailed him. His mother was going to be home in a couple of hours. He needed a drink. He couldn't face her stone cold sober. He made for the door. When he was at the hotel, he'd buy a bottle of vodka to drink on the way. He stopped. "The girls at the hotel were saying Mum was bringing Nathanial, her Aussie…friend home with her." As soon as the words left his mouth, he knew he'd put his foot in it.

Rayan froze. "That's a lie! Nathanial…has other things to keep him in Perth," she hissed.

Isaac looked at her dumbly. "I'm only telling you what I heard. Does he know about the—"

"No! He does not. Nor is he going to," Rayan said emphasising every word.

"Could help—" Isaac started to say…

Rayan's face went puce with rage. "Get out! Get out. And get my ticket," she shrieked slamming the door after him.

She scrunched her eyes tightly shut in despair. Was losing the tickets a 'sign' she should give birth and make Sue a mother? She knew Sue had been praying to St Jude, the saint of hopeless cases. Rayan gasped as the baby kicked as if affirming her thoughts.

"I don't believe in that religious claptrap," she sneered to the empty kitchen. "If I stay in Ireland much longer, I'll believe in fairies, secret waterfalls and the pot of gold at the end of the rainbow that shines over Muckish after a rainstorm."

She startled as Mac O Lochlainn's voice clear as a bell, as if he was standing beside her, filled her mind. *Scoff all ye want. But you could believe in worse, girlie*, she thought she heard him say. Emotionally exhausted, she sat down remembering Mac's concern for her when she found out her appointment at the London Clinic had been cancelled.

She had had taken the doctor's advice and contacted the British Pregnancy Centre in London. It had caused some confusion when she tried to explain her circumstances. Yes, she explained, she was presently living in Ireland and seeking a termination in England. But, no, she wasn't an Irish citizen. She had only been living at her address in Ireland for a short time.

There were more searching questions. Yes, she was an Australian citizen. Yes, born and bred, she assured the cool voice on the other end of the phone. There was a pause. Rayan could hear the scratch of a pen on paper—then another question. This time there was a note of curiosity in the voice... Rayan had breathed past the grip she had on her temper. No, she wasn't pregnant when she came to Ireland in March. Sick with nerves, she'd clutched the phone until it was slick with her sweat. She hadn't expected there to be so many personal questions. And then the question she had been dreading the most; the question of parentage. Was the father Irish? Yes, he was Irish. Yes, he was happy for her to have the termination. And, yes, he would be coming with her to the clinic. She thought she had detected a small involuntarily murmur of surprise that Isaac would be accompanying her. But the woman on the phone, obviously satisfied, picked up pace and explained there would be counselling session and medical questionnaires to complete when Rayan got there.

Then she finally gave her a date and time.

She had been over the moon. She felt as if one of the big boulders on the summit of Muckish had been lifted off her. She'd began been marking off the days on the calendar. Those rows of neat crossed out dates bringing her visually nearer to the termination date.

She made her plans. Isaac would drive her to the airport. She would book a three-day parking spot for Imelda's car. It would be costly but it would be worth it, she might not be feeling…fragile. Having the car would be more private than using the airport coach. There was sure to be local people on it. They'd assume she had been on holidays and would want to hear all about the sights of London. They'd want to chat. Donegal people loved to talk and share news. She didn't want to be the local news item that week, she mused.

More to reassure herself than anything else, she had phoned to double check the date only to be told her appointment had been rescinded. Shocked, she had more or less told the receptionist she was incompetent and to do her bloody job right and check again. When it was confirmed that, yes indeed, her appointment had been cancelled, she had felt impotent, helpless. The cool voice on the other end of the phone had accepted her apology and put the phone down with a decisive click before Rayan got a chance to make a new appointment.

She had been distraught, outraged, and ready to emotionally disintegrate when Mac and Raphael had sauntered through the back door. Mad as a bag of frogs at what she was sure as his interference she'd went at Raphael, yelling it was his fault.

Mac had stood back, bemused. Then he had sat down across the table from her, gave her a kindly look and asked her if her Australian boyfriend knew she was pregnant. She'd glared at him. How did he know about Nathanial? And how dare he ask her such personal questions? It was a bad habit they had in Donegal; people wanting to know the intimate details of your business.

Yet, sensing he meant well, she'd shaken her head mutely.

"Not his baby, then," Mac had enquired.

Rayan had shaken her head.

Mac had leaned back in the chair and gave her a thoughtful look. "Your boyfriend wouldn't be the first to take on another man's offerings and rear it as his own. Why don't you tell him? Let him make the choice," Mac had said in his Donegal burr.

Rayan's eyes had sparked fire. "You don't understand. I never wanted to be pregnant." She found once she started to talk, the words poured out of her like the water that rushed from the waterfall on the mountain. "When I was young, I made myself a promise…"

"Mac had chuckled softly. Ochs, sure, darlin' when we're young and have no sense, we all make promises, we can't keep," he said giving her hand a fatherly pat.

She had dragged her hand away and rushed on. "I swore I would never be a mother—never be like my mother—dependent on a man. And I am not breaking that promise. I will not bring another human being into this world. Not every woman wants to have a child. I'm one of them." She'd gulped.

The click of the timer on the range sounded loud in the silent kitchen. It broke her melancholy and Rayan realised Isaac should have been back ages ago.

Chapter Twenty-Three

Imelda longed for the antenna to announce her flight from Dubai to Heathrow was boarding.

They had taken off from Perth over thirteen hours ago. Now they were grounded in Dubai for "technical" reasons. All she wanted now was to get home to the Manse. She glanced surreptitiously at the male passenger sitting opposite her. If the seats were any closer, we'd be touching, she thought. His left hand rested on his knee showing off a gold signet ring on his pinkie and a gold wedding band on his third finger.

Ayeman would be forty-two now, Imelda thought, about ages with this man. She had been thinking about him since she'd seen the security man guarding President Clinton in Derry that day she'd had dinner with her twins. An audible wistful sigh escaped her. The man looked up, raised an enquiring eyebrow then went back to reading his book.

An image of Ayeman when she known him in Belfast in the mid-seventies flashed into Imelda's mind: Curly black hair, cleft dip in his chin, the way he tossed back his head just like Isaac did when he laughed. His reticence when he was in a crowd. She glanced in the direction of the man again. Reality check, Imelda, her inner voice scoffed. It's not him.

Gathering up her things she paced between the waiting area and the coffee shop. Had he ever married? Did her boys have siblings somewhere in the Middle East? She stared unseeing into a gift shop window. Would he have married her if his family hadn't intervened? Her mother hadn't helped in that direction either.

Discovering Imelda was pregnant with twins was bad enough for her mother Norah. Finding out the father was Muslin was shocking for her. Horrified at the thought her daughter had sex with a black man, she'd forbidden Imelda to dare to show her face with twins in Donegal. 'Give them to the nuns in the Nazareth House in Belfast. People know you're studying; carry on with your law course—nobody will be any the wiser,' she ordered. Norah kept the twins' birth a secret from her husband. And alternated between angry telephone calls of righteous recriminations and crying copious tears about the shame Imelda had brought on the family. If Imelda ever brought them home, *she'd* ensure the authorities took them away and hid them in a children's home far away from Donegal with strict instructions they were to be split up and never be given the name or address of their mother.

Fearful she would succeed Imelda fought tooth and nail to keep them. Moving into the Manse had been an act of sheer desperation to get the twins away from her mother's religious fervour and to a place where she could keep them safe. She'd fully expected to be evicted and charged with breaking and entering. But it was either that or wait until her mother wore the old priest down to take them away.

She shivered. If only the twins knew how close they had come to being torn apart and separated for the rest of their life, she thought.

But what if she should meet Ayeman again? She was now forty and he was forty-two. They were no longer young adults at the mercy of their respective parents. Would the love they felt for each other still burn fiercely between them? Did she still carry a torch for him and him for her? He had sworn he loved her; loved his unborn babies.

Despite the heat she shivered. His family had whisked him off and sent her packing. She grimaced remembering overhearing Mac O Lochlainn's wife, Mary, describe the twins' father to their local butcher. "From what I hear, he's neither Irish nor Catholic. Skin the colour of a bar of chocolate; hair like a gollywog," she said in a stage whisper. "And Imelda, the brazen hussy, the breaking of her poor mother's heart…swanning about with them two half-cast children as if she'd won the Pools."

She'd startled when the butcher had looked over her gossiping head. "What can I get for you, Imelda," he'd asked his fat cheeks turning crimson.

"Can I offer you a coffee?"

Imelda startled back to the present. The man who had been sitting opposite her was smiling down at her.

"No, no. We'll be boarding shortly."

"We have time," he said smoothly.

"I'm fine. But thank you," she said politely.

The man smiled again. "My wife is meeting me in London. It can get lonely when you're travelling alone."

Imelda considered. He looked respectable and charming. What harm could it do? Just for a while with him by her side she could dream of what might have been if Ayeman had married her.

As she sat down in the coffee bar Imelda knew she should get up and leave but just for a while she could allow her mind to play, what if. What if, by some stroke of karma he was Ayeman? He was the right age and height. It would be amazing just to spend one more night with him; feel his arms around her. Dream on, Imelda, you've had too much Aussie sun, her inner voice giggled.

"You are returning from holiday?" he asked signalling for the waiter.

Imelda nodded. "First real holiday since my twins were born." She watched his face for any flicker of recognition.

He lowered his gaze and fiddled with his spoon. "My wife and I…we do not have children."

"Oh, I'm sorry…"

"No, no, you misunderstand me. *We* do not have children. I have children from a former relationship but I do not see them," he said a wistful note in his voice.

Imelda's heart hammered against her ribcage. "Broken marriage," she managed to get out.

What the friggin' hell do you think you are doing, Imelda? her inner voice remonstrated. He is *not* who you want him to be. You have as much chance of meeting the father of your boys again as you have of winning the lottery. Now get out of there and into the queue before he gets the wrong idea. You know what Middle Eastern men think about western women—they think they are all whores. Imelda started to gather up her belongings. "No, no, don't answer that. It's really none of my business. I see people queuing up… Thank you for the coffee," she yelped, fleeing in the direction of the boarding gate.

The 747 was choc-a-block. Passengers elbowed and jostled their way past each other as if the plane was about to take off without them. Imelda saw the Muslim man heading for First Class. She paused just for a second and drank in his appearance. We were little more than children enjoying our first taste of freedom away from our parents, she thought her thought returning to her and Ayeman. I wonder did ever he reach the inner circle, the higher echelons of the justice system his family had planned for him. "Getting lumbered with a pregnant first year undergraduate definitely wasn't in their plans," she murmured.

Squeezing past a man who was stacking his overhead luggage regardless of the bottleneck he was creating behind him, Imelda moaned. "Why do they have to make the seat numbers so bloody small," she complained squinting at what she thought was the right seat number.

"Yeah, reading glasses and hearing aids, that is all we can look forward to at our age," a woman passing down on the other aisle announced cheerfully.

Imelda squeezed in. "The cabin crew can change me if I'm in somebody's else's seat," she puffed pushing her bag down to her feet until she had space to stand up and stack it in the overhead compartment. Adjusting her seatbelt, she arranged the pillow in the small of her back, closed her eyes and waited for take-off.

The smell of food woke her. She smiled at the proffered enquiry of what she'd like from the food trolley. "Coffee, black." She glanced down the aisle. There was a long queue for the toilets. Her eye travelled behind the partially open curtain in First Class. She could always use their toilets. She checked on the cabin staff. Quickly, she unbuckled and walked purposefully through the open curtain that separated the cabins.

A short queue formed. In front of Imelda, a mother soothed a fractious child. "Mama Mama, pee, pees," the child kept repeating.

I know the feeling, Imelda sympathised, silently willing whoever was in the toilet to come out.

"We meet again," a voice said behind her.

She didn't need to turn her head to know it was him. "Yes. We meet again," she responded hoping he wouldn't see her desperate need for the loo etched on her face.

"You are in First Class. We should have that drink," he grinned.

Imelda glanced at the cabin crew readying the drinks. Any minute now they were going to cotton on she was on the wrong side of the curtain.

"It's free now. You should go in," he advised. Embarrassed at her obvious need for the loo, Imelda scuttled inside. She double checked the bar had connected with the keeper. She could still hear the child lambasting her mother. Eventually, she opened the door. He was gone.

Bored with searching for a film without subtitles, she switched to the music channel. Clamping the headphones slightly away from her ears, she drifted with the music. "Imagine, listening to music thousands of miles in the sky as if I was sitting in my own sunroom," she thought. "My own sunroom," she mused.

"Except of course it belongs to some rich American guy who thinks it's been on the market for sale for years." The thought unsettled her.

What if the Manse did sell one of these days, she mused. Ireland is full of millionaires now thanks to the Celtic Tiger. Some entrepreneur somewhere is bound to think he could snap it up and make a fast buck developing it into a housing estate or a caravan park, she thought.

Disgruntled with her thoughts she sat up and looked around her. The cabin crew had lowered the window blinds. Most people had turned off their reading lights and had cosied up in the blanket ready to sleep. She wished now she hadn't slept earlier.

Her thoughts turned to home. Now that the twins were ready to fly the nest maybe she should seriously think what she going to do with the rest of her life. Would she go and live in Australia if Nathanial asked her? Nah, she didn't think so. Nathanial was a nice enough guy but as changeable as the Irish weather, she thought. Not that's there's much chance of him asking anyway, she mused.

She wondered what Nathanial had ever seen in Rayan. She's not his type at all, she thought. He's not yours either, her inner voice sniggered. She shrugged. He wasn't, as if happened. But that was fine. It was a pity she couldn't persuade him to come back with her. It would have given her great satisfaction to see the incredulous look on Vivian's face when she walked in with him on her arm

She wasn't looking forward to going back to work under Vivian's tyranny. But what else could she do. She wasn't trained for anything else. She shrugged. She'd decide after the twins graduated. Consulting the music list again she picked a 70s hit record that had been popular when she was studying at Queens. Adjusting the earphones, she settled down to listen.

It was a few seconds before she realised the attendant was vying for her attention. She removed her headphones. "Sorry, what did you say?"

"A gentleman in First Class has requested you meet him for a drink," the flight attendant smiled, a twinkle in her eye.

"It's the middle of the night!" Imelda protested waving her hand at the sleeping passengers.

"He is a very nice man—one of our regulars."

Imelda closed her eyes. A very nice married man whose wife is waiting for him at Heathrow, she thought. "Tell him I'm asleep," she said softly.

"You are not asleep," a male voice said. "Glass of bubbly while we chat," the man grinned.

"It's the middle of the night," Imelda protested.

"It is champagne time somewhere," he smiled sliding into the empty seat beside her and handing her a champagne flute.

Imelda wanted to feel annoyed at his cheek. But she had to admit she admired his tenacity. "You don't give up, do you?" she said in a low voice. Oh, what the hell, I know he's not Ayeman but a girl can dream, can't she? Being picked up by a handsome traveller would be a nice end to her holiday.

He gave her a wolfish look as his free hand found her thigh.

She was glad now she had bought the figure-hugging top with its front string opening in the Duty Free. She knew she wasn't as toned as she had been when she worked out in the gym in the Spa but this guy doesn't seem to have any problems with the few extra pounds, she thought as his fingers caressed her ribcage. She knew he would revert to type once the little wife kissed him at Heathrow. But in the meantime, he'd help while away the long flight, she thought.

"A toast to the Mile High club," she giggled as the wine tickled the back of her throat.

Playing with the string of her blouse, he let his fingers lightly fan her breasts as his hand slipped between her legs under cover of the blanket.

Chapter Twenty-Four

Rayan listened to the fading hum of the engine of Isaac's car on the road. One of these days he's going to lose his licence for drinking and driving, she thought. She hoped it wasn't today.

She thought fleetingly that there was a deepening animosity developing between him and his twin. She had been impressed at their close closeness to each other when she first arrived. She hunched her shoulders. She had more important things to worry about today. You can't trust anybody, she thought. She was certain Raphael and Sue had planned between them to keep her here until Imelda got back and put a stop to the trip to London. And Nathanial's emails had petered out again.

She went to the gate and looked up and down the road. She could hear the distance toll of the midday Angelinos Bell. There was no sign of Isaac. He'd tricked her. He wouldn't be back, she thought going back inside.

The dog stretched and nudged her elbow. "Go away. No walking on the mountain today," Rayan shouted. The dog persisted. "No walking on the mountain," she repeated. The dog's ears flattened. He scraped at the door. The sound, amplified in the silent kitchen gnawed on Rayan's taut nerves. "The farmer will shoot you if he finds you in his fields again," she warned opening the door. Dizzy shot past her and disappeared around the gatepost.

Rayan wondered if Mac was dropping off climbers at the makeshift car park in the lower foothills. He might be going back into Derry. A faint hope rose in her. It had been on the news that some flights were delayed because of some official visit to Stormont.

The mountain guide pushed his beanie hat off his forehead and gave a bemused nod. "Thinking of having a go at climbing the north side," he joked glancing at her pregnant shape and her dishevelled state.

"What the blazes is keepin' Mac O Lochlainn. He was supposed to pick my group up an hour ago. He must be running late," the guide grumbled.

A hysterical gurgle started in Rayan's chest. "Aren't we all?"

The guide shaded his eyes. "What the hell."

Rayan looked to where he was staring; a group of walkers were striding towards them. "Bus driver couldn't make it. Had other business to attend to, so we walk," the first guy to reach them said in a deep German accent.

The guide cursed behind his gloved hand. "That your dog," he asked Rayan as Dizzy raced madly between the climbers before racing away again.

Rayan whistled to the dog but it came out shallow and squeaky.

"Here, use my spare whistle," the guide offered.

Rayan hesitated. "He'll turn back in a while," she muttered.

"Take it," he insisted, anxious to be away.

"I might not see you again. I'm going away for a…holiday," she added quickly.

The guide checked his gloves. "No panic. Leave it in Paddy's Pub—"

"You might not be there."

"Ah, for god sake; it's a bloody whistle, not the crown jewels," the guide barked, thrusting it into her hand.

"Thanks," Rayan said moving awkwardly out of the way of the line of climbers. "How far to the healing waterfall that doesn't freeze over?" she asked.

The guide raised his eyebrows and smiled sardonically. "You mean the one that is supposed to have magical powers?"

Feeling foolish, Rayan turned her face away. "Forget I asked," she snapped.

"Mac O Lochlainn still spinning that old tourist folklore?" He laughed. "You stop believing in tales like that that when you've lived here for a while." He looked at her. "You're not thinking of going up the mountain today, are you? Weather forecast only favourable for experienced climbers like these guys. You're the Australian woman the paramedics rushed to hospital with the head injury. You made a good recovery, then?" he said his attention on the climbers. "Sorry, have to move on with these guys," he apologised. "Pay no attention to what old Mac tells you. The tourists love the Irish folklore. Old Mac spins those yarns to get them interested in the mountain—good for business," he chuckled, "See you," he said moving off.

Hope of keeping her appointment in London shrivelled up like dead leaves. In despair she watched the climbers and the guide until they grew into small distant humped shapes.

There was only one option left to her now. Veering into one of the slopes, tears blinding her, she began to climb. The rough terrain hurt her feet through the thin leather soles of her court shoes. She stumbled on, higher and higher. Overhead, the sky turned a mottled grey. Dark clouds low and ominous hung over the summit of the mountain.

A slight rumble carried on the wind reached her. She veered to the left her mind centred on finding the waterfall. It was her only hope now. Panting, she pushed on ignoring the spasm of pain in her back. Everything would be alright once she reached the waterfall.

The rumble came again. Suddenly, lightning streaked across the sky followed by a roll of thunder that seemed to shake the terrain beneath her feet.

The dog gave a plaintive howl, turned and. raced back the way they had come. Another roll of thunder was followed by forked lightening. Rayan stopped to get her bearings. Had Raphael turned right or left after the old mine? She turned right.

As abruptly as the storm had started, it stopped. Now the mountain was eerily silent. Rayan was sure she could hear the waterfall. She retraced her steps and came to a smoother path. She had been right. The sound of the waterfall was louder, nearer now.

She felt a tremor beneath her feet; followed by what sounded like more thunder. She stopped and looked upwards. Too late, she realised she was in the path of falling rocks. She turned clumsily in the vain hope of getting out of the way.

The boulders thundered over her. She screamed in agony and fell headlong into the boggy green moss.

The last sound she heard was the rush of the nearby waterfall.

Chapter Twenty-Five

Isaac drove into the yard of the Manse, the two plane tickets gripped in his hand. The kitchen was empty. The jubilation at extracting the tickets from Sue fuelled by several drinks he'd had in the hotel bar evaporated. He tossed the tickets on the table. Where the fuck was Rayan?

Taking the stairs two at a time, he rapped on her bedroom door. "I've got the tickets," he called out edging the bedroom door open a crack. The room was empty. His eyes fixated on his mother's hairbrush on the dressing table. Shame burned in him remembering how Rayan had humiliated him. He hadn't told anyone, not even Raphael about the beating.

He went back to the kitchen. He noticed her handbag partly concealed where it sat on the seat of one of the kitchen chairs. Idly, he checked the various small zipped compartments inside. His eyes widened when he saw the rolled-up wad of sterling notes. He knew instantly it was the money to pay the clinic for the termination. He pushed it back in beside Rayan's passport and zipped up the bag.

Taking the half empty bottle of vodka from his pocket, he took a deep swallow. He wandered around the kitchen trying not to think of the feel of the wad banknotes Rayan had in her bag.

Picking up the plane tickets, he checked the flight time. They'd never make it on time. He took another swig from the bottle and thought how Rayan had belittled and humiliated him. "I'm fucked if I am driving that bitch all the way to Belfast when it's too late for the flight to Heathrow," he muttered draining the bottle. "I got the tickets back for her. She can drive herself to the airport. I'm going back to the bar…"

Out on the road he heard the familiar rattle of Mac O Lochlainn's tour bus. Quickly, he unzipped the handbag and drew out a twenty-pound note. "I might as well be hung for a sheep as a lamb," he grinned pulling out another twenty and stuffing them both into his jeans pocket. Pulling the door shut behind him, he sprinted down the yard and into the middle of the road almost under the wheels of the tour bus. "I need a lift back into Derry," he panted as the bus door hissed open. He'd have a good drink and then he'd come back and face his mother.

Mac fixed him with a look that could kill. "It'll be the feckin' morgue you'll be goin' to if ye pull a trick like that again," he bawled two angry red spots spreading across his wrinkled face. "Get in."

Isaac flung himself into an empty seat beside a large woman who was dozing. He fingered the money he had stolen from Rayan's bag. His stomach knotted. She still has plenty left, he reasoned.

He settled back in his seat and watched the hedgerows flash by. If she hadn't got herself into this shit I wouldn't need her money for drink to get me through it, he thought.

Mac dropped him off on the Strand Road. "Tell Raphael to see me later—wee job needin doin'," Mac said under his breath as Isaac descended the bus step. "And here, young fella," he said in a louder voice, "get home te that student flat o' yours and don't come out the night again." Isaac looked questioningly at him.

Mac glanced over his shoulder at his passengers. Most of them were dozing after a day of sightseeing, eating and drinking. "The place is hivin'wi' Brits and our friends in the RUC. There'll be a bit o' recreational rioting later," he smirked, giving Isaac a wink.

Isaac shrugged. He couldn't care less. That was Raphael's department. Rayan's money was burning a hole in his pocket. He was more concerned with getting to the nearest off licence and getting another bottle of vodka. "Thanks for the lift," he said his thoughts already on whether to go drinking with the winos in John St or find a dark spot on Derry's Walls. With the entire tourist walking tours finished for the day it would be quiet on the Walls now.

Stiff with cold, Imelda shuddered awake as Raphael stopped the car. "Are we home?" she yawned.

"We're stopping for something to eat. Mind your feet, the ground is covered in puddle holes," he warned.

"What kind of a place is this," Imelda asked looking around the low beamed room and the warren of little room that seem too veered off it.

"It's a country pub. Sit over beside the fire and get warm," Raphael said heading towards a buxom woman serving drink behind the bar.

"You're late. Your full Irish was ready half an hour ago," Kate said with a pout.

"Took the back roads—place is crawling with Brits and the Royal Ulster Constabulary," Raphael growled. There was a general muttering of curses from the men sitting at the bar.

The barmaid bent down to gather up glasses giving Raphael a clear view of her shapely thighs.

"Now I know I'm back in Ireland," Imelda said watching Raphael wolfing down a huge platter of bacon, sausage, fried bread, wheaten bread, fried eggs topped with beans. "There's enough food on that plate to feed a small family."

She wondered what Nathanial would think if he saw so much calories and fat on the one plate. Nathanial is a ten-inch steak man, she mused thinking about the steakhouse he had taken her to in Perth. And the sex they'd had in Rayan's bed afterwards. She snapped her mind away, embarrassed to be thinking such thoughts in front of her son.

A man with a neck like a tree trunk and feet encased in mud splattered boots came in the door and made straight for their table. "You're late," he said without introduction. He swept his eyes over Imelda. "You're this boyo's mammy," he stated casting an appraising eye over her. "The grannies never look like you in my day," he chuckled. Raphael choked on the piece of bacon.

"Manus," Raphael interrupted hurriedly signalling him to say no more.

"What? You didn't tell her? He didn't tell you you're going to be a granny?" he said turning back to Imelda.

Ice was forming in Imelda's veins despite the heat coming off the turf fire. Jesus! What Rayan had hinted at was true.

"Could be worse, could be my daughter your son put up the pole," Manus commented, throwing a glance at Raphael.

Imelda's narrowed her eyes at him. "Don't be ridiculous. Isaac is studying to be a barrister. He wouldn't be interested in a country girl," she said glancing at the barmaid. "That's more your type," she said turning to Raphael. "You've had more woman like that than you're had hot dinners."

The chattering in the bar died to a murmur.

It was for the best Rayan was taking that little flirt Isaac had been partnering at tennis to England. Judge's daughter or not she wouldn't be the first Irish girl to do go and she'll not be the last, Imelda thought. Isaac couldn't get bogged down with a *baby*. It would be like history repeating itself. He needed to finish his studies and marry a girl with connections. Like Shawnee, the judge's daughter, her conscious sneered.

Raphael speared a sausage with his fork. "Stop staring at Kate, Ma."

"Who?"

"Kate, the barmaid, Manus is her da."

Manus looked at the audience of drinkers who were pretending not to listen. "Kate, a whiskey for Raffi's Ma. Best thing for shock." He motioned to Raphael. "Leave that," he said motioning to the food on Raphael's plate. "I have a wee job for you."

"Kate!" he bellowed when the barmaid didn't respond straight away.

"Comin' Dada, coming."

Manus paused at the pub door; the bulk of his belly filling the opening. He turned towards the drinkers at the bar. "Loose tongues cost lives," he thundered pushing Raphael out in front of him.

Imelda waved the drink away Kate put down in front of her.

The barmaid folded her arms under her breasts and planted her feet firmly on the floor in front of her. "When my dada, Big Manus, says you're to have a drink, you have a drink," she said an intimidating note in her tone. "Sit where you are," she advised as Imelda made to get up.

"I've had a long international flight. I want to get home," Imelda said icily.

"You'll be home soon enough. Drink your drink."

The men at the bar were chatting again but she could sense a kind of tense undercurrent. Imelda gulped at the whiskey.

"Nice tan you got in Australia," Kate smiled, keeping a sharp eye that none of the drinkers went out the door. Every few minutes she'd bend her ear as if listening for a signal from outside.

Imelda listened too but all she could hear was the rain lashing against the window. "What is Raphael doing out there? We should be going."

"You'll be on your way soon," Kate assured her.

"Do you go to university?" Imelda asked, thinking that was where Raphael knew her from.

Kate laughed. "Nah, book learning is not for me. I'm more a politics of life kind of woman. But Raphael, now, he's taught me a thing or two…"

Abruptly, Imelda put down her glass pushed her chair back.

Startled, the barmaid gripped her arm. "Wait, you don't want to go out there. Dada wouldn't like it," she said tersely. Imelda shoved her aside and made for the door.

Outside, the rain was coming down in sheets. It took a minute for Imelda's eyes to adjust to the darkness. A man coming from the shadows of the pub brushed past her carrying something. As she watched, he opened the boot of her jeep. Imelda heard herself shout out. She turned back towards the pub, "Somebody's breaking into my car!"

She heard muted swearing. In the pool of light from the open pub door, she caught a glimpse of the violent expression on Manus' face. Gripping her arm like a vice, he yanked her forward. She heard the slam of the pub door and a bar being drawn across from inside.

"Shut your trap, woman," he hissed in her ear.

"He was opening the boot… He put something inside."

"He was doin' nothing of the sort." His grip tightened as he manhandling her into the front seat and slamming the door shut. "You saw nothing. Your son is in enough bother without you slabbering. Make sure she keeps her trap shut if them limey bastards stop you on the road," he growled, breathing hard, spittle dripping from his chin. "Fuck this one up and you're fodder for the fish in the Foyle," he promised Raphael.

Raphael nodded mutely. The brakes squealed as the car accelerated and shot out on to the main road.

They were over the Glenshane Pass before the thumping in Imelda's chest allowed her speak.

"He put something in the boot?"

"Nothing was put in the boot, Ma," Raphael muttered.

They drove on in silence. "When were you going to tell me Isaac and Rayan were taking Shawnee on a…trip to London."

Raphael glanced at her. "You picked it up wrong, Ma. It's Rayan that's going to London. She's going for an abortion."

Imelda laughed.

Raphael gave her a perplexed look. It definitely wasn't the reaction he had been expecting from her.

"It's true, Ma. Isaac got Rayan pregnant," he blurted out.

Imelda was speechless. She opened her mouth but no words came out. "She's old enough to be his mother," she finally croaked out as they crossed over Craigavon Bridge.

Raphael glanced at the street drinkers huddled together sharing their booze. He prayed Isaac wasn't among them tonight.

Suddenly, he was furious with Imelda. "Why did you have to go and leave a...*virgin* like Isaac with a woman like Rayan? Was it deliberate to get him interested in women?" he shouted. Slamming his boot to the floor, the car shot forward.

Thrown forward Imelda braced herself against the dashboard. "For god sake, Raphael, slow down," she screamed as they narrowly missed a bus coming in the opposite direction.

Raphael veered left into Abercorn Road. A passing army patrol land rover drove slowly past reminding him of the guns old Manus had hidden in his boot.

"Isaac got Rayan pregnant," Imelda gabbled out, her voice rising. She rolled down the car window and gulped in mouthfuls of cold air. "That's you...he's imitating you. You set him a bad example with all your womanising."

Raphael threw his mother an incredulous look. "You're some piece of work, Ma. Isaac and me have had a string of 'uncles' since you took us to live in the Manse. It took me a while but I figured out why none of them ever stayed. They were all married men with their own families." Imelda put her hands over her face.

They were only streets away from the student flat he shared with Isaac. His mother was in shock; he shouldn't say any more. But the words were queuing up to leap from his mouth. "You picked carefully, didn't you, Ma. A chef, you got that fancy kitchen from him; and the landscape gardener," he sneered.

"It was all for you and Isaac. If your granny Norah had her way, you'd end up separated and adopted. I couldn't let you be separated. I did what I had to do to keep us together."

Raphael hardly recognised the derision in his voice. "Imelda making a home for her wee half-cast bastard sons," he mocked as the car shuddered to a halt in front of the student flats.

Chapter Twenty-Six

The shaking began in Imelda's legs again as soon as she opened the back door and stepped into the familiar kitchen. "I'll see to the range," Mac offered, fiddling with the temperature gauge on the oil-fired stove.

Imelda shivered into her coat and stuck her shaking hands up the sleeves. "Thanks for bringing me home."

Mac O Lochlainn shifted from one foot to the other. His heart felt like a lump of lead in his chest. It saddened him to see Imelda and the twins at loggerheads with each other. "Not a bother, girlie."

The adrenalin, fuelled by Imelda's fury against the twins drained away leaving her feeling utterly devastated. She was shocked beyond words at the dishevelled drunken state of Isaac and the terrible animosity between her boys.

"Things always seem worse when you're tired out," Mac said soothed. "A good sound sleep in your own bed an' things will look different in the mornin'."

Imelda gazed out at the desolate gaunt silhouette of the trees under a sky as bleak as her mood. All Isaac kept saying was that Rayan had tricked him; made a fool of him.

Mac glanced worriedly at Imelda. She was taking this thing about Isaac and Rayan bad, very bad. She was in bits. Her fingers twitched, her body slumped in on itself. He could see she was in a state of utterly exhaustion and shock. She seemed to have aged ten years. He wondered if he should call in and have a word with the local doctor on his way home. Get something to settle her. Gone was the feisty woman who faced down the bible thumpers and the village gossip in defence of her twins.

"Does everybody know?" Imelda asked him.

"Ach, sure, something else will come along. Like the news about Sue and Vivian."

Imelda felt as if her brain couldn't work out what Mac was saying.

"Sue and Vivian?"

"Ach, you know the gossips—nothing else to do wi' their time. A'll make a brew of tea—heat ye up," Mac blustered evasively. "You go up and get the bed ready. I'll call you when it's stewed a bit," he offered chancing a smile. Realising his words had not come out the way he had intended, Mac's face reddened. "Ah didn't mean… Ach you know what ah mean, Imelda."

Imelda extracted her trembling hands from her sleeves and gave him a wan smile. "You may be many things but you're no womaniser, Mac. I'll have the tea and then I'll go up."

"You goin' back to work at the hotel?" Mac asked changing the subject. It was the only safe topic he could think to talk about.

Imelda hunched her shoulders. She'd emailed Vivian to tell her she was coming home early but she'd heard nothing back. "I suppose so." She wrapped her hands around the mug of tea. "Rayan's away to England," she said.

Mac jiggled the tea past the lip of the cup. He cast around for something to mop up the spill. He took a gulp of the scalding tea before he answered. Wherever Rayan was, she wasn't away to England unless she had managed to get to the airport and get another flight, he thought blowing on the steam curling up from his cup. He was sure Imelda would agree with them stopping Rayan from doing that terrible thing to a wee innocent babby nearly ready to be born.

He looked at Imelda from beneath his eyebrows. She was a flighty bit and not too keen on the priests or the chapel but she'd never be agreeable to what Rayan had planned for her first grandchild. Well, the first we know about, he mused, his thoughts on Raphael's womanising.

He rose to his feet. "The wife will be wondering what's' takin' me so long. She can be jealous when she takes it into her head," he said jovially to cover up his confusion.

"Thanks again for bringing me home. Raphael wanted to stay with Isaac. I'll make a sandwich and take it up to bed with me," She groaned. "The bread bin's empty."

"Here, wait there; I have a few bits of shoppin' in the boot—got for the wife while I was in Derry," Mac offered.

He pushed the guns Raphael had transferred to his car to one side and picked up the shopping. "Fresh loaf o' pan bread and a pot o' homemade jam," he said coming back in and plonking them down on the table.

"Takes me back to when I was at home, with Norah," Imelda murmured uncorking the pot and dipping in a spoon. "How is my dear mother these days?" She asked licking the sticky spoon.

Seeing Imelda lick the jam off the spoon reminded Mac of when she'd brought the twins home. What a stir that had caused. "Eating red jam with a spoon is one of the dirty habits she's picked up living in Belfast," her mother had complained to his wife Mary.

He dragged his mind back to the present. "Will you be all right on your own?"

Imelda nodded. "I'm going straight to bed." Every bone in her body ached. The long international flight, the row with Raphael in the car and finding Isaac in such an inebriated state, had left her reeling with shock.

"If you need anything give me a shout. You sure now you'll be alright in the house by yourself?"

"I'm sure, Mac."

"You'd be very welcome and stay with the wife and me…"

Imelda shook her head. "I've been looking forward to getting into my own bed since I left Perth. Go home. Mary will be waiting for you. Tell her thanks for the bread and jam. I'll return it as soon as I get to the shop."

Mac straightened his flat cap and chose his next words with care. "Would you…like me to tell your mother you're back?"

Imelda shook her head emphatically.

"Well, if you're sure…"

Imelda listened to Mac smashing the gears as he tore out the gate.

Carrying her tea to bed, Imelda couldn't help smiling at the idea of Mac's wife being jealous of him. What woman would be interested in a wee roly poly balding man like Mac, she thought. "She'd need to be very interested in the folklore of Ireland and its politics," she mused.

She peered out at the black outline of Muckish. Lights flickered and bobbed against the rock face. It was late to be on the mountain. Probably some hill walkers, she thought. She hoped they got down safely.

Her thoughts turned to Dizzy. He must be off chasing foxes, she mused. He'd be back in the morning.

As she switched off the bedroom lights, her thoughts went back to the pub they had stopped to eat at. It was really to see that barmaid, Kate, she mused. She stilled remembering the old man Manus steel grip on her arm and his warning to keep her mouth shut. "Old buffoon," she scowled. It was probably illegal cigarettes or drink, she mused. "Cross-border smuggling racket," she murmured, settling into the comfort of the bed.

"Isaac is not throwing away a promising career on a woman as old as Rayan," she yawned. Pulling the bedcovers up to her chin she let her weary body sink into the mattress. And then, despite her troubled thoughts, sleep washed over her.

Mac slowed at the end of the lane leading to Imelda's mother's place. No love lost between mother and daughter, he mused. He sighed. There might have been some chance of reconciliation before Imelda's father took his heart attack and died but the mother blamed that on Imelda too, he mused.

That old bitch, Norah, has a lot to answer for, he thought. She'd never put out a hand to help Imelda bring up the boys. If anything, she put up as many obstacles as possible. "Waiting and hoping for a day just like the day," he growled. Aye, she'd delight in Imelda's boy's downfall, the hypocritical old witch, Mac mused.

He let his mind drift back to Imelda as a young mother; her long marmalade coloured hair streaming out behind her in the wind. Striding down the main street of the village, in a mini shirt showing off her shapely legs, pushing her babies in a big old-fashioned twin hooded pram she'd bought from an advertisement in the Donegal Democratic; like the ones he'd seen the posh nannies wheeling their charges in Hyde Park when he had been a navvy in London.

No hiding behind net curtains for Imelda, he thought. "Not a bit of it," he smirked. "Whatever her faults, she dug her heels in and got away from that holy joe of a mother of hers. Aye, made a good home for her boys," he mused. Och, there had been talk and whispers behind hands that she was no better than the woman who worked Foyle Street; selling her services to the highest bidder. His thoughts turn to the old Manse. Well, if she did it went into that old barn of a place. It was falling' to bits before she started to fix it up, he thought.

Taking the bend after the Bridge of Sorrows he noticed the flickering lights on the mountain. "Some poor soul is stranded on Muckish," he said out loud. He resisted the nudge of curiosity that prompted him to check it out. He still had the guns in the boot Raffi brought from the oul Manus. They had to be taken to the arms dump before he went home. Yet, some instinct told him to check it out. Swinging the car around he took the narrow bumpy road to the car park at the foot of the mountain.

An ambulance crew was setting up. "Somebody injured?" he asked a paramedic in a green luminous jacket.

The man held up his hand to silence him as he listened intently to a crackling radio message. "They need to come down a bit more before they try an airlift?" The paramedic frowned. "Tell them they'll need to be quick, weather boys at Mallenhead reporting the weather closing in."

Mac got back into the car and swung the car around so he could train the full beam on the mountain. Other cars arrived and did the same. Soon the car park was half full of locals offering what help they could.

"Who do they think it is?" Mac asked.

The paramedic humped his shoulders against the rising wind. "Not sure, but a guide taking up a party of climbers earlier in the day reckons he was talking to a woman who was acting a bit strange. She kept asking him about a magical waterfall. He said she seemed a bit…distracted and heavily pregnant…"

A chill started in the pit of Mac's stomach. He'd told Rayan all the oul stories he told all the visitors—about the flowing waters of the waterfall that rush and tumbled down Muckish having magical powers; that if you bathed in its waters as the sun was going down, it took away all your troubles. But surely, Rayan wouldn't go up Muckish in her condition, he thought.

Why not? A voice in his head railed at him. You and Raphael put Sue up to stealing her plane ticket. Maybe she decided to…end her bothers for good. Mac snapped off his thoughts; you're letting your imagination run away with you, he told himself. But he'd wait a while, just in case…

"What's happenin' now?" he asked moving to where two Garda stood talking.

The female Garda shrugged. "The Mountain Rescue team are still up there. They had to be dropped off. It was too windy for the Sligo Rescue helicopter to land. It's a woman. But they're having difficulties getting her down. A guide," she said nodding towards a cluster of climbers, "who was with that group earlier warned a woman about the danger of climbing the mountain given the weather warning. They think it's probably her."

She gave Mac a searching look. "Aren't you the bus driver who ferries the tourists back and forth across the border?"

Mac cursed silently. The last thing he needed was the Garda poking their nose into his business.

"Aye, that's me."

She faced full on with him. "Where were you earlier today? The guide mentions he had been waiting for you and you didn't turn up," she shot at him. "Did you have some other business to attend to?"

Mac stilled. Had he been spotted checking on the arms dump this morning? If he had that meant the guns would have to be moved again.

He feigned a deep sigh. "Another tour operator's bus broke down. Had to pick up and drop off a group to that cruise ship that's docked in Greencastle; didn't get been back in time to pick up the climbers." He gave her a sheepish grin. "Don't tell me I was clocked for speeding?"

Her eyes bore into him. "Just keeping tabs on all cross-border traffic," she said crisply.

"Aye? Sure, they'd be nothing going on now with the ceasefire in place in the North of Ireland," he said blandly.

"Safe home to you, Mr O Lochlainn. Take care where you're driving."

Mac felt an icy finger travel down his spine. "I'll do that, Garda," he smiled. "The wife will be wondering what's keeping me," he said moving off. "It's too risky to hide the stuff Raphael brought tonight," he muttered. "It'll have to stay in the boot."

Chapter Twenty-Seven

Rayan gagged as fingers deftly cleared her mouth and nose of the slimy bog algae she had been lying in. She screamed in agony as hands freed her trapped legs from the iron grip of the bog. She felt the hands probe her.

Bradley, the mountain team rescuer and paramedic drew in a shocked breath. The woman was in an advance state of pregnancy, maybe even labour and had lower limb injuries. This was going to be a difficult rescue, he thought. "We'll soon have you down the mountain and into hospital."

"I don't want to rescued," Rayan croaked out.

The paramedic stilled. Had she come up the mountain deliberately to…harm her…and her baby?

The wind tore at his waterproof. He shook himself like a wet dog. This wasn't the time to think about it. Getting her and the rescue team safely off the mountain was that he needed to concentrate on right now.

He patted her arm. "I'm Bradley, the guide you spoke to earlier. It's lucky I saw you, struggling up the mountain earlier," he said close to her face. "Drink this it'll help clear the bog water from your throat," he said holding a flask to her mouth. "We're going to put you on a stretcher now. We have to get you further down the mountain and then attempt an airlift. It's too windy for the Rescue helicopter to land on this side of Muckish."

Wind whipped around them as they started their descent. The paramedic swore as he misjudged his footing. "Move forward slowly." he warned as the stretcher bearers manoeuvred down the cliff face. "Be careful. The ground is littered with loose rocks and debris from the landslide and it's fucking slippery as an eel's belly," he cursed. There was a murmur of assent as another of the volunteer rescue team slipped on the rocky terrain.

Rayan slipped in and out of consciousness. Time stretched into a long jagged series of rolling movements and jerky stops and starts. She cried out as spasm of mind-blowing pain rolled over her so bad she thought her heart was going to burst out through her chest with its intensity.

"Nearly there just another mile and we'll have you down far enough to attempt an airlift," a voice said.

"Must be...a fucking Irish mile," Rayan panted as the pain receded.

There was a titter of laughter.

"There's your lift. We do it in style for our visitors to Donegal," someone joked. Above the black mountain peaks the inky starless sky was suddenly washed with lights disturbing the eerie stillness and showing the danger and devastation caused by the rock fall.

Hysteria gripped Rayan. "Mac Lochlainn a liar. The waterfall has no magical powers at all," she screamed out. "I still need to get to London..."

"London? What's taking you to the Big Smoke?"

"*Please!* I have to go. I have to go," Rayan cried out as another pain gripped her. She clawed at the restraints.

"Lie back," a voice said sharply, "unless you want us all to end up in a bog hole."

Pain, intense and violent gripped Rayan's belly as if it was intent in ripping her apart. She screamed out. "Stop! Please stop," she gasped.

The rolling motion of the stretcher steadied and slowed but didn't stop. "Hang in there, we need to get as far down the mountain as possible so that there's a better chance of a pick up," a voice soothed.

"She's in labour," Bradley said. "It's a miracle we found her. She was well off the usual paths. Why didn't you use the whistle I gave you? We might have found you sooner," he chided Rayan.

"Get stuffed, drongo," Rayan wheezed past the pain.

There was a titter of laughter. "That's you told," someone sniggered good-humouredly.

Rayan tugged at the covering. "Stop..."

"We can't stop, love," a different voice rebuked her. "The paths are blocked with the rock fall. We're had to take a longer route. You're doing well," he soothed.

The wind screamed around them like a banshee. Above it Rayan heard another sound: a high-pitched whooshing sound. Somewhere round the edges of her mind she knew what it was but its name kept floating just out of reach.

The steps of her rescuers slowed and then, on a terse command, stopped. Bradley's face loomed over her again. "We going to fasten you securely and winch you up to the helicopter."

Rayan shrieked in terror as she felt herself swing out over the mountain; felt the wind whip her about like a flag on a flagpole. Any second now she'd be smashed against the rock face like a rag doll.

Below her she could hear snatches of shouted instructions. Above her the whoosh, whoosh sound of the helicopter 'propellers drowned out her screams of agonising pain.'

Hands grabbed for her. "I have her," somebody yelled. "Breathe in, breathe in," a voice ordered pushing something over her face.

She felt the helicopter shudder and tilt precariously as it faced into the full force of the wind. Somewhere near, a man was talking urgently. "Permission requested to use the Heli-Pad," he kept repeating…

"I have to go…to London," Rayan tried to say past the oxygen mask. "It's my last chance—last chance," she sobbed.

Chapter Twenty-Eight

Her eyes sticking together with sleep, Imelda jerked upright.

The phone was ringing. She scrunched her eyes and tried to focus on the small luminous hands of her watch. Five o'clock in the morning! It had to be something urgent for someone to be ringing at this bloody hour, she thought, groping blindly for her clothes.

Too fatigued to search the drawers or fight the combination lock on her case the night before to get nightwear, she'd crawled into bed in her bra and pants and wrapped the bed clothes tightly around her. She pulled on the bottoms and the top she had worn for the journey home. Fumbling her feet into her shoes she reached the bottom of the stairs just as the phone stopped ringing.

The kitchen was cold as ice. She reset the timer gauge on the oil-fired range and listened hoping she'd hear Dizzy scratching to get in. Everything was silence, except the wind whispering through the bare trees. Turning, she went back to bed and crawled in fully clothed. Raphael's wounding words came back to her. She twisted in the bed. Tear swelled at the corners of her eyes. In the dark room she let them run unchecked. How could he say such things to her? She'd never forget the repugnant scrunched up ugly twist to his face when he hurled the accusations at her; if his intent was to cut her deep, he had succeeded. She wrapped her arms around her body as if to protect her from the deep hurt his words had caused her.

He must know I would have done *anything*—fought windmills to keep him and Isaac with me. Could he not see that?

The twins had been young when she'd broken into the abandoned Manse. Initially, to get away from her mother's constant barging and fault finding about the work the twins made for her in the house not to mention the shame, she said Imelda had brought on her and her father; she'd brought them for walks to the orchard where the grass was a tall as they were. They'd picked armful of wild bluebells and ate the wild blackberry and she'd let her imagination believe it was her and Ayeman's secret garden.

The house had been boarded up for years. She remembered it when the owners had posh parties there. She'd worked at a few of them as casual labour when she was doing her leaving cert.

It had started to rain heavy one day. Reluctant to go home she'd taken shelter under the trees. The twins thought it was great game to hold their faces up to the branches and let the drips from the sodden leaves fall on them. As she'd stood, shivering in the rain she'd noticed some of the rotting boards on the windows at the back of the house had been pulled off. She'd cupped her hand against a cracked pane. There was a pile of ash in the middle of the room where somebody had lit a fire.

She'd tugged at the sash window. It made a sucking sound and slid up enough for her to get her fingers under.

Her mother Norah had been contemptuous in her scorn that Imelda would even consider letting the twins live there. "They'd be better in Care and I'm making it my business to see that's where they'll go," she'd promised. "And I will be only too happy to sign you into St Columbus' mental hospital. It's where they put women like you years ago," she'd sneered. When she persisted in living in the old house, Norah reported her to the Garda and Children's Services, screeching her grandchildren were in physical and moral danger.

Imelda got out of bed and pulled on the big man's dressing gown from behind the door. One thing Raphael had said had been right. Every man she had every slept with had been carefully chosen so he could help her get the Manse renovated, modernised; a home where Raphael and Isaac could bring their friends. It had taken her years to fix up the old house. But little by little, room by room, by fair means or foul, she had done it.

Raphael must some memory of how dilapidated the place had been. The rusty brown water that spurted out from the kitchen taps; and clattering and clanged of the pipes. And how disgustingly brown the inside of the toilet bowl was.

A garda sergeant had arrived from Letterkenny in a squad car. Imelda's hands tightened on the lapels of the dressing gown as she, remembered. Quacking in her shoes, she'd faced him likes a tiger protecting her cubs. "My mother is more concerned about her reputation than about the twins' welfare," she'd cried.

The sergeant had stuck his thumb in the broad black straining belt of his uniform. He'd walked through every room in the house, wrinkling his nose at the smell of the neglect and decay. Imelda had trailed behind him, the twins holding tightly to her. When he'd finished his inspection, he'd stood in the middle of the orchard looking around.

"Nobody has lived here for years. I'll make it into a home for my boys…"

"I understand you're in a fix. Breaking and entering is a crime…"

"Would you rather the hillwalkers and weekend drinkers burn it down?" she said to him her knees shaking.

He'd rubbed his protruding belly that flopped over the band of his regulation uniform trousers. "Somebody living in the old place would save me having to dispatch a patrol car to keep it from being vandalised," he admitted. "But I have a job to do," he said heavily.

Scratching his ear and pursing his lips, he'd smiled at Raphael and Isaac. "Which one of your twins was born first?" he asked in a kinder tone.

"I was," four-year-old Isaac answered before Imelda got a chance to reply.

"As soon as you take my boys away, my mother is going to sign me into St Columbus."

Wet-eyed Imelda watched the night sky lighten outside the Manse window. Even now, years later she felt the tears flow down when she recalled how close the twins had come to ending up in Care.

The sergeant's eyes had hardened. He'd looked over her head. "My mother ended up in a place like that all because she gave birth to me and my twin sister. We were brought up separately in the Children's Homes."

He'd turned his uniform cap in his hands. "Would you be willing to be an unofficial temporary caretaker of the old place, at least until I find the time to track down the owner of the property?" he'd asked her.

Imelda remembered how her heart had leaped into her throat and how in the middle of the weed-choked orchard, waist-high in yellow gorse she had swung first one twin and then the other high in the air with pure joy, hardly able believe she could stay.

"Mind you don't make me regret it. I'm taking a big chance here," he'd warned, fixing his peaked cap on his thinning hair and heaving his belly in behind the wheel of the patrol car.

"But what if my mother comes with the social workers?" Imelda said, her happiness dimming at the thought.

"You leave that to me," he'd said gruffly as he gunned the engine and passed out through the broken-down gateposts.

Moving to the bedroom window, Imelda gazed out at the trees in the orchard. Devoid of their leaves their naked branches looked like long clutching fingers. She wished Dizzy was here, her tail thumping and her eyes followed her every movement.

Tightening the belt on the dressing gown she went downstairs and pulled back the bar on the door. Out in the yard a white frost speckled the top of the hen coop and sparkled like cut diamonds between the cobbled stone in the yard. As if the faint light spilling out from the open door had announced it was a new day, the rooster opened his throat and crowed loudly.

"Loud and proud, that's you, rooster," Imelda smiled as he strutted haughtily past her, his red cockscomb quivering. "I hope you have been keeping the hens happy in my absence?"

A movement near the corner of the house caught her eye. She hesitated. Was it a fox come to raid the chickens? Or someone prowling about? It was almost December. "Could be burglars doing their Christmas shopping," she murmured, her breath forming a nervous cloud in front of her mouth. She started back towards the lighted kitchen. A weak keening sound emanated from the shadow of the house. Imelda hesitated. She whistled softly. "Is that you, Dizzy?" There was a scraping noise and a faint sound like a dog's tail against frozen ground.

Picking up a hawthorn stick she used for walking on the mountain, Imelda moved in the direction of the sound. She raised the stout stick above her head as something crawled out of the shadows towards her.

"Oh Dizzy, it's you," she said with relief. "Oh my god, you're hurt," she cried, kneeling down beside the bleeding dog.

Chapter Twenty-Nine

Rayan's dazed eyes followed unseen the strip lighting of the hospital corridor lit up like a runway. Her hands gripped her abdomen. It felt hard to the touch and icy cold. She had a strong urge to go to the toilet. She gritted her teeth and cried out as another pain gripped her.

There was a flurry of activity and the squeak of rubber soled shoes on a polished surface. She screamed manically as she was transferred from the stretcher to a trolley. A nurse bent close to her and stroked her arm. "We going to cut away your clothing so the doctor you can examine you," she said.

"You are soaked to the skin from where you were laying half in and half out of the bog," the doctor said her plaited ponytail swinging over her shoulder as she examined Rayan.

Rayan cried out and tried to roll away.

"You and your baby are safe now." The nurse soothed, gently wiping at the dried blood on Rayan's face. "Lie as still as you can while doctor examines you."

"You have injuries to your legs and ankles. We'll not know the full extent until we get X-Rays. You have hypothermia. That's to be expected. You were on the mountain for quite a number of hours. But you are still shaking so that's a good sign," the doctor said. "It will pass as your body temperature rises. We'll get you a hot cup of tea. That will help warm you up; make you feel better."

Rayan gave an irritable moan. "Ireland's answer in every crisis."

The doctor ignored her barbed comment. "What were you doing up the mountain so far advanced in your pregnancy? Bradley, the paramedic mountain guide advised you about the impending storm? You put a lot of the rescue mountain team's lives in danger as well as your baby's and your own," the doctor commented, straightening up. "You were lucky to be found in this weather."

Despair crept over Rayan. It didn't seem like luck to her. She had welcomed the bog sucking at her, filling her mouth and ears with its slimy stagnant water. She had waited to die, not to be rescued; Rayan thought her whole body trembling. She closed her eyes against the question in the doctor's eyes. "I wanted to see the waterfall…before I went to England," she croaked out.

She heard the doctor draw in an irritable breath. She cast her eyes over the mound of Rayan's belly. "Are there twins in your family?"

Wearily, Rayan shook her head. Then her eyes flew open and she stared at the doctor. "Why are you asking me that?"

"I thought I detected two heartbeats."

Rayan felt shock reverberate through her. A hysterical laugh caught in her throat and turned into a sob. "That's why I look like an over-inflated water balloon," she whimpered a blog of spittle escaping from the corner of her mouth.

There was an exchange of glances between the doctor and the nurse. "You didn't think you might be having twins? When is your due date?" Rayan didn't answer. Due dates had not figured in her plan.

She detected the changed note in the doctor's voice. "I didn't know I was pregnant until recently," she said her tone mutinous.

"I need a sonogram to check the gestation period," the doctor said wearily turning to the nurse. "I think this patient is in early labour."

Wracking sobs shook Rayan's body. Despite the heat of the examination room, she felt the deathly grip of the mountain bog still on her. Her due date had been when she reached the waterfall. She hadn't planned on the rock fall and weight of her belly tipping her off the path before she reached it.

The springy heather had broken her fall but the bog water beneath it had suck at her dragging her deeper until her clothes were sodden and weighting down in thick black mulch and stagnant water green as the sea.

Her plan had been to drown in the pool of water below the waterfall Mac O Lochlainn so eloquently described. Instead, she'd fallen into the rocky mossy ground behind it. She'd have crawled to the swirling water pool is she could have but she couldn't move.

She hadn't struggled against the cloying bog. *It's better for everybody, this way*, she'd thought. Nathanial and Sienna would go on with their lives; Isaac could follow the career Imelda had mapped out for him and her parents would be free of her at last.

She'd lost consciousness and come around to the baby kicking. It kicked again and again, stronger, fiercer than the time before forcing her out of her sense of futility.

Above the rising wind; her cries had bounced around the rocks and echoing back to her. She'd screamed for the dog until her voice was just a whimper; clawed at the clumps of weeds and stumps of trees that bordered the waterfall. She could hear the water hurtling headlong down the mountain; feel the pull of the wind rising to a fierce gale.

She didn't want to die on the mountain and be fodder for the wild fowl. She wanted to go home; find out why her father had never allowed her mother to love her. She screamed out, reliving the terror.

"Stop it, Rayan," the doctor's voice ordered bringing her back to the present. "You're safe now," she said softening her tones, noting the abject trauma registered on Rayan's face. "Your babies are showing feeble signs of movement."

Rayan felt herself jerk. "It's still alive?"

Dr Blanid Breen looked into Rayan's eyes. It was best practice to always tell the patient the truth. "Yes. But your babies may not survive." Is that not what you wanted, she silently judged. Swiftly, she rebuked herself. Her job was to save lives, not pass judgement. Something compelled her to grasp Rayan's hand. "You are not alone anymore, Rayan, I'm here now," she said softly. "I will do my best for your babies…"

Chapter Thirty

Finding poor old Dizzy dying had been the final straw.
Imelda tried hard to concentrate on what Raphael telling her but her ears felt as if they were full of cotton wool. "What did you just say?"

Raphael rose from the side of her bed. "Ma, I said. Isaac is to go back into Falcarragh later to find out about Dizzy. The vet might know what happened to him. I have to go. I can't miss any more time study time."

"Where's Isaac?"

"He's down in the kitchen. He's still not sober from the feed of drink he had yesterday."

Isaac sat, his body hugging the arm of the sofa, his fingers shredding the frayed fringe of Dizzy's old tartan blanket. Raphael headed for the door then turned back. "No drinking. Right. You have that meet with Hilary Houston, Head of Studies in the morning."

Isaac's fingers quickened their twisting. "You hear me, Isaac. No drinking. If she finds out that it's me that's putting in both our work this semester, they'll chuck us both out."

"What does she want to see me about?"

Raphael stared at his twin. "Take a wild guess, bro. It's not to ask you how much vodka you're pouring down your gullet, is it? Look, they can't tell the difference in us...except for our grades. Your grades are down. So now, they think you are me." He didn't bother to say that since he was now attending all his lectures, his grades had improved.

"How will I get to the vets if you take Mum's car?"

Raphael glanced towards the stairs. "Don't tell Ma. Granny Norah is lending me her car."

"She doesn't speak to us. Norah crosses over to the other side of the street when she sees us coming. Won't she guess if the car is parked at the back door?"

234

"Tell her Mac O Lochlainn gave me a lift. I saw granny on the road. It was pissing down. I stopped and offered her a lift." He paused and grinned at his twin. "She's old now and short-sighted. It was only when she got in, cleaned her glasses and got a good look at me that she recognised who I was. Don't tell Ma! She'll flay me."

"Remember, Ma, no drink for Isaac," he said as Imelda came into the kitchen. "Somebody from Alcoholics Anonymous is coming to speak to him when he gets back to Derry."

"You are not an alcoholic," Imelda said appalled looking at Isaac. "You don't need to talk to some recovering *drunk*. You're not even twenty-one; too young to have a drink problem!"

Raphael glanced at her surreptitiously. She looked haggard, worn out. Not like a woman who had just spent time on holiday. He didn't want to have another row with her.

He turned to his twin. *Tell her, go on, tell her,* how your drunken binges have you on the verge of being thrown out of university, his stare said.

Isaac locked eyes with him. Tit-for-tat, brother, tit-for-tat, the look said. You tout on me and I'll tout on your involvement with the Derry paramilitaries.

Imelda looked from one to the other. Animosity sparked like electricity between them. She put a protective hand on Isaac. After Raphael's savage verbal attack on her yesterday, she didn't trust him not to start on his brother.

Jet-lag was making her head feel empty and her legs like lumps of lead. Her eyes were gritty from crying and her body felt as if she had been hill walking on Muckish.

Her heart ached for poor old daft Dizzy. She'd tried moving him but he was too heavy. She'd covered him as best she could. Nobody else had wanted the big lumbering dog so she'd taken him.

No doubt the local sergeant would be around soon to inform her he'd caused an accident or worse.

Sensing her distress, Raphael moved beside his mother folded her in his arms. "Dizzy knew you were home, Ma," he said softly. "He made it home to see you before he died. I am sorry about Dizzy and I'm sorry for all the things I said yesterday. Ma," he mumbled into her hair. "I had no business saying what I did. You did a good job bringing Isaac and me up on your own," he said his voice thickening.

Imelda shrugged him off. "You better get going." She knew her tone was cold and dismissive but she couldn't so easily forget the hurtful things he had accused her of.

Feeling rebuffed, Raphael turned to his twin. "Bring Dizzy back here. We'll bury him under the slabs where we used to have the swing. That way, the foxes won't dig him up," he said. He cast a look at Imelda, hoping she'd show some sign of forgiving him. When she didn't, he felt his heart harden. She'd said hurtful things too, he thought.

Imelda turned to Isaac. "Don't you have classes to go to?" Isaac shook his head and shrank back into the chair.

It's as if they have switched personalities, Imelda thought in confusion. Raphael was now the studious one.

The kitchen was silent after Raphael left. Isaac hunched into the end of the sofa. "I'll have a shower and see about the dog," he said.

Imelda looked at her son as she spooned tea into the pot. He had that look he always had when he was hiding something from her. "Go on, have your shower," she relented. "But I want a talk when you finish. I want to know how you and Rayan come to be…sleeping together." She gulped at the hot tea.

Isaac kept his head down and shredded the fringe on the dog's rug. "It just happened. She was here. I was here," he mumbled, his ears beginning to redden.

Imelda could feel a nerve starting to beat in her temple. "Tell me, Isaac, before Mac O Lochlainn or somebody else tells me."

Isaac felt as if his stomach was inhabited by a flock of trapped birds that were beating their wings against his insides. He needed a drink. "I'm glad you are home, Mum. What about a drink to celebrate your homecoming?"

"It's ten o'clock in the morning," Imelda said irritably trying not to breathe in the smell of his unwashed body and the smell of drink that wafted over her when he talked. Her heart felt as if it was torn in two. He looked nothing like the boy she had left eight short months before. Or bore no resemblance to the image she had of him suited and booted and working as a barrister in the High Court in Dublin or Belfast.

"Why did you have to pick *her*, Isaac?" Imelda said. "Why not a girl your own age…your own kind…" Shocked at her own words, Imelda's voice cracked. It was pretty close to what *her* mother had shouted to her twenty years before when his father Ayeman had come to Donegal looking for her.

"She was here," Isaac said so quietly that Imelda wasn't sure she had heard him. He shook his head from side to side. "Oh Mum, it just happened. You kept at me to find someone—"

"*But not a woman the same age as me,*" Imelda exploded.

"It just happened…"

"No, Isaac, it did not *just* happen. Rayan took advantage of your innocence—she knew you were a virgin," Imelda bawled. Shocked at the words she'd just uttered and their implication, she snapped her mouth shut. Hate for Rayan welled up in her. And guilt for having left Isaac in her care overwhelmed her.

"I almost wish my first instincts about you had been right," she quaked.

Isaac lifted his head. "You want me to be *gay*!"

"No! But at least you'd have been safe from Rayan," she said her voice barely audible.

"It just *happened*," Isaac repeated beginning to get riled up. "We got on well together. She liked me and I liked her." How could he find words to explain to his mother what being with Rayan had been like in the beginning? That he had been besotted with her, couldn't keep his hands off her. How did he tell his mother it had been *him* that lusted after Rayan; day dreaming of thrusting his penis deep inside her as she lay naked beneath him? His studies no longer held his attention. His only lucid thoughts had been to get back to the Manse and into bed with Rayan.

He jerked his thoughts back to the present and glanced at his mother's face mottled with rage against Rayan. He couldn't tell her any of that. It was easier to let her believe Rayan had taken advantage of his youth, his lack of experience. And she did, in a way, she did, he reasoned.

Unable to sit still, Imelda got up and starting to fling things from the worktops into the cupboards. "What about that girl?"

"What girl… Shawnee?"

"Were you and Rayan planning to take her to England for an abortion?"

Isaac turned shocked eyes on her. "No! Where did you get that idea?" Relief made Imelda's legs feel weak. At least that was something. Isaac wouldn't be hauled up before the Bench on charges.

She stopped what she was doing and sat down beside him on the sofa. "Tell me the truth, Isaac. Rayan…forced you…that first time, didn't she?" Her cheeks tinged pink with embarrassment, Imelda watched him closely. His shocked reaction convinced her she had been right. Rayan had taken unfair advantage of an innocent child in his own home. *Well, we'll see what the Guards have to say about that*, she thought grimly.

Isaac stared in shocked disbelief at her. This was turning into a nightmare. He wished now he'd waited and gone to London with Rayan. He shuddered. He'd be the talk of the place. And the story of the thrashing with the hairbrush was sure to come out.

"Why did you move out of the room you've shared with your brother since you were little?" Imelda shot at him.

"Rayan thought we were too old to be sharing bunk beds," he mumbled.

"I'll bet she did," Imelda said through gritted teeth. "I swap houses with that middle-aged dog-on-heat so she could look after you and Raphael while I had the first real holiday since you were born and what does she do? Takes full advantage of the situation, the sleazy bitch!"

"I'll go and see about Dizzy," Isaac stammered rising hastily to his feet.

His mother looked at him. "You can't go into Falcarragh looking like that. Take a shower, change your clothes. Take my bag and cases upstairs when you're going," she said nodding to the overnight case sticking out from under the kitchen table.

Isaac wondered if there was any duty-free drink in it.

Imelda gave him a feeble smile as he came back downstairs, showered and dressed in clean clothes. "I'm glad you didn't go on…holiday with *her*," she said. "You can't afford to be mixed up in…things that might be considered illegal," she said picking her words carefully. "There'll be plenty of time to see the sights of London when you graduate with honours."

Isaac pushed down his irritation. "Yeah, I'm studying hard," he lied.

"That's good, Isaac. You were always a top student." She hesitated. "Once Rayan comes back from London and goes back to Australia, things will go back to normal."

Isaac licked his lips. His throat felt as hot and dry as desert sand. He glanced surreptitiously at the kitchen clock. Were the hands even moving? He had to get a drink.

"Your career—your future is what is important. I haven't worked all these years to throw it away…on a summer fling." She stood for a minute scrutinising him. It was foolish of Raphael to say his twin should avoid drinking. Everybody can drink in moderation, she thought. Granted Isaac had really tied one on yesterday. But it was just exuberant first term back at uni. Once he settled to his studies and with this thing of him and Rayan behind him, the drinking to excess would stop. "I'll get my coat and come with you to see about the dog," she said.

The phone started to ring just as she pulled the door of the house behind her. Imelda hesitated.

"You should get that, Mum," Isaac said. "I can see to the dog."

"That's who it probably is—the vet phoning about Dizzy. Let it ring. We'll be there in ten minutes. Time enough to hear the bad news," Imelda sighed climbing into the driver's seat of the car.

Isaac swore under his breath. He'd have to find a way to get her off his back. Give her the slip when they got to the vets—say he was going to get petrol. The local garage sold alcohol. He'd get a bottle—if not vodka, then something—wine, anything as long as it cured his terrible thirst and stopped his hands shaking.

"Rayan never got the better of the rooster, then," he muttered as it strutted past the car. "When she came at the start, he didn't trust her near the hens."

Imelda's stiffened. "Wise old cockerel. Wish I'd had as good a sense of judging her," she muttered jamming the gearstick. "We wouldn't be in the mess we're in now."

A horn blasted behind them. Imelda checked her mirror. "It's Mac O Lochlainn. What does he want?"

"He probably wants to find out what time Raphael gets back," Isaac muttered. "Pull into the side of the road before he runs over us."

"Don't youse ever answer the phone in your house? Ah've been trying to get you since the early hours of this mornin'," Mac roared in the car window.

"We were at the vet's... Dizzy..."

But Mac O Lochlainn wasn't listening. "You better get yourself into Letterkenny hospital..."

Imelda's hand flew to her mouth and she emitted a cry. "Raphael—it's Raphael—he's had an accident. "The row from yesterday and her coldness to him this morning rolled over her in waves. What if he's dead or badly injured...? Then a thought struck her. "How did he have an accident if he's not driving? We have the car," she demanded.

"Mum, be quiet!" Isaac said sharply. Something in the expression on Mac's face told him it was bad news.

"Rayan fell into a bog hole on Muckish an' had to be airlifted to Letterkenny Hospital last night." Mac took off his flat cap and ran his hand distractedly over his balding head. "The mountain rescue team said the woman they plucked from the mountain was in a bad way. Broken bones and in danger o' losin' the babby," he panted. "You need to get up there right away, Isaac. Ah'll see your mother gets home," he said wrenching open the car door and helping Imelda out.

Imelda twisted free of his hand. "Isaac's not driving anywhere. He's been drinking…"

A car coming on the opposite direction blew its horn imperiously. "Go on to fuck wi' you," Mac roared at the driver stepping back on to the grass verge and waving the car around the parked busload of passengers.

Isaac looked at him in bewilderment. "Rayan's away to England."

Mac shook his head doggedly. "She didn't get away. The tickets got lost."

"She's away to England. I know because I got the tickets back from Sue and stuffed them in her bag…" Isaac stopped. Cold sweat broke out all over him. There had been a handbag on a kitchen chair but he had assumed it was his mother's. And the case he had taken upstairs hadn't been Imelda's. It had been Rayan's. He had searched it looking for drink. It hadn't dawned on him to wonder why she hadn't taken it if she'd gone to England.

"Get away wi' ye, man! You should be there to see your child born. It'll likely not live long," Mac said mournfully.

Imelda felt the ground tilt before it rushed up to meet her.

Chapter Thirty-One

"Take a seat. I'll get someone to see you."

Isaac's guts were in bits. Every nerve in his body screamed at him to tear out of the hospital and into the nearest pub. Mac had spilled his guts to Imelda about Rayan's attempt to have an abortion and his and Raphael's part in preventing her getting it.

She demanded he apologise to Shawnee, his summer girlfriend, for two-timing her with Rayan. He felt the bile rise in his throat. It wasn't that his mother was affronted for Shawnee; it was so her father would still consider him as a possible candidate for a leg up the career ladder.

"It's for your own good," Imelda berated him. "Shawnee's father has *contacts*. All Rayan will do is name you as the father so she can get Irish passports for her babies."

He was brought out of his reverie as a dark-haired middle-aged nurse with a purposeful stride entered the room. "I'm Sister Hampton," she said. "You're here to see about Miss Ritchie? Are you relatives of the patient?" She smiled. Isaac noticed the smile didn't reach her eyes as she scrutinised both of them.

Mac O Lochlainn coughed nervously and nodded at Isaac. "Well, he is…maybe…or maybe not, as the case may be," he admitted his neck beginning to redden. "You see, nurse, Rayan… Miss Ritchie…is…was renting Isaac's mother's house at the foot of Muckish…" He jabbed Isaac with his elbow. "Tell the nurse the way of it, young fella," he ordered.

Isaac gave him a mutinous look but didn't speak.

"Anyway, it's…about the babbies she expecting," Mac went on, "he wants to know if he's the father or not, you see."

Alice Hampton snapped her gaze from the older man to the glowering youth. She'd put the older man in his sixties and the young man in his late teen or early twenties. "Are *you* the father?" she asked crisply.

Under the nurse's searching gaze, Isaac's insides curled like the dead leaves under the bushes along the side of the road. How was he supposed to know if he was the father or not? Rayan had said he was. But it could just as easily be Raphael.

His mother and Shawnee's father, the judge, had warned him to admit to nothing. "Play down the affair with Rayan," his mother urged him. "You have your whole life in front of you. Don't throw it away like I did…" Imelda had stopped when she'd seen the look on her son's face. "No, I don't mean… I have you and Raphael. I love you—wouldn't be without you. But it cost me my chance to have what you are about to throw away…if you're not careful," she finished.

She had gone to the university and 'explained' the situation. Whatever yarn she had spun had been enough to get him reinstated on his law course. He cursed inwardly. He didn't want to be a solicitor, barrister or judge. His apology had gotten him back with Shawnee. He felt his groin tingle. He smirked. Rayan had been a good teacher. And he had learned well. Shawnee was impressed by his artful lovemaking.

But she's not going to be impressed for long if you turn out to be the father of twins, his inner voice sneered. What way did her daddy put it? "My daughter is not going to mother offspring from some bush woman from the outback."

"You think you *might* be the father?" Sister Hampton repeated emphasising her words. He seemed to have a smirk on his face, she thought. Was he even listening to what she was asking him? It was obvious he was only here because the older man had made him come.

She held fast to her patience. They were short-staffed and it had been a long day. All she wanted was to go home, get in the bath, swill down a glass of wine and go to bed. She cursed the young trainee nurse who had shown this pair into her office. Her feet ached and her brain felt frazzled.

She'd had her fill of this bloody Australian woman and her problems. Now, it appeared an Aussie ex-partner had arrived asking to see Rayan and the bold *Miss* Ritchie was refusing to see him. Christ, nothing. Not even a visitor—except the dolled-up beauty therapist from the hotel Spa—in the three weeks Rayan had been in the hospital and now the boyfriends were coming out of the woodwork, she fumed.

She scrutinised Isaac. He was very young. Rayan Ritchie was forty if she was a day. She shrugged mentally. Some younger men like older women, she thought. "Are you Miss Ritchie's boyfriend?" she asked.

Isaac shook her head emphatically. "No. I am not."

"Do you want to be the father?"

Isaac shook his head.

"Then what is your interest in her pregnancy?" she asked coldly. Jesus! We get all kinds of weirdoes in this bloody place, she thought. It's all that newspaper and radio coverage Rayan got about surviving her fall on the mountain.

"I *was* her boyfriend for a…short time but my new girlfriend wants to know if I'm the father…before she'll get serious…about me," he finished lamely.

Alice Hampton threw her pen on the writing pad in front of her. "So you could be the father?"

"Or it could be my brother," Isaac blurted out.

Mac O Lochlainn swore to himself and made the sign of the cross on his chest.

Alice Hampton ears pricked. What did he just say? I could be the father. Or it could be my brother. What was going on? She thinned her lips. It was no wonder *Miss Ritchie* didn't want to keep her babies. Or see her ex-boyfriend of six years. She's been playing away from home, literally, and now she has no idea who the father of her children is she thought in disgust. She wondered how old this guy's brother was and was the older man also involved sexually with Rayan?

"Your brother…*he* was also Miss Ritchie's boyfriend at the same time as you?"

"In a roundabout way," Isaac said feeling like a deer caught in headlights.

For a fleeting moment Sister Hampton wondered if these two were a couple of cowboy schemers—hoping to cash in on the media coverage, money and gifts that had been pouring in from all over the country in what the papers were calling a 'miraculous' survival on Muckish.

"Did you know she was pregnant?"

Isaac licked his lips not sure how much to disclose. He nodded. "But you see… I didn't expect her to have it." Mac gave Isaac a warning jab with his elbow to say no more.

The nurse drew the writing pad towards her. It was obvious something underhand was going on between these two, the brother and *Miss Ritchie*. "Why was your heavily pregnant ex-girlfriend climbing alone on Muckish?" she shot at Isaac. "It's hardly the place to be with a storm forecasted from Mallenhead Lighthouse Station." She turned the pages of notes in front of her. "And it appears a local hill walking guide *did* warn her it wasn't a day for inexperienced walkers to be on the mountain."

Isaac humped his back and let his arms dangle between his knees. He could feel his gut heaving. He threw a killer sideways look at Mac. If him and Raphael and Sue had minded their own fucking business, he thought, Rayan would be back from London now and I wouldn't be sitting here being grilled by this poker-faced bitch of a nurse, he thought savagely.

"How should I know what she was doing on Muckish? She had an appointment to go to Eng—"

Mac jabbed Isaac with his elbow. Enough said, his eyes warned.

Sister Hampton raised her eyebrows. "Where was she planning to go?"

Isaac licked his lips. "London—for a holiday. She missed her flight," he stammered out.

The hairs on the back of the nurse's neck stood up. So that was the story. She shivered. Rayan had missed her flight and presumably, her appointment for a late termination. She pretended to read her notes as she gathered her composure.

"Rayan is Australian?"

Isaac nodded.

"Does she have any relatives in Ireland we should contact?"

Isaac shook his head. "I've only known her since she did a year's house swap with my Mum," he said evasively.

"When was that?"

Isaac shuffled his feet, looked up at the ceiling and then down at the floor. Fuck! It was worse than being questioned by the Royal Ulster Constabulary and the Brits, when he crossed the border checkpoint between Donegal and Derry and they mistook him for Raphael!

"I don't know, do I?" He said belligerently. "March, April—she was here for Mother's Day," he said, remembering him and Raphael had bought her a parka as a present. He sat glaring at Mac.

Mac shrugged and crossed his arms across his barrel chest. Don't blame me. Blame your Ma. It was her idea we come here, his exasperated sigh said. He wouldn't have come either except Imelda had hinted she'd tell the wife his part in it if he didn't come with Isaac to try and find out what the hospital knew.

The nurse threw them both a baleful look. It was like talking to a delinquent schoolboy and his lying grandfather in the headmaster's office. Swiftly, she calculated when Rayan had become pregnant. Without the exact date of her last period, it was a best guess sometime in May.

"She tricked me. I was only trying to help her…"

The nurse's head snapped up. "Who tricked you? Miss Ritchie?"

"He's not the father," Mac O Lochlainn put in hastily, visions of them both being arrested if Isaac blurted out about arranging to take a woman to England for a termination. "We've taken up enough o' your busy time, nurse," he blustered.

"Rayan tricked you? What do you mean? And how were you going to help her?" Nurse Hampton said ignoring Mac's insistent input.

"What he means is she's trying to trick him into naming him as father…so she can apply for Irish passports," Mac blundered on.

"She's older than me….my first girlfriend," Isaac said speaking over the top of Mac.

The nurse looked at him in astonishment. "Miss Ritchie is your first girlfriend?" She wondered with his little boy petulant look did he have problems deciding his preferred gender partner. He certainly seemed too old to be having a first girlfriend—especially one twice his age.

"She knew things," Isaac blurted out sensing her interest.

Sister Hampton raised her eyebrows. "She didn't know that much did she? No pre-natal scan or doctor's visits. As far as I can gather, she made no effort to help these babies to survive in the womb. Was she…unhappy about being pregnant," she asked perceptively. "Is that why she climbed the mountain…?"

Visibly shaken, Isaac stumbled to his feet. "You can't blame me if she thought about drowning herself in a bog hole on the mountain. It was Raphael who took her up the mountain. I only went to the doctor…so she could get the name of—"

"Sorry for takin' up your time, nurse," Mac blustered leaping to his feet. "His mother thought…. it'll keep 'til the babies are born."

Sister Hampton felt a sickening realisation creep over her. Rayan Ritchie hadn't planned for her babies to be born. She rubbed her throbbing temple. The unborn babies were underweight and underdeveloped. She obviously had been starving herself to hide her condition. Or possibly in the hope of causing a miscarriage, she mused.

She checked Rayan's injuries from her fall on the mountain. Both her ankles bones had been shattered. And she had fractures in her right leg. If she needed further surgery, giving birth with casts on would be problematic, especially with twins.

She stilled. But what if what she now suspected was true and what Isaac, the young boyfriend, had hinted? She had arranged to go to England for a termination? And failing to get it became suicidal and in desperation set out to end her life and her babies' lives? Would she try it again before the babies were born?

She could hear the two men arguing outside in the corridor; "Couldn't keep your mouth shut, could ye, young fella. Ye're about as useless as an ashtray on a motorbike, so ye are." She heard the gravelly voice of the older man say in a derogatory tone. She'd get no help from that quarter, she thought as their voices faded and died away.

Her tired mind struggled with what was the best course of action to take. They could put Rayan on suicide watch. But they simply didn't have the staff.

She rubbed at her temple. "A fine mess this is going to turn out to be," she muttered, reaching for the phone. "The media will have a field day when they find out the woman they have taken to their hearts as a survival was planning to commit suicide. Not only was she planning to end her own life but also the life of her unborn twins!"

She checked the proposed birth date—14th February—Valentine's Day, six weeks from now.

Will they even see their birth date? she wondered as she waited for the hospital social worker to pick up.

Chapter Thirty-Two

Stamping the snow off her boots, Sue made her way into the hospital foyer taking care the elaborate bouquet of Christmas roses cradled in her arms didn't get their heads snapped off in the heavy doors.

A group of school children their faces shining with exuberance, their voices soaring as they clustered around the floor to ceiling Christmas tree were lustily singing *Mary Boy Child*. Sue's thoughts flew to the following Christmas. This time next year the babies would be old enough to take to Santa's Grotto. Old enough to visit baby Jesus in his crib in the Cathedral. She might even bring them here to see the lights on the tree change colour making the baubles and golden streamers shine and sparkle. She hugged the thought to herself. It would be wonderful. Her dreams come true.

Her thoughts sobered as she waited for the lifts. First she had to get Rayan through the remaining weeks of her pregnancy.

She felt sure Rayan would be in a good mood today seeing she was getting the cast off her leg. She'd still have to wear the ankle support boots for another while but at least she can hobble about, Sue thought. She hoped being mobile again would improve Rayan's black mood. The pregnant women who came to the Spa seemed to glow. Rayan glowered, she mused. Plastering a big smile on her face, she pushed open the door to Rayan's private room.

Propped against a mountain of snowy white pillows, her face sullen, Rayan greeted her with a frown.

"You got your cast off," Sue said brightly as Rayan scratched irritably at the scarred skin on her leg.

"You didn't tell me Nathanial was still here, in Ireland."

Sue gave a short laugh. "I didn't think you'd be interested." She still couldn't believe it. Rayan was expecting two babies—*twins!* And she had agreed to let her adopt both babies! It was like a miracle; an answer to her prayers. At least that had been the story until Nathanial had appeared on the scene.

Sue's mouth turned down. Vivian was less than OK with the idea of them adopting twins. She straightened her spine. She can bloody well suck it up and get used to the idea, she thought grimly as she arranged the roses in a crystal vase and placed them on the bedside locker. She let her gaze wander over the snow filled fields behind the hospital window. She'd win Vivian around. And if you don't, her inner voice asked. What will you do then?

Rayan gave her a dour look. "You could have told me."

"Has he been in to see you?" Sue asked with trepidation.

Rayan looked down at her huge protruding abdomen. She felt ugly and unattractive. No way was she going to let Nat see her like this. She thought how she had planned to be slim and glamorous when she'd see him again. "I told the nurses I didn't want to see him—not looking like this."

Sue's gut contracted. "Planning on staying…until after the birth, is he?" She wondered if she should tell Rayan that he was staying at the Manse with Imelda. Sue's lips curled. She was showing him off like a prize bull. It was disgusting to watch. She decided against it. "How are my…the babies doing today?" she asked.

Rayan scowled. "Kicking like Freemantle footies and keeping me awake at night," she grimaced. "I am so *bored* looking at these four walls and listening to the nurses telling me how lucky I am," she muttered.

Sue felt envy stab at her. What I would give to be carrying those babies inside me, she thought. I wouldn't be moaning about *anything*. I'd be thanking God my babies were alive and kicking after what they have been through.

She glanced surreptitiously at Rayan. What has she to complain about? she thought resentfully. Bored with the room, she fumed. It's me footing the bill for all this, she thought her eyes sweeping around the room.

"I'm glad Vivian put me on the Spa's private health insurance to give the babies the best medical care," Rayan said as if she had read Sue's mind. A shudder passed through her. "I'm terrified of giving birth. But when the bog swamp was sucking me down the baby—babies—kicked and kicked. They wanted to live." She gulped. "I knew then they were real—not just tissue and missed periods like I had been telling myself," she choked out. "They're determined to be born."

Sue watched with greedy eyes as Rayan, her eyes filling with tears, absently stroking the bump. "Now that you have your cast off, you will soon be able to come home—home to the flat."

A silence fell between them. "Vivian has agreed to me being there—until the babies come?"

"She will," Sue said resolutely.

Rayan pushed her legs over the edge of the bed and stood up holding onto the bedside. It felt strange to be upright after weeks of being immobile. Her thoughts went to Dr Breen. She had ordered complete bed rest until they had gotten the early contractions under control. She'd kept her promise and made sure the staff saw to anything Rayan needed. Rayan knew initially it was because they were watching her in case she'd harm herself. She smirked. She couldn't get to the toilet without a junior nurse or nurse's aide watching her pee.

She looked out at the snow laden sky and thought of Perth. It was summer there now. The temperature would be in the thirties. With only days to go to Christmas shops would be buzzing. Preparations would be underway to barbecue Christmas dinner. The beaches would be crowded with Sienna look-alikes sun worshippers and swimmers. Surfers would be riding the waves; ducking and diving into the waters of the Indian Ocean. School would be out and the 'schoolies' would be heading east with their parent to Paradise Island or Bondi Beach.

A great wave of homesickness washed over her. She desperately wanted to be there. She was tired of the harsh Irish winter weather "I wrote to my father and mother," she said turning to Sue.

Sue felt the hairs stand up on the back of her neck. Ever since Rayan had had the near-death experience on Muckish she had been different, softer, and less dogmatic. But surely she hadn't forgotten the way her parents had treated her, especially her father. She suspected Rayan's father had seen Rayan's birth as an intrusion in his lifestyle—and his wife's time and attention. Was Rayan hoping the birth of grandchildren would change their cold attitude towards her?

"Did they write back?"

Rayan opened the drawer of her locker and drew out an envelope and silently handed it to her. Inside was a white business-type postcard addressed to the hospital. She turned it over. There were no words of greeting, just a curt message. *Do not give away your own flesh and blood to strangers*, her father had written.

Sue's knees buckled under her and she slumped into a chair. Was Rayan telling her she was taking the babies back to Australia?

Chapter Thirty-Three

"Is that you, granny?" Raphael asked pointing to an old photograph.

Norah leaned over his shoulder. "It is," she said.

Raphael took the photo over to the window and pulled back the thick net curtain that blocked the light. "You looked a lot like Ma when you were young," he observed.

Norah snorted. "Indeed I did not! She favoured her father's side of the family. Cut from the same cloth, the pair of them."

Norah sank heavily on to an old flowered patterned ottoman heaving with blankets and sheets that hadn't been used in years. She cursed her forgetfulness. It had completely slipped her mind that the old photographs albums were hidden amongst all the stuff Raphael was helping her clear out.

"Who took all these? Ma definitely looks like you in this one," Raphael said holding it out for her to see.

"Come on, less looking at old photographs and more work," Norah said forcing a smile.

"Give these old sixties clothes a few more years and they'll be vintage in the new millennium, 21st century fashion," Raphael quipped, sneezing as the dust motes floated in the airless room.

A distant look came into his granny's eyes. "I put them away after your grandfather died…"

Raphael let her talk as he turned the pages of another old album. "Wow, look at Ma. She was a stunner even as a baby," he exclaimed. "There's a lot of Ma as she was growing up…"

A film of sweat gathered on Norah's upper lip. "Your granda was always taking photos of her…. They're only fit for the bonfire," she said tossing the photos aside.

"I like looking at old photos of the sixties and seventies, when Ma was young," Raphael protested retrieving the album. "Some great pictures here, Granny."

"Put it away—there's a good boy. It brings back too many bad memories."

Raphael looked enquiringly at her. "Bad memories?"

"It's a sin to be so conceited about your looks," Norah stated staring at a photograph her grandson was holding in his hand. "Yes indeed, that's your mother... She was barely thirteen there. Soon as she turned a teenager, she started tempting the men."

Raphael chuckled. I can see how that could happen, he thought. She was a stunner. His smile dropped when he saw his granny's face.

"I brought her up decent. It wasn't my fault she turned out to be a sinner."

Raphael laughed. "Granny, you take all that religious stuff too serious. Mum was a good looker—still is." Men still look at her, especially Nathanial, he thought.

The springs of the old bed squeaked under Norah's weight as she sat down beside him. "Imelda was always one for showing off her body," she said curling her lip at a picture of Imelda in a pair of shorts and halter top.

Raphael had to admit it give him a jolt to see his mother dressed like that. But it was the mad sixties, he reminded himself. He wanted to make a joke of it and say don't hide your light under a bush. But the closed look on Norah's face warned him to keep his flippant remarks to himself.

"Her father gave in to her every whim," Norah said staring at the image of her daughter's youthful face and figure. "Never saw the badness in her like I did. Swimming in the reservoir—no swimming pools then; skinny dipping the young ones called it." A look clouded Norah's eyes. She stared across the room into the falling shadows. "I went out to the hedge, and cut a good strong sapling. I had to force her father to take the stick in his hand and chastise her—do his moral duty like any good Christian father would."

A shiver crawled down Raphael spine. His granny's tight-lipped mouth was unnerving.

"Did he beat her?"

Norah rose from the bed and smoothed down her apron. She staggered as she crossed to the room door. "He never beat her. It wasn't his way; but he did that time," she muttered a triumphant note in her voice. "He finally saw her for what she was," Norah murmured, looking unseen at the wrinkled skin on her hand as it rested on the doorknob.

Raphael couldn't believe what he was hearing. "She was just a young girl. What harm was she doing?"

"She did plenty of harm. Men, aye, and young boys were attracted to her like flies to jam. She knew what she was doing, alright. I saw it in her, plain as day. She was at the devil's work. Aye, it was always Imelda this and Imelda that—boasting about how well she was doing at the school. Pride! She made her father commit the sin of pride. She deserved what she got," Norah said unrepentant.

"A mother is supposed to protect her child; not encourage it to be abused," Raphael spluttered out.

His words seemed to jerk Norah back to the room. "It was a chastisement—for her own good. Not that it did much good. Look how she ended up." Oh, how she had thrown that in her husband's face. She tightened her lips. Even in the face of the shame Imelda had brought on them, her father had dared to show affection for his daughter's illegitimate sons. Imelda still had first place in his life, she thought bitterly.

Raphael felt his temper rising. He had to get out of there before he said or did something he regretted. "This lot is ready for the bonfire," he said curtly gathering up bags of old clothes. "I'll get it started. Mac O Lochlainn is calling for me shortly."

He wasn't burning the photo albums. He was taking them home. He was certain Imelda's mother had never let her father show her any of the photographs.

Guilt settled like a lump of cement in his stomach. His mother had been telling the truth when she said she had moved them into the Manse to save them from her mother. What he would give to take back the words he'd flung at her, he thought as he watched the grey smoke from the bonfire curl upwards.

Mac O Lochlainn slammed his hand down hard on the bus horn and kept it there. "What the feck is keepin' that young fella. I'm sittin' here like an eejit for the past ten minutes," he muttered as he lit up another cigarette.

Norah opened the kitchen window and shouted something. Mac ignored her. I'm not in the mood for her oul prattle today, he thought.

Norah pulled her cardigan across her chest and hurried towards the bus. "What's keepin' him?" Mac asked.

"He's burning stuff out the back."

He looked away from Norah's steady gaze. He always got the feeling Norah's eyes saw more than he wanted them to see. "How are things in the North?" she asked.

Mac tossed the cigarette butt out of the open window. "Wonderful what a bit of a ceasefire can do. Mind you, am not sure for how much longer it will last," he commented.

Norah gave him a look. "It'll last. If folks let it be," she said succulently.

"He'll soon be puttin' on the gown and the oul mortar board. That'll be a proud day for you all," Mac said changing the subject. A frisson of guilt jabbed at his stomach. Manus at the "Top of the Hill" wanted to see Raphael. If things went arse up at the meeting, it might be a wooden overcoat the lad would be wearing rather than a graduation cloak.

"Graduation?" Norah shook her head. "Not that one in there," she said decisively jerking her head towards the house, "never was much of a scholar. That was all Imelda's doing." She snorted. "Now, the other one, Isaac…. pity, he couldn't keep his zip closed on his trousers." She sniffed. "I hear the Australian woman will soon be out of hospital." Mac nodded in a non-committal way.

"Jimmy, the bread man, tells me she's got the cast off her leg and she going to live with that pair from the hotel 'til the birth. Is there any truth in that?"

"Could be true alright."

Norah pursed her lips. "Don't know what Holy Ireland is coming to letting the likes of them pair live together. Say what you like about the North. People are burned out for less there. Imagine my great-grandchildren being exposed to the carry on them pair would get up to." She leaned closer. "I heard the Australian woman is no better. It seems her and that Sue one have a thing going and the other one is jealous," Norah said making a snorting sound and crossing her arms across her chest.

Mac leaned his right arm, tanned to the elbow from driving with the window down, on the window ledge and willed Raphael to come soon.

"I suppose you heard she left word with the nurses that she doesn't want to see the Australian boyfriend—after him coming all this way to see her," Norah said indignantly.

Mac shook his head. He hadn't heard. He had kept well clear of the hospital and Imelda since the night the nurse had grilled him and Isaac about the parentage of the babies.

"Who's the father, Raphael or Isaac?" she shot at him.

Mac threw her a scathing look. "If any of your grandsons fathered them babies, it was Isaac. He was beddin' her every hand's turn, woman."

"It's all Imelda's fault," Norah said vehemently.

Mac stared hard at her. "Your daughter was away on the other side of the world!"

Norah folded her lips together. "She's an unmarried woman living alone in that big barn of a house. What kind of a moral example is that to set her sons?" She tightened her cardigan. "Not content with that, I hear she's throwing herself at that Australian gigolo."

Mac tried to keep the smirk off his face. He hadn't heard anyone called a gigolo in years.

Norah put her hand on the rail and stepped up the first two steps of the bus and leaned closer to Mac. "I hear when those poor wee innocent souls are born, they're going into care."

"Isn't t that what you want?"

Norah took a step back. *That's all you know, bigshot Mac O Lochlainn*, she sneered inwardly. It's the last thing I want. I want Raphael to look after them brats and me. I'm getting too old to be living alone. Hadn't she given him and his twin a home when their mother had landed with them in 1975? He owed it to her.

"Why don't you ask your daughter which of her sons is the culprit?" Mac said acidly.

Norah's face contorted. "I haven't spoken to Imelda in twenty years. I don't intend to start now."

She thinned her lips. If they turn out to be Isaac's brats, no way would Imelda let *him* wet nurse two babies and me, she thought.

"You're a god fearin' woman, aren't ye?" Mac said exasperated. "The church says to forgive?" Mac ground the gears, willing Raphael to come before he said something really offensive to this oul bat of a woman.

"Her behaviour sent her poor father to an early grave."

"Your husband died from a massive stroke. He'd angina for years. Isn't that why he wasn't able to run after the salmon poachers and the lads settin' the mountain alight?" he said as evenly as he could manage.

Mac recalled the look of awkwardness on Imelda's father's face when the locals commented on the twins' lovely Mediterranean skin colouring. He sighed.

The saving grace was that their swarthy skin and dark eyes colouring was just light enough to pass for the 'Spanish Irish' complexion. A throwback to the Spanish Armada, Mac mused.

"Imelda killed him." Norah's face had a determined set to it. It dawned on Mac that she had told this story for so long she believed it.

"He scrimped and saved—made me go without—so he could send her to *Queens University in Belfast*," Norah sneered. "And what did she go and do? Open her legs to a black man and expected me to welcome her half-caste sons with open arms," she spat. "*They're Imelda boys*," she said imitating her dead husband's voice. "Wouldn't have a word said against them."

Mac gunned the engine, anger mounting in him.

She let her voice dropped to a hoarse whisper as Raphael stepped out on to the gravelled drive and started towards them. "Raff...thinks of those babies as his. I'll help him rear them."

Mac looked incredulous. "Norah, you're too old to be bringing up babies. And Raffi...mightn't always be here..."

Norah's eyes narrowed. "You see that he does. You forget my husband was a sergeant in the Garda. One word is all it will take..."

Mac recoiled from the steely look in her eyes. "You're a mad oul bitch, Norah, you know that!"

"I know a lot more than you give me credit for. Raff and me...we're like that," she said holding up two fingers close together. "He tells me *things*..."

Mac's hand closed like a vice around Norah's arm. "You keep your trap shut. And them oul eyes of yours on your rosary beads. Pray for a happy death, in your own bed," he snarled.

Norah shook herself free. "I'm not afraid of the likes of you, Mac O Lochlainn," she spat at him.

Mac started the engine. "You should be, old woman, you should be," he said ominously.

Chapter Thirty-Four

"I'll drive. It's what I hired this heap of junk at Belfast International Airport for," Nathanial scowled as Imelda stepped out onto the icy backyard of the Manse. The wheels spun precariously as Nat smashed the gears. "Bloody rip-off this piece of tin. The heater's buggered now too," he growled fiddling with the knobs on the dashboard.

Imelda fixed her eyes on Muckish. Its snow-capped peaks looked like a picture postcard. An ache deep and sorrowful squeezed her heart. She could visualise Dizzy leaping from boulder to boulder as he raced through the rocks and bracken his brown dappled shaggy coat melting in with the grey sheen of the mountain terrain. They'd buried him in the foothills. He's free now to roam and chase the goats and mountain wild life, she thought.

An icy wind, with a promise of more snow whipped her legs "Get in before we freeze to death," Nathanial howled huddling into the fur lined sheepskin he'd bought in Letterkenny. Imelda stood for few seconds more soaking up the panoramic view before clambered in beside him. Her thoughts went to the twins. The boys' reaction to the dog's death had been very different. Suffering from a hangover and sulking from the bollocking she had given him after Mac emptied his belly about Rayan's planned trip to England, Isaac had distanced himself from burying the dog. Raphael had gently covered the big dog's head and face with his old tartan blanket before lowering him into the bog hole. "The house is not the same without the big mutt," she murmured.

Nathanial eased the car on to the narrow country road. It had snowed every day since he had arrived in Ireland. And each night a bitter frost fell below freezing point. He had never experienced anything like it before. The roads were like skating rinks. Snowdrifts banked both sides high enough to partly obscure the poles along the hedgerows that carried the electricity.

Field after fields of virgin white spread like a bride's wedding train; an artist's Christmas card work of art. "Christ, I'm snow blind," he growled. Taking one hand from the steering wheel, he rummaged in the glove compartment for his sunglasses. The car swerved on the icy road and ploughed into tracks made by a tractor. Nathanial swore and abandoned his search.

He breathed in relief as he edged out of the minor road and on to the main highway. Here, the wind had blown the snow into drifts that resembled sculptures. Long trailing fingers of icicles hung from the roofs and guttering of houses like expensive silver Christmas decorations. Here and there a scattering of grit lay in a haphazard fashion in the middle of the road tossed there by Donegal Council snow gritters. "Like using a sticking plaster to stem a flood," Nathanial muttered as the car skidded dangerously. "What did you say? You miss Rayan not being in the house?" Nat asked cagily. He'd gotten the impression Rayan and Imelda were arch enemies now.

"What? I was talking about Dizzy." Imelda clenched her gloved hands. "Rayan took him up the mountain. He got caught in that rock fall and had to be put down."

Nathanial whistled in shock. "Rayan is one lucky lady to survive—especially when she was in the family way." It gave him a spine-chilling feeling to think Rayan could be lying dead at the bottom of a ravine.

Imelda glared at him. "Your little *bitch Biscuit* is in the family way. How would you have felt if I'd let her out to play with the traffic in the highway outside your front door in Perth and she got run over and killed!"

"Yeah, I suppose," Nathanial admitted. He shifted in his seat. He'd reckoned it was the start of a new year—him and Rayan might get back together. He'd imagined the surprise on her face when she'd see him. His hands gripped the steering wheel. It had been him who had been surprised—shocked—to find his ex-partner who swore she'd *never* get pregnant was having twins! Would you have come running to Ireland if Sienna hadn't cast you off, his inner voice smirked. It still rankled that *she'd* dumped him. It had been good to show her off. She had been like a piece of new body art, arm candy, he mused. But it was like taking out a kid, he thought, pouting, huffing and tantrums. He gave a mental shrug. No worries, mate. She's not half the woman Rayan was in bed, he thought.

Imelda stared out at the fluffy blanket of white. It seemed incredible to think that this time last year she had been upbeat; planning her trip of a lifetime to Australia. Couldn't wait to get someone to life swap with her; had leaped at the chance of swapping with Rayan. That bitch! If she had only had taken time to, what her mother, Norah, called get the measure of her, she'd have never let her anywhere near her boys' or her home. Now she was going to make her a granny!

They took a right turn for the hospital and parked up. She looked sideways at Nathanial's taut profile. The holiday and the sex is well and truly dead and buried, she sighed. Admittedly, when she came home she had enjoyed flaunting her Aussie conquest—her real he-man oozing sex appeal.

"What will you do if Rayan still refuses to see you today again?" she asked keeping her eyes on her gloved hand on the door handle.

Nat retrieved the keys from the ignition. "I reckon my chances of seeing her are betta this time. Sister Hampton is putting a good word in for me," he said turning up the collar of his coat against the icy wind.

"What about the…babies? Have you thought anymore about taking them back to Perth when they're born?" She held her breath. If he did, she'd make sure his name as the father and not Isaac's was on their Irish passports.

Nathanial scowled. It was the question he kept asking himself. His gut tightened. How often had that skinny runt of a school boy had her? The thought gnawed at him, tortured him. Visions of Rayan naked writhing beneath that paltry face college kid consumed him. Rayan was *his*. He had shared her bed; put up with her jealous crap, her moods, damn it, for years! But would he want to father *her* kids?

"I'll meet you in the foyer after visiting time," Imelda said.

Nathanial nodded, his thoughts still on Rayan. He'd asked her, no, begged her, to have *his* kid? He had even tried to sabotaged her birth control, pretended to run out of condones in the vain hope once pregnant she'd go with it. Now, having travelled eleven thousand miles to tell her he wanted her, only her, no strings, no baby, here she was with not one but two kids in her belly! Momentarily, he recalled the violence that was part of their relationship. Yeah, but things would have been different this time, he reasoned.

He hunched his shoulders against the falling snowflakes and started for the main entrance to the hospital. He started as a snowball caught his square between the shoulders.

"At least somebody is enjoying the snowstorm," a man beside him chuckled as a group of youngsters ran past laughing and hurling snow at each other. "Ah to be that age again with nothing to bother ye," the man laughed. Nathanial grunted a response and headed for the lifts.

He passed the florists bright with festive blooms. He'd bring Rayan flowers. His hands stiff with cold, he fumbled out the Irish money. Shit! He'd never get used to this damn currency. "Forget it," he told the florist. Rayan's not a flower person anyway; he told himself as too impatient to wait for the lifts he took the stairs.

Imelda, seated behind a huge Santa Claus, watched Nathanial stride towards the stairs that led to the wards. He hadn't shaved since he'd come, she noted. His beard added to his rugged, masculine physique. She felt her nipples harden. Despite the anger that simmered like hot molten iron beneath her skin, Imelda felt her heartbeat quicken imagining the muscled sinews rippling beneath his clothes as he bounded up the stairs. Too late she realised Nathanial was looking down at her from the turn the corner of the first landing. Colour sufficed her face. Her affair with him ended for her the day she'd booked her ticket home.

Nathanial's eyes widened. There was no mistaking that look. Imelda was hot for him. She had been a real hot cougar when she was in Perth, he thought. It was ludicrous to think of Imelda as a granny. When he thought of their sexual encounters and how energetically she made love to him, he had trouble even thinking of her as Isaac and Raphael's mother.

He retraced is steps. "I was thinking," he said, "why don't we hang about? With this snowstorm, I haven't really had a chance to see your beautiful Donegal. You could show me the sights?"

Imelda's anger dissipated. It was his ex-partner's fault not his that she'd come home to this chaos. He had his own things to deal with. "It's been a while," she said almost coyly. She was owed at least one worry free night. The last weeks had been like being in a nightmare with your eyes open and your ears on full alert. The local gossips were chattering like the crows on the telegraph wires spreading the news far and wide that Isaac was going to be the father of twins and she was going to be a granny. She never thought she'd be grateful to Vivian but thank god Vivian had been short staffed and had needed her to work 24/7. It meant she was so drained when she got in at night she fell into bed wiped out.

You couldn't make up what was happening, she contemplated: First Isaac and the drink. Rayan, pregnant and hell bent on having an abortion; Raphael and his granny Norah, thick as thieves. What could you make of that? Norah couldn't stand the sight of Isaac and Raphael when they were growing up, she thought. Now she's coming over all maternal about *Rayan's twins*; knitting bonnets and bootees! What fragging planet is she living on! Imelda snorted. She startled. Nathanial was waiting on her answer.

"We could go and see the beautiful Nativity Crib in the Cathedral," she suggested.

Nathanial gave her a wry smile. "Forget the birth of Baby Jesus," he said tersely. "Why don't we stop off at a pub, have a few bourbons." He caught the familiar tang of her perfume and leaned in to her. "Afterwards, we could go home—listen to music—have an early night?" There it was an offer, plain as day. She hesitated. It was one thing dating Rayan's ex as a holiday fling but with Rayan ready to give birth to her grandchildren…

Imelda jutted out her chin. That bitch took my son's virginity. She owes me big time. Why shouldn't I take what is hers? She took what was mine, she thought. She smiled at Nathanial. "Yeah, OK—why not, sounds like a plan," she smiled.

She sipped her latte and gazed around the hospital coffee shop doubts crowding in on her. *Are you mad? Taking myself off to Australia, beginning of a new stage of my life? Yeah, right*, she mocked, vigorously stirring the hot creamy liquid. "The old one hasn't even ended yet," she muttered.

Raphael was planning to move in with her mother! Was it possible *she* had been wrong about her mother? Had she done wrong in keeping Isaac and Raphael from knowing their granny all these years? Imelda felt her body tremble with fury. Vehemently, she shook her head. "My mother is not to be trusted. It's not for the love of Raphael or the babies. She has some other plan in that manipulative, devious head of hers. Raphael might be fooled by his granny's talk of family. But I know better."

Imelda's hand shook so much the hot liquid sloshed against the rim of the cup. She smiled robotically as a woman glanced her way. She should go. Her muttering was beginning to draw attention. She gathered up her bag and headed for the ladies. She was going to have one last fling with Nathanial before Rayan forced her into granny mode.

Chapter Thirty-Five

"Nathaniel sure is a man who knows his way around woman's body," Imelda murmured her tongue licking the residue of the sweet tasting strawberry jam off her fingertips. She smiled stretching her hands above her head in yoga pose. It was the first morning she had woken with a smile on her face since she'd come back from Perth. They'd had a lovely meal in the Cuckoo's Inn followed by a bottle of prosecco by the fire in the front room of the Manse and a long night of lovemaking.

She looked around. Nathanael was enthralled with the oldie worldly style and 'vintage' furnishings of the Manse. "Like what you see in the old movies," he'd drawled putting on an upper crust British accent. "I love the old house and its buxom servant girl," he'd said pretending to leer at her as he held her captive within the circle of his arms. Thrusting her against the solid oak dining room table, he'd glided his hand up her thigh.

Her face sobered. Nathanial was on his way this morning to see Rayan at Sue and Vivian's staff accommodation flat in the grounds of the hotel. He had been absolutely livid with Rayan when she discharged herself from the hospital without seeing him. She had made him look a fool in front of the nursing staff.

Imelda had never seen him so het up. He had ranted on and on. He was getting away from the damn snow and icy roads; he was going back to Scarborough Beach, to the sunlit was over between them for sure this time. But when he'd calmed down, he had still wanted to see her.

Imelda shrugged. When he saw the size of her swollen belly, he'd realised she hadn't wasted much time jumping into another man's bed. A frisson of guilt stirred in her gut. That 'other man' had been her son. Did that make her, Imelda, responsible for Rayan's dilemma? "Rayan must be crazy to let a man like Nathanial slip through her hands, especially in her circumstances," she said reflectively. "Instead of pushing him away, she should be grabbing him with both hands and holding on like a drowning woman to a life raft."

Her loss is my gain, she mused. He was considering a trip to Europe—France and Germany—before he went back to Australia.

She stood for a minute looking at her reflection without really seeing it. She had decided to try and persuade Vivian to create a temporary spot for Nathanial as a Yoga/Pilates instructor at the Shingle Beach. It might fill bedrooms during the quiet months of January and February and would create a customer base for the spa, restaurant and hotel bar.

She had to admit her real reason was to keep Nathanial in Ireland until Rayan gave birth. That way he might take her and the twins back to Perth. And with a bit of luck she'd never see sight or sound of her or her babies again. And life for her and her boys could get on with their lives.

But somewhere deep inside running parallel with the guilt she felt at leaving Isaac to Rayan's wiles, anger smouldered at the bloody mess he had plunged them all into and was now more than willing to walk away and leave her and Rayan to deal with it. She shook off her worries. It was a bloody awful mess but she wasn't spoiling her happy mood by dwelling on it today, she resolved.

She heard male voices outside. Hurriedly she tightened the belt on the white raw satin dressing gown she had brought back from her holidays. It had cost the price of a fill of oil but she didn't care. It had been a special treat; a present to herself. She chortled softly wondering what the stuffy old rooster would think of it if she dared to collect the hen's eggs while wearing it. She held its silky fabric to her cheek. It wasn't going to of much practical use now that she was home. But it was perfect for her and Nathanial's little play fantasies.

The voices became more distinct. Her heart raced. It was her boys. Hastily she pulled on a duffle coat that was hanging on the back of a kitchen chairs to cover her near nakedness.

Raphael was first in the door. He's the new leader of the pack, she thought. "It's only us, Ma," he smiled pulling out a chair and slouching down at the table. Isaac came in slowly. He gave her a cautious smile. "Missed you," he murmured leaning in and giving her a kiss.

Imelda laughed. "What's all this? Missed me or missed my cooking?" she joked.

Isaac stomach rumbled as if on cue. "Any chance of a fry-up?" he asked opening the fridge. His face fell when he saw the empty shelves. Imelda wanted to giggle. Nathanial had a ferocious appetite. She'd need to go and do a full shopping.

"Why don't we go down to the Fleets Inn? They serve a full Irish breakfast all day long; my treat," Imelda offered. "I'll scoot up and change…won't be a tick…"

Isaac shook his head. "Can't do, Mum. I'm off the booze. I've been sober for twenty days."

Raphael leaped to his feet. "My name is Isaac and I'm an alcoholic," he intoned in a singsong voice as if he was at a Twelve Step meeting.

Imelda turned on him. "Don't mock. Addiction is nothing to make fun of." Then, remembering the terrible drunken state Isaac had been in the night she had arrived back from Perth, she offered up a silent word of thanksgiving for Isaac's sobriety. Twenty days since he'd had a drink? That was good, wasn't it? Not that I believe for a nanosecond he had a serious drink problem, she thought. It was all that stress and I wasn't here to help him through it. Her inner voice smirked. That's the point; if you hadn't been swanning around the beaches of Western Australia your son wouldn't be in the trouble he's in. And you always thought it would be his twin that brought bother to your door. Think again!

Isaac and Raphael laughed in unison at the stricken look on their mother's face. "It's a joke, Ma," Raphael said. "But Isaac could be alcoholic. He has addictive tendencies…"

"Don't be ridiculous," Imelda cut across him. "You and your brother share the same genes, for god sake; talk sense, Raphael. He's no more alcoholic than you are! There have never been any addicts in our family."

Raphael snapped his lips together and clamped down hard on what he was thinking. Your father was pretty fucking addicted to taking photographs of you, Ma, he was tempted to say. He glanced at his twin. He'd shown Isaac the plethora of photographs their grandfather had taken of their mother and voiced his concern.

Isaac had laughed. "Yeah, a happy snapper," he said. "Granda probably couldn't believe granny Norah had produced such a beautiful feisty daughter," he said dismissively. These days his twin was so bogged down in his own problems with study pressure, keeping sassy little Shawnee happy and trying to figure out his next move when Rayan gave birth, to concern himself about his camera-obsessed grandfather who was long dead, Raphael thought.

Imelda breathed deep with parental pride. I must have done something right, she thought looking at her sons. Clean shaven and sober, clad in good quality jeans and a nice chunky cream cable stitch Aran sweater, Isaac already had the cut of a successful man. She could see the influence of Shawnee's father on him already. She could imagine him vying with the best of them, confident, competent and handsome in his court robes…just as his father no doubt was doing in some other part of the world, she mused.

Isaac didn't know it but she had taken her courage in her hands and had a word with the judge. She wasn't about to let all her years of hard work and Isaac potential career go down the drain that easily.

She'd explained how Rayan, a mature woman on the rebound from a long-term relationship, had taken advantage of Isaac's naivety with women. He had understood. Isaac and Shawnee's relationship was stronger than ever. Isaac had even been invited to spend time at their Dublin residence. Imelda felt her chest puff up in gratification. Like sticking a pin in a balloon, the invitation had deflated the gossip mongrels tattling overnight.

But she had to get Isaac to drop this idea that he was alcoholic; that he couldn't trust himself to go into a pub. "It's great you're not drinking bottles of vodka anymore but surely you can go into a pub; have a glass of beer and something to eat…?"

Isaac hesitated. "I suppose… I will have to meet clients in places where they sell alcohol… If I monitored my drinking, I could do it."

"Good boy. I'll go and get dressed, then," Imelda said, rising.

Raphael rose too. "Ma, Isaac's AA sponsor advised him to avoid people, places and things that might lead to him going back on the drink."

His mother threw him a bemused look. In an army styled khaki bomber jacket and crumpled jeans, he looked every inch the student. "I know you mean well, Raphael, but your brother does not have a drink problem. He's been under a lot of stress… Now, I'm going upstairs to get dressed and we are going as a family to eat at the pub like we have done dozens of times before I went to Australia…"

Raphael's eyes fell on the red rooster storage pot sitting on the worktop. "I have an idea. It's years since Isaac and I cooked you breakfast. Remember how we used to do that when we were young. Go on. Get dressed. Isaac and I will cook you eggs Benedict on toast," he said playacting a wild chef look with a tea towel.

Imelda glanced at Isaac. "You're OK with that?"

Isaac nodded sulkily. "Yeah. It's one day at a time, Mum. We can go another day."

"It'll be like old times," Imelda laughed. "Hold on, not so fast you two. Who's going to clean the kitchen? I remember the mess you little chefs used to leave behind you," she chuckled heading for the stairs. It's good we're eating here, she thought hurrying into her jeans and sweater and her old comfort house shoes. It'll give me a chance to tell them Nathanial and I are together, at least for the time being. She shrugged. "That suits me fine," she said to her reflection in the dressing table mirror.

"Ready to dish up," Raphael called up to her.

Taking the pan, he skilfully slid a pancake of golden eggs and peas onto the three plates. "How are you both getting on with your project work?" she asked as she speared a piece of egg on the end of her fork.

Isaac gave a smug smile. "The uni has given me a month to resubmit some of my papers. I'm trying to improve my grades." He gave his twin a grateful glance. If it hadn't been for Raffi covering my assignment work, I wouldn't be there at all, he thought.

Imelda looked from one twin to the other. The bitter anonymity between them seemed to be gone. She glanced at Raphael. "Is everything all right between you and Norah? You seem a bit…flat."

Raphael pretended to chew his eggs. "You know your mother. She's a black widow, literally. Devours everybody that comes near her." He could feel his Adam's apple bobbing nervously. "I need to ask you something…about when you were growing up," he said looking into his mother's eyes. If she told him a lie, he'd know it.

Imelda wondered what was coming but she didn't break eye contact. "Ask me anything. What was it you wanted to know?" she said steeling herself for whatever rubbish her mother had filled his head with about her when she was a teenager. She smiled to cover her apprehension. "I was no angel when I was young—no wings on my back," she quipped.

"How did you ever live there?" Raphael asked. "She's a religious nutcase. I understand a lot of things now, Ma; why you left there and brought us to live here when it was a vermin-infested dump." Uttering the words Raphael wondered had his mother come to live in the Manse to get away from her mother and her father.

"Do you two remember your Granda Bobby?" Imelda asked as if she had read her son's mind. They both shook their heads. Imelda smiled. "He was a good man; a good father. He only ever lifted his hand to me once in his life…"

her voice trailed off. "I suppose your granny Norah told you about me and the local lads skinny dipping in the reservoir." She was thirteen. It was a hot summer; the sky blue as a sailor's suit. The boys were shoving and pushing each other around the water's edge. Soon they had stripped off to their boxers. Then the horse play began. In the tussle one boy's boxers came off. He jumped into the water to cover his nakedness. Soon all the boys had jumped in the water and were shouting the girls to come in...

"She told me," Raphael said.

Imelda focused on the distant point of Muckish she could see through the window. "We were only children—an innocent summer prank that got out of hand. Your granny was obsessed with sin. She turned it into something dirty." She remembered her mother was so uncomfortable with her daughter's budding figure she had bought Imelda a bra even though she had nothing worth to put in it.

She was the only girl there wearing a bra. As the boys shouted encouragement, she'd pulled her summer dress over her head revealing her new bra and pants. In her mind it was like the bikinis she saw models wearing in teenage magazines. A great cheer went up as she hit the water. She remembered the feeling of exhilaration as she swam about. It was only when she started to tread water that she realised her pants and bra were clinging to her, revealing her nipples and her thighs.

There had been a stunned silence as the boys she grew up with gaped open-mouthed at her body glistening in the sun. Their stares awoke something in her.

Imelda waited for her heart to stop jumping about in her chest. How do you look your sons in the eye and tell them you discover young the female form had power. It had been the catalyst for her sexual relationship with men.

There was silence in the kitchen. "It was the only time my father gave in to my mother and beat me. She stood there, watching..."

Raphael licked his lips uncertainly. His mother had looked so happy when they'd come in. Now there was a frown between her brows. He didn't want to steal away her happy mood but for his own peace of mind he had to know about the photographs.

He cleared his throat. "When I was clearing out the spare room at Norah's, I found albums full of photograph," he said. He scrutinised his mother's face. Her eyes didn't flicker away from his.

"Yes. Your grandfather was an amateur photographer. He was always snapping away. He had a dark room out the back where he developed black and white photos. I used to help him pin the negatives up to dry on the washing line he had strung around the room." Sadness filled Imelda's face. "I loved being in there with him; safe from Norah's preaching, nagging tongue. He took pictures of everything: St Patrick Day parades; class photos of the local school children, priests' ordinations, Garda passing out parades."

"There are albums and albums of photos of *you* from you were a baby until…adolescence."

Imelda raised her eyebrows in surprise. "I thought Norah had destroyed or burnt most of those? Every time she had a row with my father about me, she'd open the range in the kitchen and throw armfuls of them into the flames."

Raphael shifted uneasily. "Is that all it was…a hobby…a way of escaping from granny's tongue?"

"What did you think it was?" Sensing her son's unease, Imelda looked him straight in the eye. A smile played around the corners of her mouth as she thought of the quiet sergeant of the Guards who had been her father. "Norah's right about one thing, for sure. My father loved me. From the day I was born until they day he died, he loved me. Norah knew it. I knew it—never doubted it for a minute." She looked at Raphael. "He loved me as a father loves his daughter, nothing more. He stopped taking pictures of me as I grew into a teenager. He said I was growing into a woman and people might get the wrong idea."

Raphael thought of the picture of his mother in hot-pants and a halter top. It had been the one that gotten him worried. Imelda laughed when he told her. "I used to pretend I was a model and strike up a sassy pouting pose. I told you. I was no angel," she chuckled. "I'd love to see those photos. Do you think you could sneak them out past Norah?"

"She said they were only fit for the bonfire… But I didn't burn them. I have them in the student flat. I'll bring them the next time I'm coming."

"There must be photos of you and Isaac in the albums? Your Granda took loads of pictures of you; carried them about in his wallet and showed them off when you're your granny wasn't there," Imelda sighed. "I wish he had lived long enough to see you as you all grown up. He'd be very proud of both of you."

Imelda gave herself a shake. "Enough talk about me and my childhood. What brought all this on?"

"Finding the albums…"

"And no doubt you're fed up listening to your Granny Norah's religious claptrap, aren't you," she said perceptively. "You want to come home and live here again."

Raphael let out a sigh of relief. He knew his mother had been rattled when he'd gone to live in his granny's house. "I'd like to—at least when I'm helping old Mac on the tour bus if that alright with you, Ma?"

He saw the hesitation in his mother's eyes and knew her answer without any words being uttered. He guessed it was because Nathanial and she were sleeping together. He'd glimpsed the skimpy dressing gown under her old duffle coat.

"Hold on, hold on, what about me," Isaac bleated. "I need someplace quiet to study. It's party after party in the student flats. I'm moving back into my own room," he announced flatly.

Imelda put her fork down carefully on the table. Both twins knew that look. Imelda had something to say they weren't going to like.

A silence ensued. "While we're on the subject of wants and needs, I think you should know there is something I want and need too," Imelda said a steely edge creeping into her voice.

"You want Nathanial to live with you," Raphael stated.

"I need him here with me, for now, anyway."

Isaac stopped eating and gave her a stupefied stare. He had been relieved when Nathanial had turned up, keen to get back with Rayan. It was his get out of jail card as far as he was concerned. He glowered at Imelda. She could bloody well find another boyfriend. She always had in the past. "Mum, Nathanial can't be your live-in boyfriend. It was one thing having it off with him on the other side of the world where nobody knew you. *But not here, not in our home under our noses*," he shouted, his face contorted with rage. "What will people *think*? What will Shawnee's father *think*! He'll think you're a slapper. Just like Granny Norah and the locals thought all those years ago!" Isaac was so worked up he was breathless.

Imelda stared incredulously at this son of hers that had literally dropped her in the equivalent of cow mature; caused her to cut short her first real holiday in twenty year and was prepared to deny two innocent children the right to life just so he could avoid taking responsibility for his sexual behaviour. And here he was, the little shit, spoofing moralistic claptrap and telling *her* what she could and couldn't do! A potent swell of rage so strong it frightened her, build inside her.

"Shawnee's father can think what he likes. We're not a kick in the ass off a new millennium. Ireland will soon be in the 21st century like the rest of the big bad world."

Incensed, Isaac clenched his fists. He could see his chance of palming Rayan off on Nathanial fading. Well, it fucking wasn't going to happen, not if he could help it. He'd had a bellyful of his mother and her boyfriends. "We are your family, *me and Raphael*," he said hotly. "We come first. Not some tattooed wallaby that's a good lay!"

"Isaac, shut it," Raphael stormed at his brother.

Imelda stared at Isaac as if she was seeing him through new eyes. She listened to the whine in his voice. He sounded like an overgrown spoiled brat; *just like his father the day he arrived unexpectedly in Donegal.* The words bounced so arbitrarily into Imelda's mind, they staggered her. She felt as if someone had punched her in the gut. The glaring truth of the words sends her into a spin. Just as Ayeman had abandoned her, Isaac was abandoning Rayan. The similarities in character between Isaac and Ayeman were so obvious they were blinding her. Had she always known Isaac had the same selfish characteristics she had seen in Ayeman? She just hadn't wanted to recognise them.

Her mind twirled back two decades. Ayeman had skipped off to London when he had discovered she was pregnant with twins. She had followed him. He had taken her for tea at a posh hotel; driven her to the airport with false promises dripping from his tongue. She'd given him her home address. He had promised when the twins were born, he would come.

She'd written to him via London University and included a photo her father had taken of Isaac and Raphael. He hadn't answered any of her letters. Then, one day, he knocked on her mother's front door.

Imelda cringed. She'd literally thrown herself into his arms. He had been dumbfounded expecting the twins' skin tone to be darker. He'd stammered out it wasn't a good time for him to have family responsibilities, when he graduated…maybe. Then he'd scuttled back to the airport. She had never seen or heard from him again.

White-lipped with the consciousness that history was repeating itself, she leaned across to Isaac. "Aren't you forgetting something?"

Isaac stopped shouting and looked at her. "What? What am I forgetting, *Imelda*," he said in a mocking tone. "Go on, tell me? What am I forgetting? I haven't forgotten you deserted me—right in the middle of my studies—when I needed you most. Run away to the other side of the world. Didn't give a fuck how I'd manage…"

"Shut up, Isaac," Raphael barked forcing his twin back into his seat.

Isaac sank into the chair and snivelled. "You abandoned me. Granny Norah is right. You're a slapper and a bad mother," he bleated.

Like the mountain mist lifting its veil to give a clear view of the summit, Imelda saw that Isaac had always taken the easy options. He had chosen, planned even, to lose his virginity, not behind a pub or in a grassy knoll somewhere as no doubt his twin had, but in the comfort of his own bed, *her bed*, with a woman who would meet all his needs; a woman who would be both mother and lover to him.

Imelda felt the ire rise in her throat. She had handed him the opportunity on a plate; a woman, running away from a broken life, an empty house and all the comforts of home. She drew in a staggering breath. Isaac should add 'poor deluded blind fool' to all the other things he had called her.

Raphael reached Isaac before Imelda did. But he couldn't stop the blow that she smashed into his twin's mouth.

"I'll tell you what you have forgotten," Imelda panted as Raphael did his best to hold her off a shocked and bleeding Isaac. "You've conveniently forgotten you are going to be the father of *twins*. Twins! A family all of your own making, which you don't want to be responsible for. And god help me, I have encouraged you dodge your responsibility," Imelda said her voice wobbling.

"But I will do it no more. You don't want to be a solicitor, fine. Open a garden centre." Imelda looked down at him, her heart splintering into shards. "And here's something Granny Norah also says, since you're so fond of quoting her. You've made your bed. You lie in it. Drunk or sober, you lie in it. Get out of here before Nathanial comes back from seeing Rayan."

Chapter Thirty-Six

Nathanial clocked the figure-hugging elegant jacket displaying the name badge on the young receptionist. "Hi Shawnee," he smiled. "I'm here to see Rayan Ritchie." Placing his elbows on the highly polished white veined marble desk, he inclined his upper body towards her.

Shawnee busied herself at the computer. "I'll just check if she's—"

"She's expecting me," Nat said an impatient note creeping into his voice. He wanted this over and done with right now.

Shawnee picked up the phone. "I'll just let her know you are here. Who should I say…?"

"Nathanial."

Shawnee's eyes widened. Nathanial, Rayan's Australian ex-boyfriend! "If you go out the front entrance and turn right past the Night Club. The staff cottages are just before the stone steps that lead to the beach," she explained. "It's the one right at the end."

Nat loitered near the desk.

"Is there something else I can do for you?" she enquired politely giving him a wide smile that showed she didn't scrimp on her dental work.

"Your name—I know a girl in Perth with a similar sounding name," Nathanial said indicating hr name badge. Shawnee glanced down at her name tag. She'd heard the girls in the Spa say he was a real womaniser. She arched her eyebrows. "Your…. friend must have Irish blood in her."

Nat snorted. "Actually, she's a bit of a mongrel…"

Shawnee lifted her handbag as the real receptionist she stood in for from time to time came to take her place. "My name is a female version of Sean. I am called after my father," she said snootily, stepping around the desk.

Nathanial's mouth fell into a gape. "Geez, you have legs to die for," he blurted out before realising he had voiced his thoughts out loud.

"It's kind of you to say so, sir," Shawnee said in a syrupy voice starting off down a corridor to their right. "Follow me. I'll show you the shortcut to the cottages via the hotel," she said caustically. "Miss Ritchie is availing of the staff accommodation." Vivian wasn't likely to put up with Rayan invading her and Sue's privacy for much long, she thought. "Congratulations to you and Rayan on the soon-to-be happy event. And you didn't even know it was twins? Wow! That's something else..." She bit her tongue as she nearly said 'and at your age...'

Nathanial pursed his lips. "No history of twins on my family tree," he said tersely as they came out of the hotel into the slushy tarmac of a parking lot.

"No? Well, here we are. If you walk straight down this path, the cottages are on your left. Keep to the path and be careful not to walk into the sea. The tide is in," she joked.

Nathanial looked about him. "Beautiful scenery in Donegal; pity about the weather," he said breathing in the salty tang of the Atlantic. "I could be teaching you yoga on the beach if we had sunshine," he hooted watching the wind lash waves on to the beach behind the hotel.

Shawnee hunched her shoulders against the cold. "I prefer to spend my time on the tennis courts. You'll find Rayan in number five," she said.

"Thanks."

Nathanial's guts clenched. Now that he was here, he was afraid to face Rayan. What if she went for him when he told her it was over between them? He drew a breath deep into his lungs. Would she even listen when he told her she should have her brats adopted and go home? He had reached an agreement with Ben Watts. *He would* not to sue *for* wrongful arrest if the police dropped the charges of domestic violence against Rayan. She was free to, go home, make a fresh start. But she would have to attend anger management group therapy.

His courage deserting him he tried to think of some excuse to keep talking to the girl. "What are you doing...later?" he blurted out.

Shawnee scrutinised him. He was quite old—nearly as old as her dad, she guessed. He was kind of sexy with all those muscles and a designer stubble beard.

"You mean you'll be free after you see Rayan?"

Nathanial looked to where the grumbling grey sky met the horizon. "Free as a bird," he quipped watching the seagulls duck and dive into the foam in search of their lunch. "What about a drink in the bar?"

Shawnee pocketed her name tag and shook out her silky strawberry blond hair. Fishing car keys from her bag, she sashayed across to a low slung red soft hooded car. Nathanial whistled appreciatively. She doesn't run that on what she earns as a hotel receptionist, he mused. He nodded at the car. "Nice wheels."

Shawnee arranged her body against the gleaming paintwork. "Daddy bought it for me. He says I deserve it for being willing to help out at the hotel sometimes," she said with a girly twirl of a manicured hand.

"Your father owns the hotel?"

"Not quite—he has shares in the Shingle Beach Groups. He's a High Court Judge."

Nathanial was impressed. Class and money, a winning combo, he thought.

The scent of her perfume was storming his nostrils. He could see the thrust of her breasts straining against the buttons of her blouse.

Shawnee's phone trilled in her bag. She stiffened. "That will be my boyfriend. He's been ringing me *all* afternoon. He's had a war of words with his mother." A look of annoyance creased her pretty face as she checked the message. "I don't believe this! "She pouted. "He was supposed to meet me here to take me for a Chinese and a glass of champers at the rugby club in town. Now, he wants *me* to drive over to his mother's house and pick him up!"

Nat stepped back. She sounded exactly like Sienna—a drama queen. He backed off. He'd had his fill of wet-nursing child-babes. They were lovely to look at and delicious to hold but damn petty. He had come to see Rayan. He needed to get it over—get his ticket booked for going back to Australia.

"Is the offer for that drink still open?"

Nathanial looked at her in confusion. He couldn't very well say I've changed my mind. He cleared his throat and put a little more distance between them. "You should pick up your boyfriend. And I need to see Rayan," he stuttered, like an adolescent schoolboy.

Shawnee folded her legs into the car. "We haven't been properly introduced," she said cattily. "I'm Isaac's girlfriend, Shawnee," she pouted.

Nathanial had heard Imelda mention something about a girlfriend. "Yes. I was his summer tennis partner. He's becoming such a bore."

"Nice to have met you," Nathanial said. He'd probably need more than a few glasses of wine when Rayan had finished with him. He'd stop at the bottle shop and buy a bottle of whiskey. Make a night of it with Imelda, he thought as the c engine of Shawnee's car purred soft as a kitten as she drove off.

Rayan shrank back against the wall of the living area of the staff condo. No way was she letting Nathanial see her fat and frumpy.

She gritted her teeth. She knew Vivian's tricks. She had set up this meeting between her and Nat, hoping she'd get rid of her. In a way she couldn't blame Vivian. Sue had simply brought her home from the hospital set her up in the cottage and then informed Vivian Rayan was staying until after the births.

There were two bedrooms and a lounge rooms in the flat. Sue and Vivian had an apartment in Letterkenny but used the cottage for sleepovers and resting between shifts and when they were working on the late shift. Already, living in such close proximity to each other was creating more animosity between them. Rayan sighed thinking of the peace and tranquillity of the old Manse. No way was Imelda going to let her stay there. Sue let slip, Nathanial was staying there.

It was going to be a long six weeks until she had her caesarean section Doctor Breen had arranged for her. She wasn't letting Nathanial see her until after the births.

She shrank further back as she heard Nat call her name through the door. Her pulse quickened at the sound of his familiar voice filled her ears. The thumping on the door grew louder more forceful. Without the hospital staff to turn him away, she realised Nathanial was not giving up this time. Anxiety made her want to pee. She daren't chance crossing the hall to the bathroom. Why didn't he just go away! Come back when she had her figure back. She'd be the woman Nathanial remembered, not this shapeless bump.

She heard voices; and the familiar tap tapping of Sue's high heels on the frozen ground outside. Shit, she forgotten Sue would be—checking if she was OK. "She's more concerned about you two in there than she is about me," she whispered fiercely glaring at her huge abdomen.

Sue came bustling into the lounge with Nathanial at her heels. "You have a visitor," she said ungraciously. Rayan sat down abruptly, her need for the loo stronger than ever.

Nathanial's muscular physique seemed to fill the small lounge. She feasted her eyes on him. He looked as handsome as she remembered. There was something different about him, she thought wildly, anxiety making her breath come in little puffs. He had a beard! She liked it. It made him looked even more rugged than before. All of a sudden she felt overjoyed that he was here in the same room with her and simultaneously mortified that she looked such as mess.

She watched as he unbuttoned his fur-lined jacket and shook the sleety rain from his shoulders. She could see gloves sticking out from the pockets of the coat. *Bit of a change from his sleeveless figure-hugging vests and shorts that drive the beach babes' wild on Cottesloe beach*, she thought.

Nathanial felt his legs shake. All the things he had planned to say flew from his mind. He felt his eyes growing round in amazement. She was *enormous*! She was as round as a hot air balloon. Yet, there was something *magnificent* about her. Gone was the long lean rangy beanpole body; and in its place was a woman of quintessence. He sucked in his breath and searched around for an analogy. In a flowing colourful caftan robe with her hair in a wild free style, she reminded him of a large beautiful exotic bird he had once seen on a visit to a protected species sanctuary.

Speechless for a moment, his gaze fastened on her. Somewhere deep within him, a fire started to burn. Strange sensations washed over him as strong as the waves that pounded the shore outside the window. *He loved her. He loved her.* The knowledge made his knees knock together like clanging symbols. Thoughts of Imelda, Sienna and the many other women he had bedded since he'd left her faded. He knew now they had only they had only been stopgaps until he got back with Rayan. Words he didn't know he was going to say rose to his lips… "You look fa—"

"Fat, Frumpy," Rayan mumbled.

Nat swallowed past the lump in his throat. "I was going to say fabulously beautiful. Being pregnant suits you," he said in a rush.

Mortified, Rayan turned away and picked up a cushion in a vain attempt to hide her bump. "Welcome to Ireland. How are you enjoying the snow storm? I would have thought you'd be back in the summer heat of Perth or Sydney by now," she said, embarrassed at him seeing her protruding stomach and frizzy hair that stuck out from her head like a wild abundant prickly bush in need of pruning.

"I couldn't go back without seeing you," Nathanial said his heart doing somersaults. He had to stop himself from rushing across the space that separated them, taking her in his arms and kissing her.

"I've missed you, Rayan," he said shakily. "There wasn't one day when the sun set that I didn't think of you. Whether I was on Cottesloe Beach or Bondi Beach in Sydney, not a day passed that I didn't think of you." Tentatively, he took another step towards her. "How are you?" he asked his words coming out jerky and disjointed. "Imelda told me about your near-death experience on the mountain."

It suddenly occurred to him just how fragile and transient life was. He could have come to Donegal only to discover Rayan had been buried alive. He touched her shoulder. "I've missed you, babe. I'm so, so glad you're OK," he said hoarsely.

Rayan had visualised this meeting so many times in her mind but not with her huge protruding abdomen between them. Looking into his face she noticed the outline of the scar at his hairline where she'd hit him with the glass in a fit of jealous rage. "I'm sorry, Nat," she said her voice quivering on the edge of tears. She didn't know if she was saying sorry for the scar, for being pregnant or for running away to Ireland.

"Why didn't you tell me about the…babies?" Nat asked.

Rayan lifted her head and looked into his eyes. "I didn't want you or my parents to know anything about it. I planned…" she stopped. Should she tell him what she had planned? And what she'd been driven to in the end? What she had almost achieved? She decided she'd only tell him the censored version. "But I did write to my father and told him…" her voice trailed off. Nathanial guessed from the drop of her head what her father's response had been.

"He told me I shouldn't be giving away my own flesh and blood to strangers."

"But you weren't to bring shame to his door," Nathanial finished for her. "Your father is a hypocritical bastard," he said disparagingly. He couldn't see him showing off baby photos of his Irish illegitimate grandchildren to his facility cronies.

"I won't be taking them home with me. I've arranged a private adoption."

Sue marched into the room and thumped a tray down in front of Rayan. Nat noticed there was only one tea mug. Obviously, his presence wasn't welcomed. "I need to pee," Rayan said with obvious embarrassment…

A thought struck Nathanial as Sue elbowed him out of the way and helped Rayan to her feet. He glanced from one to the other and dismissed the idea. *No way.* Rayan is too hot to be in love with a *woman,* he mused. But it was clear from Sue's attitude that she believed she had some kind of claim on Rayan. "Why don't you leave that?" he said, nodding at the sandwich. "What about a short walk and then we can go and get something decent to eat."

"Won't Imelda be waiting for you?" Sue cut in before Rayan got a chance to answer. "I hear you and her might be going travelling," she said glaring at Nathanial. All she needed was him and Rayan getting all lovey-dovey and deciding to keep the babies. She glanced surreptitiously at Rayan. The rift between Rayan and her parent was no closer to being resolved. And that was the way she wanted it to stay until the adoption was legal and finalised.

Sue smiled with grim satisfaction when she saw Rayan's body stiffen at the mention of Imelda and Nathanial's plans.

Nathanial had no doubt Sue had been drip feeding Rayan all the gossip about him and Imelda. "Yeah, Imelda has said if I wanted, she'd show me around Dublin and the Lakes of Killarney," he countered angrily, conveniently forgetting he had talked about a short tour of Europe. He dismissed the thought. That was before. Things were different now.

He turned back to Rayan. "I wanted to come and surprise you for Christmas. *We* could have gone travelling. When you wouldn't see me, I thought of going home but now…" Quickly, he placed his hand over Rayan's where it rested on top of her belly. "I can wait."

The babies began to kick. Nathanial stared mesmerised at the strong inward force of the baby causing Rayan's belly to move. He felt the soft heat radiating off Rayan's skin; felt the movement of the babies beneath his hand. His heart contracted. *If only the babies she was carrying were his.*

He allowed the fantasy he had harboured for so long of being a father, of having a son, rise to the surface of his mind. He imagined showing the curvy woman who came to do yoga on the beach, pictures of his son. He visualised them flocking around him admiring the photos.

He snapped his mind back to the present. It was a fantasy, a dream. Rayan had already made plans to have the babies adopted. "Come on, Rayan," he said, helping her to her feet. "Let's go for a walk."

Rayan looked incredulously at him and then down to the bump.

"It's OK. We'll find a seat—a sheltered spot."

Sue snorted and waved her arm towards the window. "That's no Bondi Beach out there with golden sands dappled in sunshine. It's the tail end of a snowstorm piled up against the harbour wall."

Sue's attitude grated on Rayan's nerves. She turned to Nat. "Maybe a cosy dinner beside the fire in the hotel would be nice," she said smiling at him.

"You got a new tattoo," she smiled touching his skin where it was showing just above the neck of his shirt.

"I got it when I was working over east, in Sydney," Nathanial laughed and launched into a funny story about how he had come to get it.

A guest at the next table smiled in their direction at their obvious happiness. Then, he looked again as he recognised Rayan. Getting up, he crossed over to their table. "We meet again. Glad to see you looking so well. By the look of it, won't be long now to the happy event." He turned to Nathanial and stuck out his hand. "Welcome to Donegal. You'll be staying for the birth?"

Nathanial exchanged a look with Rayan. She shrugged. The man looked vaguely familiar.

Embarrassed, the man straightened. "I'm sorry. There I go again jumping in with both feet. I'm Bradley, one of the mountain guides. I'm the one that lent you the whistle and went up Muckish to help find you," he explained seeing the look of incomprehension on Rayan's face.

Blood rushed to Rayan's face. She hadn't recognised him. She hoped he wasn't about to give Nathaniel a blow-by-blow account of the mountain rescue. She remembered he liked to talk. Relieved, she saw he was preparing to leave. "I'll let you get on with your meal. I'm sure you have a lot to catch up on…especially the near fatality of your girlfriend and your baby on the mountain," he said starting to turn back to his own table.

"Twins."

"What?" the guide said turning back.

"Rayan is pregnant with twins," Nathaniel said, the words coming out in a rush accompanied by a sense of pride.

The guide chuckled. "Fair play to you, big fella," he said pumping Nathanial's hand. "When the happy event is over, come and find me in Paddy's Pub in Falcarragh—that's where all the hill walkers usually hang out," he said with a grin.

Giving them a cheery wave, he made his way to the cash desk. It was only as he was putting his change in his pocket that he remembered he'd heard the Australian boyfriend wasn't the father. "Pity," he murmured looking at them deep in conversation, "they look like a couple in love to me."

Chapter Thirty-Seven

"If you want Nathanial, you need to make your move before Rayan snatches him from under your nose," Sue said, glowering at Imelda. Imelda was seething inside but she wasn't about to let her work colleagues see it. Nathanial had dropped her faster than a hot brick and picked up Rayan again.

She breathed deeply fighting to maintain her outward appearance of nonchalance. The staff was having a great time sniggering and laughing at the latest turn of events. It's your own fault, her inner voice reminded her. Parading him around like a something you found in a Christmas cracker. Well, newsflash Imelda, Christmas, like the snowfall has passed. The winds of 1997 are blowing new changes.

"That's the question, isn't it? Do I want him?" Imelda said with a flippant toss of her head. She gave Sue an exaggerated wink. "Maybe I have bigger fish to fry," she said.

Sue wrinkled her nose. "You mean the old American guy who has booked into the hotel?"

Imelda pretended to flick a roll of notes. "After my stint on reception I've booked a full Brazilian bikini wax and a few sessions on the sunbeds to brush up the tan I got in Aussie," she smiled sashaying out of the staff room.

Out of sight of Sue's penetrating stare, her mask of carefree nonchalance fell away.

The American businessman was a red herring to fast-track Sue and the other's minds off her and Nathanial. "Like greyhounds on speed when it comes to gossip," she muttered heading for the hotel reception.

She trailed her finger down the booked appointments for the Spa. She sighed. Her client base had dwindled away while she was in Australia. The old discontentment and restlessness that helped spur her to take the year's sabbatical in the first place surfaced again. "As old Mac O Lochlainn would say," she muttered, she had neither chick nor child to hold her back now. She was free as the seagulls that swooped and dived on the seafront. She could go wherever she wanted.

With the twins gone the Manse felt more uninhabited than it had been the day in desperation had gathered an armful of sticks from beneath the trees in the weed choked orchard and lit a fire in the abandoned fireplaces. Taking umbrage the crows had left cawing loudly at being evicted. A bit like Isaac, she mused. He had left spewing bitter words of recrimination and threatening to quit his law course.

Imelda's shoulders sagged. She had failed spectacularly as a mother.

Buoyed by the arrogance of youth she was sure she would succeed where others had failed. She had boasted about her boys; set them on a pedestal above the local lads. She cringed with embarrassment realising how self-absorbed and egotistical she must have sounded. What have I to show for it? She asked herself. A house renovated within to an inch of its life that doesn't even belong to me. A son who was a potential college dropout; and another involved in a paramilitary organisation. Despite her best efforts, a tear rolled down her cheek.

"Trying to scare off whatever few customers we have on this bleak February day," Vivian's voice said at her elbow.

Imelda startled and slapped on her professional cheery faced look. Vivian had only taken her back part-time basis. "Sorry, short lapse—won't happen again," she apologised.

"I suppose you've heard the hotel including the Spa is ripe for a takeover," Vivian stated.

Imelda nodded.

A faint smile played around the corners of Vivian's mouth. "Be nice to our American guest. He seems interested in the takeover."

Imelda raised her eyebrows. "I'm always *nice* to our guests; especially the well-heeled males. I thought that was one of my character defects."

Vivian's cheeks tinged with pink. Despite her disparaging attitude towards Imelda, she was loath to admit it but she had a grudging respect for Imelda's tenacity and her ability to rise above the hits life hurled at her. She studied Imelda surreptitiously. Even now with her life and dreams in tatters, she's come out fighting, Vivian thought. She envied her strength of character.

They both turned as Rayan with Sue at her side waddled across the foyer in the direction of the restaurant. "Your advice didn't pan out, did it?" Imelda said thoughtlessly.

Vivian snapped her head around. "What do you mean?"

Imelda wished she could bite off her tongue. "I better get on with what I'm supposed to be doing," she said hurriedly.

Despite the cold of the day, Vivian began to sweat profusely. It was obvious Imelda knew about the advice she had given Isaac and Rayan on how to go about getting information on a termination. A hot flush crept up her face. Her heart began to pound. It was a criminal offence in the Republic of Ireland to provide information on abortion. She could be in big trouble. She gritted her teeth. She might have known lily-livered Isaac would spill his guts and try to shift the blame onto somebody else.

"What exactly did Isaac say? What *advice* did I give him?"

"It's okay," Imelda said hastily seeing the alarm on her boss' face. "It might have saved us all a load of trouble if it had worked out," she mumbled, backpedalling furiously. "You don't want to adopt Rayan's babies. I don't want to be a granny."

Vivian's body seem to lose stature. "I don't have much choice, do I? Sue moved Rayan into the flat without even consulting me. To all intents and purposes, the unborn babies are already living with us. Sue thinks of them as hers. It's all she can talk about," Vivian choked out.

She wrinkled her nose. The thought of smelly nappies and baby paraphernalia cluttering up their pristine apartment and taking over their lives was giving her nightmares.

"We'll need a bigger place to live. The Celtic Tiger boom had sent house prices sky-high," Vivian burst out. Despite the medical health insurance, Rayan's hospital bills were depleting Sue's saving by a shocking amount and still Sue continued to spend lavishly on Rayan's every whim. Agitated, she rubbed her temple. Jesus! All this was driving her crazy! Her arms fell limply to her sides and her shoulders sagged as if under a great weight.

Imelda couldn't help but stare at the ravaged look in Vivian's eyes. She had never seen Vivian lose her composure before. It wasn't a pretty sight. It was as if the painted façade that was Vivian was falling apart. Her mascara was smeared and her carefully applied makeup was blotchy. She shrugged. It's called Karma, she thought. "Maybe Nathanial will take Rayan and the babies back to Perth."

Despairingly, Vivian shook her head. "Sue has signed a private pre-adoption agreement. She has agreed to pay all Rayan's hospital care including the costs of the Caesarean section because Rayan refuses to have a natural birth."

"But that is like… Like a contract…paying for them as if they are a…product!" Imelda gasped. Fleetingly, Vivian thought on the emotional pain Imelda would suffer, especially if the babies were born identical twins. Despite what Imelda said about not wanting to be a granny, she'd love the babies once were born. Vivian mused.

She gave Imelda a mollifying look. She shared Imelda outraged at her unborn grandchildren being reduced to a sordid business arrangement but for a very different reason. "I'm sorry. It's dreadful that the lives of two small unborn helpless infants should be subject to the law," she sympathised.

She almost choked at her blatant hypocritical words given that it was only a matter of months since she had advised Rayan and Isaac to passing Irish law and go to England for an abortion.

She crossed the foyer to meet Sue and Rayan as they emerged from the dining room. "Take the shortcut to the parking lot," she said. "Drive safely," she smiled ignoring Rayan but giving Sue a brief hug.

Once home, Sue helped a sullen Rayan into the extra-large deep buttoned armchair she had ordered. It had cost a packet. "I'm not comfortable," Rayan whined.

Sue gave an audible sigh of frustration. She was sick of all this: sick of the constant attention Rayan demanded of her, sick of the rows she and Vivian were having about money and depleted savings, sick of listening to Rayan complaining *all* the time, sick of Nathanial disappearing for weeks and just when she felt sure he'd given up the idea of fatherhood, he turned up again with some cheap gaudy touristy gift for Rayan he'd bought in Killarney or the Giant Causeway. There can't be much of Ireland, North and South; he hasn't seen while he's been waiting for Rayan to give birth, she thought sulkily.

It will all work out in the end, she reassured herself pouring a large glass of Chardonnay. She didn't usually drink but she needed it today. Rayan had been up half the night moaning about back pain and insisting Sue gave her a massage.

The wine relaxed her. She smiled mechanically at Rayan. At thirty-five weeks pregnant, Sue thought Rayan resembled the beached whale Vivian had insisted on dragging Sue to see on the banks of the River Foyle in Derry City. People said it was a bad omen. She had to admit it was freaky to see such a huge manual lying there gasping for breath. A shiver went down her spine. Stop it! You're getting to be as superstitious as old Mac O Lochlainn, she berated herself.

Rayan shifted uncomfortably in the chair. "My back is killing me. It kept me from sleeping most of the night," she lamented.

Tell me about it, Sue thought, and pretended not to hear. But finally, as Rayan's complaining got louder, she plonked her almost empty glass on the table. Reaching down, she picked up the soft cushion that seem to be her constant companion these days and thumping it into shape, she pushed it behind Rayan's back.

"That better?"

Rayan nodded.

"I think I might be in labour," Rayan moaned after a few minutes.

Sue rolled her eyes to the ceiling light. "You're not in labour. Remember what the hospital midwife said when I phoned this morning? It's just that there is less room in there and the babies are pushing against your back," she said through gritted teeth. "And even if you are in the early stages, there is no rush. It can take hours. Even days, the midwife said."

"I want to go to the hospital. Something is not right. I feel strange..."

"*Jesus!* Rayan, will you give me five minutes of peace? The way you're going on you'd think you were the only woman was ever pregnant," Sue burst out. "Didn't Doctor Breen say you were better at home until you were sure you were in labour? How many times is it now you thought you were in labour?"

Looking down at her unsightly swollen ankles that overflowed onto the soft leather cuffed shoes Sue had bought her, an irritable frown creased Rayan's forehead. She hated them. "My leg hurts where I broke it," Rayan muttered.

"It knit back OK. Everybody's bones hurt in the cold weather if they'd had a break."

"I hate these boots you bought me. They're old ladies' boots," Rayan lamented staring down at her feet.

Sue had to admit the boots were really ugly but they were the only things that didn't hurt Rayan's ankle bones which were still tender from when she injured them on the mountain. Norah, Imelda's mother, had been wearing a pair just like them when she'd paid them an unannounced visit and insisted Rayan and the babies should share her house after the birth.

"I'm going to be their great-granny, after all," Norah had said stiffly. "We'll see about that," she said stridently when Rayan informed her they were being adopted.

"Crazy old biddy," Sue murmured.

"I feel funny…unwell. I want to go to go back to bed," Rayan whined.

"Can't you just *wait!* I'm exhausted but you don't hear me complaining," Sue retorted, draining her glass.

Rayan shifted in the seat and glared angrily at Sue. It was dawning on Rayan that Sue didn't have the caring temperament she'd thought she had. Had she made another bad decision? Would Sue have the patience to mother two small babies? It's a fulltime job if the women who come into the salon were anything to go by. She'd watched young harassed mothers trying to snatch the time to have their hair styled while entertaining small fractious children.

She looked at Sue's immaculately coiffure hair, manicured nails, matching sweater, designer jeans and imported Italian boots. She looked like she'd stepped out of the pages of a top-drawer fashion magazine. There won't be much time for her to keep looking like that when she has two hungry crying babies to see to, she thought.

Something gushed down the stretched leggings she wore under her caftan. Emitting a smothered scream, she looked down in horror at the pool of wet forming on the carpet.

"Oh my God, your waters have just broken," Sue squealed in delight.

Mesmerised, Rayan looked down at the wet stain, panic rising in her.

Chapter Thirty-Eight

Rayan gripped the headboard of the bed. "The hospital said to come in *hours* ago and they'd see about an emergency caesarean. I can't wait any longer." The contractions slow and unevenly timed that had started after her waters broke like bad menstrual cramps were now like the violent waves that battered the rocks on the beach outside the bedroom window.

Sue ran her hand through her hair. "You're getting me all flustered. It's not my fault you started early. I'm your birth partner. I'll need a change of clothes. I might have to be at the hospital a while," she said frazzled. "But with you moaning all the time, I can't decide what to wear."

"I need to go to the hospital *now*, Sue!" Rayan screamed, the pain in her lower back growing more persistent.

"I want to look my best," Sue huffed. It's not every day I become a mother, she thought. "I'm nearly ready now. All I need to do is pack a small bag in case with my makeup and stuff…"

The twenty-mile journey to the hospital seemed to take forever. By the time they'd reached the outskirts of Letterkenny and the hospital, Rayan felt as if somebody was ripping out her insides.

Sue clattered into the examination room in her high-heeled boots behind the nurse. "Doctor Breen arranged for us to have a caesarean section," she stuttered excited the birth was going to happen soon.

The midwife examining Rayan pursed her lips. You never could tell if the 'partner' was going to be a man or a woman these days. She sniffed. She preferred the days when the labour ward door was closed firmly and the work of birthing babies left to those who had been trained for the job. "Dr Breen is finished for the day."

"I am not giving birth…naturally," Rayan moaned. "I have a birthing plan for a c section!"

Sue caught the look that passed between the midwives as they fitted the monitor. "You took your time getting here," the older of the nurses scolded. "You might have to have a vaginal birth. What date did your obstetrician book you for your caesarean birth?"

Sue fumbled through the large case of clothes and makeup she had with her. "February 14th," she said. "We're two weeks early," she apologised.

The midwife studied the flickering movements on the screen. The date was irrelevant. Baby A was fully engaged. She drew in her breath. Baby B was breech. "Were your other children born by c section?" the nurse asked carefully.

"It's her first," Sue interjected.

The midwife's breath came out in an irritable snort. That was all she needed after a twelve-hour shift in the labour ward; a geriatric first-time mother in an advanced state of labour with twins and only the briefest of medical notes.

"See if you can get Doctor Breen on her private number," the midwife instructed her junior. "And check if the emergency c section has been set up and team ready," she murmured. "This patient is pretty well dilated at eight centimetres." We'll take you down to the birthing unit as soon as soon as we can," she said to Rayan.

"I am not giving birth without an operation. I am not," Rayan said mutinously, gritting her teeth as a pain tore through her.

"Your medical notes say *only* if a natural birth is not possible," the nurse said coolly. "These little ones are in a hurry to be born," she said tersely.

"Slow it down...until the doctor gets here," Sue stammered out. She felt lightheaded. She hadn't thought about the labour. It was awful. Rayan's face and neck glistened with sweat. She didn't know how she could stand it.

The younger midwife smiled at Sue. "The midwives have done this many times before. Don't worry—most twins are born safely. We'll get you something to take the edge off the contractions. You're in good hands," she said turning to wipe the sweat of Rayan's face. "All the pain will be forgotten as soon as you hold your babies in your arms," she assured her.

"I don't *plan* to hold them. Does this hospital ever get anything right?" Rayan said through gritted teeth. "That's going to be Sue's problem, not mine."

Sue felt her panic escalating. This wasn't the way she had pictured it. She had brought scented candles and soft music with her. She envisaged giving Rayan a massage and looking into her eyes in gratitude as she gave birth to the babies.

"Where the bloody hell is Dr Breen?" the midwife snapped. These babies were birthing much too fast for their own good. She doubted there would even be time to set Rayan up for a 'C' section. "Don't push," she ordered sharply.

Terror-stricken Rayan clutched at Sue. "I want them out. Get them out of me," she screamed. As another contraction gripped her, she began to hyperventilate.

"Calm down, Miss Ritchie. Women give birth every day. It's not that difficult," the midwife said curtly.

There was a muttered relief as a doctor arrived. "This patient is booked in for a C-section but labour started early and is well advanced. It's going to have to be vaginal births," the midwife said succulently, shoved the clipboard with the information at him as Rayan opened her mouth and screamed manically.

"Stop it. Stop it now," the midwife ordered sharply. "Your babies are becoming distressed."

"I am *not* having a vaginal birth," Rayan screeched back into the midwife's face. "I want Dr Breen. She promised I wouldn't have to give birth naturally...*gave me her word*!" Rayan screeched. "I want her here, now!"

"I'm Dr Breen's intern..."

"I don't want you. I want Dr Breen," Rayan gasped, a stream of obscenities rolling off her tongue. "She promised I could have these damn babies by caesarean section. She promised," Rayan panted beating at the doctor's hands.

The doctor's voice lost its pleasant tone. "Getting hysterical is not going to help you or your babies," he reprimanded her. "Stop screaming obscenities at the staff. They are here to help ensure you have a safe delivery..."

"I'm not swearing at the staff. I am swearing at Isaac Wright and bloody Ireland. I wish I had never set foot in it!" Rayan gasped as she felt something move inside her.

The doctor frowned at the babies' heart monitor. Time was not on these babies' side.

"Doctor Breen is not answering," the junior midwife said under her breath. "And these babies are not going to wait for her."

"Epidural?"

The nurse shook her head. "Baby A is in the birth canal. It will be born vaginally whether this patient likes it or not. It's almost ready to crown."

Rayan went rigid with fear and rage.

"Don't you dare start screaming like a banshee again," the older of the two midwives warned Rayan. "Now, breathe and count," she ordered holding the gas and air mask over Rayan's face.

A smarting sensation made Rayan draw in her breath. "Don't bear down. Take short panting breaths. You want your babies' entry into the world to be gentle… Don't you dare push. Don't push," the midwife ground out in panic.

"What's keeping that porter?"

"Baby B is breech," the midwife nodded grimly. "Emergency section set up for delivery."

Every fibre of Sue's being shook with fright. This was turning into a horrendous nightmare. She breathed deep trying to calm her palpating heart. She could feel sweat trickle down her face; smell her own perspiration through her clothes. She stared at Rayan. Rayan's body was slick with sweat; her cheeks bellowing out and then deflating like air leaving a balloon.

The labour ward was hot as a sauna. She had to get out. She tried to move but Rayan's grip on her wrist was like iron. She was trapped. She needed air.

She tried to draw air deep into her lungs like she did during her meditation class. But the best she could manage was short shallow rasping breaths. She hadn't thought it would be like this. She had pictured a smiling nurse placing the twins, first one and then the other into her arms.

Teetering on her heels, she turned to the nurse. "I need to go out," she said shakily.

The midwife eyed her coolly. "Does Miss Ritchie have another birthing partner who might want to be present at the births?"

Sue wilted under her gaze. She shook her head. "I thought I could do it," she gulped shamefaced.

The midwife turned away. "There's a family room. Wait there," she said.

Glad to be free, Sue breathed in great gulps of air. She felt mortified about leaving Rayan to go through it without support. She pressed back against the wall of the corridor as the porter swung Rayan's bed out of the room and towards the lifts. "You'll feel the pressure, but don't push," Sue heard the midwife say urgently to Rayan.

"Follow us down to theatre two, second floor," the junior midwife said softly, giving Sue's arm a light squeeze. "I'll help you gown up. Baby A is minutes away from being born. Your…friend is in good hands," she said her cheeks reddening. Quickly, she followed the gurney down the corridor. She wished she was as confident as she sounded. Baby B's heart rate was fluctuating wildly. It wasn't looking good…

Sue slumped against the wall. She couldn't do it. She felt tears of self-pity well up in her. The young midwife had assumed she and Rayan were partners. She wished that was true. But Vivian was her partner.

She tapped in Vivian's number wondering if she asked her, would she come to the hospital. The phone went to the answering machine. Vivian's crisp voice said, "Leave a message." Sue hesitated. What could she say? Rayan is in labour? Vivian already knew that. The whole village probably knew it by this time. Rayan, her pregnancy and her near death on Muckish had turned into a local legend. Sue licked her lips. "I'm frightened," she whispered down the phone. "Please come."

She startled as someone touched her elbow. It was the junior midwife. "Baby A is born and on her way to the special baby unit. Rayan is prepped for her C-section. She's asking for you."

Sue stilled. She was letting Rayan down. She was letting herself down; all because she was afraid of a little sweat and pain.

"You won't have to see anything if you don't want to."

Sue felt tears gush down her face as Baby B was placed briefly in her arms. She looked mostly through her tears at the masked and gowned assembled medical team of surgeons, anaesthetist, midwives and paediatricians.

She felt her knees shake; felt a supporting arm steady her. "I'm a mother," she said incredulously, gazing down at Baby B.

Chapter Thirty-Nine

Rayan shifted carefully in the bed. Twenty-four hours had passed since she'd given birth. She had refused to hold her daughter or her son when they were born; refused to look at them. She had left that to Sue. She was going to be their mother.

"Miss Ritchie," a voice said. Rayan snapped her eyes closed and pretended she was asleep. Staff, even reporters, wanted to talk to her. This amazing Australian woman—who had survived a rock fall and given birth to twins she reportedly didn't know she was expecting.

A real survivor, a reporter from the Donegal Chronicle hailed her. He wanted to get photos of the babies; wanted her to tell her story.

The local radio station phones were blocked with calls about the lack of services for pregnant woman living temporarily in Donegal. Other callers were complaining about 'foreigners' coming to Ireland to have their babies 'free' on the struggling health service. Depressed, Rayan buried her head in the pillows. If only they knew the real story.

"I missed the big event. How are you feeling?" a female voice said moving to the side of the bed.

Rayan opened her eyes. Doctor Blanid Breen was reading her chart. Rayan thought again she looked too young to be a doctor. Her hair was pulled back into its usual ponytail and her white doctor's coat lay open to show a red blouse with little hearts tucked into a straight skirt.

"I've come to check your incision and your stitches," the doctor said.

"My breasts hurt," Rayan moaned. Even to her own ears, her voice sounded like a petulant child.

"Have the nurses been talking to you about breast feeding when your milk comes in? And going to see your babies?" the doctor asked as she examined Rayan's abdomen.

Rayan couldn't hide the anger and hostility that surged through her. What you care, she thought. You said you'd be there when I needed you and you weren't. Self-pitying tears smarted at the back of her eyes and coated her eyelashes. She blinked them away. "I am *not* breast feeding," she said through stiff lips.

"You could always use a breast pump and express—"

"No!"

"Have you seen your twins yet?" the doctor asked unperturbed.

"No. Nor do I want to see them. I am having them adopted."

The doctor pulled up a chair and sat down. "You've been through a lot since you came to Ireland less than a year ago," she said placing her hand on Rayan's. "And despite what you have been through, you have given birth to two beautiful babies." She smiled. "That's a lot in anybody's book," she smiled.

Rayan snatched her hand away. She wondered would the doctor be so kind and easy with her praise if she knew what her intentions and her fatalistic thinking that almost led to the death of the babies. She shifted in the bed. "Are they OK?" she asked tersely.

Doctor Breen cleared her throat. "Lack of nutrition during pregnancy has left them significantly underweight and underdeveloped." Blanid Breen watched closely. She saw the shame and guilt register on her patient's face. She let out a sigh of relief. That was a good sign. It showed she had a feeling of remorse about her treatment of her babies while they were in the womb. Miss Ritchie cared about her new-born infants at some level. Whether it would be enough to help the staff to get her to care for them was another matter. "Your son has significant problems. I think you owe him to do what you can for him after what you have put him through," she stated bluntly.

Rayan shrank back against the pillows. The doctor had gotten it in one. She had literally almost starved them to death, hoping she'd miscarry. Helpless tears seeped from Rayan's eyes. "I never wanted to give birth or be a mother," she gulped.

The doctor touched her hand. "I'm not judging you. Who knows what any of us might do if we were in a strange country without family." She paused. "You have already begun to make up for what went before."

Rayan looked at her.

"Despite everything, you gave birth *not once but twice*. Your body did the job it is designed to do. You are now a mother. Your daughter came hurtling into the world vaginally—couldn't wait to be born. Sometimes having to face our fears is the best solution to our problems."

Despite herself, Rayan smiled. "When I lay in the bog hole, the baby kicked furiously. The kicking kept me semi-conscious. I didn't know I was carrying twins." She closed her eyes and wondered if her daughter had saved all their lives on the mountain by her persistent, relentless kicking inside the womb. "I gave birth. They're no longer my responsibility. I have arranged to have them adopted. All I want to do is get out of here and forget it ever happened. When can I be discharged?"

Doctor Breen pursed her lips. She didn't t like the idea of having the babies adopted right away. Rayan was on the cusp of menopause. Given her aversion to birth and motherhood, she'd have no other children. Would she regret having her twins adopted later on?

She knew nothing about this woman except what bits of gossip she'd heard yet, something urged her to support, befriend her.

She'd read the social worker's report. In his opinion Rayan was neither physically nor psychologically fit to mother twin babies. She has no family support, he'd pointed out. And according to the staff present at the births, Miss Ritchie exhibited strong neurosis symptoms around birthing and motherhood. She sighed. As far as he was concerned, placing the twins for adoption—it was a *fait accompli*.

Blanid paused. She was away out on a limb here—stretching her brief as a doctor. But something forced her to say, "Rayan, your children need you. You are their mother. My advice—takes a month *after* you are discharged; rest and get better before you make a final decision." She snapped her lips together as if to stop any more words seeping out.

Rayan felt her heart wobble. *Your children,* the doctor had said as if it was the most natural turn of phrase in the world. As if they were real little people connected to her. *You don't give away your own flesh and blood*—her father's words filled her mind. A keening sound she hardly recognised as coming from her filled the room. She couldn't think like that. They were Sue's now.

Her mother wouldn't want to know. She'd be too busy nursing my father after his stroke—attending to his every utterance, she thought. And Nathanial was away sightseeing. She hadn't heard from him in a while.

The doctor checked her watch. "Remember what I said," she felt compelled to add. "There is no rush..."

Agitated, Rayan thumped her head on the pillows. "You don't understand. I'd make a terrible mother. They're better off without me."

The doctor carefully masked her feelings before she spoke again. "I think, having carried them to within weeks of full term, you owe it to yourself…and your son and daughter to at least go to the nursery. If you do that and are still adamant they are to be adopted, I will personally help you…if that is what you really want. Agreed?"

Chapter Forty

In stunned silence, Imelda stared through the glass partition at the babies. She waited to feel a sense of connection to these small scraps of humanity, her grandchildren. Everybody seemed to set such store by bloodlines. She should feel *something*, some connection, if they had her son's blood pumping through their veins.

When her boys had been born, she'd had an immediate fiercely protective feeling that they were part of her. Jesus! Her twins had fathered twins!

What colour was their skin? She drew back. What if they were black or darker skinned like their great-grandparents? She still hadn't had the conversation about who their father was with Isaac and Raphael yet. She realised she was panting as if she had been running. Ayeman's mother was American. Would another generation mean the babies would be lighter, like their mother Rayan? Or a Mediterranean colour like Isaac and Raphael?

She motioned for a nurse to bring the special cots a little closer. Sometimes the genetics missed a generation. She focused her gaze on the cot nearest to her. The baby was a patchy yellowish colour. Her hand flew to her mouth.

"This little one was born very badly jaundiced," the nurse's voice said through the glass. "It will clear up." Imelda's eyes swivelled to the other cot. The baby's skin looked like it had a holiday tan. She let out a sigh she hadn't been aware she had been holding in. *She looks like what the older generation in the Ireland used to call the 'dark Irish'*, she thought. They were brown skinned but not quite black.

She scanned the babies' features. She couldn't tell if they were identical or not. She looked to see if she could see any resemblance of Isaac in their tiny screwed up faces with so many wires and tubes attached to their tiny, bodies it was difficult to tell. "Which one has the problems?" she asked Raphael lightheaded with tension.

"They're both alive and that's all that matters," Raphael retorted touched his mother's arm. "Come on, granny Imelda," he smiled, "time to celebrate."

Imelda was far from ready to celebrate. She'd be asking for a blood test to prove they were Isaac's before she started to call him the father or her grandmother.

"*Somebody* should go and see Rayan since Nathanial is away kissing the Blarney Stone at the other end of Ireland," she said belligerently.

"I've seen her. She wants Isaac to come and see her."

Alarm bells started ringing in Imelda's head. She was glad to say Isaac was showing no interest in Rayan or her twins. "Hasn't she done enough to him already?"

"She has named Isaac as the father on the hospital records."

Imelda stiffened. "Why did she do that?"

"Maybe it has something to do with the adoption."

Imelda snorted." She wants a father's name on the hospital records so that she doesn't look like a whoring cradle snatcher—"

"Ma!"

As they waited for the elevator to the front hall Imelda cast a covert glance at Raphael's face, black as thunder. She was becoming concerned at how possessive he had become of these three-day-old twins.

As they walked out into the chilly late-February day, Imelda placed a comforting hand on Raphael's arm. "Sue is adopting Rayan's babies," she said careful to mask her sense of relief. "Isaac is not old enough to take on the responsibility of raising two small premature, sick babies. Let Sue and Vivian have them…it's for the best…"

A small glimmer of understanding of where her mother had been coming from when she had demanded that Isaac and Raphael be adopted so she, Imelda, could continue on with her university education, flittered across Imelda's mind.

Raphael zapped the car and opened the passenger door for his mother. "I've arranged to have a paternity test." He got in the driver's side and sat; his hands clamped on the steering wheel stared straight ahead. "You know those games— swapping over—Isaac and I used to play. We did that with Rayan too."

Imelda covered her ears with her hands. She could feel the pressure in her chest increasing. This thing was going to give her a heart attack or a stroke. She had hoped, even prayed, there would be some release from this nightmare. Instead it was getting worse.

"You had sex with Rayan and let her think you were Isaac!" she said horrified.

"I'm sorry, Ma," Raphael said shame-faced. "I didn't know her then. The strange thing is I really like Rayan now."

Imelda slumped in the seat. *God Almighty,* what was she going to do!

"Did Rayan know it was you and not Isaac?" she quaked stunned.

"I don't think so, at least not the first few times. I...always kept the lights off and made love to her by moonlight," Raphael confessed. Imelda felt a manic guffaw rise in her throat. If it wasn't so serious, it would be hilarious, she thought.

"Sister Hampton at the hospital thinks I am Isaac. He and Mac went to see her when Rayan was admitted. She thinks I am Isaac. They tell me how the babies are doing because they think I am the father," he insisted. "And who's to say I'm not. I could be the father," Raphael said doggedly.

"They think you are the father because you never leave the special nursery unit... You spend hours gawking all dewy-eyed at the babies!" Imelda screamed, beating at him with her fists. She stopped and rubbed her chest hoped it was just her reflux playing it up and not an angina attack like her father had died from.

There was utter silence between them as they drove home. Her mind going round and round in confused circle, one of her mother's religious rants came to Imelda's mind. "Pray, pray, not to be put to the test," she used to preach. Imelda swallowed. She had been put to the test and failed miserably and more was to come, of that she was sure.

Raphael dropped his mother off at the Manse and went back to the hospital to see Rayan and the twins. The young female doctor with her hair in a long plait was in the nursery checking the equipment and the sick babies in the special cots. She'd arched her eyebrows when he asked how the babies were doing.

Dr Breen scrutinised him. He must be Isaac. The man named as the babies' father on the hospital forms. He looked distraught. Most young fathers would back off at the mammoth task of sick pre-term twins but not this one.

"Looking after premature twin babies is a tall order. Miss Ritchie will need all the support you can give her," the doctor stated covertly watching him. "Baby B was born quite malnourished and underweights. His lungs had not developed as well as his sister's and as a result he had quite serious breathing problems; the possibility of transfer to the Children's Hospital in Dublin 100 miles away might have to be considered." She'd stopped abruptly as if afraid she had revealed too much information without her patient's consent. But she couldn't help being pleased he was showing an interest in the babies. Maybe he could persuade the mother to do the same.

Shocked, Raphael looked at her. He realised she was telling him Baby B, the boy, could deteriorate further—even die. Raphael felt as if somebody had rugby tackled him. His month went dry. She thought he was Isaac. He started to explain and then drew back the words. He could be the father! Shame coursed through him remembering slipping into Rayan's bed pretending he was Isaac. He squirmed under the doctor's steady gaze.

"Have you and Miss Ritchie discussed the future welfare of the twins?"

Numbly, Raphael shook his head.

A look of something approaching irritability with him flickered across the doctor's face. "You do know Miss Ritchie is making arrangements to have the babies adopted?"

He nodded.

"Don't you think that is something you need to discuss with Miss Ritchie?" the doctor said baldly.

Rayan was lying staring at the far wall without blinking. Raphael explained about going to the nursery to see the babies most days. "The nurses keep calling them Baby A Ritchie and Baby B Ritchie. Have you decided on names for them yet?"

"I hadn't planned on naming them," Rayan said. "Sue can do that."

Her disinterest stoked Raphael's anger. "They are real living human beings with beating hearts and flesh on their bones—not much because you starved yourself trying to hide them—not balls of tissue like you lead that fucking moron brother of mine to believe. If you want, I will give the boy my name and the girl your name!"

Rayan stirred in the bed, a perplexed look on her face. "Why would you give the boy your name?"

Raphael clammed up, realising he had nearly let slip about the game he and Isaac had played on her. If the paternity test was positive, he would have to tell. No way was he letting Sue and Vivian—two gay women—adopt his babies. The thing was, he couldn't bring them to live with granny Norah. She was as crazy as a box of frogs.

He thought of his mother's shocked stony profile as he'd driven her home. She might help him if it meant letting drunken irresponsible Isaac off the fucking hook, he thought.

Chapter Forty-One

The squealing tyres of the wheelchair mimicked the silent wailing going on inside Rayan's head. She caught a glimpse of her reflection in the high gloss steel of the lift as it rode upwards to the intensive care baby unit. She barely recognised the ashen-faced dead-eyed woman that stared back at her. She looked like she felt, depressed and morose.

"I am only going before I am discharged because Doctor Breen forced me into it," she mumbled as Sister Alice Hampton pushed through the double doors of the care unit and placed the wheelchair between the twins' cots.

Rayan recoiled at the sight of the babies' tiny bodies crisscrossed with oxygen tubes and wires. As if on cue, the puckered skin from her c-section wound began to throb. A coat of silvering had begun to form on the wound just below her bikini line but it was still red and ugly.

"Why are they in here?" Rayan quaked, staring at all the equipment.

Alice tried hard to mask her irritation. "Babies born below a certain weight and born before their birth date spend some time here. The special cots help to replicate the environment in the womb."

Rayan covered her face with her hands. "This was a mistake. I can't look at them all wired up," she gulped panic rising in her. "They looked little half-starved rabbits."

Alice stilled the judgemental words that rose to her tongue. Carefully, she put her finger through the little opening in the specialist crib and gently stroked Baby A's leg. "You have given birth to a beautiful daughter," she said.

Rayan forced her eyes to focus on the name tag on the cot. *Baby A: mother, Rayan Ritchie,* it read. Seeing her name threw her. She couldn't deny it to herself any longer. It was there in black and white. She shrank back. She thought of them as Sue's twins.

Rayan realised the nurse was talking. "...She was just over two pounds in weight when she was born; the bigger of the twins and the oldest by twenty minutes," she said. "She lost a small amount of weight the first few days. But she is gaining weight steadily now. Overall, the prognosis for her is promising." She stroked the baby's hand. "The nurses call her Angel. Because you have such an angelic wee face," she cooed to the restless infant.

Rayan felt herself stiffen. Despite her attempts at indifference, it irked her that the staff had taken it upon themselves to name the baby. *Raphael did ask you to name them, and you refused*, her inner voice remonstrated with her.

"As you know, she was born naturally." Sister Hampton smiled down at the baby. "You couldn't wait to get into this big bad world, could you, little one?" She glanced surreptitiously at the mother, willing her to show *some* flicker of maternal interest.

"Why is she wearing an eye shield? Has she no eyes? Rayan stammered out all sorts of imaginings leaping into her mind."

Alice Hampton cursed her own insensitivity. She had forgotten how shocking it could seem to a parent who had never been in a specialist baby unit before. Again, judgemental words raised their ugly head. If you had visited a midwife, obstetrician or paediatrician during your pregnancy, she would have told you about the baby unit, she thought.

"She was jaundiced when she was born. She is receiving phototherapy to help clear it. The eye shield is to protect her eyes. It usually clears up within a week or so."

Rayan closed *her* eyes. She had wondered if instinct would take over and she would feel some form of attachment when she saw them. She was struggling against it. These were Sue's babies, not hers.

"Would you like to feed her?"

Rayan shook her head vehemently. The feelings she was experiencing would pass. Her hormones were playing havoc with her emotions. These babies were not hers to keep and care for. They were Sue's. Growing attached to them, even temporarily, would just cause problems.

Mutely, Rayan swivelling her gaze to the other cot forcing herself not to cry out in alarm. Even to her inexperienced eye, she could tell Baby B was very sick.

Despite her opinion of Rayan, Sister Hampton felt pity rise in her. Rayan was obviously shocked to the core to see Baby B's little chest heaving up and down.

"Why can he not breathe properly?"

"His lungs didn't develop in the womb." She laid a caring hand on Rayan's shaking shoulders. "He's a little fighter. I have seen sicker babies than him survive. But it will be a while... Wouldn't you like to stroke him...?"

"No! I don't want to touch either of them. I did what Doctor Breen wanted. I came and saw them. Now I want to go back to my room."

Sister Hampton let her judgemental emotion surface. How could a mother gaze so impassively on her sick babies and not show a scrap of feeling for them? She ground her teeth. Some days she hated this job. Dr Blanid Breen would be hoping her patient had shown *some* kind of interest in her babies. Alice snorted. I'm a nurse not a bloody miracle worker, she thought.

"Your friend Sue has chosen names for them."

"I don't want to know."

Alice Hampton clamped her lips together and reminded herself that this patient was still suffering physically and psychologically from the trauma she suffered being submerged for hours in a bog swamp and having to be airlifted from Muckish in early labour. Her feelings were bound to be stunted, she reasoned. Perhaps with a bit more coaxing and encouragement she would take more of an interest in the babies.

"Branna is an old Gaelic name," Alice said stroking Baby A's head. "It means a beauty with hair dark as a raven. It suits her," she smiled. "With her dark looks she will be a beauty—envy of her friends as she grows up," she murmured gently massaging the baby's cheek. "You do it," she said.

Rayan felt her hand move involuntarily.

Alice held her breath. For a brief few seconds, she thought she had made a breakthrough.

"No! The doctor asked me to come. I did that. Now I want to go back to the ward."

Her patience evaporating rapidly, Sister Hampton changed tact.

"Excuse me, I'll be back shortly. Keep a check that the protective goggles stay in place on Baby Branna," she said acerbically.

Left alone to sit between the two cots Rayan felt panic rob her lungs of air. What if Baby B stopped breathing while she was sitting here trying not to look at him? Sister Hampton hadn't told her what his name was. Had Sue not picked a name for him or was he not expected to make it...?

Anxiously, she looked around. Sister Hampton was helping a mother to get started on breast feeding her baby. Rayan's hand went to her own breasts swollen with milk; they hurt like hell. She had asked for something to cease the pain and stop the milk. She gritted her teeth. She knew the nurses were holding off hoping she'd change her mind and breast feed the babies. She had refused point blank to even express her milk.

Your children need you, the doctor had said. Of their own accord her eyes went to Baby B, frail and helpless fighting for every breath.

Guilt assailed her as she remembered how frenziedly she had sought the termination. He was suffering and it was all her fault. If he died, she would be to blame as surely as if she had aborted him.

Sitting there looking at her twins she realised she was glad she hadn't succeeded. She was glad she had given them a chance at life.

The thought surprised her.

She edged her way out of the wheelchair and stood up holding onto its sides. She took an uncertain step towards the cot. Heart drumming in her chest she edged her fingers through the opening and touched Baby B, shocked to feel his bones beneath his stick thin legs. Letting out a moan, she withdrew her hand.

The baby stirred.

"He knows it's you," Alice Hampton said softly behind her.

Rayan fumbled her way back into the wheelchair. "I'm not some young mother you can trap into caring for her infant," she said casting a look across at the other mother. "I'm a forty-year-old, middle-aged woman soon be menopausal," she said, angry more at herself that the nurse.

"Age has nothing to do with motherhood," Alice Hampton snapped, finally losing patience. "*You're his mother.* You gave him life. All babies know their mother's touch."

"As soon as I get back to the ward, I'm discharging myself and getting on with my life," Rayan said quaked.

Two red spots coloured Sister Hampton's cheeks as she pushed Rayan into the lifts. I did my best, she thought angrily. Dr Breen will have to accept this woman has no maternal feeling for her babies.

Rayan sat mutinous in the chair. *Age had nothing to do with it!* She inwardly mocked the nurse's tone of voice. In my case age had *everything* to do with it, she raged.

Her mind went back to her own doctor. Stupid senile old bastard, she fumed balling her fists. She had felt insulted, aggrieve and relieved all at the same time. Telling me it was doubtful I'd get pregnant at *my age.* She had something to tell the stupid old decrepit. It was time he retired before he gave another woman the same advice.

Mentally bushed, she looked up at the grim-faced nurse. "Age has everything to do with it," she cried out as she helped her into bed.

"I'll get you something to help dry up your breast milk," Sister Hampton said with a sigh.

Rayan wanted desperately to sleep and put the images of Baby Branna and Baby B out of her mind. She wished the nurse hadn't told her the name. It made them real. Thinking of them as Sue's wasn't working anymore. She squeezed her eyes tightly together but the picture of the intravenous tubes Baby B was being fed through and the protective sun goggles covering Baby Branna's eyes was seared in her mind's eye. Every time she closed her eyes the images of the tiny babies attached to the wires and machinery flashed across her lids.

Distraught, for the first time in years, she sobbed for her mother. Doctor Breen had asked about contacting a relative. It was pointless to think her mother might help her. "My father would forbid her to have anything more to do with me."

Her mother wouldn't go against him. She never had despite the many beatings. "My wife is rather clumsy. She has had another accident," he says jovially to account for her bruising.

Great wracking sobs shook Rayan's body. "Why would she help me now? She never once saved me from his belittling tongue or demeaning fun making in front of his friends and colleagues when I was growing up," Rayan sobbed brokenly. "If she had, just once, maybe things might have been different. I wouldn't have had to run away from home at sixteen. And I wouldn't have to give my babies away to a stranger," she wailed to the quiet room.

She buried her head in the pillow to smother her sobbing. A strict rule of "respectability for mother and me," she gasped, "While he hid his many clandestine affairs with his female students."

Distraught, she shook her head from side to side. "He would never allow me to bring home illegitimate by-blows born of an Irish father." A hysterical giggle rose up her throat and burst out her mouth. "It's as ludicrous and unthinkable in his eyes as getting pregnant by an aboriginal man," she spluttered. Taking the twins back to Perth was out of the question. She swiped at the tears dripping down her cheeks. She was mad to even consider it.

Fatigued and depressed she moved her face from the soggy tear-stained pillow. There was a light tap on the door. "Sister says you are to have these," a young nurse said proffering two tablets.

"What are they?"

"They're to dry up your breast milk."

Rayan lay back on the bed and stared at the small orange coloured phial holding the tablets. "I don't want them," she said handing them back. The only thing she could do for her babies before Sue adopted them was to sustain them with her breast milk.

Chapter Forty-Two

"The very spit out of your grandfather Wright," Norah declared as Raphael held Baby B up so that his great granny could get a good look at him through the glass panelling of the nursery.

Raphael tucked the baby gently in the crook of his arm. "Breathing on your own now wee man," he murmured. "That's good." He touched his lips to the baby's forehead and tenderly placed him back in his specialist cot. He stood looking down at his little screws up face preparing to cry. His own heart ached. At six weeks the baby was still as small as the new-borns on either side of him.

"No name, I see," Norah said staring at the "Baby Ritchie" card index above the baby's cot. "Nurse," she called brusquely, as Raphael joined her in the corridor outside the nursery. "From now on this baby is to be called Bobby..."

Raphael shook his head at the nurse.

"You can't give the baby Granda's name... Sue will name him like she named his sister. They *are* going to be *her* children."

Norah cast a disparaging eye on her great-granddaughter who was crying lustily. "I never heard of a saint called Branna. It's not even a Donegal name. It's easy seeing Sue's from down the country. *You* have *every right* to name him," Norah rapped out. Well, he's either yours or Isaac's, she conceded silently. It didn't matter a jot to her as long as Raphael got custody and brought them home to live in her house. She wrinkled her nose. She didn't fancy nappies and squawking infants but it was better than living out her time in a bloody old people's home, she reasoned.

She took a sneaky look at Raphael. "I hear the Australian gigolo has booked his flight home." Maybe Rayan will go with him, she mused. It would be easier for Raphael to stake his claim for the infants, she'd keep at him.

Raphael spread his hands in exasperation. "How do you hear all these things?" He'd heard Nathanial was toying with the idea of staying in Ireland with Rayan.

"A fine solicitor you'll make if you don't keep your ear to the ground," Norah mocked. ". She leaned towards him. "Strike while the iron is hot. That's what your granda used to say."

"I had a paternity test. What the fuck else do you want me to do! Sorry," he apologised. "C'mon, let go home." He put his hand under her elbow and hurried her towards the lifts.

Norah shook her arm free of Raphael's grip. It was her sixty-fifth birthday today. She was officially a pensioner but nobody cared. They're all too busy with their own lives to take any heed of a poor old woman she thought despondently.

"This way," Raphael said heading across the packed car park.

Norah supported herself on the open door frame before sinking heavily into the driver's seat.

"Want me to drive?" Raphael offered regretting swearing at her. It was just with this business with Mac O Lochlainn and old Manus at the Top of the Hill, and Rayan and the babies, his nerves were stretched as taunt as the wires strung between the electricity poles.

"I'm not decrepit yet," Norah said dolefully staring at the cars parked bumper to bumper wondering how she was going to get out without hitting something. "Like sardines in a tin," she muttered. "In my young days there was hardly a car on the road. Even the Gardaí walked or rode a bicycle."

Raphael sank back in the passenger seat. Norah was going to recount the good old days.

"When your grandfather was transferred as a young Garda from Mayo to Donegal, he'd only the use of a rickety bike. It was only when the Troubles along the Border got bad in the late 60s that he got the use of a shared car."

Raphael closed his eyes and pretended to doze. His granny talked on. "Then when we could have been enjoying the benefits of his long years of service, he died leaving me on my own. "She sighed theatrically. "The old folks' home is all I have to look forward to now," she said mournfully.

Raphael glanced at his granny's sour face as the ticket barrier slowly rose and the car careered out into the main road of the hospital. "That's going to be a while yet," he smiled attempting to cajole her out of her black mood.

"I'm glad you think so. The only daughter I have is cavorting with that American man old enough to be her father. It turns out he owns the Manse. She'll not take me to live with her that's for sure," she lamented. Tears of self-pity blurred her vision. She fell silent. The reality of her situation was beginning to sink in. Imelda hadn't spoken to her in years. And as for Isaac, her grandson, depending on him was like depending on a broken stick. She glanced surreptitiously at Raphael. He was her best bet.

"There must be *something* in those law books of yours to keep that Australian hussy from signing away the twins to those two sinful women."

Raphael felt himself shrivelling up inside. He gripped the dashboard. "Nothing I can say will make any difference!"

Red blotches stained Norah's neck and cheeks. "How can you sit back and let it happen? Where are your Christian values to even *think* about allowing your son and daughter to be brought up by that pair? It's an abomination that women like that should be even considering rearing children," she spluttered spittle beginning to form on her chin.

"I can't do anything to stop Rayan adopting the babies because I can't be one hundred percent sure if I'm the babies' uncle or father," he choked out. "We're identical twins, Granny. We have identical DNA. All the paternity test has proved was it could be me or Isaac. So, the test made no difference…"

A feeling of hopelessness like swimming against the tide filled Raphael's body and mind. No judge would let him bring the twins up on his own without proof of parentage. The situation was as fraught with barriers as climbing Muckish in winter time.

I'm fucked, he thought. Everything is conspiring against me. And now old Manus is trying to get rid of me out of his daughter's life.

Chapter Forty-Three

"No crying today, little Branna, you're going home," Sister Hampton soothed as she walked past Sue and placed the fractious baby into her mother's arms. The baby screwed up her face and sneezed as the angora blanket snuffled her nose.

Bitch of a nurse. She doesn't like me, Sue thought. The smile on her face felt as if it was frozen in place. Her arms ached to hold the sweet little pink bundle. It should be *me* carrying her home, she thought resentfully. After all it is *me* who is going to be her mother. "She's a great little screamer," she smiled to hide her chagrin.

"You're going to miss your brother when you wake up tomorrow. But he's getting stronger and will hopefully be home to join you soon," Sister Hampton said smiling down at the baby girl. She cast a surreptitious glance at Sue, the potential private adopter. Her sense of foreboding deepened. She'd voiced her concerns only to have them waved aside.

"It's a good arrangement," Doctor Breen said. "It will give both Rayan and the potential adopting mother time to get used to caring for one baby to begin with." Mentally, she crossed her fingers hoping it would allow a space for Rayan to reach her decision whether or not to finalise the adoption. "It's a big step. Not one she should take in her present emotional state following trauma."

The social worker had backed the doctor.

Alice Hampton sighed, not at all happy about this discharge. The twins had been sharing a cot for several weeks now. Baby B had thrived noticeably better when he was with his twin. She feared that without his sister, he'd slip back. Like the rest of the nurses, she'd grown fond of the little twins. At six weeks old Baby Branna was marginally over the weight she should have been at birth. "She is a very fussy feeder," she explained, stepping back so that she was addressing both women. "Feeding her little and often—the nursery nurse tells me works best for her."

She stroked the baby's head. Dr Breen felt the mother was forming a bond with her babies. Rayan had voluntarily agreed to continue to express her milk and had attempted to bottle feed Baby B. She was convinced his mother's presence with him in the nursery had helped him pull through. And since she was going to live, initially, at any rate with the proposed adoptive mother and her partner, they felt that it was safe to discharge baby Branna to her care. Alice hoped she was right. It was lovely for this little one to be going home. It was just that her gut feeling told her something wasn't quite *right.*

There was no sight of the "father" today. A frown creased her forehead. *He* had done a complete 360 turnaround from the night in her office when he acted like a sullen schoolboy. Strange carry on that, she thought. He certainly didn't want to be considered the father. Now, he was in the nursery *every day*, telling anybody who'd listened that *the twins were his.*

Fathers display all kinds of emotions at the sight of their new-born's son or daughter, she mused. But this guy—this guy loved this little one and her brother; of that she had no doubt, she thoughts looking down at Baby Branna fretting and fussing in Sue's arms now.

She glanced at Rayan. She had made a good recovery from the births and her near death experience on Muckish. She did wonder about her mental state. She looked depressed.

"When do you think the other baby will be ready to be discharged?" Sue asked brightly bringing Alice out of her reverie.

Sister Hampton pulled back her shoulders and drew herself up. Sue's possessiveness of the babies irked her. You're not legally the mother yet, she felt like responding. She turned to Rayan. "Baby B will be discharged as soon as he is well enough to go home. Would you like me to take you to see him before you go? It would be no problem," she assured Rayan. "The breast milk really made a tremendous difference to him," she added quietly.

Sue shifted from one foot to the other like a little girl impatient to play with her new doll. "Why don't we go home, get Branna settled, introduce her to Vivian and tomorrow we can come and check on her twin," she said persuasively patting Rayan's arm.

Chapter Forty-Four

Vivian could clearly hear the baby screaming long before she got near the staff apartment. She quickened her steps and stuck her key into the lock. For a small baby she had a fine pair of lungs, she thought. If this noise kept up it wouldn't be too long before the other staff living in the adjoining accommodation began complaining.

"Why is the baby screeching like a fishwife? I can hear her all the way to the Spa," she snapped as she stepped into the lounge room.

"She's hungry," Sue huffed.

"If she's hungry, get up and feed her instead of sitting there with your hands over your ears!"

"She doesn't like that breast milk Rayan is always expressing. And even if she does take it, she's screaming with hunger again almost as soon as she's finished. She's a greedy demanding baby," Sue mumbled. "Those nurses spoiled her; feeding her every two hours when she had the jaundice," Sue complained.

"Look at the state of this place," Vivian scolded looking around the lounge room of the two-bedroom staff cottage. It looked as if a baby bomb had hit it. Every square inch seemed to be covered in baby equipment and baby clothes. The neonatal nurses at the hospital had clubbed together and bought a huge cot that turned into a bed. She had tried to persuade Sue she didn't need to assemble it yet but she had gone ahead. The locals and the general public enamoured with the story of the twins' survival covered by local media, had sent a load of gifts. They were piled high on every spare surface.

A rank smell made Vivian draw in short breaths. "What is that smell? Have you changed her today?"

"I can't remember." Sue yawned.

Vivian ran her hand through her hair as the baby continued to howl lustily. "Where is Rayan? I thought she was supposed to be here helping you."

Tears of self-pity welled in Sue's eyes. "She's probably walking on the beach or out somewhere with Nathanial."

Vivian picked her steps around the small chaotic space. Bending, she began to gather up the dirty dishes strewn on the small occasional table. Whatever stupid notion I had that I'd give this crazy idea a try and make this work for Sue's sake is fading fast, she thought curling her lip in disgust at the state of her partner. She obviously hadn't showered or washed for days. On the table lay grease-encrusted takeaway boxes. Sue had always been choosy about what she ate. Now she is gorging on this stuff, Vivian thought in alarm. She wasn't going to keep her shape if it kept up. What the hell was happening to her?

"Sue, do something about that screeching," she said sharply.

"You try and stop her. She cries night and day. Please, Vivian, help me," she begged, beginning to sob.

Vivian retrieved a man's sneaker from beneath the sofa. "Don't tell me you have been letting Nathanial stay here," she said incredulously.

Sue hiccupped tearfully. "He's good with the baby. He stays at Paddy's Pub most nights."

Vivian stopped picking up the mess of clothes and stale food. She'd send in housekeeping. There would be snide remarks and gossip. "What the hell," she muttered, "let them talk!"

At least one of my problems has resolved itself, Vivian thought. The American businessman she had thought was scout for the takeover bid for the hotel had turned out to be the tycoon owner of the Manse—bought as an investment during the Celtic Tiger years with the intention of setting up an exclusive club for well-heeled businessmen and politicians from Northern Ireland as a safe haven out of the glare of the media.

Now, he had moved in there with Imelda. And if the rumour mill was to be believed, they were happy as the rabbits that played in the surrounding fields.

Imelda is a cat. She always lands on her feet, Vivian thought enviously. Who would believe that when she was at her very lowest ebb, a rich sugar-coated daddy Romeo would materialise as if out of the mountain mist albeit in a chauffeur-driven Rolls.

Even stranger was that he remembered Imelda as a teenager working for him at the lavish parties he used to host before he abandoned the whole thing and moved back to New York. Now he was back hailing Imelda as an 'entrepreneur' at the job she had done on the house.

"And here am I on the verge of losing the Spa business I sweated blood and tears to build. If this takeover bid goes through and I'm saddled with a frigging screaming kid," she growled slamming her keys down.

She marched into the bathroom and shoved the stopper in the bath. Angrily, she slapped at the hot and cold water as she dumped bubble bath into the rising froth. She'd bath the baby—get rid of that revolting smell!

She caught sight of her face in the steamy mirror. It was mottled red with anger. No wonder Sue looked a mess. After a few days of this, I'd probably look as bad myself, she conceded.

A sense of guilt pervaded her. This mess was partly her fault, she knew. After two weeks of the baby screaming morning and night, she had packed a bag and went to stay in one of the spare chalets. She sighed. Well, she couldn't ignore the situation any longer. Sue was not coping. As usual, she would have to take charge of the situation. She balled her fists. She needed to do *something* to get Sue and herself out of this chaotic situation before the pressure of living under this stress broke their already tenuous relationship.

Maybe if I could get Sue away from here even for a few days she might begin to realise motherhood was not all it was cracked up to be, Vivian thought. "Damn hard work, if you ask me," she muttered swirling her hand around in the foaming bathwater. "Maybe I might be able to convince her that some women are just not cut out to be mothers."

She dumped more bath scents into the rising water. She'd bathe Sue first. Rayan Ritchie could bloody well come and take care of her own baby. Sue needed a break. This obsession with babies had been hogging their lives for too long. She was putting a stop to it right now.

"Your bath is ready."

Sue closed her eyes and lay back in the chair. "I'm exhausted. I'll take it later."

"You'll take it now. I will help you," Vivian said forcing a conciliatory tone into her words.

"I've missed you being here with me," Sue gulped. For a minute the two women held each other.

"Come on. I'm here now. I'll help you into the bath and I'll see to miss-screamer-of-the-year and tidy up here," Vivian quipped forcing a smile on her face.

Sue's body sagged. "I know it's in a bit of a mess, Viv. But I'm always so tired," she said petulantly.

Gently, Vivian reached for her by the elbows and helped her to her feet "Have a lovely long soak. I'll come in and help you wash and condition your hair," she said softly.

Vivian listened for the sound of the bathwater slushing against the side of the tub. Satisfied Sue was well and truly ensconced in the warm bubbles, with a purposeful step, she crossed the small hall and into the bedroom that had been her and Sue before Rayan and the baby came. She wrinkled her nose as she looked in distaste at the rumpled bed. Nathanial had obviously stayed last night and he and Rayan had had a good old romp by the look of the bedclothes.

She snapped up the phone extension beside the bed and rang the hotel coffee shop. Sure enough, Rayan and Nathanial were there. "Take the mobile phone down to Miss Ritchie's table," she ordered in a clipped tone.

The manageress hesitated. Vivian could be a real bitch when she was in a mood. And going by her angry tone she was in a mood today. She shrugged. It was none of her business. But everybody was saying her and Sue's relationship was in the toilet since the baby had arrived. There had been raised eyebrows when Vivian had moved out and the Australian woman had moved in. There were even rumours that it was all planned. That Sue and Rayan had been lovers. That Rayan got pregnant on purpose. That they were setting up house together with the twins.

"Vivian for you," she said handing over the hands-free phone and running her eyes over Nathanial's biceps. Nathanial caught her look and smiled at her. If it was a toss-up between him and Sue in bed, she thought, it was a no-brainer. She'd take him. But what did she know?

"Rayan," Vivian said tersely.

"Yes."

"Get your ass up to the cottage, *now*. Your daughter is screeching like a banshee," Vivian said giving vent to her anger.

There was a beat of silence.

"My daughter's what?"

"*Never mind—get your arse up here NOW!*" Vivian bellowed.

In the background she could hear Nathanial's broad Australian accent asking Rayan what was going on.

"*My* daughter? Have you forgotten something?" Rayan said icily. "Sue is the baby's mother now?"

Fear struck at Vivian heart. Sue would never tell her what stage the adoption was at. Oh God. Had Sue signed the final adoption papers without telling her? Cold sweat formed on Vivian's brow. What would she do if Sue was now the legal lawful mother of twins?

"Sue is not fit to mother one baby let alone two," she said ominously quiet. "If you are not here by the time I have Sue out of the bath, I am ringing Children's Services. Do you hear me, Rayan Ritchie! I am ringing Children's Services. It's what I should have done months ago before all this madness got out of hand," she shouted slamming down the phone.

"Why were you screaming at Rayan?" Sue's voice called out from the bathroom.

"I was bawling her out for not helping you."

"Will you see to the baby now?"

Vivian grimaced. "OK," she said reluctantly.

"Thanks Viv, I would be lost without you," Sue smiled closing her eyes and sinking deeper into the frothy bath water.

Vivian picked up the screaming infant. "Stop that racket, this minute," she ordered. Stripping off the saturated clothing, she tried hard not to breathe in the smell of sour feeding mixed with urine. "Towelling nappies are better for the environment, my ass." She muttered mutinously pulling the stained terry squares off the baby. ... "I'm not washing this shit. Housekeeping can send them out with the laundry," she muttered. She plucked a clean nappy and a vest from the pile of new outfits. Despite her annoyance, she couldn't help smiling at the hiccupping baby. "It's not your fault, baby. You have two mothers and no mother when it comes down to it," she murmured.

The baby laid its soft downy head against her shoulder. For a moment Vivian allowed herself to remember a time when she'd considered hiding behind husband and children. Was Sue giving her a chance to have the best of both worlds? Was the decision not to have children in the normal fashion one she regretted? She shook her head vigorously. She'd loved Sue from the first day she'd met her at a health and beauty trade fair. And despite the difference in their ages—she in her late forties to Sue in her twenties—they had hit it off.

Now Sue was infatuated with idea of being a mother before she became menopausal. Vivian sighed deeply. She'd thought what harm would it do to indulge Sue's mothering instincts? But she'd been secretly relieved when they local authority had turned them down as adopters. *Then Rayan had to come along with twins*, she thought grimly. *Yes, one child she could have possibly managed but not two!*

She wrapped the snuffling baby in the expensive pure pink angora blanket Sue had insisting in buying in a baby boutique to bring *her baby* home from the hospital and went to figure out how to mix the formula for a bottle.

Alone in the kitchen, Vivian wondered what would become of the babies once she phoned Children's Services? She hoped they would be kept together. Fleetingly, she thought of Imelda. She knew Imelda's greatest fear had been if her own sons had been taken into care as babies that they would be separated.

She didn't want that either. But Sue knew nothing about the daily drudgery of bringing up children. She was a brilliant aunt to her nieces and nephew. Sending presents and took them to Dublin Zoo once or twice. But she had never had to cope with them on a seven day a week basis. It was a real shock for Sue to discover that Branna didn't understand Sue was tired and it was time to sleep. "Or, like now, if her bottle is long in coming, she will scream nonstop until she gets it," Vivian murmured shakily hurrying back to the baby.

In many ways, Sue is like a little girl, Vivian mused. Motherhood was, dressing up your baby and walking her out in her pram so that people could admire her. And Branna, as Sue called the baby, with her dark skin and startling big eyes was already fulfilling that dream for Sue from the Spa staff and guests.

Branna sneezed and despite her despondent mood Vivian felt a smile tug her lips upwards at the surprised look on the little screwed up face. Clearing a space, she secured the baby in a corner of the sofa propping the bottle on a cushion. "Enjoy your bottle, little Branna," she murmured. "When you are finished, you are going to have a nice sleep and so is Sue," she said firmly. The baby gave a slow gurgly milky smile as if she understood. Vivian could see how quickly you could become attached to her.

"Why did you call her Branna?" she asked sitting on the edge of the bath rubbing the conditioner into Sue's hair.

"Why? What's wrong with it?"

"It's a Gaelic name. She's not Irish…"

"Her father is Irish. It's a beautiful name," Sue retorted. "It suits her with her dark hair."

"She's not yours yet, is she?" Vivian held her breath waiting for Sue's to confirm if the adoption was legally signed and sealed.

There was a beat of silence. "If you'd had your way, she'd be ashes in some hospital furnace," Sue said shaking her mass of hair so the droplets from it showered her partner. "I know you were only trying to help Isaac and Rayan. But it's a terrible thing to do an innocent baby." She reached out a soapy hand and gripped Vivian's arm. "You pick a name for Baby B. What would you like him to be called?" she asked softly entwining her fingers with Vivian's.

Vivian looked down at their entwined hand and watched the diamonds on Sue's glitter through the rainbow of coloured bubbles.

Under Irish law, they couldn't be legally married. But they'd each taken their own vows had given each other the gift of a gold bejewelled wedding band.

A dull pain started a drum beat in Vivian's temple. What was it about this woman, about Sue, that she loved so much? Even in her dishevelled state her face naked of makeup she had a raw beauty about her. Was that it? Was it that, unlike her, Sue didn't need to hide behind a mask of cosmetics and a relentless routine of toning and firming to look and feel confident in her own skin? Vivian shivered. She knew she wasn't worthy of Sue. She had always known she would lose Sue's love one day. Vivian stood up abruptly. If Sue ever found out about her terminations when she was a teenager, she would leave her for sure and never come back.

"I've phoned for Rayan to come and take her baby."

Sue's eyes filled with tears. "No!"

"Yes. It's too much for you, Sue. What you need is a holiday. We both need a break away from all this chaos. Let's go on that cruise you always wanted to go on."

Sue let go of Vivian's hand. "Go back to the Spa," Sue said clambering out of the bath. "It's your real, love," she said wrapping her body in a large towel.

"Sue, that's not true. I love you."

"You have no time in your life for anything else." There was a note of finality and a touch of cold steel in Sue's words Vivian had never heard before.

Shaken, Vivian went back into the lounge room and placed the sleeping baby in the wicker bassinette. "I'm doing this for you…and your brother," she murmured. "You need to be adopted far away from here where the pointing fingers and gossip mongrels with minds like sewers don't know anything about you," she said tucking in the blanket.

"She's lost weight since I started to take care of her," Sue said coming up to look over Vivian's shoulder at the baby.

"She's not the only one. You're worrying yourself into bad health," Vivian said tucking a stray hair behind Sue's ear.

"She's missing her twin," Sue gulped. "If he was with her, here, she wouldn't cry so much."

Vivian threw her hands up in the air. "Sue, look at yourself. Look around you at the state of this place. You can't manage one baby. How are you going to manage two babies?"

"Baby B will be getting out of hospital soon. Branna will stop crying when her twin is here with her," Sue said stubbornly.

This has to end here and now, Vivian thought wearily sinking into a chair. It might also mean the end of your relationship if you force Sue into give up the babies, her inner voice warned. It might, Vivian admitted. But I can't stand by and watch Sue being torn apart trying to be a mother. She stood up and took a deep breath. "I'm going to talk to somebody—get help," she said.

Hope flared in Sue's eyes.

"I think Rayan is hoping Nathanial will take on the babies. If he doesn't there are…agencies that look after children…"

Sue's face paled. No! No! "Please Vivian… You don't like Rayan," Sue shot out. "You're jealous of her; jealous of her friendship with me! That's why you hate Branna."

Vivian gasped. It was true she had never liked Rayan; sensed Sue was keen on her. She'd seen Rayan as a threat to her Sue's relationship. She swept an armful of soiled baby clothes beside her off the sofa on to the floor. "Yes, you're right, I was jealous of your friendship—still am," she admitted. "But I don't hate a wee helpless infant. It's just ridiculous to say that—shows how stressed you are that you would even *think* that."

"It's not ridiculous, it's true!"

"It's not true." Vivian stood up her back as straight as a ramrod. "L knew *you* fancied Rayan. A blind man on a motorbike could see that. It was the talk of the salon when the staff thought I wasn't around. Remember that night you stood me up and went *au naturel* with her in the Sauna? You're not going to tell me that was just friendship?" Vivian mocked.

Sue clenched her jaw. "Your problem, Vivian, is you think everybody is like you—self-serving enough to take what they want without thinking about other people." She picked up the sleeping baby and gazed down at its little pouted mouth with traces of milk at the corners.

Vivian smirked. "It's you who are self-serving—you, paying all Rayan's hospital expenses so you'd be guaranteed she'd keep her word about letting you adopt the twins. But she's not so sure now, is she?" She took a deep breath. "I'm doing what I'm doing because I love you, Sue."

Tears splashed down Sue's cheeks. "Please Vivian; please let me keep the baby. Rayan doesn't want her. She'll end up…"

"She will be adopted by a family who will love and cherish her." Vivian held up her hand as Sue started to speak again. "Have I ever refused you anything in the years we have been together?"

Sue shook her head but tightened her grip on the baby. Here within her grasp was everything she had ever wanted and Vivian was taking it away from her. In that moment her love for Vivian turned to hate.

Vivian turned away from the look on her face.

"Where are you going, Vivian?"

"To make arrangements for the babies."

Sue hugged the baby to her breast. "Please, Viv, please, I'm *begging* you. Don't do this. If you do it's the end for you and me," she sobbed. "I promise, I *promise* I'll clean the place up…not let the baby cry," she said her voice rising hysterically.

The words that rose to Vivian lips remained unsaid as Rayan spoke behind her, "Nathanial wants the boy but not Branna."

Chapter Forty-Five

The brakes squealed in protest as Mac O Lochlainn brought the bus to a shuddering stop. He robbed the sleep from his eyes and squinted near-sightedly at the figure looming up like a ghost out of the early morning mist. He put his hand on the horn.

At the shrill sound Rayan jumped into the shallow drain that ran alongside of the narrow strip of road barely wider than a broad path.

"What the blue blazers are ye doin' walkin' in the middle o' the road in the dark," Mac bawled out of the window of the bus. "I might have run over you," he bellowed.

Rayan startled. In the shadowy dawn light, the bus looked like a huge prehistoric animal with blinking eyes.

"You should wear your glasses like your wife says, then you'd see where you were driving," Rayan shouted rudely. The truth was she had been so caught up in her own distressed thoughts she hadn't heard the rattling of the old bus.

"Get in before the battery dies. It's not right charged yet," Mac said sourly seeing her staring at the flickering headlights.

"Top of the mornin' to you too," Rayan said bitingly in a mock Irish accent.

"Get in. Ah thought since the babies were born, you'd stopped tramping about the roads at all hours of the day and night," Mac grumbled focusing on the swell of her breast under her coat as she stepped up to the second step. He shifted his eyes. What I'd give to be thirty years younger walking arm in arm with a feisty woman like Rayan, he thought. Give over, he berated himself, there's enough gossip. You could write a book about this poor woman and her unfortunate babies without you adding to it.

"You're incorrigible, Mac O Lochlainn. Do you know that? And at this hour of the morning too," Rayan reprimanded him, seeing the gleam in his eye.

"What?"

"Don't you dare say it, Mac," she warned.

"What? What was ah goin' to say," Mac frowned and settled back into the drivers' seat.

"What you always say every time you look at my breasts," Rayan retorted dropping into a seat. "The Donegal air is doing you a power of good," she mimicked; she threw him a scathing look. "I'm not in the mood for your old blarney given the kind of week I've had," she warned him.

Mac released the handbrake. "Can't a man pay a lovely girl a compliment?"

"Not today."

"What about Sue and wee baby?"

"Don't ask."

Mac got the message. She didn't want to talk about it. The bus rattled over a deep pothole. Mac swore.

"Get out of the wrong side of the bed this morning?" Rayan asked noting the absence of Mac's usually cheerful disposition.

Mac grunted. Usually, he loved showing the visitors around his lovely county of Donegal. But today his heart felt heavy as a cement block in his chest. How was he going to do oul mad Manus' bidding. Jesus! He'd bounced Raphael on his knee as a baby. He wiped his hand distractedly across his stubble. Anxiety like an iron fist gripped his guts. It was going to be bad, very bad.

Mac's gaze swept over the face of the mountain range and he shuddered. He never saw its beauty like the tourist did. He spun the tourist's yarns about its magical wishing wells and waterfalls. That's what they expected to hear. But he knew the mountains' deep dark secrets hidden below the mossy bog's scenic beauty held the bones of men thought to be traitors—informers—touts to the *cause*.

His father and his grandfather had been in the old IRA—the Irish Republican Army. He had been reared on stories of the suffering of Irish people at the hands of the English Crown. He had been soothed to sleep on tales of the 1916 Easter Rising, the Partition of Ireland that and the Civil War of the 1922 that followed, where brother killed brother.

He shuddered. In the night when sleep refused to bring relief from his guilt, the stories and the voices of the dead on the mountains came to him. And now Manus wanted him to add Raphael's voice to their clamour.

"Are you OK, Mac?"

Realising Rayan was scrutinising him Mac slapped a grin on his face. "Ah, ye know, was just thinking about the old folk."

"What old folk? You mean Raphael's granny, Norah?"

Mac snorted. "Not that oul hag! No! Ah was thinking about me father and his father before him...and all the seed breed and generation o' them." He coughed nervously and changed the subject. "How's the wee lad's lungs coming along now?"

Rayan bit her lip and didn't answer. It was a subject she didn't want to have to think about right now. She tugged at the hem of her glove unravelling the stitching. The illuminations hands on her watch showed 4.55. "You're out earlier than usual this morning—busy day ahead?" she said side-stepping his question.

"Paddy's Pub in Falcarragh phoned—tourist is looking for a lift into Derry. Ah offered to pick him up before ah picked up my crowd." Mac threw her a look as a thought struck him. "Were ye going in that direction yourself," he asked perceptively. "Is that not where that boyo that came to see you is stayin'?

Rayan nodded. "It's probably him you're going to pick up." She lapsed into silence. She'd woken up with a vague, apprehensive feeling that she shouldn't let Nathanial go away without saying goodbye to him properly.

Rayan ducked her head into her chest. She couldn't believe she had turned down Nathanial's offer. She shook her head in bewilderment. All she had thought about *wished for* with all her heart was for Nathanial to say he forgave her and wanted her back. He'd done that and more and she'd rejected him. A sense of agitation filled her. What was wrong with her? She knew in her heart that he'd never ask her again. His disappointment had been palpable. Their parting had been acrimonious.

"I thought I'd go and see him before he goes. I don't think I'll be expected at Paddy's or made welcome," she mumbled.

"It's as well for you ah decided to take the mountain road, isn't it. You're no Maureen O Hara. It's a fair stretch o' the legs from the hotel to Paddy's Pub," Mac said grumpily.

Rayan gave him a perplexed look and then a wan smile. "Oh, I get it. John Wayne and Maureen O'Hara in the film, *The Quiet Man*. Do you know before I came to live here that was the image of Ireland I had in my head along with pictures of quaint wee whitewashed cottages with roses growing around the door. I even asked Imelda how I'd get about and she told me she had a pony and trap," sarcastic bitch, Rayan muttered.

The silence enveloped each of them in their separate thoughts as the bus left the back roads and on to the main road leading to Falcarragh. "And why would ye not be welcome? Wasn't he your live-in partner for years? He'll be needin' a farewell kiss." Mac caught her eye in the mirror. "Did you have a row?" he enquired his natural nosiness getting the better of him.

"He wants me but only one of my babies," Rayan blurted out.

Mac said nothing as he chewed over this bit of information. He had heard Vivian had booked an exclusive holiday for her and Sue. He wondered did that mean she had put a stop to the adoption.

"What's going to happen to the babies?"

Rayan drew in a deep breath. "It's all up in the air at the minute. The social workers are dealing with it."

Mac sighed feeling genuinely sorry for Rayan. "And ye say that boyfriend of yours wants to separate them? That's a pity."

Rayan looked unseeing out of the bus window at the fields as the shadows of night shortened and the cows began to lumber away from the shelter of the hedges. She knew what she confided in Mac would be common gossip before the day was out. "Yes. He wants to keep the boy and let Sue adopt the girl."

Mac didn't add that the wicked old bitch of a Norah was spreading rumours that the wee lass had hair black as a raven hair and as wicked and bad-tempered as Imelda had been as a child. Poor Sue was nearly ready for the mental hospital; the child was so uncontrollable.

Loose pebbles skidded beneath the wheels as Mac drove into the forecourt of Paddy's Pub. "Ah'll come in win' ye—just in case, he cuts up rough," he offered as Rayan stepped with an uncertain step from the bus.

Nathanial couldn't believe his eyes. As Rayan stepped into the kitchen of the pub, his heart jumping like a jackhammer, he fumbled out a chair for her at the kitchen table. "I'm glad you came," he said hoarsely. Without asking, he poured her out a cup of tea.

Rayan's tongue seemed to be stuck to the roof of her dry mouth and her hands shook. She glanced at the owner of the pub, Paddy Francis. Despite the early hour, he was already busy frying up platters of bacon and sausages as part of a full Irish breakfast for the hill walkers.

"The things ye find on the back road o' Donegal in a mornin' mist," Mac joked winking at Nathanial. Sitting down uninvited he poured a mug of tea and tucked into the ratchet of warm toast.

Paddy Francis glowered at him. "Help yourself, why don't you."

Unperturbed, Mac buttered a round of the toasted bread. "What about a bit o' bacon and eggs," he asked.

"Paying guest first," the owner said sliding a plate of food in front of Nathanial. "Can I offer you a bit of breakfast?" he said in a gentler tone to Rayan.

Rayan shook her head. She didn't think she'd be able to get anything down past the lump in her throat. She looked in amazement as Nat tucked into the heaped plate of bacon, sausages, fried wheaten bread, black pudding, fried tomatoes and double yoked eggs. He certainly has changed his eating habits, she thought in amazement, watching him shovel it into his mouth.

Like a kid caught with his hand in the sweetie jar, Nat gave her a bashful look. "Back to full on training when I touch down in Perth," he grinned.

A sudden onset of homesickness engulfed Rayan. She thought what it would be like to walk out of Perth Airport and go home to her own house and business. An ache started in her stomach. She wanted to go home; feel the heat on her skin and hear the familiar burr of the Australian accent. I wish I was going with him, she thought. But things were different now. I am a mother.

Nathanial ate in silence. Rayan glanced at Mac tuned in to every look that passed between her and Nat. There was no way they were going to get a chance to have a private conversation. No way was she going to have the opportunity to tell him the adoption had been shelved—at least until a proper assessment of the needs of the twins could be properly made. She gulped. In the meantime Children's Care Service would be taking care of the twins.

"Are ye packed yet, young fella," Mac asked sourly. "Ah haven't all day to sit about while you chew the fat. Ah have—"

"Yeah, mate. I'm packed and ready," Nat said resignedly.

"You'll find his bags at the door of the house—if you have a mind to drag yourself away from that breakfast table," Paddy Francis barked at Mac giving him a dirty look that said he should shift his arse and give the parting couple a private moment to themselves.

"Hillwalkers' needin' a lift to the foothills o' Muckish or Errigal?" Mac asked in an attempt to placate the pub owner.

"The answer is in the question," Paddy Francis barked banging another tray of sausages into a double oven. "*They're walkers.* They don't need a fecking lift."

"Don't you to be long, fella," Mac growled at Nathanial.

Nat nodded his assent as he wiped the last of the egg yolk off the plate with the last piece of toast.

Rayan's heart plummeted to her feet. She felt light-headed as if she might fall over. This was it. Nathanial was going out of her life forever.

"Put the mug o' tea and toast on me bill," Mac said sarcastically as he left the kitchen.

"Nosy freeloading bastard," the pub owner muttered as he slammed the oven door shut. He cleared his throat as if getting rid of a bad taste and turned to Nathanial. "See to things, while I give them shower of dozy headed Germans another shout," he said wiping his hands on the tea towel he had tucked into the belt of his trousers.

"Sure thing, mate," Nat said thankful for the man's tact in letting them have the kitchen for themselves.

Tears prickled behind Rayan's eyes. "I wish I was going with you," she said attempting a smile.

Nathanial rose and took a step towards her. "Why don't you. You haven't anything to keep you here now." Rayan opened her mouth to speak. "Shush," Nat said cupping her face in his hands. "I love you Rayan. I didn't know how much until I saw you again. I'd marry you in a heartbeat on top of Muckish—if you want."

Suddenly, Rayan was kissing him passionately.

In one fluid movement Nat encircled her in his arms again. She could feel the power and security of his body as he pressed her to him. "Come with me," he murmured into her neck.

Rayan stood stock still. She wished right at this moment it was as simple as that. "I can't," she mumbled. "I have the babies to think about now and the adoption and Sue…"

"Branna is in temporary foster care and her brother is going there once he is discharged from the hospital. And as for Sue in the adoption… I can't see it happening, Rayan," he said stroking her back. "Have you your passport on you?" he jerked out.

Rayan nodded. She always carried her passport and her bank book. There had been several break-ins at the staff cottages.

"Come with me," Nat urged. "What have you got to look forward except being chucked out of the cottage when Vivian brings Sue back? Come with me," he pleaded.

"It's winter in Perth…"

"But a hell of a lot warmer than spring here," Nathanial argued.

"I can't…just run away…from my responsibilities again."

Nathanial stopped cajoling her and let his arms fall to his side. "I have to go, Rayan…"

Panic gripped Rayan. Her gut told her if she let Nathanial walk away this time it really would be the end of them. "What about my clothes and all my things? I can't go home with just the clothes I'm standing up in!" she stammered out.

Nathanial swung her around, jostling the table and making the milk dance about in the jug. "Who needs clothes," he said seductively running his index finger around her lips. "Anyway, we're touching down in London and Dubai. You can buy all the clothes you want, babe."

"Ready?" Mac asked coming back in.

"We sure are, mate. Any objection to another passenger?" Nat chortled.

"Not a bother. Tell him to shift himself…"

"Ready, babe?" Nathanial said, grasping Rayan's hand.

Mac looked from to the other. "Rayan's going as far as Derry with you?"

"All the way, mate."

Mac's jaws dropped. "She's goin' back to Australia, now, today?"

Nathanial nodded.

Mac swung around to eyeball Rayan. "You sure about this, girlie?" He gave her a dazed look. "It's all a bit…rushed. What about your ticket for the flight?" He scowled at Nathanial. That fella could sell snow to the Eskimos; especially if they're women, he thought.

Rayan hesitated. Mac was right. She should take a step back and think about this? Wasn't it a crazy impulsive decision that brought you here and got you into all this mess in the first place? Her inner voice remonstrated with her.

She fingered her passport in her pocket. The temporary foster mother had promptly changed Branna's feeding from breast milk to bottled formula. And the nurses at the hospital had followed suit with Baby B.

She took the passport out and held it in her hand, fingering the binding.

Nathanial took it from her and flicked it open. "Decision made," he stated triumphantly. "Your visa expires today. There are always seats in First Class…"

Chapter Forty-Six

"Have you seen much of Raphael lately? I was hoping he'd be with you today," Kate said wistfully. "Its weeks since I saw him."

"See to the regulars," her father Manus ordered and jerked his head in the direction of the Hill Top pub door indicating Mac should follow him.

Outside, the bright May Day sunbeams smiled graciously on the yellow gorse that decorated the mountainy fields turning them golden.

Like a badger leaving its sett the old man scanned the picnic area. Satisfied he wouldn't be overheard by tourists snapping photographs of the fields and the mountains, he lowered his body down onto a seat.

"Wright's a tout," he ground out without preamble. "I'm ordering you to sort the wee bastard out."

"You're wrong there, boss. Raphael Wright is a sound man."

Manus' brow darkened. "You callin' your superior officer a liar."

Mac steeled himself. It was dangerous, very dangerous, to cross swords with the old man.

Manus shifted his gaze and looked across the fields and hedgerows dressed in late spring foliage looked fresh and green. What he was ordering O Lochlainn to do was personal—and abuse of his power as unit commander.

"Raphael has served the IRA well carrying information, shifting guns and ammunition from one arms dump to another," Mac said.

"He's loose cannon now after that business with Big Brendie arrested and the Garda finding the arms dump," Manus growled. He sighed. Kate was besotted with Wright. He sighed again. Wright was a womaniser. He was making his daughter a laughing stock courting half the country including that big-mouthed Australian woman who had blabbed to the Garda. He'd deal with her later.

He watched Mac O Lochlainn surreptitiously. He looks green about the gills, Manus thought. It will test his loyalty to me, he thought. He spat on the ground. "Touts are lower than the rats that scuttle through the sewers," he snarled.

He breathed deep into his chest. Younger men in the organisation were snapping at his heels keen to show their mettle. He'd show them he still had the balls to order his long-standing comrade to execute the boy O Lochlainn had nurtured in the absence of a father.

"How did the Brits know Big Frank would be crossing the Border the night of that party last May? Only you, I and Wright knew."

A group of tourists came and sat down at the nearest bench to them.

Manus lumbered to his feet. Mac followed until they were standing on the bend of the road that led to the GlenShane Pass and Derry City. "Don't question my order. Find out who Wright's Brit's handler is and what information he's passed on then put a bullet in the bastard's head."

"Raphael's no informer—I'd stake me life on it."

Manus swivelled his huge body around. "If it wasn't Wright it must have been you," he shot out.

Mac's Adam's apple bobbed up and down in fury. Red hot ire exploded in his brain driving him past reason or self-preservation. White lipped with rage he turned on his unit commander all sense of levels of authority wiped away. "There was never any touts in my family connection," he said furiously. "My father and his father, every breed, seed and generation o' them to a man—and, aye, womenfolk too, fought to free Ireland to the very marrow in their bones. What about yours? Maybe it was yourself who gave the Brits the information, Raphael, me *and you* knew where the arms dump was!"

With a bellow Manus' face turned a mottled purple; his tree trunk of arms came up, his hands shot out. Mac thought he was going to throttle him where he stood.

"Your loyalty is with Wright," Manus roared. "Get in your bus and get to fuck out of here. The bloodhounds will do it." He puffed with exertion as he pushed up the steep incline and in through the pub door.

Mac acknowledged the insanity that now glittered in the old man's eyes. The sadist's thugs used during the Troubles were nicknamed the bloodhounds because they literally tore men from limb to limb to get information from them. He shuddered. He'd shoot Raphael himself before he'd let him fall into their hands.

"I'll do it," he quaked, caving in. "What about Kate?"

"She'll get over it. What about that big-mouthed Aussie hoor?" Manus asked almost conversationally, spreading his weight on a barstool.

"She's back to Perth."

Manus scowled and looked around for his daughter.

Kate left the customer she was serving. "You want a drink, Dada," she said a surprised note in her voice.

He smiled at her. "I do, Daughter. No, not that stuff," he said as Kate reached for a bottle. "Pour me a good measure out of that bottle of Bushmills I keep for toasting special occasions."

"Can I toast it too, Dada."

Manus felt a beat starting to throb in his neck. Wright was the only man she'd ever known. She thought she loved him. What did she know about love? But if she guessed he was having his shot…

"Go on, darlin' find the bottle…"

"I know where you keep it, Dada."

"I don't want her to *ever* know," he snarled when Kate was out of earshot.

"Here you are, Dada," Kate said plonking the bottle of single malt whiskey on the counter.

Mac watched as Manus lost his antagonistic grim expression and smiled with unbridled love at his daughter. Leaning across Kate kissed him on the cheek. "We'll keep the rest for when Raffi asks me to marry him," she confided.

Manus raised his glass so that the sunlight from the open door illuminated the golden liquid. He hoped he was long dead before she found out what he had done for love of her and love of his country. "Aye, we could do that, I suppose," he responded avoiding her eyes. He put the drink to his head and threw it back.

"Another one to keep the first one company, Dada?"

"No, darlin', I need a clear head." A shadow crossed his face. "You're the best daughter a father could ever wish for," he said. He cupped her face in his hands and looked into eyes so like her mother's. A deep guttural sob escaped from his throat. "Remember anything I did was for you and your children's children. See to O Lochlainn, there," he remonstrated with her gently as she hugged him.

He shoved his belly against the bar and levered his bulky body off the bar stool. Kate's smile left her face. "Are you feeling unwell, Dada?" Her father waved her concerns away.

"My mother left when I was a baby," Kate explained to Mac. "But I'm lucky. I have the best dada in the world," she smiled. "Same again?" she asked dimpling at Mac.

There was no time to spare if he was to get Raffi away to some place where he'd be safe, Mac thought. He licked his lips, dry despite the whiskey he had just sunk. "Ah don't want to lose the oul bus licence," he quipped.

"Give the man a double whiskey. He's going to earn it." His melancholy forgotten, a malicious smiled played around the corners of Manus' thickset lips. "Did you know this bottle of whiskey was matured for twenty-one years? It's as old as young Wright."

Mac got the message. The maturing of the whiskey has to come to an end just like Raphael. Wright's life had.

"What about you, Dada?"

"No, not for me; I have things needing seeing to. Keep the bottle handy. We'll celebrate later—just you and me."

The sadistic bastard, Mac thought. He would let his daughter unwittingly toast to the brutal death of her boyfriend. He threw the whiskey into the back of his throat.

"Bring Raphael the next time you come," Kate smiled, refilling his glass.

Mac could feel the amber coloured liquid burn all the way down to his feet. What had he to lose? He was already a dead man walking.

Mac shook his head. "Can't do that, Kate. I wish I could."

"Why can't you?"

"Following your father's *orders*," he said emphasising his words.

Kate's round face blanched. "Dada gave you orders…to do with my Raphael?"

She gripped Mac's hand tightly. Her eyes widened with horror. "It's about that party and that bouncer, isn't it? Dada's getting Raffi dealt with, isn't he? That's what he was celebrating, wasn't it?"

Mac nodded. He was signing his own death warrant but it might save Raphael time to get away.

"*He knows* it was that Australian woman and now she's gone…somebody has to pay," Kate said her voice rising. "Well, it is not going to be my boyfriend," she bawled.

"Shush girlie!" Mac looked around uneasily. "Walls have ears."

"Dada has no right! I'm not a wee girl anymore." Fire danced in her eyes. Slapping down the tea towel she had been vigorously polishing glasses with, she glared at Mac. "Here have the rest of the bottle. I need a word with my father."

A hush fell over the bar. Drinkers down their drink and headed out the door. A storm was brewing and they wanted no part of it.

Mac put the bottle of whiskey to his head. He wasn't getting out of here alive. He had touted to Manus' daughter. He might as well die drunk. The whiskey gathered in the pit of his stomach. He waited.

After what seemed like a very long time, he heard the heavy tread of Manus' step behind him "Bring Wright to the waterfall on Muckish at six o'clock," Manus snarled.

Mac breathed out in relief. "Thanks Boss," he mumbled.

But he knew Manus. Like a cornered animal, his authority challenged by his own daughter at Mac's doing and in front of the drinkers, his old commander was twice as dangerous now. He needed to act fast.

Kate had bought her boyfriend a compromise; he would suffer a humiliating brutal beating and be shot in both knees. He would never walk into the Hill Top pub again nor be permitted to see Kate but as least he'd be alive, Mac reasoned.

Mac had no doubt there was a bullet already marked with his name.

He hoped they'd shoot him on the mountain—leave him to die behind the waterfall.

As he drove away despite the bottle of whiskey he'd just drunk, his head was as clear as a bell. Waiting for six o'clock to bring Raphael to the mountain was a possible decoy to appease Kate. The hound dogs were probably on their way to Norah's house right now.

Raphael's smile faded as Mac, shouting out his name, leaped from the bus even before it stopped. "Get across the fields—make for the Border; you might have some chance there," he panted in a highly agitated state. "Manus' shower of mad dogs is on their way for you. Don't stand there with your mouth hanging open. You knew it might come to this. That murdering oul bastard is having you done away with…"

"Get out of my house, Mac O Lochlainn. Raphael is going nowhere. I'm calling the Guards," Norah bawled reaching for the phone.

"I'm no tout. You know that… I'll tell them…" Raphael said.

"When will ye tell them? After they'd torn you limb from limb and dumped you in the bog as fodder for the wild fowl," Mac bawled. He could feel the froth coming out of his mouth and running down his chin.

Above the melee, Mac heard the sharp crack of booted feet on the loose gravel outside.

He grabbed Raphael. "Get out to fuck—over the fields. Don't go to the mountain," he bawled.

"I'll explain—"

"Suffering Christ, man, they're here to murder you and me," Mac bellowed as the door of the house banged open and a group of men wearing balaclavas crowded into Norah's living room.

Chapter Forty-Seven

Rayan gasped as she stared at her father. Gone was the arrogant puffed-up man who had bullied and belittled her. Here was a man reduced in prominence but his eyes hadn't changed. Ice cold, they stared into her shocked face.

He sat in the armchair he claimed was his personal seat padded upright by a mountain of pillows "Get her...out. No visitors," he choked out slapping at her mother's hands; his words coming out garbled and distorted.

"You have upset him, as usual. You should have telephoned—see if he was seeing visitors," her mother admonished edging her out of the lounge room. Her mother's chastisement sounded like an echo from Rayan's childhood.

"I didn't think I'd need an appointment to see my own father or you, Mother. I thought you might be glad to see your only daughter, only child, after being on the other side of the world for over a year."

There was no welcome on her mother's face. "You took your time coming to see us. It's June now. You've been back in Perth since April."

"I'm sorry. It took me a while to get my business back on its feet, settle back in..."

"Your business could have waited. I needed help with your father. "A thought struck her and she cast a horror-struck look around. "You haven't those *babies here*, have you?" Her hand flew to her chest and she plucked at her blouse. "The doctor says another stroke will kill your father," her mother's chin wobbled. Without warning, loud choking sobs filled the quiet kitchen.

Icy fingers shivered their way down Rayan's back. The sound of her mother crying dragged her back to the sleepless nights she'd been woken out of her sleep by her mother's cries as her father struck her in the middle of the night.

"Your grandchildren are in foster care in Ireland," Rayan said reaching for her bag. "I have pictures..."

"*No!* Your father...has forbidden me to have anyth—"

The familiar feelings of pity mixed with rage Rayan had felt against her mother as she grew up rose in her again. "He has ordered you to have nothing to do with me or them, hasn't he, Mother?"

"He's my husband...."

"Yes, he is. And I am your daughter and these are your grandson and daughter," Rayan said spreading out the photos the social worker had sent her on the kitchen table. She took a deep breath. "Look at them, Mother. Just for once, ignore what my father says and put *me first*."

Her mother hiccupped struggling to regain her composure. "You have brought a good father's and husband's name down...again," she said glaring at the photos of Baby B and Branna.

Rayan stared at her mother incredulously. "He is domineering, controlling and abusive. How can you say he's a good husband! Despite his stroke he is still controlling you; forbidding you to even look at a photograph of the only grandchildren you will ever have," Rayan hissed.

Her mother eyes focused somewhere behind Rayan's left shoulder. "He is the way he was because of you." She drew in a deep breath and rushed on. "When I got pregnant on our honeymoon and had a son he was delighted. He only lived for a day. I never forgave myself for that," she choked gulping back tears. "Your father would have been a very different man had his son lived."

Rayan's ears popped. Had she heard right? "You had a son before you had me? I had a brother?"

Her mother nodded. "Your father insisted I get pregnant right away again. He was adamant it would be another boy..."

"But instead he got me," Rayan finished for her.

"Yes," her mother affirmed. "If I had known you were going to be a girl...but they couldn't tell in those days."

Rayan felt as if her lungs had stopped functioning. She felt the ground shift beneath her. For a moment she felt as if she was going to keel over. She fought for air. Like a fish out of water she opened her mouth wide and drew in great gulps of air. Her mother was saying if she had known she was carrying a girl she would have had an abortion.

The old familiar feelings of helpless rage rose up in Rayan. She clenched her fists. "My being born didn't make my father a controlling abuser," she choked out. "He was like that before I was born, and you know it, Mother!"

Her mother, Dawn, sniffed. "I wanted for nothing. He was a good man…before you were born."

Rayan could hardly believe what she was hearing. "He controlled the amount of money *he* deemed to dole out to you. *He decided* what friends were suitable for you as the wife of a man in his respectable position in the community." Rayan paused to draw a calming breath. "Was that why he never let you love me because I wasn't a son?" she asked.

Her mother startled. Rayan's words resonated with her. Her husband had been devastated when she'd given birth to a daughter. It was the first time he'd struck her. Behind the privacy of the curtained bed, he had slapped her hard across the face with his open palm. She had been so shocked she hadn't even cried out. The next day he brought her a huge box of chocolate and flowers.

The nurses thought him charming. But behind the curtain when she breastfed the baby, he became incensed, demanded she stop. Saying he loved her beautiful breasts and didn't want them spoiled by breastfeeding.

As soon as she got home from the hospital, she'd stopped breastfeeding Rayan. But paying Rayan the slightest attention when he was around drove him into a temper and finding fault with her care of him.

Then he had an affair. He said the affair was because he couldn't make love to her while the Rayan was sleeping in their room. She'd moved Rayan's cot out into another room and closed her ears to the baby's cries.

She jumped as the sound of Rayan's voice brought her back to the kitchen.

"I'll leave the photos."

Her mother narrowed her eyes. "Giving birth hasn't changed you. Even as a small infant you were defiant and rebellious." She looked at her daughter's closed face. "You were such a time-consuming baby—looking for my attention all the time. Your father needed me to spend time with him but that wasn't always possible because you were such a demanding baby—looking for attention." She broke off remembering how happy it made her feel to hear him say he wanted to be with her even after she had failed him by giving him a daughter and not a son… She swallowed hard. "Your father found you a hard baby to love. He changed after you were born. You made him the way he is. I wanted for nothing before I gave birth to you."

Rayan's eyes opened wide in shock.

"You wanted for *everything* that makes up a normal relationship between a husband and wife," Rayan said gathering up her bag. It had been a mistake to come back here. Her father had done a good job on her mother. She'd defend him to his grave.

"You were brought up in a good home. Your father's friends and colleagues said we were the perfect family."

Rayan held fast to her rising temper. She hadn't come to fight with her mother. She had come hoping their time apart might have healed some of the old wounds. "You helped him maintain that illusion of a happy family, Mother," she said striving for calmness. "You were always careful to wear something that hid the bruises when we had guests. *He* always played the devoted husband praising you in front of people on the way you kept the house and the meal you had just cooked. There was no mention of how he berated and belittled you. That was kept for later when everybody had gone home, wasn't it?"

Dawn wiped at the tears that had dried on her cheeks. "You don't understand. You never understood. Your father had a position to maintain. I had to be there to support him," her mother whimpered like a wounded animal. "I failed him before. I didn't want to fail him again." Failing her husband by not giving him another son had driven him to be unfaithful to her. She looked at her daughter. In a way she was partly to blame. If she'd been born a boy, things would have been different.

"You never loved me. Why did you never love me? You lavished more time and attention on my father's bloody rose bushes than you did on me," Rayan burst out. "All because he insisted on wearing a fresh white rose in his buttonhole every morning. Do you know why? What he didn't tell you was that all your hard work was done for the benefit of whatever young teacher he had within his wandering womanising eye. It adorned the chosen one's desk every day—until he tired of her and moved on to the next."

Dawn glanced nervously in the direction of the lounge room. She could feel her husband listening to every word. She shivered.

She looked at her daughter's stricken face. Tentatively, she reached out her hand. "It's just the way he is. He loved you…"

Rayan went to stand beside the window. Her heart felt as if it was torn and bleeding. She looked out at the garden with its bushes of white roses; the day unusually overcast for spring in Perth "Do you know what his kind of 'love' did for me, Mother?" Rayan ground out. "It left me feeling reviled and unwanted all my life. So much so that I promised myself I would never be a mother; never expose a vulnerable child to the feeling of rejection I felt." Abruptly she turned from the window. She knew her father had heard every word.

He recoiled as she neared his chair. "Do you know what your twisted mind robbed me of, *Father*," she said her voice low and menacing. "It robbed me of a mother's love," she said through bloodless lips as she stood over him. "And if it hadn't been for right-thinking people in Ireland—strangers—it would have led me to abort two innocent babies and kill myself."

Her father froze beneath her steely gaze. With grim satisfaction Rayan saw his pale eyes like a trapped animal flood with fear. For one wild moment she had an insane desire to reach for him and shake him; spew hurtful belittling words at him as he had her as a child.

She drew back as her mother rushed into the room. "No need to panic, Mother. I was just saying goodbye to my father," she said without turning. She leaned closer until her eyes burned into his. "If only your son had lived. You could have twisted him into a bully and an abuser just like you did me," she said sneeringly.

Her mother tugged at her arm. Rayan shook her off. "You let me think I was a big disappointment to you. But it was *you, the bigshot college administrator,* who was the big disappointment as a father!"

Her father opened his mouth wide. Garbled words came out in spittle. Rayan smiled savouring his agitated state. "All that control and power your personal weapons—taken away from you in an instant," she said through clenched teeth. "Now you don't even have power over your own body movements, do you, *Father*," she said contemptuously, wrinkling her nose at the repugnant smell of urine.

"You never loved *me*, your own flesh and blood, so why did you tell me not to give away my babies to strangers?"

"Family name, the Ritchie family name," her mother burst out. "Your father is the last of his generation to bear the Ritchie name. A man needs a son...or grandson to carry on his name." Distraught, she wrung her hands. "You were a girl—you would marry and change your name...but...you gave him a grandson...to carry on the family name forward..."

Rayan whirled around then turned back to her father. Selfish and twisted to the end, she thought. She felt her lips draw back baring her teeth. "You lousy bastard. You knew once your grandson was adopted, he'd take on his new family name. You would let *him* languish in the Irish Care System so that the Ritchie family name could be preserved." Fighting for control she leaned even closer. "Your grandson will *never* carry the Ritchie name The Ritchie name will die, with you, *Father*."

She arched her chin. A small silvery scar glittered in the light of the table lamp. "This is what you gave me for daring to compare you to the man you called a beach bum—remember him, *Father*? Nathanial, he's a better man than you ever were. *Your grandson* will bear *his* name, not yours."

Chapter Forty-Eight

Isaac walked desolately through Dublin's city centre after another crappy day of kow-towing to whining well-heeled clients with nothing better to do than send solicitor's letters to their neighbours about cutting or not cutting dammed bushes on their shared driveways.

His body felt as dehydrated as a fish washed up on the banks of the River Liffey. He wished he could get drunk in one of pubs that were on every corner. Was it worth the risk? Shawnee's father had spies everywhere.

He had been in Dublin for month now. And yet was still as much out of step with the roar and beat of the city that milled about him with its rush of people and traffic as he been the first day he came here.

For a second, he thought he saw a familiar figure from home on the other side of the street. He shrugged. It was all in his head; his mind playing imaginary tricks on him. He often imagined the turn of a head or a laugh belonged to someone he knew from home.

He shoved his hands deep in his pockets and blew out through his mouths. Even if he did meet someone from Letterkenny or Falcarragh or north-west Donegal, according to Shawnee's father, the best thing he could do was to turn and go in the other direction.

He caught sight of the woman again. Was it Sue, Vivian's partner from the Spa? He couldn't be sure. The woman looked dishevelled and seemed to be walking aimlessly her long coat blowing about her in the wind.

He slowed his step as the woman crossed at the traffic lights on O Connell Street. Now she was on the same side of the street as him. The pavement was crowded with people hurrying along but he would literally be rubbing shoulders with her as he passed.

Isaac felt indecision rise in him. If it was Sue should he say hello in passing, stop and chat as he would at home? Shawnee's father had warned him to stay well clear of anything or anybody to do with Donegal if he didn't want to be tarred with the same reputation as his brother.

He was closer to the woman now. If it was Sue she had certainly changed. The hair was the same. But gone was the up-market sophisticated well-dressed woman he remembered from his summer working at the Shingle Beach Hotel.

The long tweed coat that flapped about her legs and the trailing scarf she wore was definitely *not* out of the top-notch Brown Thomas Department Store on Grafton Street. It looked more like something out of a charity's shops. Oh, how the mighty have fallen, his granny Norah would have sneered, he thought.

"Hello Sue," he said as they drew level.

Walking with her head down against the wind, Sue started. For a moment Isaac thought she was going to walk straight past him.

"Hello, Isaac," she stuttered. "I thought I was hearing things. It's not often people call you by your name in the city," she said attempting a smile. She looked at him and then looked away. "I heard you had moved to Dublin. You are looking…looking…" Her face tinged with colour and her words trailed off.

Isaac's smiled. "I'm looking sober. Is what you're trying to say?"

Sue blushed. "No, I didn't mean that," she protested. "I just meant…suited and booted…you looked…the way your mother hoped you'd turn out."

"Yes? Well, you know, Imelda always gets her way in the end." He wondered if Sue had heard his mother had thrown him out.

They stood together awkwardly as people pushed past them on the crowded pavement. "How is Raphael," Sue finally asked. "I heard…about him and old Mac."

Isaac clenched his fists in his pockets. "I don't have any contact with him," he lied. "I don't know where he is. Shawnee's father thinks it's better that way."

He shifted his eyes from her face. "Granny Norah phoned the Guards because Mac O Lochlainn wouldn't leave. But the Guards already had their suspicions about Mac and gun smuggling. They clocked him speeding crossing from Derry into Donegal and tailed him to Norah's house." He shivered involuntarily. "If they hadn't been there, the IRA would have shot both Raphael and Mac."

Sue touched his sleeve. "I'm sorry, Isaac. I really am. I know how close you and Raphael were growing up. You had your difference—like brothers do. But it can't be easy being separated…not knowing where he is—you being twins." Sue's voice trailed off.

A gust of wind blew off the Liffey sweeping empty cigarette packets and crisp packets into piles like some form of modern art. Another silence fell. Neither of knew what to say next.

"Well, it was nice talking to you," Isaac said turning up the collar of his coat.

"You too, maybe I'll see you around," Sue muttered moving past him as she tried in vain to keep her hair from lashing across her face.

"Yeah, maybe," Isaac said sounding doubtful. He'd like that but Shawnee wouldn't. As far as she was concerned, his connection with Donegal was over.

He stood in a doorway and watched Sue as she crossed the street again. She must spend the day walking around the streets, he thought. What the hell was going on? Was she homeless? He caught a glimpse of her hunched shoulders and long hair lifting and falling in the gusts of wind. She looks as lonely and forlorn as me, he thought. On impulse, he shouted after her. "Sue. Hold on, wait." A few people turned and gave him a perplexed look.

Sue quickened her step and kept walking. She wasn't in the mood for reminiscing about home today.

Isaac cursed as the lights changed and three lines of Lorries, cars and motorbikes revved up their engines, tearing off in the direct of O Connell Bridge like racing drivers in the annual Donegal Rally.

He was panting for breath when he caught up with Sue. Stepping in front of her, he blocked the way forcing her to stop walking. "What the hell are we doing a hundred miles from home talking like two bloody polite strangers? C'mon," he said, reaching for her arm, "let's get out of this wind and have a drink."

Sue shook her head vehemently. "I'm carrying enough guilt without having the added grief of putting you back on the booze."

Isaac stood uncertainly as people jostled him and Sue. A sleety rain began to fall.

"Go home to Shawnee. It's Friday night… You must have something better to do than spend time with me."

"She's staying at a friend's this weekend. I'm in no hurry. I have nowhere else to go."

Sue caught the lonesomeness in his voice. "How often does she stay the weekend with friends?"

"As often as it suits her. And that's pretty often."

Sue knew Isaac had been a little shit when he worked the summer at the hotel last year partnering Shawnee and her posh girlfriends on the tennis courts. And he had treated Rayan disgracefully. But he was still Imelda's son. She had literally worked her ass off and put up with Vivian's shit to get him where he was now. A young man like Isaac shouldn't be alone in a city like Dublin with its buzzing night life on a Friday night. How *dare* Miss Snooty—judge's spoiled daughter treat Isaac like a spare accessory.

"Why do you put up with it?" Sue asked, some of her old feisty spirit surfacing.

Isaac hunched his back. "I'm living in the garden apartment of her parents' home in Dublin 4. And her father is keeping me in a job—such as it is."

A small uncomfortable silence fell.

"You fancy coming back there?" Isaac offered impulsively. "It's only a few stops on the DART."

Sue shook her head. "Thanks Isaac but I don't think that's a good idea."

"You'd be out of this wind and rain."

"Shawnee's parents wouldn't like it. It might make matters wor—"

Isaac snorted. "The judge and his wife are always invited to some function or other at the weekends. We can order something in and talk," he said persuasively.

Sue felt the wind press her wet coat against her legs. The rain that had started as a drizzle was becoming more persistent. Soon it would turn into a downpour. "C'mon, there's a cafe up on the Quays. It's not the Shelburne Hotel but they do a nice fish supper," she said.

Seated across the table in the dim interior of the cafe Sue got a really good look at Isaac. He looked hollowed eyed and haggard. He was obviously missing Imelda's cooking. The move from Donegal wasn't working out for him. *He looks almost as unhappy as I feel*, she mused.

"You finished with studying, then?" she said trying to smooth down her windblown hair with her hands.

Isaac heaved a sigh. "I am. I went back and then left again." He sighed. "So much for the First-Class Honours Mum had planned for me." He fumbled with the salt and pepper, obviously embarrassed. "The judge has me working as a clerk—smoothing the feathers of old biddies." Isaac looked around the cafe without seeing it. "I suppose I should be grateful to be gainfully employed, within such a prestigious law firm," he said with a sardonic smile.

Sue raised her eyebrows. "Why?"

Isaac shrugged. "I was too drunk to submit last year's coursework. Raphael did it for me and impersonates me in the law exams. If it ever comes out, Shawnee's father wouldn't let me within a mile of longstanding clients like the old biddies in case I gave them the wrong information." He gave a brittle laugh. "How's that for a start and finish to my career as a lawyer," he smirked. "If he ever finds out I'll be walking the streets of Dublin too."

Sue said nothing. She had no wish to be privy to any of Isaac's or Raphael's deceits. It had been their deceitfulness over who was the father of Rayan's twins that had finally turned Vivian off the possibility of adopting them. If Mac O Lochlainn was to be believed, they had impersonated each other in Rayan's bed.

Sue felt nausea rising like bile in her throat. It had been a low thing to do. Now it was unclear who the father of the twins really was. She cast a surreptitious look at Isaac. Was he man enough to seduce Rayan and father twins? She felt her lips narrow. There was no denying Raphael's reputation for manliness, she mused. As old Mac would say, he'd get up on a broken stick.

Isaac searched in his inside pocket and produced a small comb. He proffered it to Sue. "I'm sure even in a place like this they'll have a mirror in the toilets."

"Do I look that rough? No wonder I can't get a job as a masseur." She held out her hand and took the comb. He's still a jumped-up little shit, she thought but he might have a point about this place she mused as she edged her way into the miniscule ladies' toilet which also housed a bucket and a mop. There was no mirror.

Vivian wouldn't be found dead eating in a place like this, she thought. The aching pain in her heart that was never far away started up again. She stood for a minute trying to compose herself.

Going back to the table she waited until the waitress had taken their order and moved out of earshot before she spoke. "I know I look a mess but I haven't been well. I've had a breakdown," she said soberly.

Isaac tried to keep the shock from showing on his face. He had heard Sue taken it really bad about not being able to adopt Rayan's twins. But he hadn't realised she'd had a complete breakdown.

Where was bloody Vivian? He remembered there was a time when Vivian wouldn't let Sue out of her sight. When she'd been openly jealous of Sue's friendship with *anyone*! The staff at the Spa used to be almost afraid to have a conversation with Sue in case Vivian, in a fit of jealously docked their hours or reduced the clients she allocated to them.

"Where's Vivian?"

Sue looked over his shoulder into the distance. "We haven't been together since… I kidnapped one of the babies and fled across the Border into Northern Ireland."

Isaac's eyes widened. Fuck! The Republic of Ireland and Northern Ireland were considered two separate countries. Kidnapping an infant and taking it to a different jurisdiction would be considered a serious crime.

Sue saw the shock register on Isaac's face. "I let my obsession about being a mother and my anger at Vivian overtake reason. I made a mistake."

Isaac furrowed his brows in confusion. "I don't understand. I thought you were just waiting to sign the final adoption papers," he said a perplexed look on his face.

Agitated, Sue leaned forward as if she was intently examining the checked oilskin tablecloth. "I was. But I wasn't coping with Branna. She cried all the time. She wouldn't take her bottle. She only slept for a few hours at a time. I think she was missing her twin. He had to stay in the hospital after she was discharged. I became distraught…" Sue gulped twisted her hands together and stopped talking.

Isaac could see she was becoming distressed. He knew he should be feeling sorry for what Sue had been through. Or guilty because he had abdicated his responsibilities as Branna's potential father. Yet, all he was experiencing was a rush of pure relief. He didn't blame Sue for not coping with a wailing infant. He couldn't have coped either. It occurred to him that he didn't like babies.

Sue cast Isaac a beseeching look. "I didn't intend to abduct her. Or, take her across the Border. When Vivian said she was going to get in touch with Children's Services, I just put Branna in the car and drove and drove. It was only when a British army patrol pulled me in for a routine check I realised I had crossed into Northern Ireland."

"Where did you stay?"

Sue smiled wanly. "I don't honestly know. I drove around. Bought takeaway food, ate it on a beach or in a picnic area. When I got tired, I booked into the first B&B I came to." She paused and a small smiled played about the corner of her lips. "The strange thing was Branna loved being in the car. She hardly ever cried. I bought over the counter formula and got eateries to make it up for me—a day's supply at a time. She took it and slept as soon as the car engine began to purr."

Abruptly, she rose to her feet and pushed aside her greasy plate. "C'mon, what about that drink we talked about earlier?"

"It's OK if you want to drink non-alcoholic beer," Sue said as they settled in a pub in Temple Bar. "They won't blink an eyelash here. They get all sorts Americans, Italians, tourists looking for the Irish pub experience."

Isaac nodded to a waiter clad in black trousers and black shirt. He thought fleetingly that the bar staff uniform was similar to the dress code Raphael used when he was attending the funeral of a republican volunteer in the IRA. He tore his mind away and focused on ordering.

"The judge or any of his cronies is unlikely to be in here," he grinned. "Forget the non-alcoholic beer. I intend to get rip roaring drunk. What about you?"

Sue laughed outright for the first time in weeks. "Let's be tourists from Donegal for a night," she said a feeling of recklessness filling her.

Sue wasn't sure how long they had been in the bar. O, even if they were still in the same bar or what she was drinking. Drink kept appearing on the table and she kept drinking it. Music pulsated from speakers. Couples danced on the postage stamp-sized dance floor.

"How did they find you?"

"Find me?"

"When you stole the baby?"

Sue felt slighted peeved at Isaac's suggestion that she had *stolen* the baby. "I didn't *steal* her. It wasn't something I planned. I just grabbed her and a pile of baby things from the mountain of gifts Branna and her brother had been given; threw clothes into a bag, lifted my handbag and car keys and ran out the door."

"But how did the find out where you were?"

Sue shifted irritably on the seat. Isaac's questioning was spoiling the lovely detached cocoon the drink had created. She wondered if it would be crass of her to tell him to fuck off to his garden flat and leave her to drink herself into oblivion in peace.

"Sue, how did they fin—"

Sue puffed out her cheeks in frustration. She might as well tell him. He was going to nag her until she did. "After three days I needed clean clothes for Branna and myself. I bought new things and paid for them with my credit card." She rolled her eyes. It had been an imprudent thing to do. But the truth was the realisation of her predicament was beginning to seep through. Where was she going to go with a small infant and half the Garda and police, no doubt, looking for her?

"I brought her back, didn't I? Didn't your mother tell you? It was in all the papers."

Isaac shook his head. "Mum and me...we don't keep in contact. She's so wrapped up in her latest boyfriend she hardly knows what planet she is on."

"Yeah, my five minutes of fame," Sue muttered reaching for another drink. "I was arrested by the Garda and assessed temporary screw balled by a psychiatrist. I don't want to talk any more about it. Tonight I am a tourist out for a good time. It's been such a long time since I had a good time," Sue said drunkenly.

Isaac's mouth fell into a gape. He was floored by the news that Sue had kidnapped one of Rayan's twins and been arrested. He was even more *amazed* at Sue's capacity to drink! Shawnee would want to know who he spent all his money on. She'd call him a liar when he told her Sue had swilled whiskey down like a navvy and they'd ended up tying one on.

Sue considered the glass in her hand. A terrible sadness washed over her. There was a time when she had been so jealous of Imelda and her boys. Now Imelda was estranged from both of them; the family torn apart. "Contact your mother," she advised. "You don't know what you have 'til you lose it," she murmured thinking of her and Vivian.

"How did you not get charged with kidnapping?" Isaac asked.

The *thump* of the music increased. Sue closed her eyes and let its beat roll over her. And there was me worried I would be responsible for the wee shit getting drunk, she thought. The one night I want to get pissed with him, he wants to stay sober and ask frigging questions, she thought.

"Vivian's solicitor persuaded the Garda and Children Service that I had thought I was the legal adoptive parent."

"And what happened then?" Isaac prompted. He wondered if Raphael knew any of this.

Sue gave up trying to recapture the warm fuzzy feeling she had enjoyed earlier. "Branna and her brother were taken into foster care. And Vivian made arrangements for me to receive treatment as an outpatient at a private clinic here." She glanced across the table at Isaac. "Do you ever want to see them? Wonder if you are the father?"

"Where are you living in Dublin?" Isaac asked changing the subject abruptly.

Obviously not, Sue thought.

"I'm not homeless," Sue said guessing what was on his mind. "I share a house with other people who are attending outpatient clinics. It's not great but at least I have a place to stay." She smiled. "I'm skint. It took all my savings and some of Vivian's to pay for Rayan's stay in the hospital as a private patient," she admitted. "How did you come to be living in Dublin 4?" she asked.

"After the attempting shooting at Granny Norah's house, the IRA ordered Raphael out of Derry. Mum was afraid I'd be shot in mistake for him." He paused. "It nearly happened. I was drinking with the street drinkers in James Street one night. A group of young thugs mistook me for Raphael." He smiled grimly. "Even the street drinkers didn't want to associate with me after the news broke that Raphael was supposed to be an informer for the Brits—said my drinking was a disguise to get information from the other drinkers."

"What about going on to a club somewhere?" Sue suggested as last drinks were called. Isaac shook his head. He'd be lucky to have enough money for a taxi back to Shawnee's house.

Sue swayed unsteadily on her feet. "Is that offer still open for a bed for the night in that flat of yours," she slurred.

Isaac shook his head. He couldn't believe *he* was going home relatively sober and Sue was going back to her shared house, plastered. As soon as the air hit her, she'd keel over, he thought.

"Awk, go on, Isaac, we can talk..."

"There's only one bed," he said as he pushed her out the pub door and into a taxi.

Sue giggled drunkenly. "That's OK. You're not my type," she burped.

The cabbie winked at Isaac. "Thinks she's a lessie, does she?" He grinned at his own humour. "All she'll need to turn her straight is a good night with a young fella like you."

To the bemusement of the taxi driver and the embarrassment of Isaac, Sue started crying great big heaving heart-breaking sobs. "I love Vivian. We're living apart...because she loves her job more than she loves me," Sue wailed, promptly falling into a drunken asleep.

Isaac clocked the driver eyeballing him in the rear-view mirror. His heart sank as he saw recognition dawn in the cabbie's eyes. "You're that guy works in the solicitor's offices around from the taxi rank," he grinned.

Isaac blanked him as he tried to shake Sue awake.

"Yeah, our guys often pick up the Judge and take him to court," he said. He scrutinised the sleeping Sue who was snoring loudly. "Like them old, gay and sloshed, do ya."

Isaac curled his hands into fists and made no reply.

"Ah well, every man to his own poison," the driver said cheekily.

Isaac heaved Sue out of the cab. He gave the driver a conspiratorial wink and tipped generously, hoping the next time the cabbie picked up Shawnee's father, he would conveniently forget he had brought Isaac and Sue home.

Chapter Forty-Nine

"Raphael is getting a place of his own, isn't he?" Nathanial said plucking a cold beer from the icebox. "Imelda did say it was only temporary, didn't she?" Yeah, Nathanial thought, it was a bummer; the Irish outlaw sharing with them in Perth.

Rayan nodded. Imelda had phoned her voice almost unrecognisable. The IRA had ordered Raphael to get out of Ireland or be shot, she'd told Rayan, her voice vibrating with terror. It would only be temporary, she pleaded. He wasn't planning on staying in any one place for long in case the IRA found out where he was.

Yeah, right, temporary my ass, Nathanial thought. The way he has settled in he could be here for a while. Too fucking long already if you ask me, he thought. "But who cares what I think," he muttered. He glowered into his chest. Things had been tops with him and Rayan since they'd come back from Ireland…until Raphael came.

Rayan was way too friendly with him for his liking. He glanced surreptitiously at her. As far as he could tell the only things between them was their common interest in the twins' welfare. Jealousy gnawed at him. How could he be sure? Every time he saw him, he imagined his twin making love to Rayan.

"Why didn't Raff come home from work with you?" Rayan asked breaking into his thoughts. Nat reached for another cold beer. He cracked it open before answering.

"He wasn't about when I was leaving. He's probably off chasing a hot babe from today's class."

Nat raged inwardly. He hated having the Irishman on the beach when he was delivering his Yoga and Pilates classes. It was like having an adult son—not a good look for my image, he thought. Raphael was drawing all the younger babes to his end, leaving Nat with the old Sheilas and distracting the women with his witty Irish humour. But Rayan insisted he take him to help build up his body after the terrible beating he had suffered at the hands of the paramilitaries in Ireland.

Personally, Nat thought Raphael had the beating coming to him. Him and that brother of his, too cocky by far, if you ask me, he thought. He sighed. But he supposed it was better the Irishman was out working with him on the beach rather than hanging around the salon all day with Rayan.

"You came on and left him there again, didn't you."

Nathanial felt irritation gather like bile in his gut. "Hell, Rayan! I'm not his minder. Isn't it enough I gave him a job."

Rayan left the cooking and leaned against his muscular chest. He could smell the heady perfume she liked to wear. He missed their spontaneous love-making; it had become less and less since Raphael came. He muzzled Rayan's neck. "It would be good to have you to myself again," he said hoarsely. His hands cupped her breasts. "We have the house to ourselves, for a change," he murmured as his groin began to respond to the feel of Rayan's body.

Rayan wriggled free of his hands. "Raffi might come in. Anyway, it's the wrong time of the month." She had got to know her menstrual cycle intimately since she'd had the twins. She wasn't taking any chances now despite being on the Pill. "It's one of my days for ovulating."

"You're on the Pill and I'll use protect—"

"No! I don't trust either of them anymore."

"Ah, good old-fashioned lovemaking," Raphael's voice said cheerfully behind them. He noted Rayan's obvious relief at his intrusion. "Something smells good. I'm starving. Keeping these Aussie beach babes satisfied is hungry work for a growing lad," he quipped ignoring Nathanial's obvious boner and the loaded atmosphere.

Nathanial dropped his hands and moved away from Rayan. "I didn't hear you come in," he growled carrying his beer to the dinner table.

Hurriedly, Rayan placed Nathanial's dinner on the table before Raphael's. She hated herself for doing it. It was what her mother used to do to placate her father.

"Thanks babe. I had a message from Bradley Dixon," Nathanial said. "He was saying—"

"Bradley Dixon, the mountain guide…"

Nathanial.

"She *knows* who he fucking is," Nat snarled. He glared at Raphael. "I'm speaking," he growled.

Raphael shrugged. "I was just saying."

Rayan felt her anxiety shift up a notch. Every conversation seems to turn into a war of words between the two men these days. "Go ahead, what were you going to say," she said letting her breast linger against Nathanial's shoulder in a half promise for later.

"Bradley was saying Sue is having a trial separation from Vivian."

Rayan looked at Nat. "Yeah? I didn't know you were still in contact with anyone in Ireland."

Nathanial sighed irritably. "Bradley contacts me from time to time," he lied. It was him who had contacted the mountain guide to find out if Imelda was right about her fucking son being ordered out of Ireland. If Imelda was exaggerating, he was fucking Raphael out.

"He was telling me about the Shingle Beach Hotel. It's under new management," he almost shouted at Raphael. "I felt a bloody fool when Bradley told me. You keep things close to your chest, don't you, mate?"

Raphael looked at him open-mouthed.

"You could have bloody said."

"I haven't a clue what you are going on about." Raphael's heart fluttered like a caged bird. What he would give to be having a pint and a chat with Mac O Lochlainn there tonight. He swallowed his homesickness and tuned back in to what Nathanial was saying to Rayan.

"Yeah, well, Imelda has scored big time. Her latest boyfriend is now the new owner of the Shingle Beach Hotel. He's throwing a party on New Year's Eve to bring in 1998. Fancy going," Nathanial said jeeringly to Raphael.

Rayan's appetite left her. She didn't like the mean-mouthed man Nathanial was sometimes since Raphael came. She gave him a disparaging look.

"You know I can't go back to Ireland."

"It was a joke, mate. I thought the Irish enjoyed a good joke—could laugh at their own tragedies."

"Did you mention to Bradley I was here with you and Rayan?" Raphael said through stiff lips.

Nathanial hesitated. "I might have," he admitted his gut tightening.

Raphael scraped his chair back and made for the bedroom. Rayan could hear him wrenching open the door of the built-in closet and the soft thud of the case as he threw it on the bed.

"Look, mate, I'm sorry," Nathanial apologised as Raphael came back into the dinette. "It wasn't intentional. We were just talking and he mentioned your name…and it kind of slipped out…"

Nathanial gripped Raphael's arm. "Look mate, don't go. The IRA is not that well connected that they will find you in Australia," he said attempting a grin.

Raphael wrenched his arm free. "That's what you think, *mate*!"

Rayan glared at Nathanial. "It didn't slip out. You did it deliberately to get rid of him," Rayan stormed at him beginning to grab up the dinner plates.

There was a sharp rap on the outer door between the house and the garage and Ben Watts stepped in. He swung his eyes to Nathanial and then to Raphael's travel bag.

"Everything good here."

"Yes. We are all fine, Ben, thank you," Rayan said her temper cooling as she stacked the dishwasher.

PC Watts removed his uniformed peaked cap. "I'm sorry, Rayan, to be the bearer of bad news," he said.

Rayan stilled. "Did my father have another stroke? Is he dead?"

Ben replaced his peaked cap. "I'm sorry to have to inform you your father died earlier this evening. He appears to have died from a drug overdose," he said very formally.

Rayan could feel her eyes widening. *Her father died from a drug overdose?* Immediately, her mind raced back to her threatening behaviour to him the last time she'd been there. She looked mutely at Ben. He was wearing his official face now.

Ben placed a hand on her arm. "You need to accompany me to the Police Station."

"But it's months since I saw my father…"

"Your mother is at the station. She is helping police with their enquiries concerning your father's death. She has made a statement…about your last visit."

Chapter Fifty

Rayan stood back from the open mouth of the grave. Many times she had wished her father dead as she grew up. How did she feel now that he was? What she felt was a detached indifference. Yet, in some part of her mind she wondered if facing him down had led him to take his own life.

Surreptitiously, she watched her mother. Ever the dutiful wife, she thought, whispering her husband's last instruction to the sombre undertaker. He nodded and taking her arm positioned her in exactly the right spot so that the single white rose from *his own garden*—as had been his specific instructions—could land exactly right angle on the gold nameplate on his casket.

Rayan felt bile gather in her throat. In control to the end, she fumed He had left a list of specific instructions. Exactly where the white rose should be placed was only the first of a long list of how his funeral service and his burial should be conducted; from the hymns that were to be song by the hand-picked sole suprema singer during the service to the readings.

Nausea rose up in Rayan's throat threatening to suffocate her. She gripped her small clutch bag until her nails made dents in its soft calf leather. Her gaze fixated on the single floral wreath in the shape of the Ritchie family crest. Her father had thought of everything.

I should be grateful, she mused. His planning for his own funeral in such minute detail, at least the police see her mother had no hand in his death. He had been planning it for a while.

Shaking visibly her mother's fingers closed on the spiky stem of the white rose. She cried out as its sharp thorns pierced her skin drawing blood. Shocked, she let the rose slip from her fingers. Falling erratically, the rose missed the nameplate and ended face down in the brown squelchy soil. For one split heart-stopping second, Rayan thought her mother was going to scramble down and retrieve it. "I failed him. I didn't do it right," she cried out. Gently, the undertaker moved her aside. Proffering a small shovel, he indicated Rayan should step forward and sprinkle some earth on the coffin.

The shovel of earth felt like a weighty bag as Rayan waited for the priest to reach the point in his long litany of prayers when she could tip the soil into the yawning hole which was now a sickly muddy brown from the rain. "Dust you are and dust you shall return to," the minister murmured. With a thrust of her arm, Rayan dumped the cold soil on the coffin and moved back.

She felt a hand on her elbow. "Let's get the fuck out of here and let the worms get started on eating the bastard," Nathanial whispered hoarsely in her ear.

"You came then," Rayan muttered mutinously. Moving away she took sheltered under the large umbrella the undertaker was offering her and her mother. He cast a discerning eye over Nathanial. His shorts and tee shirt clung wetly to his chest, showing off his muscular physique.

"The limousine is waiting at the cemetery gates to take you to your late father's club for refreshments," he said turning back to Rayan and her mother. Rayan wondered if he had heard Nathanial's inappropriate remark. Should she apologise? She decided against it. Her father had said much worse things about Nathanial.

Rayan's lips felt stiff from repeating her thanks to the long line of people who had come to pay their last respects. Her brain was in overdrive listening to stories about her father. Try as she might, she couldn't keep the incredulous look of disbelief off her face. These people were talking about a man she didn't recognise. He was one of the great and good: a thoughtful and kind employer, an exemplary administrator, a true friend and a pillar of the community.

They made him sound *normal*—a good man who would be missed.

They were seated beside a table where a large head and shoulders smiling picture of her father displayed in a silver frame took centre stage surrounded by vases and vases of white roses from her mother's garden. Their pungent smell was beginning to make Rayan feel sick. She glanced at her mother. "We've been here for *hours.* Can we go now? "Most people have had their say," Rayan said just as a colleague of her father's came back to offer his sympathy again before he left.

She'd had enough. Turning the photograph of her father face down, she went in search of Nathanial.

"Yeah, kinda freaky weather for Perth," Nat was moaning to a man in the public bar. "The old bastard is probably reorganising the seasons," he chortled as Rayan slipped onto the stool beside him. She saw the other man scrutinise her appreciatively. She knew the sleeveless black designer knee length dress and light jacket made the most of her curvy figure and the discreetly applied eyeshadow and a light touch of tinted moisturiser gave the right impression for a parent's funeral. She offered up a silent thank you to Sue who had drummed into her to style her hair and pick her clothes and makeup according to the occasion.

"It's not right to bad-mouth the dead," she said quietly. "Haven't you heard? Happy is the corpse the rain falls on."

Nathanial drained his glass. "You're not in Ireland now. Your father never put his foot inside a church door, except to be seen at some nob's funeral. Don't think just because he topped himself, I'm going to say he was anything but a bastard."

"Show some respect, mate," the man beside him said.

Rayan cast him a look. "Thank you." She turned back to Nathaniel. "I'm going back with Mother," she said.

"Why would you do that? She treats you like shit."

Aware of the man's presence beside her, Rayan felt the heat rise in her face. "Nat; she's just buried my father. She shouldn't be alone tonight." He followed Rayan's gaze to where her mother was being comforted by a young woman. "Just like your old man. One face for all these fuckers and another for you," he grumbled and signalled the bar attendant.

A woman near them swept her eyes over Nathanial's muscular physique. "Not exactly yoga on the beach weather is it?" she smiled.

Like waving a magic wand, Nat's scowl disappeared. "You've been to some of my classes?"

"Doesn't it show?" the woman smiled.

"I should start charging more if all my babes shape up like you," he smiled.

The woman preened. "Your glass is empty. Can I buy you a beer?"

Nathanial nodded.

"Nathanial, don't forget Biscuit. She's been home alone all day," Rayan said as the woman and Nathanial grinned at each other like two teenagers on the make.

"Biscuit? Who's Biscuit?" the woman asked drawing back a little.

Nathanial placed a hand lightly on her knee. "No worries. She's my dog."

The woman giggled.

"Yeah, I'll walk her when I get home."

When she reached her mother, Rayan looked back. Nathanial and the woman heads were close together. Maybe her mother was right. If you didn't look after your man, another woman would. Lately, she had been too preoccupied with what she was going to do about the twins and with Raphael's problems.

When they reached her mother's house, everything looked exactly the same from the last time she'd been there months before. The blinds were all at the exact same drop on the windows. The usual bowl of fresh roses stood on the hall table.

Mentally exhausted, she walked through to the lounge room intending to sink into a soft chair. She stopped in her step. Her father's chair was still there; still overflowing with pillows and cushions as if waiting for him to come back. She thought she even sensed his presence in the room.

Overwrought, she felt tears well up. She hadn't cried when Ben Watts told her father had killed himself with an overdose of his prescribed medication. In fact, she had secretly toasted his death. She hadn't cried when she'd gone to the Chapel Of Rest and saw him laid out dressed in his best suit and freshly laundered crisp shirt and 'old boys' tie. A white rose in his lapel. She had looked at him and felt nothing.

Now, tears ran unheeded down her cheeks as she looked at his empty chair and recalled how shocked she'd been to see him in pyjama top and slippers, his haggard features and the loose skin on his neck making him look like an old man. A feeling of desolation and guilt engulfed her. She remembered the angry, menacing words she had hissed at him the last time she had been here.

There was a sound behind her. For a second she half expects it to be him; to hear him berate her for something she had omitted to do at the funeral.

Her mother stood there, pale and drawn. Rayan wanted to comfort her but she didn't dare. Her mother had never liked her to touch or hug her, especially if the father was about. And unreasonable as it seemed, Rayan felt he was still here in this room with them.

"Did I drive him to take his own life?" Rayan said.

She felt rather than saw her mother shake her head. "He had been hiding his medication for some time. That's what I told Constable Watts," she said woodenly.

Chapter Fifty-One

Rayan stood at the open screen door looking in incredulity at the lightening streaking across the Perth midnight sky like fireworks on Australian Day. There was a deafening clap of thunder and the ominous looking low hanging black clouds erupted. Rain lashed the patio turning it in a river.

Rayan's phone rang. Turning, she went inside closing the screen door against the torrential downpour. "Yes, Mother," she sighed picking it up. "I know. It's a freak heat storm; it'll pass."

"Hello Rayan," a familiar voice said tentatively. "Is this a bad time?" Sue said. "It's just I wanted to talk to you…about Branna."

Rayan's heart started to rattle against her ribcage. She hadn't spoken to Sue since she had taken the baby and disappeared for three whole days and three nights.

A plethora of mixed emotions rushed over her. Hearing Sue's voice on the other end of the phone was the last thing she'd expected. Should she berate her for abducting Branna? Or, should she get indignant and slam down the phone? Or, should she pretend it was a social call from an old friend? Her throat felt as dry as chalk. She took a deep breath and opted for the latter.

"I thought it was my mother. She's phones constantly. We're having an electrical storm…unusual for us," she finally got out.

Sue was sobbing. Rayan could hear her gulping back the tears. "I could have written but I wanted to say sorry to you personally for what I did. By the time I got back from the cruise, Vivian insisted on taking me on and you were gone." She stopped to draw breath. "I am so, so sorry that my stupid running away ended with darling wee Branna and her brother ending up in care," she gasped out her deep distress obvious even over the phone. "I'd give anything to turn back the clock."

It was on the tip of Rayan's tongue to ask Sue had she felt entitled to take the baby because of the money she had 'invested' in the baby—in both of the twins.

She clamped her mouth shut reminding herself Sue had been a good friend before the issue of Rayan's pregnancy drove a wedge between them. "Yeah, well, none of us can turn the clock back," Rayan said woodenly.

Overhead the thunder rolled away. Rain lashed the windows; the raindrops running in rivulets down the panes like fat tears. "You brought her back. She came to no harm," Rayan heard herself say. There was silence on the line. "How did you and Vivian enjoy the cruise?" It seemed such a trivial polite incongruent question almost a year on, under the circumstances.

Sue gulped. "I don't remember much about it except Vivian frogmarching me from deck to cabin—afraid I might jump overboard." She gave a slightly hysterical giggle. "As soon as we docked, she booked me a health assessment for me at the Black River Clinic." She paused. "I spent weeks there as an outpatient having treatment." She drew in a deep breath.

Rayan licked her dry lips and wondered had the treatment cured Sue of her obsessive yearning to be a mother.

"Vivian and I have put the whole baby thing on hold for a while," Sue said as if reading Rayan's mind. "We're having a trial separation while I have aftercare. I'm living in Dublin and Vivian is still in Donegal."

"Whose idea was that?"

"Mine—about the separation and Vivian's about the babies."

There was another awkward silence. "Now that I have said what I wanted to say to you, I won't bother you again," Sue said beginning to wind up the call.

"You haven't asked about Branna."

"If you have the twins adopted, will you do something for me?" Sue asked. "Could she keep the name I gave her?"

Rayan's heart twisted in her chest. She didn't have the right to ask that of the twins' new adoptive parents. Now, she realised, like Sue, she'd always think of them as Branna and BB.

There was another long pause. "Sometimes in the night I think I hear her screeching," Sue whispered.

"I do too," Rayan admitted. "And believe it or not, when I came back here, I actually missed the flailing fists and the screaming. My mother told me when I was a baby, I was a screamer too," Rayan said afraid Sue was going to start in about the adoption again. It was too late for that now. The Children and Family Agency's social worker had told her in no uncertain terms that private adoptions were not permitted in the Republic of Ireland. "It seems I was always screaming for attention too—just like Branna. So her screeching wasn't entire your fault," she said as kindly as she could.

Sue drew in a shuddering breath. "That's good to know. I had such hopes of being a mother. Now all I feel is guilt. I made a real mess of it, didn't I?"

Rayan's hand holding the phone shook. "I should have helped you more, Sue. I got caught up with BB being sick and Nathanial…" Her voice dried up.

"BB?"

"Baby B, that's my pet name for him…"

"How is he? You didn't call him Bobby, then, like great granny Norah demanded?"

Rayan was relieved to hear the little chuckle in Sue's voice. "He's not as robust as his sister. I worry about him," Rayan admitted, surprising herself. "But as for calling him after his great grandfather, absolutely not." She felt her face grow grim. "The twins' social worker thinks Norah is an interfering old bat."

Sue laughed outright this time. "No change there, then," she chortled.

Rayan felt the icy coldness she'd harboured against her friend beginning to melt.

"I met Isaac in Dublin quite by accident," Sue said. "We had something to eat and then he took me for a drink," Sue said feeling the clutch of nerves in her in her stomach beginning to loosen their grip. A note of sadness filled her voice. "Imelda and her boys were *so close*. The envy of the village, truth be told. Now, Isaac isn't even on speaking to his mother and he doesn't know where his twin is." She paused. "Do you know where Raphael is, Rayan?" she asked.

"How's the big romance between Isaac and Shawnee coming on?" Rayan asked hurrying away from the subject of Raphael.

Sue grinned even though her friend couldn't see it. "She can't whip him into shape the way you could, Rayan."

"Oh, right. So you heard about that?" Rayan said wincing, the blood rushing to her face in humiliation. How crazy had she to be to do such a thing, she asked herself.

"Yeah, he told me." Isaac had been hungover and in the mood for sympathy the morning after their drinking session. Sue could hardly keep the smirk off her face when he was telling her about Rayan putting him across her knee and whacking his ass. "The little shit deserved it—leaving you for her when he—"

"It wasn't my proudest moment," Rayan interrupted. "I was supposed to be the adult."

"Anyway," Sue went on, "the big romance between him and Shawnee might be over by now. He was supposed to be on the wagon—part of the agreement for Shawnee's coaxing her father into giving him board and lodgings and finding him a job." She paused remembering when she and Rayan used to swap confidences. "If I tell you something, will you swear never to tell Imelda or Vivian?"

Rayan wondered what it was that had to be kept a secret. She didn't really want to know Sue's secrets but she missed the gossipy, girly get-togethers they used to have over a bottle of wine and a curry.

"Is it about Imelda and her new boyfr—"

"I slept with Isaac."

Rayan dropped the phone in shock. She could hear Sue's voice babbling away as she retrieved the receiver.

"...A pub crawls around Temple Bar pretending to be tourists. I got sloshed and ended up in Isaac's bed—in the garden apartment he shares with Shawnee..."

"What! Was Shawnee there too?" Rayan couldn't imagine miss snooty daddy's girl, in a compromising love triangle. She wondered if Sue was on heavy medication and suffering from hallucinations. "Slow down. Start from the beginning—again!"

Sue chuckled down the phone. "Shawnee's daddy and Isaac's addiction counsellor are not going to be too pleased. Isaac was blocked."

Rayan gripped the phone. "Never mind about Isaac's addiction counsellor or Shawnee's father, tell me everything from the beginning!"

"You missed the craic."

Rayan smiled down the phone. She remembered when she arrived in Ireland and heard them talking about the *craic*, she'd been appalled until she learned it was an Irish word for having a bit of banter. Her heart lifted as Sue gave her old familiar chuckle and recounted the events from, when she'd met Isaac in Dublin City Centre until she woke up beside Isaac in the bed the following morning.

"I was naked. He was naked." Sue was helpless with laughter now. "Ugh, it was not a pretty sight." Then just as quickly as it started, her laughter died.

Rayan was so flabbergasted she was speechless. She couldn't remember Sue telling her if she'd ever been with a man before she met Vivian.

"Promise me you will never tell Vivian," Sue pleaded.

"You don't even have to ask that. I never would." She gave a small awkward cough. "Was it…was he…any good?" She wondered if Isaac still made love like a schoolboy. But she remembered what he lacked in technique he made up for in enthusiasm.

A chuckle started in Sue's throat. "You tell me! I don't remember. I think we were both so pissed we both passed out. How are you and Nathanial getting on?" Sue said changing the subject. "Mac told me you left with him…on an impulse."

Rayan shrugged. "My visa was about to expire. It worked out OK. When I got home, I found out my father had had a stroke." She drew in her breath. "He has since died."

Sue's mind flashed back to the cold unfeeling blunt words Rayan's father had written on a standard white postcard after the twins were born. No congratulations or enquiry for his daughter's or his grandchildren's wellbeing, just a blunt rebuke that said, *You don't give away your own flesh and blood.* But the message was clear. Don't bring your illegitimate brats back to Perth.

His self-righteous rejection had hurt Rayan deeply. Wrapped up in my own fear of something preventing the adoption from going through, Rayan's feelings of abandonment had barely registered with me, Sue thought sadly.

She forced her mind back to the telephone conversation. "I'm sorry about your dad, Rayan."

"It's OK. Anyway, with both the twins in care, there was nothing to keep me in Ireland."

Sue heard the pain in her friend's voice. "Oh, Rayan," Sue said so softly that Rayan had to strain to hear what she said next. "I'm here. Your children are here. Come back to Ireland. You don't want the authorities to take the decision about the twins out of your hands."

How could she tell Sue that she, Rayan, didn't know what she was going to do—couldn't make a decision about the future of the twins? If she didn't make a decision soon, that was exactly what was going to happen. The Children and Family Agency would make the decision for her.

Rayan traced her index finger over the small faces of Branna and her brother propped up with cushions side by side on a sofa. She noticed at eleven months, Branna, despite her dark colouring and her shock of black, frizzy hair looked surprisingly like *Imelda*. Beside her, Baby B, or BB, as she thought of him now, looked paler and fretful; a worried frown puckering his brow above eyes that stared worriedly into the camera's lens. A tweed flat cap perched on his high forehead gave his thin cheeks a rounder look. Compared to his sister he looked emaciated and sickly. He didn't appear to have gained weight from the last set of photographs she had received from the social worker when he was six months. Her heart twisted. He looked so *unhappy*. Like a wee old man with the weight on the world on his shoulders, Rayan thought.

She put the photos down and picked up the accompany letter. It had the tone and format of a formal letter attempting to be friendly, she noted. It talked about the twins' developmental stages and the milestones they had reached. As expected, given Baby B shaky start, Branna was more advanced in crawling, even attempting to walk. BB was doing much better now. They were being well cared by their foster mother. Rayan cast the letter aside and picked up the photos again. The photographs looked like they had been taken by a professional photographer. Branna was holding a doll and BB had a toy train clutched in his hands. Why go to that expense, she mused. Up to now the photos had been snapped by the foster mother. Were they being photographs by a professional in preparation for prospective adopters?

She read the letter again. It assured her the twins were fine but the underlying message was crystal clear. It was time for her to either make a long-term commitment to the care of her children or place them for adoption, properly. It wasn't stated in so many words but she got the impression that if she didn't make a commitment very soon the twins would be placed for adoption *without* her consent. Despite late autumn borrowing summer's heat she felt chilled. She wondered could they do that. It was something she'd need to discuss with Nathanial…and their new lodger Raphael.

Rayan glanced across the table at Nathanial. He had been in a stroppy mood since Raphael had arrived. No, the two of them were beginning to act like marauding bulls for her affection. She pushed the letter towards Nat. "I'm not sure what to do," she said. It had all seemed so cut and dried when she had agreed to let Sue adopt the babies.

"It seems straightforward enough to me," he said tossing it back. "They want you to agree to have them adopted…and soon."

Rayan turned her back to him. "I want them to come here."

Nathanial did a double take. "You *want* both of them to live with here, with us? I suppose this is Raphael's big idea. He still fancies himself as their father?"

Rayan swung around. "It was you that suggest we keep BB. What difference will one more make?" She pushed the photographs towards him again. "Look at BB, Nat. He looks so miserable. He's not thriving in foster care."

Nathanial gave her a brooding look. *Yeah,* he mused. *I did think about taking the boy. Not any more—not with Raphael here. They're his brother's kids. No way am I getting into that*, he thought.

"It's already overcrowded with Raphael here. What would it be like if there were two small babies and all their stuff?" Nat countered, a mental picture of the chaotic state of Sue's flat covered in baby stuff rising up before him like a mirage.

"Raphael and I have talked about it. If it doesn't work out, he will find a place of his own and take the babies with him."

Nathanial looked at her grim-faced. "Oh, so it's Raphael and I now. He'd want to play surrogate father. It's a wonder you're not asking me to move out and let you and him play mamma and papa!" His eyes widened when he saw just that mirrored in Rayan's eyes. "You're asking *me* to leave so he can live here and help you bring up the twins?"

"You don't have to move out permanently. And it's only if Branna and BB both come…"

Nathanial shook his head. "You can forget that little plan. It isn't going to happen, babe."

She's a sexy woman, Nat thought. She had kept her curvy figure after the birth of the twins, still wore her hair in the windswept style she'd had when he first saw her in Sue's flat in Ireland. She looks fantastic, he thought. No way am I moving out and leaving her alone with fucking Raphael.

Nathanial sighed and sank into the corner seating. They had been getting on really well since they'd come back from Ireland. But this thing about the twins' future was hanging over them like a storm waiting to erupt.

He had to admit the birth of the twins had changed Rayan for the better. Who knows? Maybe it could work, he mused. Prompted by Ben Watts who was a regular visitor to the house—to the consternation of the nosy curtain twitching neighbour across the way—Rayan had signed up for an anger management programme. She had short flare-ups of jealousy but nothing manic like before. They'd not had a single row about his 'beach babes' since they'd come back.

He watched her covertly. But she'd had been in a funny mood lately, he mused. It had started after her visit to her parents. She never talked to him what had gone on but whatever had happened had had a profound effect on her. After the visit, she'd started to brood about the children; nights he'd wake up to find her looking out the window, a look of deep sadness on her face. He was beginning to feel anxious being around her again. He could see the cracks coming. Soon there would be a blow out and he would be in the firing line. Maybe she was right. Maybe he should move out for a while.

Pushing down his anxiety, he smiled at her. "Let me think about it," he said.

Rayan rushed over and threw her arms around him. "Thank you, Nathanial. You are a good man."

Chapter Fifty-Two

The summer heat was despairingly oppressive. It had been years since Perth had had a heatwave like this; Rayan thought as she padded out of the bedroom into the lounge room in her bra and pants and slumped down in a seat under the wall mounted air conditioning little Biscuit lifted her chin from the cushioned rim of her basket, yawning prettily she stretched, sticking her little butt up in the air;. Rayan smiled as the dog's tail curled over her back like a fluffy ponytail.

For no reason Rayan's mind flashed back to big awkward Dizzy stretching his huge paws as he lumbering off the sofa in the kitchen in the Manse, his tail thumping a welcome on the tiles.

The phone rang. Rayan sighed. It would be her mother. Ever since her father's funeral, her mother had taken to phoning her several times a day to ask her 'advice' about things she'd been coping with for years. She knew, despite their troubled marriage, she missed her husband. But her helplessness act was driving Rayan up the walls.

"Hello Mother," she said.

"I can't sleep with this heat," her mother lamented.

"Maybe it will break soon."

"I don't think the air con is working as well as it should."

"Did you get the maintenance company to look at it, like I told you?"

She heard her mother snort. "A *child* came and fitted some new parts; tried to sell me a new unit. If your father had been here, he'd have—"

"Mum, you know you always made decisions about the appliances—"

"But your father always checked it out," her mother interrupted in a shaky voice. "Will you come over make sure he fixed it right?"

Rayan held fast to her patience. "It's a work day," she said wiping the sweat off the back of her neck.

There was a short silence.

"Did you think about what we were talking about—taking up voluntary work—maybe a few hours in one of the op shops?" The sullen silence continued at the other end of the phone. "I know it's hard for you to meet people…after my father's…sudden…passing," Rayan said carefully. "But it would give you some interest outside the hou—"

"You don't understand. You have Nathanial and that Irish bloke. *I have nobody*," her mother wailed. "I miss your father. He was a good husband. I wanted for nothing."

Rayan gritted her teeth. Her mother's words had become like a mantra; as if repeating them made them true.

"This heat wave has to break soon," Rayan reiterated, lifting her hair off the nape of her neck. "I'll call on my way back from the salon," she said putting down the phone before her mother thought up another excuse to drag her over there.

The phone rang immediately again. Rayan was tempted to ignore it. It was her mother again.

"Your father left you well enough off so that you can take a day off."

"Mother—"

"He bought out the deeds of that hairdressing business of yours, didn't he? The least he would expect is that you would look after *me*—now that he is gone," her mother said a belligerent note in her voice.

Rayan pushed the phone away from her ear. It was going to be one of her mother's days for challenging her and pushing her guilt buttons.

She had been more than surprised to find out at the reading of her father's will that he had bought her the building that housed her salon and put the deeds in her name.

"I'll phone you later," Rayan said shortly putting the phone down again. She hurried into the bedroom and dressed. Her mother would ring again and again until she got Rayan to do what she wanted.

Biscuit picked up her ears expectantly as Rayan hurried back into the lounge room. "Get your lead," she said to the little dog. Biscuit ran and sat below the peg where her lead was kept.

Rayan knew when she got back there would be a long line of missed calls from her mother's number. "She needs bereavement counselling," she muttered.

On the short walk to the park, Rayan noted that despite the early hour the volume of traffic heading for the Cannington Bridge was picking up. "Workers getting an early start on the day before the temperature soar into the 40s," she mused. She'd noticed that since the heat wave had started some of her mid-afternoon customers were young construction workers finishing work before the intense heat become too unbearable to work in.

Despite her despondent mood, Rayan chuckled. Business was booming and so was Sienna's love life. She had been down in the dumps and depressed at Raphael's departure. Her pining for him hadn't lasted long, though, Rayan mused. In Sienna book when one door closed another opened. She had had her pick of boyfriends from the new male customers. She was sashaying about the salon giving the young builders her full undivided attention and a clear view of her shapely thighs as she bent to retrieve towels from the lower shelves.

She's getting on with her life, Rayan's inner voice murmured. You'd do well to do the same. Rayan knew it was good advice but she didn't seem to be able to move on. Her thoughts were constantly on the adoption—should she or shouldn't she?

She wondered if she hadn't listened to the Doctor Blanid's advice to wait a while before signing the adoption papers could she have done just that—moved on with her life. The decision would have been made. It would have been out of her hands what happened to her twins.

Resolutely, she shook her head. Sue wouldn't have been able to cope on her own and Branna and her brother would have been made Wards of the State. She couldn't see Vivian getting her manicured hands reddened from washing towel nappies. And Imelda was adamant she had reached a point in her life where her time was her own. At least this way she had some power over what happened to them. For how much longer, her inner voice asked. She lengthened her stride. They were still her children. She still had a legal right to have a say in their future.

The park was empty except for the occasional jogger. Biscuit's little fluffy tail started to wag excitedly as she caught sight of her friend, the wire-haired terrier, and his owner jogging towards them. The man nodded a hello to her as he passed. Then, he stopped and panting, hands on his knees, he called to Rayan. "I've been around twice. Let her have a run-around."

"She might run away."

"Murphy won't go far without me," he said breathlessly moving to sit on a seat under a tree. He patted the seat.

Rayan hesitated. Nathanial would never forgive her if the dog got lost.

"Go on, let her have some fun with Murphy," her neighbour called as Biscuit strained on the leash.

Yeah, why not, Rayan thought. It's time somebody had a bit of fun around here. "Don't run away," she warned freeing the little dog.

"Murphy, play nice, mate," the man warned as the two dogs started to play-fight.

Taking refuge from the heat under the tree's spreading branches, Rayan slid onto the seat. It was huge tree but the rough bark reminded her of the trees in the Manse's orchard. Its winter time there now; she thought. The trees will be bare; their twisted limbs reaching towards a cold overcast sky. She looked up at the reflection of the sun glinting through the tree leafy canopy. She wondered if Raphael was sweating in the Aussie heat somewhere and thinking of the approach of Christmas and his beloved Muckish.

She wished she could discuss what was best for the babies with him. But it was too risky to have contact with him even if she could. She sighed. Nathanial had decided he had said all he was going to say on the subject. After a row about the twins she'd thrown a glass jug at the wall. He'd decided to move into the condo for a while.

She felt ashamed about the jug throwing incident. She shouldn't have done it. It was a step backwards when Nathanial had arranged some beach work for Raphael out east and temporary accommodation to make up for blowing Raphael hiding place. She wasn't sure Nat fully believed Raphael the IRA could track him down. But he was glad to see the back of Raphael.

She gave a wry smile. The tables had certainly changed. *She* had worked out her insecurities around her mindless jealously of Nat's beach babes thanks to her sessions with her counsellor and the 'anger' group she had joined. She understood now it stemmed from her poor self-esteem. Now it was Nat who was acting like a possessive lover.

She lifted her face and blinked at the shimmering sun slipping through the tree's branches. The thing was the more possessive Nathanial behaved, the more she saw her father's attributes in him, and the less she wanted him.

Chapter Fifty-Three

A week after Sue's unexpected phone call, a large brown official looking envelope arrived for Rayan. She checked its post markings as she carried it out with her morning coffee to the patio. It was from Ireland. Her heart lurched in her chest. She had been putting off replying to the last letter from the social worker who had been pressing her to come to a decision about the twins' future.

With mounting trepidation, she tore open the special sealed flap and peer inside. It could only be one thing, an official letter from Children's Services. It was a booklet. Probably rules and regulations about absent parents, she thought. She tipped the envelope and to her utter surprise, out tumbled a large beautifully gold embossed card.

Baffled, she picked it up and turned it over in her hand. Her breath faltered. It was a bespoke invitation for her and Nathanial to the official opening of the refurbished Shingle Beach Hotel and Nite Club on New Year's Eve.

A titanic feeling of relief washed over her. It wasn't the dreaded forms, after all. With relieved inquisitiveness, she sank into the nearest wicker chair and shook out the remainder of the contents of the manila envelope.

A property portfolio fell into her lap. What was this? Why would anyone be sending her a catalogue of houses for sale in Donegal? Bemused, she thumbed over the glossy pages. Her breath caught in her throat. There, on a two-page centrefold, was a stunning aerial photograph of the old Manse and its ground.

Rayan's heart filled with pure joy at the sight. For long moments she just sat there drinking in the sight of the house tucked under the protective shelter of Muckish. Its double-fronted windows illuminated by the rays of the setting sun looked so surreal and peaceful.

Sitting there, memories crowded in on her; arriving home to find the house humming with life and laughter, loud voices and the clinking of beer bottles floating in the open kitchen window as Raphael entertained his friends gathered beneath the trees in the orchard; the smell of cooking, wafting through the house when the chef from the smallest pub in Donegal came to cook for them all.

Unexpected tears clogged Rayan's throat. She hadn't appreciated any of it at the time. It had been a whole new unfamiliar way of living, of being young, being carefree. She thought about the friendship that had developed between her and Sue; about the 'girls' nights in' when Sue and some of the other girls from the Spa gather around the kitchen table, drank wine and ordered a curry takeaway. She gulped. She missed it. She never thought she'd ever say that, but she did. She glanced around her. With Raphael gone and Nathanial moved out the house was as quiet as the grave.

Fighting against her acute sense of loneliness Rayan flicked to the next page of the portfolio. There were individual shots of each room and featured images of the gardens and the orchard. The photographs had been taken when the trees were bowed down with fruit. Ripened apples and pears hung like shining globes against the green foliage. It was like a picture postcard image.

There was even a shot of her old arch enemy, the rooster, striding across the yard on his webbed feet; his red comb blazing out as he kept a haughty eye on his harem. "Obviously jealous of the photographer's close proximity to his broody hens," she said smiling through her tears.

At the bottom of the page there was a note. *See the sign in the garden,* it read in Imelda's untidy scrawl.

Rayan focused in on the glossy professional photograph of the garden. What was she suppose to 'see'? All there was, was a 'For Sale' sign. Nothing unusual about that, she thought. She hadn't expected Imelda and Bill to live in the isolated old house. With Bill's wealth and his business connections, he'd want to live somewhere more central, she mused, remembering how the winter weather could turned nasty overnight. Like it had the time the twins were born, when the road became almost impassable.

She scanned the photograph again. The 'For Sale' sign was lying half propped up against the gate post. Perplexed, she furrowed her brow and looked closer. Scrawled in sprawling lettering were the words, *Australian woman needed for old Manse in Donegal.*

Gobsmacked, Rayan stared at the words. Her heart beat faster. Why would Imelda write such a message? Was Imelda *mocking* her? Reminding her of her affair with Isaac while she was renting the house? She studied the words until they were imprinted in her mind. That must be it, she thought. Imelda was being malevolent. "She knows perfectly well I have no plans to go back to Donegal again, let alone *live* in the Manse." Blood pumped through her in suppressed rage. "Didn't she tell me never ever to set foot in it again?" she fumed. So why would she even bother to tell her the Manse was for sale?

She went back and read the scrawled words again. A little arrow she hadn't noticed before indicated she should turn the page to read the rest of the message. *My gift to you for all you have done for Raphael*, Imelda had signed off.

Rayan felt the glossy portfolio slip through her fingers. Was Imelda holding out an olive branch? Incredulously, she drew in a shuddering disbelieving breath. Was she letting her know that in helping to save Raphael from the death promise of the IRA, she had earned Imelda's forgiveness for robbing Isaac of his virginity?

Was it genuine or just a gesture on Imelda's part knowing full well Rayan was never going to take her up on her offer? Her old mistrust of people's motives rose up like a spectre in her mind. That was it, Rayan thought. Imelda was appeasing her own conscience. She knows I can't take her up on her ridiculous offer, she moaned. No way can I just run off to Ireland *again*! Look what happened the last time! I ended up with twins!

Unexpectedly, she began to bawl like a baby. Tears spurted from her eyes and coursed down her cheeks. Her father had been right. He always said she created chaos and mayhem wherever she went. It was no wonder her father and mother had never loved her. She was an unlovable, despicable person.

Nobody had ever loved her enough *for herself*. Yes, Nathanial loved her but in a possessive way while his eyes roamed over other women. She rubbed her streaming face with the cuff of her tee shirt. She knew her jealousy and her violent angry attacks on Nathanial had driven a wedge between them. She had been too fucked up to have Nathanial's child and now she was offended because he wouldn't see it her way about the babies. Great big wracking sobs shook her whole body.

Little Biscuit climbed out of her basket. Crawling onto Rayan's lap, Biscuit licked her wet cheeks. Rayan hugged her close as she rocked back and forward. All her life she had fought against turning into a doormat like her mother. She fought against having children or a permanent relationship that involved giving a man power over her.

You achieved that, her inner voiced mocked. But, in doing so, you turned into a violent, controlling freak like your father. She jerked upright trying to push the dark thought from her but they clung like limpets. I am a violent self-seeking person. Like him, she thoughts. I use anger to manipulate and get my own way, just like he had. She shuddered as the truth of the realisation hit her. Stunned she clutched little Biscuit to her and howled like a banshee.

After a while, wiping at her ravaged face with the palms of her hands, she put Biscuit back in her basket. Blowing her nose, she tried to get a grip on her ragged breathing.

She looked at the gilded invitation for the New Year's party propped up against the table lamp. "Oh, how I wish I had the courage to take Imelda at her word," she quaked. She emitted a jagged sigh. "Despite everything, living in the Manse was the only time I ever felt I belonged; was part of something—part of a community. And my friendship with Sue was the nearest I got to having a family—a sister," she hiccupped.

There's always the Midnight Flyer. You could be in Ireland in twenty-six hours, her inner voice whispered.

Chapter Fifty-Four

"Children Services selling houses now?" Nathanial said in a tight voice catching sight of the Harp on the postage stamps and the content of the envelope spilled across the table.

"Oh, Nathanial, you're back. Did little Biscuit enjoy her run in the park? I didn't hear you put your key in the outside door."

Nathanial's eyes scanned her face naked of makeup. It occurred to him that Rayan had changed…a lot. These days she rarely went anywhere without being fully made up and dressed to impress. He thought how the men's heads turned to check her out at her father's funeral. Even the wimpy guy in the park with his shaggy haired mutt that Biscuit loved fooling about with had asked after Rayan. It irked him. He liked the old skinny beanpole Rayan and her temper tantrums. At least he knew where he was with her.

A slow anger started in his gut. She certainly wasn't dressing to impress him today. This morning she was in the old pair of shorts and a sleeveless vest and no bra. These days it seemed it didn't matter how she looked for him. She wasn't even jealous of his beach babes anymore. Not that he was getting much attention from them these days either. His nails dug into the flesh of his hands. His beach groups had dwindled. The babes preferred the younger coaches. Raphael had seen to that.

"You left the door on the latch when you brought in the mail," Nathanial retorted. He picked up the manila envelope. "Impressive," he drawled. "A bespoke invitation from the lovely Imelda for the grand opening on New Year's Eve…" He held the glossy invitation afloat as if testing its weight. "Money's no problem now."

Rayan looked at him.

"No worries about the cost of postage," he scoffed. "When she was here, she wasn't so free in flashing the cash," he said in a derisory tone. "She expected to be wined and dined for free."

Rayan stood up wearily. "When did you become so mean-spirited and fault-finding, Nat? You're sounding more and more like my father every day." When he didn't answer, she proffered the glossy realtor's catalogue. "Imelda is hinting I should rent the Manse."

Nathanial startled and then let out a sarcastic snort. "Don't talk so stupid! She is putting it up to you—showing off her newfound wealth."

Rayan showed him the scrawled message on the For Sale sign.

Nathanial flung it away from him. "Giving birth has scrambled your brains," he said in a mocking tone. "Imelda hates your guts. Have you forgotten? You had sex with her teenage son. Maybe with Raphael too since he came here," he mocked, jealousy tightening his gut. "You were supposed to be a surrogate mother to them. And give Raphael safe house here."

Rayan stared at him. "Isaac was almost twenty-one. I never promised to be a mother to Imelda's boys. They were supposed to be self-sufficient, living in students' accommodation in Derry City."

"You are a liar! You knew they'd be home for the summer vacation. Isn't that when you got pregnant?"

Rayan looked at Nathanial's twisted countenance. Somehow, he always managed to drag her affair with Isaac into the row; and he knew she had never had sex while Raffi stayed with them. How dare he insinuate she had? She glared on him her temper rising.

"Believe me; having sex with any man was the last thing on my mind when I went to Ireland. But yes, yes, I *had wild* passionate sex *every chance I got* with *both* Isaac and Raphael," she lied. "It was incredibly, unbelievable self-affirming. Finally, I *was* somebody men desired…"

There was utter silence in the room. Rayan stood completely stock still, shocked at the words that had literally flown out of her mouth. Then she shrugged. There, she'd admitted it. Not only had she had great sex but she had *enjoyed it.*

Nathanial smiled. "I'm glad to see the old feisty Rayon is back. I missed her," he said moving closer. "C'mon, let's share a shower. You can soap me down. It's been a while," he murmured.

Nathanial rolled up her vest top. Freed, her breasts sprang forward. Like strawberries ripening with the kiss of the sun, the nipples hardened and peaked.

"Raise your arms," Nathanial ordered beginning to pull the vest over her face and head. For a moment it got entangled in her hair. Rayan stood still. In one fluid movement, Nathanial unzipped her shorts. She heard his chuckle as they fell about her ankles. "You wanton woman. When did you stop wearing panties?" he said in a pleased tone. Then his tone hardened. "Is not wearing underwear something Raphael liked?" Possessively, he grasped her bare buttocks.

Rayan cried out at the viciousness of his grip. "Nat, you're hurting me."

"Was Raphael right-handed or left-handed. That is how you knew the difference in them, wasn't it?" Nat said holding her prisoner against his torso.

Rayan could feel the rough sandy texture of his hands against her skin and his familiar smell of sand, sea spray and aftershave. "Nat. I've told you! At first I could only tell them apart because Raff had a birthmark. When he wore his hair floppy fringe style, it was impossible to tell which twin was Raphael and which Isaac was. It took me a while to realise one was right-handed and the other left-handed!" She gasped in shock as Nat's palm smacked her.

She struggled to break away from him. "Nathanial, that's not funny. Let go of me." She cried out as his free hand slapped her twice in quick succession. Nat had never raised a hand to her in all the time they'd been living together. He had barely raised his voice to her when she'd lashed out at him and berated him.

"I should have done this every time you attacked me," Nat said reading her mind. She could feel the muscles of his rock-hard torso against her. She struggled but she was no match for him. She felt her fear rising. In the anger management group, she had heard of cases where a placid compliant partner had flipped and killed or seriously maimed his or her partner. Why would he flip now? Why not when *she* had been abusive to him?

Her heart began to palpitate. She had to free herself. Her mind whirled. Nat was proud of his muscled physique. And he loved sex. Could she stroke his ego sufficiently for him to let her go?

"Remember our holiday in Bali? We made love on the floor of the hotel's balcony. And under the stars at the beach with the Indian Ocean crashing over us, remember? Nat, take me into the bedroom," she whispered relaxing against him. For nanoseconds, she thought she had succeeded. Then Nathanial emitted a low chuckle.

"Ah yes, the bedroom. How many times did you make love to Raphael in our bed when I was at work?"

"Nathanial, you know I have never even kissed Raphael…"

A shudder washed over Rayan. Nathanial was going to exact his revenge on her. She wondered if she screamed, would the nosy neighbour across the street call the cops. She twisted her body around. "I swear on my father's grave. I didn't sleep in our bed with Raphael."

"What about when you were in Ireland? In that cosy little love nest with only the mountain goats to see your goings-on?"

She wanted to yell that *he* had been bedding Sienna. From the tenseness of Nathanial's body and his grip on her, she knew he was in no mood to be reasonable.

He nuzzled her neck, seemingly mollified. "Yeah, we had a great time in Bali, didn't we?" Nat mused. "You dragged me around the Monkey Temple and all the other temples but you wouldn't marry me in any of them. Then, you humiliated me by attacking the cabin staff and being taken off in handcuffs by the air marshal."

"I'm sorry. It was a stupid thing to do—"

"Yeah, she was paying me a bit of attention—most women did…until Raphael came along with his Irish fucking charm…." Nathanial stopped talking. Rayan twisted her head. There was a faraway glazed look in Nathanial's eyes.

"Nathanial," she said schooling her voice into a soft promise. "Let's have a shower together."

"How many times did that bastard make love to you in *my* bed?"

"Let me go. You're hurting me."

"Admit you and fucking Raphael had sex."

A terrible helplessness came over Rayan. She had promised she would never physically or verbally attack Nathanial again. But pleading with him or stroking ng his ego wasn't working. She twisted her upper body around. "How many times you have fucked Imelda in *my bed*," she roared.

Nathanial's grip loosened momentarily.

Rayan angled her neck backwards—for once thankful for her height—her mouth was close to the side of Nathanial's head. Sick with desperation, she sank her teeth into Nathanial's earlobe.

Nathanial swore voraciously. He released her, his hand flying to his ear.

Shaking uncontrollably, Rayan lurched to the other side of the room the taste of Nathanial' blood in her mouth. Revulsion at what she had done flooding her mind. In a state of abject terror, she glanced at the door half expecting Ben Watts to be standing there summoned by her neighbour. How would she tell him all his good counselling and support had been a waste of time? She was still an abuser.

Nathanial shocked, staggered to the bathroom leaving a trail of blood on the tiled floor.

Her head throbbed and her body stung like she had been out in the sun all day she leaned against the seating and fumbled her juddering body into her clothes.

The shock of her attack seemed to have brought Nathanial to his senses. "Fuck! I must be going off my head," he said in a shocked voice reaching out a trembling hand in her direction as he came back in the room.

Rayan backed towards the door.

"Rayan, please, I… I love you. I would never harm you. I'm sorry, babe. It's all this stuff about the babies and Raphael and your father topping himself." Distractedly, he took the wet cloth away and gingerly felt his ear. "I will never lay a finger on you again, ever," he said emphatically.

"That what all abusers say," Rayan said shakily her hand on the handle.

Nathanial gave her an incredulous look. "I'm the abuser because I slapped your butt? You have been beating on me for years. What about my ear?"

"Get out, Nathanial," Rayan ordered her voice shaking uncontrollably. "Get out!"

Chapter Fifty-Five

The yellow roses' vibrancy mocked Rayan's black mood. "They're from Nathanial," Sienna said. "They came yesterday."

Rayan grabbed up the roses and carrying them out the back hurled them into the dumpster. As soon as Nathanial had left the day before, she had phoned Sienna to say she wouldn't be in; she'd set the alarm system and crawled into bed, emotionally shattered and physically hurting.

Sienna cast a surreptitious glance as Rayan, pale-faced, prepared to wash a chatty woman's hair. Geez, Sienna thought, if that's what spending a day in bed with the hot beach gym guy does for you, I'm glad I have other guys in my sights, she thought giving the construction worker she was just finishing off an especially bright smile. He hadn't asked her out yet but he would.

Rayan's thigh throbbed where Nat had slapped her with his open palm. Her hands shook as she massaged the woman's scalp. What the bloody hell came over him, she wondered. It was so out of character for him. Guilt assailed her. It had to be her fault. She had driven him over the edge by trying to wheedle him to take both babies to live with them. Had she unconsciously turned her attention to Raffi knowing he was keen to care for the twins? She gave a wan smile pretending an interest in the story the customer was sharing with her.

It had been a big mistake having Raff to live with them. It may have saved Raphael's life but it sounded the death knell for her and Nathanial's relationship, she mused. Nathanial had begun to act like a jealous possessive adolescent; glowering at Raff and leaving the house in a huff when she and Raffi talked about the babies.

The salon phone rang jarring on her taut nerves. "It's your mother," Sienna said.

Rayan shook her head resolutely.

"You should take it. She rang every ten minutes yesterday. She didn't believe you weren't here."

"Finish off here," Rayan said snatching the phone from Sienna.

"Why aren't you answering your phone?" her mother's voice said peevishly.

"I wasn't in the salon yesterday."

"You're not answering your house phone either." There was a disgusted snort from the other end. "Sienna told me. You were at home with that beach bum. Your father always said you were too weak when it came to men—"

Rayan gripped the phone. "Sienna was wrong. I was sick." Nathanial's attack on her had left her feeling badly shaken and biting his ear filled her with guilt, leaving her heartsick in body and soul.

Her mother went on as if Rayan hadn't spoken. "I need a new hairstyle." Rayan was surprised. Since her father's death, her mother had let her appearance go; playing the sorrowing widow to the hilt; receiving visitors in her dressing gown and slippers. Hiding behind closed blinds; convinced everybody was talking about her.

"Sienna will do it for you. I'm still feeling unwell so I'm taking the rest of the day off and going home to rest up."

Her mother drew in a deep breath. "I don't want your *assistant* to restyle my hair. I want *you*. It's the least you can do after your father—"

"I never asked my father to buy out…never mind, I'll do it," Rayan hissed down the phone aware that the chatty customer was listening with interest to her conversation.

"I need you to do it," her mother said in a small voice.

Rayan held back the sharp retort that rose to her lips. She wanted to shout—there was a time when you went to another hairdresser because my father forbade you to have any contact with *me* while I was living with Nathanial, she thought as she put down the receiver.

"My mother is coming in for a restyle."

Sienna raised her eyebrows.

"I'm going home to check on little Biscuit. I'll be back to do it." Rayan stopped on her way out of the salon. "Just so you know. Nathanial and I are over. He won't be coming back."

Sienna's eyes widened. "But Nathanial *loves* you. He always has," she blurted out. "So you won't try to kill me if I ask him out for a drink?"

Both Ben Watts and her mother were parking outside the salon when she got back. Ben was carrying a huge bouquet of mixed flowers. Despite his nosy manner, Ben had turned out to be a very good friend. "You old romantic—surprise for your lovely wife," she quipped.

"These are for you," Ben said proffering them.

Rayan was aware her mother was watching. She could almost hear the cogs in her head clanking away. Her daughter was now cavorting with a married police officer. "Flowers! Oh, thank you, Ben. They are lovely," Rayan said deliberately bending forward to inhale their fragrance.

Ben Watts blushed. "They're not from me. They're from Nathanial."

Rayan shoved them back at him. "Take them home to your wife."

Ben lost his smile. "Nathanial came to see me this morning. He's really broken up about what happened. He loves you, Rayan."

Glancing over his shoulder, Rayan checked if her mother was eavesdropping. "Mother, go on in. I'll be in straight away."

Her mother stayed there. "A married officer of the law is giving you flowers!"

"You're interrupting police business here. Wait inside," Ben barked. Her mother gave Rayan a baleful look and scurried into the salon letting the door bang behind her.

Ben put a soothing hand on Rayan's arm. "Nathanial told me *everything*. What he did was driven by insane jealousy. He accepts he was well out of order."

Rayan felt her face go crimson at a flashback of being held naked in Nathanial's muscular arms. She hung her head. "It was completely out of character for him. I saw a side of him I have never seen before... I... I deserved it...after the many times I beat on him," she whispered her lip beginning to tremble.

Ben shifted uneasily from one foot to the other. "Nathanial is at fault here, not you. He accepts that. He has promised me he would never do anything like that again."

Rayan gave him an incredulous look. "The first blow is followed by guilt and remorse but the abuser becomes less remorseful after that! Isn't that what you say?"

Ben knew he was skating on thin ice here. "I have advised him to go back over east again. Give you both a break." He hesitated. "You haven't reported it yet, have you?"

Rayan drew in a sharp breath. "You're condoning what he did! He held me prisoner, beat on me...and touched me!"

Ben shook his head vehemently. "No, Rayan, not for a single moment am I condoning the wrong Nathanial has done." Despite his earlier mistaken beliefs about the guy, his gut told him Nathanial was no abuser. "I'm here as both your friend." He hesitated. "There is something else."

Rayan saw his change of expression. He was wearing his officer of the law face now. "I've received a formal request from the Irish Police for character/police check on you."

Rayan's heart ricocheted into her throat. For a moment she couldn't hear. All she could do was watch Ben Watts' mouth moving. Had Isaac reported her for beating on him? Or, worse still, had somebody reported her for attempting to secure an abortion; a criminal offense in Ireland. Sweat broke out all over her body.

"What do they want a police check for? I'm an Australian citizen. I'm no longer living in Ireland," she bawled.

Ben held up his hands. "Don't go off on me, Rayan. I'm giving you a heads-up here. Yeah, you're an Australian citizen but your son and daughter were born in and live in the Republic of Ireland. That makes their welfare the responsibility of the Irish State."

Rayan's anger wilted. "Sorry, Ben."

Ben folded his arms across his chest and spread out his feet. "How did your kids come to be in the care of the Irish State?" he asked.

"They were taken into temporary foster care." Rayan stilled. "That's what they want the police check for, isn't it?"

"I take it the father is an Irish citizen?" Ben said sidestepping the question.

Rayan nodded. "I didn't plan to give birth to them," Rayan confessed. "I planned to have an abortion." She looked away from Ben's steady gaze. "That didn't happen so I made a private arrangement with, Sue, the woman I worked with at the Spa, to adopt the babies. Sue had a breakdown and the adoption was never finalised," she said succinctly, reluctant to go into all the dreary details on the street. "I know I don't want them adopted without my consent," she said flatly.

Ben fell silent. It was a messy complex situation. He doubted if Rayan would be allowed to take the kids out of the care of the State in Ireland. He wasn't convinced she really wanted to. From what she'd just admitted she had broken the law. He wished she hadn't mentioned it. It put him in a very awkward position. Now he was duty bound to take it under consideration when he wrote his report. Ben felt his heart sink down to his shoes. He was sure his report would be used to determine whether or not Rayan was fit to parent the twins she'd given birth to.

"Your mother is waiting," he said abruptly turning away from Rayan.

Chapter Fifty-Six

Nathanial watched Sienna in her skimpy bikini working the male sun worshippers on Scarrbough beach. You have to hand it to her, he mused. She knows how to move on. Once she had realised he was no longer interested in her, despite being apart from Rayan, she had cast her eye around for new conquests. He sighed. How he wished he could forget Rayan so easily.

He swung his eyes to the parking lot on the right-hand side of the beach where an old beat up faded blue Ute had pulled in. It was the same make and model as the one his dad used to drive. He looked down at the corn coloured sand between his toes. How long had it been since he had been home? Or had even written or phoned his parents? How many years since he left… Eighteen or twenty years? He had left straight after high school. He had always intended to go back but he never had. He didn't even know if they were alive or dead. The thought saddened him. They had been good parents. They deserved a better son.

He looked back at the parking lot. As he watched an old weather-beaten potbellied guy in a vest top stepped out of the truck; and jammed a wide brimmed white hat on his bald head before hurrying around to open the passenger door and help a woman of similar age on to the stony uneven ground.

"He reminds me of my dad," Nathanial murmured leaning back on his elbows. Good-natured like him too, by the looks of it, he thought as the old man took his wife's hand to steady her before helping her to a bench beneath the shade of a tree on the edge of the beach. Country folk—probably from the outback like my folks, he thought.

He drew a circle in the warm sand with his heel. He wondered what his father would think of him now. Would he even recognise the muscular tattooed man he was now as the skinny kid who had begged to be allowed to go sheep shearing across Australia all those years ago? He doubted it. He looked nothing like the kid he had been then. Rayan had rubbed the rough edges off him; infused him with some class and an appreciation of the finer things in life.

Guilt rose like bile. One thing he knew for sure, his old dad wouldn't approve of his present lifestyle, his womanising or the appalling way he had treated Rayan. His parents were old school. Small farmers prematurely aged: struggling to rear him and his sister Sally. Hard work and the 'Good Book' and church on a Sunday were enough for them.

A clutch of scantily clad girls passed by and gazed admiringly at Nat's toned body. Nathanial felt his spirits lift and then plummeted again. His father wouldn't understand his constant need for the attention of beautiful woman. Nat sighed dejectedly. He didn't understand it either. But something in him craved their admiration.

He drew his eyes away from the old couple and scanned the beach for Sienna. He wondered what she would think if he told her he had initially got his muscular physique from travelling like an itinerant from town to town across Australia shearing sheep faster than the other shearers. He didn't think she'd want to know he was nothing more than a dirty farmer's adopted son.

Or, that it was by pure chance as he worked out one night on a beach in preparation for a big money shearing competition that he had been' discovered' by a guy who thought Nat would be good eye candy for the rich babes that frequented his upmarket gym.

Nat shaded his eyes against the blue sheen of the merging sea and horizon and saw Sienna near the water edge lazily smoothing sunscreen into the pale skin of a redheaded guy. She gave him thumbs up. "Straight off a flight from Ireland, I'd say," Nat mused, "poor guy. Unless Sienna stops batting her boobs at him and works faster at covering him in sun cream, he's going to look like a lobster in the morning," he chuckled, rising to his feet. Rayan wouldn't want to see him. But he had to see her.

Biscuit's tail thumped out an excited welcome as he stepped in through the screen door. He stood in the centre of the lounge room and listened. The house was silent. He knew Rayan was at home. She'd have set the alarm system if she'd gone out. "Play ball, Biscuit," he coaxed, conscious he needed to make as much noise as possible so Rayan wouldn't accuse him of sneaking about her house.

After a while, he opened the connecting door to the bedrooms and shouted hello. He waited. Had she heard him come in and was *hiding* from him? "Stop fucking about. I have a plane to catch," he said under his breath. Maybe she was in the shower and didn't hear him over the hiss of the water, he thought. He cupped his ear to the bathroom door and heard the hiss of the water against the shower tray. He raised his hand to rap. Thinking better of it, he let it drop.

After what seemed like forever, he heard the familiar click as the water heater shut off. Quickly, he returned to the kitchen. He didn't sit. He knew he wouldn't be welcome.

Rayan's hostility towards him was palpable. "Get out! Come back to have another slapping game?" she said icily tying the belt of her robe tightly around her waist.

"I came to tell you much I deplore my behaviour," Nat said.

Rayan swung her hair forward. Wrapping her head in a towel, she fixed Nat with a frosty stare. "You've said it. So why are you still here?"

Nat swallowed nervously at the lack of feelings in her voice. He thought of the old couple on the beach still in love like his father and mother had been despite the hardships and lack of material things in their lives.

Rayan and he had everything going for them; money, status and a full life. And yet they couldn't get past their own failings and make a lifetime commitment to each other.

"I brought this for you," he said proffering an envelope with a logo on it. "It's a return plane ticket from Perth to Dublin…"

Rayan dropped the envelope as if it was burning her fingers. "You *are* completely insane! Why would I go to Ireland with you of all people?" she said incredulously hardly able to take in what Nathanial was suggesting. "Didn't your *best buddy* Ben Watts tell you? I can't *ever* go back to Ireland? The Irish police are likely to arrest me! And the social workers are going to have my babies adopted without my consent!" Rayan said unable to stop the tears that sprung to her eyes.

Clumsily, Nathanial tried to take her in his arms. "I didn't know, Rayan. I swear I didn't know. But that's all the more reasons for you to go—"

Rayan wrenched away from him. "Get out! Leave your key when you go. I don't want your stupid peace offering of plane tickets. And for fuck sake, stop sending flowers. The salon is beginning to look like a cemetery."

Nathaniel took a step towards the door and stopped. He had the strangest feeling of deja vu. His mind flipped back to the night Rayan had beat on him and Ben Watts was waiting outside to arrest him. He'd known that night he and Rayan's relationship was dead in the water. He had accepted it. He had agreed with himself if he stayed, he'd probably end up beating on her too. Why or why hadn't he listened to his gut feeling? At least they could have ended on an amicable footing. Now Rayan hated the sight of him.

He turned back to her. "Take the tickets. You turned your back on Ireland; walked away. Go back. You have unfinished business in Donegal. Go back and sort it out."

Rayan gasped. "You are the one who talked me into coming back to Perth in just the clothes I had on my back."

"Use the tickets, Rayan. If I hadn't let my ego and jealousy over Raphael get in the way, the twins might be living here now." He tapped the travel agency's logo on the envelope. "Get over there and straighten out the mess you created." He paused. "Branna and her brother didn't ask to be born. You and that lily-assed college kid made it happen. Get over there. Get those kids out of the care system. Let a family that will love them, adopt them."

Rayan stared open-mouthed. "How dare you tell me what I should or shouldn't do?"

"Get over there and sort it out," Nat retorted as he made for the door.

"You bastard," Rayan yelled as she lifted the table lamp and hurled it at the door as it banged shut behind Nathanial.

Ben Watts grinned at Rayan's flinty face. "The little woman has bullied me into taking a holiday in Europe," he volunteered in response to Rayan's mumbled enquiry why he was having a head massage, his hair restyled and a facial. "She says I'm stressed. That I work too hard; take my work home with me."

Sienna working on another male customer giggled. "Just as well you don't put it into practice." She chortled. "Going somewhere nice?" she smiled.

"London, England—in search for my roots," Ben said with a dramatic wave of his hand. He laughed. "Get it, girlie? That's what you call a pun," he called to Sienna who was touching up the roots of a customer's hair. Sienna giggled.

"Nathanial visiting his folks for Christmas?" Ben asked.

Rayan shrugged. "I don't know and I care less."

"It's good for parents and their children to be together at Christmas," Ben sad pointedly.

Rayan stared at him. So Nathanial had told him about buying her the plane tickets. The envelope had lain on the floor for days until Biscuit picked it up and carried it into her bed. Rayan had retrieved it and taken it into the travel agency where a snooty-nosed girl told her it was a special non-refundable ticket.

"Yeah, travel is good for you. Let's you see things from a different perspective," Sienna tittered to her customer.

"Smart girlie you have there," Ben Watts said admiringly as Rayan brushed the loose hair off his shoulders.

Rayan lost the battle over her tongue. "If you think I am taking a twenty-six-hour flight to the other side of the world so I can be turned back by border security or arrested as soon as I put a foot on Irish soil, you can forget it," she hissed into Ben's ear.

Ben shrugged nonplussed. "It's your babies' first Christmas," he said softly. He admired the end result. "You think Mrs Watts will approve?" he asked turning to Sienna.

"She will. She might fall in love with ya all over again," Sienna giggled. "You enjoy your holiday. I think you could squeeze a little one like me into your suitcase," Sienna teased openly flirting with Ben now.

"If I was forty years younger, I might take you up on your offer," Ben said jovially to Sienna. "Don't tell the little woman I said that," he added hastily his ears beginning to turn red.

The brightness of his ears reminded Rayan of the day she had accidently cut his ear when she let the scissors slip. She grimaced; what it is about me and ears, she thought. She wondered if her bite on Nathanial's had left a scar....

"Who will take over your important policeman duties when you are on holiday?" Sienna asked high on Ben's attention.

Ben snorted. "Some baby-faced *boy* barely out of basic police training. You be sure to tell him he has big boots to fill if he's taking on my job," he said winking at Sienna.

Rayan walked him outside. "Ben, about the police clearing—"

"It's ongoing," Ben said evasively. "But if I was you, I'd be in Ireland and take charge of your babies before it arrived there," he advised.

Chapter Fifty-Seven

I must be insane letting Ben Watts bully me into coming back here. It's like sticking my head through the bars of the lion's cage in Perth Zoo, Rayan thought trying not to look nervous. Her knees knocked together partly from exhaustion after the long-haul flight but mainly in trepidation as she waited third in line for security clearance at Dublin Airport expecting any minute to be pulled out of the line of weary travellers and arrested.

Was it her imagination or were the staff more alert and vigilant that when she and Nathanial had been flying out from the airport the previous April. She could hardly believe that had only been eight months ago? It felt as if her whole life; her whole existence had changed since then.

Grudgingly, she silently agreed with what Nathanial had said. Branna and BB hadn't asked to be born. If Isaac hadn't caved under pressure from Sue and cancelled her first abortion appointment and had gone on a drinking spree when he should have been going with her to England for her last chance appointment… Well, he would bloody well help her get this whole travesty straightened out now—if she got out of the airport.

She was next in line to show her passport. She steeled herself for the inevitable convinced the security staff was watching her. She'd either be turned back from entering the Republic of Ireland. Or, she'd be arrested.

She watched the passenger in front of her straighten her back and plant her feet firmly on the floor as she argued in a belligerent manner with the guy who was checking the passports. He tapped her passport and said something to her. She argued back and then took off her dark glasses. "These are not sunglasses. Can't you see I am blind? There are Braille dots on my passport."

Nonplussed, the security guard indicated his head to a uniformed woman standing to the right-hand side of his glass booth. Still arguing, the traveller was taken aside into a curtained off area.

Rayan shook involuntarily. Her feet inched forward until her legs came to a trembling halt on the outer edge of the yellow line she was supposed to wait behind. Like a runner waiting for the sharp retort of the starting pistol, she waited, jumpy as a cat.

The passport checker looked in Rayan's direction but didn't immediately indicate she should move forward. It couldn't have been more than a minute or two until he indicated she should move towards him but to Rayan it felt like an eternity. Adrenaline flooding her body she jerked forward getting the belt of the long coat she had bought to save her from the wintry December weather entangled in her hand luggage.

Impatiently, the passport checker waited until she'd freed it. "Sorry," she said in a voice she hardly recognised as her own.

Wordlessly, he held out his hand for her passport. The silence between them lengthened. "Travelling alone or with a companion," he finally asked eyeballing her.

"Alone." Rayan wished her voice didn't sound so quivery.

"Your first time in Ireland?"

Rayan shook her head. "No. I lived here for a year."

He raised bushy grey eyebrows. Rayan knew he was thinking what brought her from the summer climate of Australia to freezing cold winter days in Ireland.

"You have family here?"

"Yes. My son BBB and my daughter Branna live in Ireland," Rayan stammered out aware in her nervous state she had added on an extra letter to her son's name and was giving the impression her children were older.

"What do the three BBBs in your son's name stand for?"

Unprepared, Rayan said the first thing that came into her head. "Brian, Boru… Bradley." She sent up a silent prayer for all the times Mac O Lochlainn had talked about the history of Ireland and its High Kings from centuries ago and for having known Bradley the mountain guide.

His face registered surprise. "Brian Boru—a fine name for a boy. His father must be Irish."

"He is."

He stamped her passport and pushed it back through the glass towards her.

Rayan stood there in stunned disbelief, looking at it. She was being allowed into Ireland!

"Don't look so frightened, Miss Ritchie. We don't usually lock up the visitors—just the locals," he murmured as the curtain into the search bay curtain was thrust back and the female searcher with a firm grip on the woman in the black glasses walked past.

"Have a nice holiday."

Grabbing up her passport, Rayan fled in the direction of Arrivals.

Still reeling from the shock of not being arrested or detained, Rayan almost let her case trundle past her on the creaking carousel. The adrenalin began to ebb away and for a moment her arms felt too weak to wrestle her case onto the floor. "I've got it," a voice said at her elbow as a tawny hair girl effortlessly lifted it off and set it at Rayan's feet.

"Thank you," she said.

"You're welcome," the girl smiled moving off.

Rayan stood for a moment in the middle of the shifting, swaying crowd getting her bearing as waves of men and women clutching children and pushing trolleys piled high with an assortment of bags, suitcases and baby buggies free-wheeled for the door marked exit.

Rayan moved to the edge of the throng and breathed easier as she passed out into the outer Arrivals area. It was almost like a mirror image of the security area. Groups of people were milling about searching the crowd for their relatives and friends.

Near her a man and a woman wrapped their arms around a slim girl travelling with a small infant. As she watched, the woman folded back the baby's blanket. Cooing and making baby noises, the woman kissed the baby's toes and the man counted its fingers one by one. "He's perfect—just perfect," the man said with a broad smile tears glistened in his eyes.

"Their first grandson in a family of girls," the mother of the baby smiled by way of explanation as she caught Rayan watching them.

"I thought the plane was never going to land so I could hold him," the granny was saying as the family started to move away.

Rayan felt a lump rise in her throat. Would it make a difference, even now, if her mother was accepting of the twins? She was clutching at straws. It was never going to happen.

She caught the tail end of the family with the new grandson as they passed out through the glass doors. The man's words echoed in her head, "He's just perfect…"

Guilt gnawed at Rayan's tired brain. Branna was perfect; quick and inquisitive and learning to walk and talk at the right time. But BB wasn't perfect. She felt it in her bones. He had come off the worst from her days and weeks of starving herself so she wouldn't show as she waited for the abortion appointment. She shuddered. She had done that to him. Would that mean that his sister would be adopted but he'd spent his childhood being shuttled from foster home to foster home? Her heart twisted at the thought of BB being separated; from his sister and passed around like an unwanted parcel.

She startled out of her reverie when she heard her name being announced over the antenna. She was to make her way to the information desk where a message awaited her. She sighed. Surely her mother wouldn't phone her *here*! Wearily she made for the information desk trailing her suitcase behind her.

When she saw Sue, her hands waving wildly in the air, she blinked and blinked again.

"Oh my god, you finally got here!" Sue squealed rushing at Rayan and squeezing her so tight she thought she was in danger of losing her breath and her balance.

Rayan was so taken aback at seeing her that for a moment she couldn't speak. "How did you know I was coming? I hardly knew myself until a week ago."

"Imelda told Vivian and Vivian told me. I've been coming out to the airport…this is my third day." Sue laughed, giving Rayan another squeeze. "C'mon, Vivian is waiting for us in the car," she babbled excitedly as she grabbed Rayan's case from her and strode forward with long purposeful strides.

Too dazed to object and still blinking in disbelief Rayan followed her out the glass doors, across the pedestrian crossing and into a car park where every car in the country seemed to be parked nose-to-tail.

"Wait. Slow down. I'm not as fit as I was when I walked Muckish, and I've just had a twenty-six-hour flight," Rayan panted, trying to keep up.

Sue stopped and scanned the various zoned areas and then veering to her left started off again. "C'mon, I think I can see the car from here."

"Has Imelda told *everybody* I was coming?" Rayan puffed.

"Just all the staff you worked with. Sorry for rushing along but it's dammed costly to park here. Vivian will have her, 'you're costing me a fortune' face on. But why she should worry I don't know since its Imelda who is footing the bill…"

"Imelda's paying?"

"Yeah! Imelda sent her personal driver to collect you and bring you to Donegal. You *are* her guest of honour, after all. Didn't you know?" Sue asked with raised eyebrows as she cast a glance at Rayan over her shoulder.

"But I booked my travel ticket right through. I'd have been OK on the travel coach. I explained all that to Imelda."

Sue shook her head as she weaved in between parked cars. "You don't want to be using the buses the weekend before Christmas. You'd be sandwiched like a sardine in a tin between baying students. The buses will be jammed packed with them rushing home to their mammies for the Christmas turkey and all the homesick emigrants remembering their Christmases at home will be returning with the offspring the grandparents haven't seen since their sons and daughters went to live America and Australia."

"But I had planned to stay in Dublin for a day or two," Rayan protested. She didn't add that she wanted to see Isaac and reach some common ground about the babies. The least he can do is have the balls to admit he's their father, she thought.

As if she had read her mind, Sue slowed her step. "We're meeting Isaac in town for something to eat and then he's coming home with us to Donegal for the grand opening," she said quietly as she stopped beside a car.

Rayan's mouth fell agape as Mac O Lochlainn stepped out of the car and gave her a broad smile. "Afternoon ma'am," he said in a mock subservient chauffeur's voice as he tapped his forehead in a mock salute.

"You're Imelda's driver," Rayan stammered beginning to feel like Alice through the Looking Glass.

Mac winked. "Indeed I am. And it's well you're looking, girlie," he beamed sweeping an appreciative glance over her legs as she clamoured into the back seat.

Vivian caught Rayan's eye in the rear-view mirror and gave her a small smile.

"Right, let's get the blazes out o' here before it costs us the price of a small farm in parking tickets," Mac grumbled gunning the car and startling the drivers on either side of him.

Chapter Fifty-Eight

Rayan and Sue sipped their drinks and watched the drunken impromptu floor show Isaac and Shawnee were putting for Imelda and Bill's handpicked influential guests at the champagne opening of the refurbished Shingle Beach hotel.

The band changed it tempo to a more upbeat number. As the music floated out over the assembled guest seated in groups at round tables discreetly lit by pure wax candles in Donegal crystal holders and dressed in Irish linen tablecloths, Isaac extended his hand and bowed to his partner. Shawnee held out her short full skirted flirty dress and curtseyed to him. Couples gathering on the edge of the dance floor clapping encouragingly.

Isaac bowed again to the onlookers and taking Shawnee's hand swung her in a wide circle as he attempted to combine a jive gig with a Latina dance. Other dances tittered and moved back to the edge of the dance floor. Isaac whirled Shawnee faster and faster.

"Shouldn't somebody tell Imelda before she crashes headfirst into a table of drinks?" Rayan suggested as Vivian joined her and Sue at their balcony table.

Sue looked at Vivian. Vivian shrugged. "Imelda is in cloud cuckoo land; has been since Bill came on the scene," she said sourly. "She'll not thank you for putting a downer on her party. Leave it," she said sharply to Sue as Imelda and Bill, arms entwined around each other's waist, sauntered by below giving them a wave.

"Enjoying the party?" Rayan asked turning away from watching the dancing couple. Vivian ignored her and slid her arm around the back of Sue's chair. Leaning in to her, she whispered something in Sue's ear.

Sue frowned and shrugged her away. Rayan guessed Vivian had been asking her had she taken her medication.

"Imelda's *little boy* has learned some fancy steps since he took up with Shawnee's high society crowd," Sue chuckled as the dance came to a breathless end with a flourish. She leaned over the balcony and scanned the guests below. "I see Shawnee's mother and father are here. I'd love to be a fly on the office wall when he gets him back to Dublin," she laughed. "Isaac is drinking his own drink and everybody else's at their table when they go out to dance."

Vivian snorted. "The way Isaac is behaving it'll be a while before he's an asset to the judge's firm. Imelda's fantasy of him wigged and gowned his fingers in his lapels, in a high-profile case, is a long way off," Vivian scoffed.

"Don't be such a begrudging bitch, Viv," Sue said sharply. "You're acting like a disgruntled employee," she said plucking a glass of champagne from a passing white gloved waiter.

Rayan hid a smile. It was obvious Sue was rapidly regaining her old self-confidence.

"I'm tired of this…this charade," Vivian said disdainfully standing up. "I'm going to bed. Are you coming, Sue?"

"No, Vivian, I am not," Sue stated. "I haven't been out in months. I plan to stay here with Rayan till the last dance is called and the last drink is served. I plan to stay and have a damn good time tonight."

Rayan saw the hurt and trepidation in Vivian's eyes. Vivian was like Sue's shadow. Rayan wondered if she was still afraid she'd steal Sue from her. "Don't worry, Vivian. Sue will be fine…"

Vivian blanked her and focused on Sue.

"You are on heavy medication. You shouldn't be drinking alcohol."

Sue exhaled. "Go away, Vivian. I told you I'm not taking any more of those mind-numbing tables that overpriced shrink prescribed. They make me feel like an emotionless zombie."

Vivian's reply was lost in the general melee as chairs were scraped back at the announcement there would be a short pause in the dancing while supper was being served.

"Why don't you join us, Viv," Sue coaxed regretting her sharp tone. She slipped her arm through her partner's. "Stay and see New Year in with me."

Rayan walked ahead of Sue and Vivian down the curved stairway; one hand holding the rail and the other holding the tail of her evening gown so she wouldn't trip on it. She drew some admiring glances. She knew she looked well in the new dress. She was glad now she hadn't worn the dress she had bought for Raphael's end-of-term party the year before.

To her surprise, all her clothes were still hanging in Imelda's wardrobe, including the dress she had bought in a small exclusive bouquet in Derry. She'd sat down on the bed and holding the dress to her face reminisced about the look in Raphael's eyes when he'd told her to buy something 'sexy'. That look, that secret dream fantasy of every girl's prom night. He would be her prince and she would be his princess. Was that what she'd been thinking when she bought it? Only the dream had turned to a nightmare that had almost ended in tragedy.

She couldn't resist trying it on. Its low-scooped neckline line revealed her cleavage. Its soft sculptured shape hugged her curves and showed off her hips to their full advantage. She gave a twirl. Strange, she thought, gazing at herself in the full-length mirror. It was to be her coming of age and first real party dress; even though she was forty. She gazed at her reflection and realised with a jolt she no longer was the person who had bought that dress.

She stumbled on a stair. It broke her reflective mood bringing her mind back to the present. Crossing the dance floor under the shimmering mirrored globe that turned the maple sprung dance floor below into a glittering array of rainbow colours, she passed through an archway of red beaded holly and mistletoe into a domed heated marquee.

"The Irish sure knows how to throw a party especially when it's backed with American dollars. What a great first night opening," a portly red cheeked man standing beside Rayan beamed, sipping his drink. From his accent and demeanour, she guessed he was an American. "Are you a friend or foe," he chuckled. Not waiting for an answer, he raised his glass in a toast to Imelda and Bill who were seated across the other side of the marquee. "The lucky dog. He always had an eye for a hot little number. And boy, Imelda sure is one hot lady," he chortled enviously.

Rayan smiled benignly. He obviously had a few too many Irish whiskies.

"Let's take the weight off," he said, gestured to two chairs. Glad to rest the aching calf of her legs, Rayan sat down and slipped her aching feet out of her shoes. She looked around. Sue and Vivian were nowhere to be seen. She wondered if Sue had gone home after all.

"My name is Walter. Met Bill when we were both rookies in the forces—was his best man twice—he's forgave me for that—still friends," he grinned.

Rayan smiled wondering how long before it would be impolite to get up and go. She scanned the room hoping to catch the eye of one of her prior colleagues from the Spa. Her gaze landed on Isaac and Shawnee standing toe-to-toe beside a table littered with empty glasses. From their stances, Rayan guessed they were having a humdinger of a drunken argument.

"Bill remembered Imelda from way back when he first bought the old house. Did you know that?" Walter said breaking in on her thoughts.

Rayan shook her head and nibbled at the food on her plate. She vaguely recalled was it Raphael? No, it was Isaac, mentioning something like that but she wasn't about to get into it now. She wished the band would hurry up and start up the music again. Talking to this old guy bloated with too much whiskey and an oversized ego wasn't the way she wanted to bring the New Year.

"Yeah," Walter went on seemingly oblivious to her non-committal interaction, "Yeah," he said puffing out his chest, "with the blessing of the Irish, British and American Governments Bill planned to use the old place as a…a secret rendezvous—if you will—under the guise of an exclusive fishing lodge where the troubled politicians of the North of Ireland could meet on neutral ground and thrash out their old animosity of—away from the eyes of the press."

He paused and beckoned a young waiter who was refilling glasses. "Yeah, Imelda was one of his favourite waitresses," he smirked. "Of course, she was just a kid then, earning money to go to college. Bill was just out of a second nasty divorce." He fell silent. Relieved, Rayan prepared to make her escape.

"Imelda had a way with her," he said reflectively. "She could always make Bill forget his troubles." Walter sighed. "And boy did he have troubles—alimony payments to two wives and child support up to his armpits." Walter sipped his whiskey. "He had plenty of other women after Imelda—hell I can't remember when he didn't have a woman—but the odd thing was he never forgot the sassy colleen with the quick banter. That's what brought him back again, you know. He never really expected she'd be here. He was like a kid in a candy store when he discovered she was and *living in his house*," he chortled spluttering into his drink at the idea of it.

Rayan raised her eyebrows. "You mean the old Manse? As far as I know, Imelda saved it from being vandalised and burned to the ground."

The man startled a little but recovered quickly. "Geez, you're that Australian woman. The one Imelda is always gabbing about."

Rayan slipped her feet into her shoes and tucked her clutch bag firmly under her arm. She was curious to know what exactly Imelda had said about her but she thought it wiser not to ask.

"It was nice talking to you—"

"Hold your horses. You're the woman who gave Imelda's kid safe harbour in Australia. That was a magnanimous thing to do—considering the Irish Republican Army was planning to shoot him for being a snitch," Walter said, his voice rising.

Rayan looked around apprehensively to see if anybody had overheard him. "Happy New Year," she said, tight-lipped, making her escape.

Chapter Fifty-Nine

"Mum moved out of here and into the hotel after Bill came," Isaac observed looking around the familiar kitchen of the Manse. He hunched his shoulders. Without Raphael, his mother and Dizzy sprawled out on the end of the sofa, it wasn't home anymore. It was just another house, he realised.

He wrinkled his nose. "The damp unlived in musty smell kind of reminded me of when Raffi and I first came to live here."

Rayan looked at him disparagingly. "You were only three then."

"It's more of a *feeling* than a memory."

"I wondered if Branna and BB will one day have a vague memory of you and me visiting them in their foster home."

"How long do you intend to stay?" Isaac asked hurriedly changing the subject.

Rayan eyeballed Isaac. "That's what I want to talk to you about."

Isaac ran his hand through his hair. "This is not a great day for discussions."

"Why is that?"

Isaac heaved a sigh. "Shawnee dumped my stuff outside her door and said she never ever wanted to set her eyes on me again. And her pissing father says I'm being transferred from the main Dublin office to the wilds of Kerry."

Rayan raised her eyebrows. Nathanial had sent her a postcard from Co Kerry when he was touring about Ireland but she had no idea where that was. "Is this because you and Shawnee aired your sexual exploits in a drunken free for all torrent of exchanges just as Imelda's party was winding down and you were polishing off the remains of the alcohol?"

"If her father thinks I'm splashing through cow manure wearing a pair of wellingtons and listening to some farmer with his hand halfway up a cow's ass complaining about his tax returns and EU grants in the back of beyond, he can forget it."

"Leave and start your garden centres. Isn't that what you said you really want to do?"

Isaac snorted. "Bill has offered me a job as a gofer."

He looked out the Manse window at Muckish. He didn't think he could watch Bill and his mother acting like love struck teenagers. It was nauseating the way they were behaving; all doe-eyed at each other as if to say 'missing you already'—even though they were in the same room.

"Take his offer. You hate what you're doing anyway." She hesitated. "Aren't you afraid being back in Donegal the IRA might mistake you for Raphael?"

Isaac shrugged. "Mac O Lochlainn is sorting it out." He tightened his lips. "I can't fucking stomach Bill playing lord of the Manor. The set of him—walking on Muckish foothills wearing a barber jacket and carrying a blackthorn walking stick." His lips curled in contempt. "Have you heard the latest? Mum has persuaded him to open a dog sanctuary for Irish wolf hounds," he said scathingly.

Rayan laughed, visualising Isaac out with a shovel cleaning up piles of huge dog shit.

"I'm glad you think it's funny," he said dourly. "Mac has Bill's head filled with stories of the old Irish chieftain Donegal Clans. He has Bill almost believing he's a far-out ancestor of Red Hugh O Donnell himself." Isaac snorted.

Rayan glanced across at him. Her heart wobbled. When Isaac scowled and pulled his eyebrows down in a certain way, there were definite resemblances to the worried little face of BB.

"I was thinking about joining Raphael in Melbourne," Isaac mused.

Rayan stilled. She didn't know Raff was in Melbourne or that Isaac was in contact with him. She wondered why he'd left Sydney. Maybe he never was there. Maybe Nathanial had told her that in case the IRA came looking for him.

"He has to keep on the move," Isaac said as if he had read her mind.

"Will he ever be able to come home again?"

Isaac shook his head. "Mac O Lochlainn doesn't think so—not for a very long time." A terrible longing to see the brother he had rarely been separated from since birth overwhelmed him.

A silence fell over the kitchen.

"What are you going to do about the twins?" Isaac finally asked. "Why are you dragging it out? The longer you put it off the harder it's going to be." He didn't understand it. She hadn't wanted them in the first place. "Sign the adoption papers," he said in an aggrieved voice.

Rayan looked down at her hands twisting in her lap. She wondered if Ben Watts report had reached Children's Services yet. Was that what she was waiting for? So, the powers that be could make the babies wards of court—relieving her of the responsibility to make the decision?

"Most couples want to adopt a cute baby," Isaac went on, sensing Rayan's growing maudlin mood. "They'll be a year old soon; getting to the age where they lose that cuddly baby thing adopters want. Your dilly-dallying is lessening the twins' chance of being adopted. If you don't make up your mind soon, they could end up in an institution. Especially BB—you know that yourself without me telling you. He's…different from Branna."

His words appalled Rayan. Was he right? Was dragging her feet lessening the twins' chances of adoption? "I have arranged another visit to the foster parents to see the twins. I have said you will be coming too."

Isaac leaped to his feet. "No way am I going back there. The foster mother literally threw us out last time. That was your fault. Who hands a massive chocolate reindeer to a toddler?"

Rayan gave a half smile. They'd taken the twins their Christmas presents including a party-sized Christmas stocking. Branna grabbed for the chocolate reindeer and wouldn't let go. In the tussle, the chocolate got all over Branna's face, hands and hair. When Isaac wrenched it from her, she had thrown an ear-splitting temper tantrum.

BB had tried to console his sister. Branna bit him. He had added his scream to Branna's screeching. In the end, the foster mother had asked them to leave.

"It's time you officially acknowledge you are the twins' father. They will not always be small babies. When they look for their birth certificate at eighteen, there is *not* going to be a blank space where *your* name should be."

Isaac looked daggers at her. Jesus! She never gives up, does she, he thought. He had enough bother with Shawnee and her bloody family without thinking about two babies who *might* want to know who their father was when they turned eighteen. He had never wanted to know. Why should they?

"Raphael could be their father. He has as good a chance as me."

Rayan stared at him, perplexed. "Why would you *even* think Raphael *might* be the father of my children?"

Alarm bells started clanging about in Isaac's head. Holy Fuck! He had completely forgotten. Rayan didn't know about the trick they had played on her.

He swallowed hard. "Raffi *could* be the father…"

Rayan looked at him in utter bewilderment. "What are you saying? Raphael and I never…"

Isaac tan skin colour paled. He licked his lips. "We often faked—let on—to be one another. You couldn't tell the difference in us—"

"You're saying sometimes it was you and sometimes it was your twin who made love to me!" Rayan said horrified, her skin beginning to crawl.

Isaac nodded feeling mortified. "It was mostly me…we often pretended to be each other…even at university…don't feel bad; not many people can tell us apart."

Rayan stared at him completely at a loss for words.

"Sorry, it was a dirty trick to pull on you—"

"Don't be ridiculous," Rayan stuttered out finding her voice. "I… I'd have known it wasn't you!"

"You didn't know the difference," Isaac said convincingly.

Dumbfounded, Rayan stared at him. "You're some piece of work. Do you know that, Isaac? You'd go to any length to avoid taking the responsibility for fathering the twins. Even to saying I had sex with your brother and didn't know it," she said a note of incredulity in her voice. "You listen to me! I'm not Imelda. You are not wriggling out of this or passing the blame onto your twin, you little shit! Raphael *never* sneaked in to my bed pretending to be you. I would have known. You make love like a…beginner. Raphael would really know how to make love to a woman."

Crimson-faced at her words, Isaac welcomed the tidal wave of relief that washed over him. She didn't believe him. He forced his breathing to calm down. He should get out of there before she started figuring the night of the party Raphael had been so drunk, he hadn't realised he was in her room and not the hillwalkers' room next door. And she had drunk champagne with Maddie the chef, until she was almost comatose. He wasn't surprise she didn't know it was Raphael and not him.

Was that the night she got pregnant?

Isaac swung open the door of the Manse and drew in a huge breath of clear mountain air. No way was he signing that form until he found out for sure which of them was the twins' father.

Chapter Sixty

"I am *not* going on any more visits. There's a mean streak in Banna," Isaac burst out. "Every time the Lego man BB and I were building was almost finished, she pretended to hug me and knocked it down again." He had felt a fool crawling about on his hands and knees retrieving the pieces from beneath the office furniture.

Rayan sighed. Branna and BB's foster mother had refused to have her or Isaac back in her house so the social worker had arranged a supervised visit in the local Social Services office.

"She was jealous. You were ignoring her."

"She was dressing that doll with you."

Isaac took another slug of his beer. "She has granny Norah's mean streak in her."

Rayan heard the slur in his voice. "You've been drinking again," she said irritably. "I thought you were—"

Isaac swore ferociously. "You'd hit the bottle too if you were stuck in an office with the ancient *Miss Moore* watching you like a hawk and guarding the keys of the safe. I'm no thief," he grumbled.

Rayan's mind flashed back to the day Isaac had stolen the money from her bag.

On the other end of the phone, she heard Isaac swear again. "Bill, the tight-fisted bastard, convinced *my mother* I need to be cut loose." He snorted. "She is so enthralled with him she *agreed*. Can you believe it? *My own mother*! Cut me off without a penny! You'd think she'd be happy to help me out—now that Raffi is not here."

Cutting you loose is long overdue, Rayan thought. She held her counsel, pretended to be sympathetic. "She did?"

"Bill said we needed a man-to-man chat. 'If you were in USA, you'd be doing your national service, son. Makes a boy into a man'," Isaac slurred, mimicking Bill's accent.

"This will be the last meeting, I promise," Rayan coaxed bringing him back to the purpose of their telephone conversation. "It's the big one; the one that will decide Branna's and BB future." She could hear the shake in her own voice and the clink of glass against Isaac's teeth at the other end of the phone as he slurped from a beer bottle.

"No! No more fucking meetings, Rayan. Accept it. It's time they were adopted. Neither the two of us know the first fucking thing about taking care of babies. No, hear me out…" Isaac hiccupped as she drew breath to argue back. "You're like me; you haven't got a maternal bone in your body."

Rayan gasped as if he'd struck her. "Don't you dare compare me with you! I gave *birth* to them, didn't I?"

Isaac gave a derogatory snort. "Only because you couldn't get rid of them," he said bluntly. "You gave them to Sue when you knew she had been turned down by the State as unsuitable," he went on a belligerent note creeping into in his voice. "Jesus, Rayan, consider yourself lucky you're not being charged with a crime and being sent back to Australia in handcuffs."

White-knuckle rage surged through Rayan. She wanted to reach down the phone and choke the life out of the self-serving little shit. But she daren't. She needed him to go with her this one last time.

"Sue and Vivian were turned down only because they were same sex couples—"

"Rayan, be reasonable," Isaac roared, his anger palpable. "What do you plan to do with *twins*? Introduce them to your mother as her illegitimate grandchildren! I didn't think so," he said sneering when Rayan didn't answer.

"They're your son and daughter as well as mine, you know," she said despairingly.

There was a long silence at the other end. Rayan prayed her outburst hadn't scared him off. She needed him beside her at the forthcoming meeting. "Please Isaac. We owe BB and Branna that much."

"We owe them nothing except to let them be brought up by somebody that *wants* them."

"You low-life lily-livered bastard," Rayan spluttered breathing heavily. "You be there and be sober," Rayan said icily, preparing to slam down the phone.

"I'll be there if you agree to sign the adoption papers and put an end to this," she heard Isaac's voice say faintly as she broke the connection.

Chapter Sixty-One

The solemn silence around the rectangle table was punctuated by the creaking of chairs and the snuffling of dry nervous coughing. Perplexed, Rayan looked at the people gathered. Her nervousness grew. There was more there than she'd expected. She had expected Mary, the social worker, her superior and the twins' foster mother to be here. But what the hell was Imelda accompanied by Bill's fat-faced friend Walter, the man who had been talking to her at the grand opening of the new hotel, doing here!

A woman near the top of the table on the left-hand side leaned slightly forward and gave Rayan a small smile. It was a minute before Rayan recognised the woman; Sister Hampton, the midwife, from the hospital. She looks very different out of her nurse's uniform, Rayan thought feeling the knot of anxiety solidify like a lump of lead in her stomach. The nurse had obviously been summoned to communicate Rayan's prenatal and postnatal state of mind. No doubt she would recount Rayan's adamant refusal to see the babies; her refusal to express breast milk to help little BB to put on weight—in short, she was there to state that Rayan's non-compliance with the medical staff had hindered rather than helped her children to survival.

Her chest tightened. She tried to breath past her rising panic. It was obvious the cards were stacked against her. The authorities were obvious going to show she was a mother to two young children with whom she had had only the briefest of contact since they were born fourteen months previously. Ignominy rising in her she returned the nurse's smile with a tentative nod. I hope you remember to include that in the end I *did* provide breast milk, did mother my babies, she hoped her look implied.

Beside Sister Hampton sat Dr Blanid Breen who had been so kind to Rayan during the late stages of her pregnancy. It's a pity she wasn't there to keep her promise when I needed a section instead of a vaginal birth, Rayan thought resentfully lifting up her chin and giving the doctor a cool look.

The man at the top table cleared his throat and straightened his file. "If everybody is here, we should get started," he intoned. "My name is John Lynch, senior social worker on this case. This is my colleague is Mary Murray," he said, indicating the woman beside him. "She is the twins' case worker."

Rayan noticed the crumpled suit jacket and the weary look in his eyes. She wondered how many of these meetings he sat through in a week, a month. Too many she was guessing. She eyeballed him. "Branna and BB's father is not here yet."

He raised his eyebrows marginally and glanced at his subordinate. Hastily, she thumbed through her papers and gave an almost imperceptible shake of her head.

"There is no father's name listed as attending this meeting," the man said not unkindly.

"He said he would be here. I want to wait," Rayan said her voice rising. She'd phoned Isaac again and again but only got his answering machine. She'd apologised for the abrupt way she had finished their conversation and reminded him of the date and place of the meeting. He hadn't phoned back but she had been hoping against hope he'd show up.

Rayan's heart was beating so fast she felt as if she was hyperventilating. She was sure the others around the table could see it pounding in her chest. She threaded her finger tightly together under cover of the table and willed Isaac to come if only for moral support—even if he was drinking. Sweat broke out on her upper lip. Her eyes ached and burned from lack of sleep. This was it. She was only delaying the inevitable. Children' Services were about to take away her parental rights and decide the twins' future.

Indecision gnawed at her. Should she fight for the twins or do as Isaac said, sign the papers to allow them to be adopted? Would she even be given an opportunity to decide? She thought not.

She glanced in the direction of the foster mother who was sitting tight lipped; her chair pulled slightly back from the table and out of Rayan's direct line of vision.

The social worker glanced at her watch, then at her boss and suggested they should get started. He nodded in agreement. She shuffled her papers and then addressed Rayan directly advising her that *she* was presently looking for separate placements for the twins with a view to adoption. "BB is a lovely wee boy but he lived in his sister's shadow. I believe that given he is late in reaching his developmental milestones, BB's needs will be best met in a placement where he can develop at his own pace without the influence of his sister," she finished.

Rayan gasped. Her worst fear was being realised. The twins were being separated. Before she could gather her thoughts, the social worker indicated that the foster mother should speak.

Avoiding looking in Rayan's direction, she explained that given Branna's challenging behaviour, she felt she could no longer continue to act as Branna's foster parent. Therefore, she was requesting that she be removed from her care.

"Thank you," the senior social worker said succinctly.

He swept his gaze around the table. "The children in this case, namely BB and Branna, are our primary concern here. Their welfare and wellbeing are paramount," he intoned levelling his gaze on Rayan.

She was dammed if she was going to sit here and listen to a bunch of do-gooders pass judgement on her children. She eyeballed him. "May I be excused?" Jesus, she felt like a kid in school asking permission to go to the toilet. She listened to the click of his pen as he considered her request.

Finally, he looked around the table again. "Is there anyone else who needs…excused—before we continue this meeting?"

No one else moved.

Rayan let the door bang behind her. Its dull thud echoed in the quietness of the reception area. She made for the doors leading to the carpark. She needed Isaac's support if she was to get through this. Frantically, her eyes scanned the parked cars in the hope of seeing Isaac's jeep. It wasn't there.

She let a guttural sound rise in her throat. "I'll never forgive you, Isaac," she whispered. "Nathanial was right. You are a lily-livered little shit. The twins are better off without you."

Deflated and defeated, she went back inside. The least he could have done was put his name on public record as their parent, she thought tears pricking the back of her eyelids.

She felt bile rise in her throat. Would there ever come a time when she could depend on a man? Her inner voice sneered. If you hadn't been so determined no man would rule you and had Nathanial's kid, like he wanted, you wouldn't be in this predicament now, and it reminded her. She closed her eyes acknowledging its truth.

Inside the reception area she hesitated, reluctant to return to the meeting and hear the scratch of the social worker's pen write her out of her children's lives.

Oh, no doubt there would be visits. But how often would she be able to do that living on the other side of the world.

Overhead, she could hear distant voices. A door opened and she heard Branna's unmistakable screeching. She looked towards the stairs. They were up there unaware their future was being decided down here. Pain gripped her heart.

"Rayan," a voice said.

Her head shot up. Relief flooded over her only to be quickly replaced by anger. "What the fuck are you playing at? You were supposed to be here an—"

"Rayan, it's *me,* Raphael."

Rayan felt her hackles rise. "Isaac, this is not the time or place for playing drunken game—"

"No, it really is me." Raphael said. Coming close to her, he swept his hair from the side of his face. Sure enough, there was the small birthmark below his eye; faded to a tan by the Australian sun but still visible. She looked at the colour of his eyes. Her own eyes widened. It really was him!

She felt her knees give way. "What are you doing here? Where's Isaac?" she croaked. She waved her hand weakly towards a door to her left. "They're in there—have just decided the twins should be kept apart and then placed separately for adoption," she quaked.

There was utter silence. Raphael looked at her incredulously.

"Where's Isaac? He should be here…"

"Never mind that," Raphael said brusquely, beginning to pull her in the direction of a door where he could hear raised voices.

"Where is he?" Rayan demanded, pulling free.

"Covering for me—building houses for the aborigines in the outback. Come on, I don't have time for long explanations, Rayan." His eyes went to the stairs. "I've just seen the twins…"

The blood pounded in Rayan's ears. She grabbed Raphael's arm. "Your mother is in there. She'll know you're not Isaac."

"She knows I'm coming," Raphael hissed, shoving her into the room in front of him.

They took their seats under the perplexed stare of the social workers and the silent appraisal of the others around the table.

Raphael introduced himself as Isaac Wright, sat down as Mary, the social worker, recounted in clipped tones the future placement arrangements with a view to adoption for Branna and BB.

Raphael sat forward purposely in his chair. "As the twins' father, don't I have a say in whether my children are to be adopted or not?" Rayan's knees began to knock together.

There was a shuffling of papers as John Lynch flipped through his file checking for any reference to a father. Finding none, he looked at his colleague and then at Raphael. "You are the father of Branna and BB—Brian Bura?"

"I am." He glanced at Sister Hampton and gave her a winning smile. "I believe you can vouch for me. I was almost a permanent fixture in the special baby unit," he laughed. All eyes swung in Alice's direction.

"Maybe this would be an opportune moment to hear your report on this case," Lynch said.

Sister Hampton gave an account of Rayan's admission and time in the hospital and the medical circumstances surrounding the twins' birth. She reported that the mother had suffered from temporary loss of mental capacity due to the circumstances she found herself in and later, her exposure to the elements on Muckish, plus a traumatic early birth had brought on post-natal depression and trauma.

Then it was Dr Breen's turn.

She looked the length of the table and smiled. "I am pleased to concur with what Sister Hampton's report and to add Miss Ritchie had a traumatic birth; with Branna born vaginally and BB born by caesarean section." She stopped and looked to the senior social worker before continuing. "Rayan has made a full recovery mentally, physically and psychologically and is a fully competent parent to her children."

Outside the door of the meeting room a footstep sounded in the hall. Rayan tensed and glanced at Raphael. He had taken a huge risk in coming back to Ireland. Sweat broke out on her and the hairs stood up on the back of her neck. She glanced at Raphael. He looked relax and unperturbed.

She realised Mary the social worker was reading her report. But she hadn't heard a word she'd said. "Can you repeat what you've just said?" she asked her voice shaking.

In a clipped voice the social worker repeated that the children had been in temporary care of the State since shortly after their birth following their mother's failed attempt to have them adopted privately. She looked directly at Rayan, her look plainly saying such an arrangement was against the law in the Republic of Ireland. "In my professional opinion, the best interests of Branna and BB will be met by remaining in the care of children's Service in separate foster placements, with a view to adoption."

Rayan and Imelda reacted at the same time. Imelda, her face red with indignation, faced the senior social worker. "You're planning to separate them?"

John Lynch cast a look at his subordinate with a look that plainly said, "Who the bloody blue blazes is this woman!"

"Imelda Wright, the maternal grandmother—minimal contact with her grandchildren since they have been in care," Mary said succinctly in an undertone.

John Lynch cleared his throat. "This was not an easy decision to reach. But I'm sure you will appreciate for the future of the children—it's for the best." He spread his hands. "As you heard the foster mother explain, BB has complex needs and Branna has behavioural issues that need to be addressed. They both need the security of a family unit where these individual needs can be met," he stated with an air of finality.

Rayan's guts knotted into a tight ball. "Do you have a home for BB?" she asked hardly recognising her own voice.

"He will be placed with a temporary foster carer until we find the right placements for him."

Rayan gulped. "You mean he may have different placements—be moved around."

"Unfortunately, that may be necessary, but I assure you…"

Rayan felt the floor rise to meet her. BB was going to be passed around the care system and it was all her fault.

"Bullshit," Imelda exploded, jumping to her feet again. "Some things never change! You tried to spin me that crap when you wanted to separate *my* twins—him and his brother," she said pointing at Raphael. "That was twenty-one years ago. It was wrong then and it's wrong now to separate two babies who grew in the womb together."

Placing a placatory hand on Imelda's arm, Walter coaxed her back into her seat. "Let me deal with this, my dear. That's what I'm here for."

He flattened his pudgy hand imposingly on his leather briefcase before unzipping it and extracting a sheaf of official papers. "My name is Walter Aimes of Aimes and Aimes Associates, New York City. I'm here today to represent Mr Wright, Miss Ritchie and the children and their maternal grandmother, Miss

Imelda Wright." He nodded in Imelda's direction and waved a florid hand in the direction of Raphael and Rayan.

There was a flurry of page turning as the social workers checked if his name was on the list of attendees.

Rising to his feet, Walter pushed back his chair and walked to the head of the table. He scrutinised John Lynch with steely grey eyes as cold as flint and proffered the sheaf of papers. "You will find all these papers, regarding my clients' son and daughter who are presently under the care of the Children Department, are all in order," he said formally. "I give you notice of one week to discharge the children from your care and return them to their mother and father."

Chapter Sixty-Two

Rayan felt her jaw drop like a stone. Her eyes riveted on the social workers' surprised faces. Jesus! What were Raphael and his mother playing at? She drew in a deep breath to steady her jittering heartbeat. Isaac must have blabbered to Imelda about her pressurising him into being here. She snapped her mouth shut. Little shit couldn't keep his water, she thought.

Chairs scraped back and people began to file out of the room. Rayan felt as if she was being swept along on a tidal wave. *One week!* What the hell was going on? Had the IRA lifted the death sentences on Raphael? Was he coming back to live in Donegal and bring up the twins there? She felt Raphael's grip on her elbow steering her away from the meeting. "Raphael," she spluttered.

"I will explain everything once we get away from these showers of do-gooders," he murmured. The automatic door hissed open and Rayan found herself out in the carpark.

"I want to know what's going on," she said through gritted teeth as Dr Breen walked past, and flicked the fob for her BMW.

Walter hurried out. "Let go back to the Shingles and discuss this in private, over a hot toddy and a pot of good strong Irish tea, my dear," he said soothingly to Rayan taking in her rising agitated state.

Rayan's hand shook as she sipped the strong tea laced with whiskey. "You should have *told me*, Imelda, what you and Raphael planned to do. A week! *One week*—until the twins are with me!" She shuddered, the full implication of what was happening sinking in. "You should have discussed it with me! I can't do it," she raged, glaring at Raphael.

"You care about what happens to BB and Branna, don't you," Imelda said. "This way, they will be safe and loved. Isn't it worth it to know they will be together, with family? It's only until Raphael gets things settled with old Manus, Kate's father. Then he will take full responsibility for the twins and you can go back to running your business in Perth."

Guilt twisted Rayan's gut. She just didn't know if she could do it, even on a temporary basis. And how long was temporary? "I'm not really the mothering kind," she jabbered at Imelda.

Rayan turned Imelda's words over in her mind. It's only until Raphael gets things straightened out with Kate's father. She gulped, remembering the hard-faced old man. He didn't look the forgiving type to her. Fear gripped her heart. What if he had Raphael shot? What then? Her stomach fluttered in panic. She felt as if her emotions were on one of those roller coasters you went on at fairgrounds. One moment she was on a high knowing BB and Branna would be safe and loved and the next she was plunged down in despair, terrified of the responsibility of caring for them, should anything happen to Raphael.

"You did agree in Perth you would take them until I got a place, got settled," Raphael pointed out, seeing the indecision on her face.

Rayan gulped. It was stretching a point to say she had *agreed*. She had given it consideration, mostly for BB's sake.

She held out her empty cup to Walter. "Fill it up, stronger this time," she croaked. It was one thing to *think* about the possibility of having both twins but to have them literally thrust on her without her consent was another thing altogether, she gulped at the hot toddy. It burned her throat but she didn't feel it.

Raphael sat down beside her. "It's the right thing to do, Rayan. As soon as I get this mess about me touting sorted out with Manus, I'm coming back." Mac O Lochlainn had kept him informed about the old man. He still was in charge but was dying from cancer. Raphael drew in a strong breath. For better or worse, he was sure Kate would marry him in a heartbeat. It's not likely oul Manus would leave her a young widow. No. It wasn't the old man that was bothering him as much as how Kate would take to the idea of mothering Rayan's twins. That concerned him greatly. No more womanising for me, he thought noticing Walter, red-cheeked, from the heat of the open fire and the hot toddy, covertly admiring Rayan.

Walter sipped his drink and admired Rayan's shapely calf. She's a strong woman, he mused. He hoped Bill and Imelda knew what they were taking on. But behind the tough façade, he could tell, she was fragile, emotionally. A light sweat rose on his brow. This was going to be a tricky case. He could tell from John Lynch's carefully schooled expression that he'd sensed an ambush when Raphael announced he was the father of the children.

He noted that the senior social worker had not gotten Raphael to sign any documents to that effect. He's gone back to his office to gather his facts to strengthen his case for keeping the children under the care of the State, he mused. He wouldn't roll over that easily. Raphael and his mother had a fight on their hands if they planned to pull this off.

And then there was Isaac, the loose cannon, the drunken twin brother. It was unlikely he would contest the parentage with Raphael as father. Indeed, he will probably welcome it, slippery eel that he is, Walter thought. But in cases like these, you never can tell what a little whiner like him might do. Walter tightened his jaw. One thing he was sure of—Isaac would wring a deal from Imelda if it came to keeping his mouth shut.

Interesting case, he mused, refilling his glass. A very interesting case, he thought. According to the DNA, either one of them could be the father. I wonder does she know which of them got her pregnant, he thought, eyeing Rayan. I'd put money on it she might. It'll be fun wooing it out of her, he thought.

Chapter Sixty-Three

"Those sons of bitches won't make it easy for you," Walter said to Rayan. "This is it. We will only get one shot at this," he warned lifting his briefcase and ushering her before him into the hearing arranged by Children' Services.

Holding grimly to his professional persona, John Lynch, senior social worker, fixed his eyes on Walter. "The welfare of these children is paramount. They are Irish citizens. They have rights. And Children's Services has a responsibility—"

"Don't split hairs with me on this, buddy," Walter had said tersely tapping the sheaf of papers that lay between them on the table. "The Irish Government is going to have egg on its face when this shit hits the national media. A mother permits her children to be taken into temporary care of the state while she flies thousands of miles to look after her sick parent who has had a stroke. And you take advantage of her family crisis to have her children placed for adoption! It's like history repeating itself."

Rayan swallowed. It wasn't strictly true. She hadn't known her father was ill when she'd made the impulsive decision to go back to Perth with Nathanial.

"The media are going to love this case," Walter went on, "history is repeating itself."

A startled look flickered across the senior social worker's face. He exchanged a covert glance with his female colleague. "What do you mean, history repeating itself?"

Walter rose from his seat again before he answered. "What do I mean? I mean the scandal of the infants of those poor hapless women who were forced by religious dogma and social stigma to sign away their babies to the care of the State? What happened to the rights of those kids?"

The charged atmosphere in the room was palpable. "I'll tell you what happened to them. The institutions of the State hoodwinked the mothers of those children and then adopted their kids to rich American families, like mine, buddy.

I'm one of those kids. I was born in Ireland. I have deep Irish roots in this country, buddy."

Rayan went hot as if she was having a hot flush and then went chillingly cold. She could see a dogfight to the death developing between these two powerful men. And her babies were caught in the cross-fire.

John Lynch squared his shoulders. "Every child in our care is found a good home—"

The lawyer made a snorting sound. "You can guarantee that, can you, bubby?"

"With respect, Mr Aimes, I am not your buddy," John Lynch retorted.

Ignoring him, Walter ploughed on. "And what about keeping records on the kids you placed for adoption overseas…?"

"This is not what we are here for today," Mary, the female social worker interjected, interrupting Walter.

"The institutions were kinda light in their record keeping," the lawyer went on, ignoring her. "If they did have records, they weren't in a rush to share with adopted kids, like me, who came looking for information on their biological parents."

"This is irrelevant…ancient history…"

"What might be irrelevant ancient history to you might be of the greatest importance to others, madam," Walter said in a frighteningly quiet voice.

A loaded silence followed his assertion. The senior social worker looked at Walter. This was supposed to have been a straightforward presentation of the facts to reach a conclusion on the future of twins. He turned, focusing his attention on Rayan. "Miss Ritchie—Rayan, you permitted your children to be taken into the care of the State of your own free will, did you not?"

Rayan nodded.

There was a beat of silences as he appraised her. "Am I to understand you are now in a position to give your son and daughter a home?"

All eyes turned on her. Rayan shivered; a feeling of stark terror gripped her. The words that came out of her mouth would shape her children's future. She could feel her throat closing in. She knew nothing about babies. What was she going to do with twins!

She felt herself nodding.

"Very well. Your children will be returned to your care *under* a Child Protection Order. You must not take them out of the country for the duration of the Order," John Lynch stated, closing his file with a decided clip.

And then the letter had arrived yesterday in the post.

Chapter Sixty-Four

Rayan stirred in the comfort of the duvet. "Today's the day," she murmured. "Easter Sunday—the day of Branna's and BB's christening." She cuddled into the warmth of the covers again. "Another milestone reached," she mused.

Despite the heat of the bed, she shivered involuntarily, recalling the first days, weeks and months she had been thrust into the role of being a parent to the twins. Days when she felt sure she had made a terrible mistake in not having the twins adopted. Days she was incapable of showing them love; sure they would come to despise her as she'd despised her parents for their cold detachment. The floorboards of the old house had creaked under her feet as she walked from room to room believing Isaac had been right all along; she had no maternal instinct.

At night she'd fall asleep, exhausted, only to wake a couple of hours later filled with dread at the task she had to face come morning—Branna banging her head on the floor, screaming manically; BB hanging on to her, his eyes swimming in tears. In desperation and fatigue, she had begged Vivian to apply again to adopt the twins through the court system.

Determinedly, she got out of bed. Today was to be a day of celebrations, not recrimination. Tightening the belt on her dressing gown, she pushed her feet into slippers and padded out onto the landing. She listened outside the bedroom that used to be Raphael's and Isaac's. It was blissfully quiet. The twins were still fast asleep. She knew if she cracked open the door, BB's bed would be empty. He'd be in Branna's bed, curled into her back.

The kitchen of the Manse was warm. The clock on the wall clicked contentedly. Drawing back the blinds Rayan's eyes linger on the fine April mist on the summit of the mountain. If Raphael was here, he'd be up there walking the Minor's Path, she thought wistfully. She wished he would surprise her by stroll in past the grumbling rooster in the yard; push opens the back door, and announce. "I'm here for you and the twins like I promised."

"Except you're not here, are you, Raffi," she murmured, "Kate's father saw to that."

Turning, she filled the kettle. She could hardly believe it was two years since he had impersonated his twin at the meeting with Children's Services, declaring he was the twins' father and he did not consent to his children being placed for adoption. It still felt surreal.

She heard the clatter of the twins' feet on the stairs. "It's my turn," Branna announced in her lofty voice so uncannily like Vivian's, as they rushing headlong into the kitchen pushing each other as they made for the dog.

Papa Bill, as the children called Imelda's partner, had brought them a dog for their third birthday. "I don't *need* an abandoned wolfhound dog," Rayan had protested.

"Every kiddie needs a dog," Bill had retorted. She had to admit, the dog, aptly named Buddy, loved the children and they him.

"My turn," BB lisped, winning the first round of the morning battle.

Throwing his arms around Buddy's neck he planted a sloppy kiss on the dog. The dog, gentle as a docile sheep, wagged his tail and licked BB's face.

"It's my turn," Branna said in an imperious tone pulling him away.

Rayan watched as she placed her cheek delicately against the dog's fur and cuddled him. Rayan gazed at her daughter in wonder. She stood a full head taller than her brother and unerringly graceful to BB's ungainly gait.

"With her head of black hair, she has the looks of me," she thought. But with her aloof mannerisms and stature, she could easily pass for Vivian's child, she mused. Yes, she had given birth to them but in a sense they *felt* more like Sue and Vivian's than her children. To her shock and utter amazement, when she couldn't cope and considered placing the twins for adopting again, Vivian's response had been to move her and Sue into the Manse so they could help care for the twins. *They* became the twins' mothers. Taking it in turn to get up in the night when the twins were sick or when Branna woke up and screamed.

Her eyes swung to a framed photograph on the sunroom wall. It was of Vivian and Branna sitting on an outcrop of slightly elevated rock with the white foam of the Atlantic in the background. It had been taken the previous summer. Branna was waving and looking directly into the camera; Vivian, proud as any parent showing off her little daughter, was smiling lovingly down at her. She is as devoted to her as if she was her own flesh and blood, Rayan thought still amazed at her turnaround. Branna will become Vivian's protégé, she thought.

Her gaze scanned the next photo of Sue with BB in her arms. BB was leaning his head against Sue's cheek. A born mother, if ever there was one, Rayan thought. Sue loved both twins but there was no doubt about it—BB was *her* little boy.

He'd be a late bloomer but he could go places, she thought. Perhaps he could be the one to realise Imelda's dream, become a high-class lawyer, she thought with a jolt.

She shook her head in astonishment. She still found it hard to believe that *she* had brought them into the world. And even more amazing that they had survived in her care.

"Wash your hands," she ordered hoping it wasn't going to be one of those mornings where they literally counted each other's sugar-coated cereal to ensure they both got equal amounts. "Do you remember what special day it is today?"

"It's the day I wear my dress Mommy Vivian bought in Dublin especially for *me*," Branna crowed spreading out her hands as if she was holding out the tail of a ball gown. "*You* have to wear a silly old tie and funny coat," she scoffed at her twin.

"Don't want a tie," BB lamented, sticking out his bottom lip.

"Nana Imelda will be there. She's bringing up your great granny Norah." Rayan smiled hoping to stop BB from blubbering.

"Ugh, she kisses us," both twins said in unison.

Rayan hid a wry smile. That was the greatest shock of all. Granny Norah *adored* the twins; announcing to anybody who would listen she was their *great granny* and didn't she look well on it.

"Is Pappy Bill coming?" Branna demanded to know, sliding into a chair at the table looking for the world as if she was in the Hilton Hotel, waiting to be serve her breakfast by a white-gloved waiter.

"You are a baby. You won't get the water poured on you because you can't bless yourself or say your prayers properly," she mocked BB. "Isn't' that right, Rayan," Branna said.

"That's enough," Rayan scolded as BB's eyes filled with tears. "Stop teasing your brother. Eat your breakfast; Sue and Vivian will be here shortly."

Both twins clapped their hands, happy at the prospect of seeing them. Rayan gave a wry smile. BB called Sue 'Mama' and Branna called Vivian 'Mommy'. And they call me Rayan, she thought ruefully.

She pushed down the feeling of jealousy that gripped her. She was ashamed to admit it but it irked her sometimes how much Vivian and Sue loved the twins. How different life would have been if I had been loved with a fraction of that love, she mused. It's not that I'm envious of how much the twins are loved. I miss Nathanial. I wish I had someone to love me, she thought.

As she listened to the children's chatter, she let her thoughts drift to Raphael. The last time she had seen him had been in the Shingles Hotel straight after the first meeting with Social Services. She remembered what he had said to her. Sitting beside her on the sofa, he had taken her hand in his. "It's not a lie. I could be the twins' father," he admitted. "What I did was terribly wrong—pretending I was Isaac when I came to your bed at night. I'm sorry," he said sheepishly. "But I am not sorry the twins were born." He took a deep breath. "This is my one chance to make it up to you and them. I told Ma what we did. She nearly flayed me alive. She is going to get Bill to set up a crèche at the Hotel for the children of staff and regular customers. Branna and BB will be able to go there a couple of days a week." He'd looked shamefaced at his feet. "It's all I can do for the time being, Rayan."

True to her word, Imelda got Bill to apply for permission to open a private nursery and play facility at the hotel. Those three days a week away from the twins had been what had saved her from going under. She'd clung to the freedom those days offered her like a drowning woman to a lifebelt. The first few days the twins went to the crèche she had taken the phone off the hook and slept from sheer mental exhaustion.

Imelda had never admitted in as many words what her boys had done. All she said was, "It's the least I can do. I remember what it was like to be solely responsible for twins. I'm their granny," she'd said dryly. Shaking herself out of her reverie, Rayan squared her shoulders. This wasn't the day for looking back. This was a day for looking forward. Her heart beat a little faster. She tried hard not to think what the future might hold without Raphael to father the twins; without Nathanial to love her.

She felt her lips curl up in a half smile. It was strange, but she and Isaac were on the one wavelength now—him on his twelve-step programme—living one day at a time away from the drink and her from meeting the challenges of coping on her own as a single mother.

I should get Bill's lawyer, Walter, to find out how I go about securing the twins' future should anything happen to me, she thought. Oh, don't be so bloody dramatic, she chided herself. Where would you be going?

She saw Maddie the chef from the Smallest Pub park in the yard. She had offered to help cook the celebratory dinner to be served after the christening. She stopped to talk to the twins who were feeding the dog, the reminder of their breakfast which was sticking in clumps to Buddy's hairy chin.

"A quick one before I start preparing," she joked, drawing a champagne bottle from her bag.

Rayan laughed. "Father Donnell wouldn't appreciate it," she chuckled. "Can you keep an eye on them for a while? Sue and Vivian are on their way."

"Not a bother." She hesitated. "Have you heard from Raphael?"

Rayan shook her head.

Upstairs, Rayan stood for a while looking out beyond the apple trees to the mother sheep feeding their new-born lambs in the field below. She wondered how each ewe knew their own mother. It reminded her of Sister Hampton the day in the special nursery when at the feel of Rayan's touch, BB had stirred. "He knows it's you. He knows you're his mother," she had said quietly.

Nature is wonderful, she thought. The lambs are born and grow, the birds nest, have their young, push them out of the nest and fly away to return the following year having survived a harsh winter.

Branna and BB had survived their trauma on the mountain and their birth. Passed through babyhood and being in foster care. One day, I might even tell them about it, she mused.

She and they had both survived the toddler stage despite her as a mother being totally incompetent. They had reached their third birthday and had realised their milestone—BB a little later than his sister. But as Granny Norah pointed out, everybody gets there in the end. Rayan wondered was it the whack on the back of the head intended for Raphael that got her there.

Rayan turned back to the room. Today, the twins would be christened in St Patrick's Catholic Church. She'd have been happier allowing them to choose their own religion—or none at all—when they were old enough. But the local school principal had said their names couldn't be added to the school register unless they were christened—something to do with them being eligible for the sacraments of the Catholic Church later on. She was really doing it so that they'd be accepted as part of the local community.

Opening a drawer in the bedside locker, she took out the letter that had come from Children' Services. She unfolded the crisp single sheet of paper and read it again. *Following a review conference, Branna Ritchie and Brian Ritchie is no longer the subject of an interagency Child Protection Plan. Their names have been removed from the Children 'at risk' Registers. You are free to apply for passports for both children.*

Rayan closed her eyes and breathed out. Two years she had been grilled, on a regular basis, by social workers, health visitors and a raft of other childcare professionals. She and the twins had been scrutinised and monitored. She replaced the letter in the drawer. Obviously, the state considered her competent to be a parent now. "If only I thought the same," she murmured.

Chapter Sixty-Five

"Manus the oul bastard is not dead yet," Mac O Lochlainn snorted, when Rayan wondered out loud if Raphael would allowed back to Ireland for the twins' christening. Despite the 1998 Good Friday Agreement in Northern Ireland eighteen months previously, it was still too dangerous for Raff to show his face in Ireland.

She had posted him the date, the church and the time in a message to the last email address she had for him. "He didn't do himself any favours slip in' back into the country for that meet in' ye all and spirit in' away Kate, the oul bastard's daughter, from under his very nose in the middle o' the day," Con pointed out. "He's hanging on hoping she'll come back before he kicks the bucket. Hell will never be full 'til he's in it," Mac had growled.

Downstairs, the house phone rang insistently. Rayan's heart began to drum against her ribs. Could it be Raphael? "I'll get it," she shouted out halfway down the stairs before she realised Maddie was already lifting the receiver.

"It's old Father Donnell," Maddie mouthed as Rayan descended the last few steps of the stairs. "Speak loud; he's deaf as a doorpost. But he can hear plenty when he wants to," she snorted.

Disappointed, Rayan stood for a minute clutching the phone.

"Hello. Father," she said her voice shaky.

"Is it still on?"

"You mean the twins' christening?"

"What else would I be ringing you about?" the old priest said irritably.

According to the locals, Father Donnell was definitely old school; none of the new-fangled changes in the Catholic Church for him. It surprised Rayan that he had agreed to christen the twins at all under the circumstances. She couldn't blame him for checking. She had changed her mind so many times that in the end when she phoned, he'd growled, "Frank, call me Frank. I have more conversations with you than I have with the Bishop."

"Yes Father, it's still on."

"You'll not change your mind between now and two o'clock?"

"No, I'll not change my mind. The twins are looking forward to it. Maddie is here making preparations for the celebratory dinner. You will come back to the Manse for something to eat and drink afterwards?"

Father Donnell gave a dry cough. "Did you do what I told you—about choosing godparents?" he said ignoring her invitation.

"Yes. It's Bradley."

"Ah, Bradley, the mountain guide?" Rayan heard the note of approval in his voice.

"Yes…him…" If he hadn't been able to say which mountain trail I had taken, Branna and BB wouldn't be here today, Rayan thought.

"And the other sponsor?" Father Donnell asked cautiously.

"Sue is the other sponsor." There was a beat of silence. "She was the first person to befriend me when I came to Donegal," Rayan explained expecting the priest to find fault with her choice. "One set of sponsors for both twins—is that OK?"

"Yes, yes. One set of godparents for twins is permissible." There was a pause. "And who will represent the male parent?" he asked.

"Isaac."

"Good, good," Father Donnell responded with much more enthusiasm than he felt. He gave a sniff. "Make sure he is free from intoxicating drink," he said sharply. The last thing he needed was a melee in the middle of the ceremony.

"He's on a 12-step recovery programme," Rayan said hastily. "He'll be sober."

"Aw, sure, it wouldn't be a christening without wetting the children's head," the old priest relented, softening his tone. "He can have a few after the christening."

Rayan felt her body relax. "Thank you, Father, for all your help and support," she said softly.

She thought about her many visits to the old priest house in arranging and cancelling the twins' christening dates. They had argued about catholic schooling and the teaching of prayers and religious instruction. Rayan insisted religion should be left out of it until children were old enough to decide for themselves.

Then, on one occasion the whole sordid story of her intention to secure an abortion had spilled out. She had tried to excuse her actions by impress on him she was a non-believer "Sorry father," she'd mumbled. "I know abortion is against the Catholic faith but I don't believe…" She had expected the old priest to react in shock and horror; put her out of his warm comfortable sitting room. Instead, without a word he had taken her trembling hands in his and bowed his head. She had got the impression he was *praying* for her. When he'd finished, he had risen, gave a dry cough, went to the door and called his housekeeper to bring in a pot of tea.

"Tell me, child, and the truth now, because God sees what is in our hearts," he had said, "what brought you to your decision to abort your babies?"

And Rayan told him of unloving parents; of her terror that she would be an uncaring mother; of the promises she had made to herself that she would *never* be a punch bag or a doormat for any man like her mother had been. Once she had started to talk, she couldn't stop. It was as if a dam had burst somewhere deep inside her. Words rushed out as fierce and as ferocious as the waterfalls that pelted down Muckish when the mountain streams couldn't contain a cloudburst during a thunderstorm.

When she had finished it was dark outside and the fire had died down in the hearth. Totally embarrassed, at her long ranting tirade, she had felt feeling physically sick and emotionally drained. But, yet, lighter in a way she didn't understand.

Without asking, he poured her a stiff brandy. "Drink that down. I think we both need it," he'd said.

"Don't be late. This is a busy parish," he was saying now interrupting Rayan's reverie. "And make sure that daughter of yours behaves herself during the liturgy," he barked out.

"I'm making no promises on that score," Rayan shot back.

Father Donnell smiled. He enjoyed the banter that went on between him and this lovely immigrant woman. He couldn't coax her into becoming a candidate for the catholic faith. But she had given him a solemn promise that she had every intention of bringing her children up in the Catholic faith. It might not be good enough for the Bishop. But it was good enough for him.

"I'll be on time," Rayan promised.

After he put down the phone, the priest stood with his elbow on the mantle brace looking into the heart of the fire. He pursed his lips. Not a sign of that boyfriend of hers that had caused such a stir in the parish. Was it him she was hoping the call was from? Her disappointment had been palpable even over the phone. The old priest's face softened into folds of wrinkles and chins. Rayan was lonely. "She needs a man in her life," he mused. He was sure there had been love between her and the Australian.

He hunched his shoulders. Her loneliness troubled him. It wasn't *right* to be alone. Everybody needs someone, he thought.

He threw another log on the fire from the stack at the side of the fireplace. She has good friends in the two gay women, he reminded himself. What was the new buzzword for women like them? He screwed up his face. "This getting old is a dammed nuisance," he grumbled. "It steals away your memory. Living an *alternative lifestyle,*" he muttered aloud, the phrase finally coming to him.

He nodded his head sagely. Yes, Vivian and Sue live as colleagues. But the whole place knows they are a gay lesbian couple. The Catholic Church doesn't approve of it, he conceded. But they stood by Rayan when others whispered behind their hands that she had stolen away Isaac's virginity—led him into sin. Father Donnell smirked. "If she hadn't, he might be still as celibate as me," he chuckled.

He wondered what the Bishop would say when he was told his parish priest permitted a *gay* woman to be godparent to twins of an unmarried mother who wasn't catholic. He straightened his stooped shoulders. He knew his parishioners. There would be a flurry of letters to the Bishop. They'll say old Father Donnell is going senile—beginning to lose his marbles—that they need rid of the old bugger.

He shrugged. Christ said suffer little children to come onto me. They were living on the cusp of a new millennium, weren't they?

He hadn't permitted Vivian, the second gay woman, to be a godparent to the girl. He shook his head firmly. No, no, given the *living arrangements* Vivian and Sue shared, that would have been a step too far. There would be the possibility of the child's soul being placed in mortal danger should the godparent ever have to take physical and spiritual responsibility for her.

His thoughts turned to Raphael and Isaac. "A fine pair those sons of Imelda's turned out to be," he muttered. "Imelda never was one to teach them morality or right from wrong," he sighed, reluctantly moving away from the heat of the fire.

He furrowed his brow as he made his way to the chapel. Isaac was sober and respectable now. But would he be responsible enough to do the decent thing and sign his name where it said *father's name* on the baptismal certificate, he wondered. And the other twin is on the run from the IRA, he mused.

His frown deepened. "Two fathers and no father at the same time," he grunted. "The way those two impersonate each other, you wouldn't be sure whose name you were writing into the parish records," he muttered. "But, for the sake of the children, if Isaac is willing to sign his name, I won't stop him," he murmured.

He made his way towards the ornate stone baptismal font in the centre of the chapel. He had had the christening font moved. Its new position meant that families could gather around the font and have full participation in the baptism. There had been complaints to the Bishop then too.

He expected a good attendance at this christening. "Nothing fills a church like a potential scandal," he said in a bemused tone. "Yes, the villagers will turn out—If only to witness my demise. And see whether Isaac or Raphael turn up to claim parentage."

His thoughts sobering, he genuflected and knelt to pray for those who had asked for prayers. As he prayed, he offered up a special prayer for Branna and BB who would be received into the Family of the Church in a few short hours' time. He prayed for their mother, Rayan, for the healing of memories and release from her loneliness. Making the sign of the cross, he rose, and straightened his cassock. He was as prepared as he would ever be for his last baptism in this parish.

Chapter Sixty-Six

Rayan drew in her breath in awe. Branna stood before her, looking radiant as a bride in her white calf-length raw silk couture christening gown. The bespoke gown rucked at the bodice and sprigged with white heather fell away in gentle folds and came to rest on the tip of her of matching ruffled ankle socks that were peeping above the white Italian hand-stitched soft as down leather boots.

Vivian had spared no expense—in spite of her not being the godparent, Rayan thought in gratitude.

Rayan glanced at Vivian. *She* looked like someone who had just stepped off a catwalk. Rayan looked down at her own stylish dress and matching bag and shoes. She had thought she looked the height of fashion before she had seen Vivian's outfit. She let her gaze settle on Vivian's face. As usual, her makeup was expertly applied. Her hair coffered to within an inch of its life. But her face had a tight closed look to it.

Vivian had been incensed when old Father Donnell had point-blank refused to let *her* be Branna's godparent. "It's because Sue and I live together, isn't it? How dare the Catholic Church judge me on my sexuality," she had stormed.

In vain, Rayan had tried to explain what the old priest had told her; it was written into Canon law. There was only going to be one set of godparent or sponsors. Godparents had to be one male and one female. But Vivian was in no mood to be reasonable. Rayan hoped she didn't make a scene during the ceremony.

"We should go. Father Frank specifically asked we not be late," she said as Vivian began to fuss with Branna's dress.

Sue took Branna's hand. "Oh, my darlin', you look just like a princess," Sue said her voice beginning to wobble with emotion.

"She looks like the picture of the angel in my book," BB said in a matter-of fact voice, "'cept she has no wings."

"You look like Lord of the Manor," Sue smiled hugging BB.

Unexpectedly, tears threatened to spill out and spoil Rayan's eye makeup Sue had so painstakingly applied. She gulped back the tears, wishing yet again that Raphael was here to see the twins baptised.

BB's hair, in a pageboy fringe and brushed to a shining cap of ebony black hair, accentuated his deep Mediterranean skin colouring. Rayan smiled down at him. He looks like a little celebrity icon from the 1980s, she thought, her heart melting.

He had wriggled and complained as Sue had coaxed and cajoled him to sit still long enough so she could style his hair and fix his bow tie. He had been adamant he wasn't wearing a tie. In the end, Bill had won him over by taking him to Harrods in London and buying matching ties—cowboy style—and matching cowboy Stetsons which BB and Bill were going to be allowed to wear after the christening ceremony was over.

In a cream linen suit and matching ruffled shirt Rayan thought BB looked uncannily like Isaac when she'd first met him. Surreptitiously she glanced at Isaac who was waiting impatiently to go. She wondered did *he* see the resemblance between them. If I believed in Father Donnell's God, I'd ask Him that the locals gathered for the christening would *see* the resemblance and stop gossiping about the twins' parentage, she thought.

That's what you'll get if you decide to live here, her inner voice reminded her. She glanced at Imelda standing serenely beside Bill. How had she put up with the villagers talking behind her back all these years? No wonder she has grown a thick skin, she thought.

"The car is here. The car is here!" BB shouted excitedly letting go of Sue's hand and rushing for the door.

"It's not a car. It's a white stretch limousine," Branna said loftily.

"I'm sitting up front with Pappy Bill," BB shouted, starting to jump up and down.

Father Donnell cleared his throat. The gathered congregation fell silent as he began to speak. Solemnly, he welcomed the parents, godparents and the twins to St Patrick's Church and invited them to take their places.

Graceful as a ballerina, Branna took her brother by the hand and glided up the centre aisle with a presence that defied her young years. At that moment the sun shone its rays through the stained-glass windows bathing the chapel in light. An audible gasp went up from the gathered congregation as the twins made their way like a little mini couple to the front pew of the chapel. Father Donnell bowed his head and offered up a simple prayer of thanksgiving. On this, Easter Sunday, it was a sign the Holy Spirit was present.

"What name do you give your child?" he asked turning first to Isaac. There was a heartbeat of a pause before Isaac answered.

"Bradley Isaac Raphael."

A slight snigger echoed from the body of the chapel. The priest paused for a moment. "Remember you are in the House of God," he admonished.

Sweat gathered in beads on Rayan's forehead. She was beginning to wish she had taken the priest's offer to have the twins baptised in private, at the Manse. She hadn't expected that there would so many of the villagers present. Out of the corner of her eye, she recognised the local reporter who had tried to coax a story out of her when the twins were born. Her heart fluttered. She wondered if anybody from the child care services was there. She hoped the godfather, Bradley, had a firm grip on Branna who was already stretching her neck and looking around her curiously.

The priest's gaze swept to Rayan. "What name do you give your child?"

"Branna Vivian Sue." A muffled snort from the pews turned into a cough when the old priest cast them a baleful look.

The priest hesitated. So, Rayan was naming the girl after the two gay women. Something else to fan the flames of gossip, he sighed. He gazed intently at Rayan.

For one agonising moment, Rayan thought he was going to insist the twins be given the names of saints. She'd heard he had even changed the baby's name to the name of whatever 'Saints Day' the baby was being christened on! A hysterical giggle threatened to escape from her throat as she wondered what saint's day it was today.

There was uneasy shuffling as the congregation and the christening party held their breath to hear what the old priest was going to say, or do.

"What do you ask of God's Church for your children?" Father Donnell finally said, moving on.

"Baptism," Isaac and Rayan responded in relieved unison.

The priest turned to Sue and Bradley. "Godparents, are you prepared to take on the responsibility for the physical and spiritual wellbeing of these children?"

"We are," Sue and Bradley answered together.

Making the sign of the cross on each twin, the priest indicated that the parents and godparents should do the same.

"It will be your duty as parents and godparents to bring these children up to keep God's commandments." the priest murmured making the sign of the cross on the chest of each child with Oil of Catechumens.

Rayan heard very little of the liturgy or the homily that followed as she watched Branna struggle to free herself from Bradley's grip and encourage BB to do the same. Unable to hold her any longer, Bradley loosened his grip on her.

The priest, hesitated as the elegant child, clearly bent on exploring, grabbed BB's hand and pulled him after her in the direction of the brimming baptismal holy water font.

Given the mischievous look on the wee girl's face, he decided to shorten his prayers. Moving, he indicated that they should all make their way to the baptismal font.

Rayan stiffened as they gathered around the font. From a nearby seat Vivian was giving the old priest a disparaging look as he invited the congregation to renew their own baptismal vows and renounce Satan and all his works.

Ignoring her, the old priest asked God's blessing on the holy water.

"Parents, you have asked for your children to be received into the Catholic faith. Is it your will that Bradley Raphael Isaac and Branna Sue Vivian receive baptism?"

"It is."

Father Lynch indicated Bradley should hold Branna over the baptismal font and that Sue should put her right hand on the child's shoulder. Branna trailed her fingers in the holy water.

"I baptise you in the name of the father, and of the Son, and of the Holy Spirit," Father Donnell intoned reverently, stopping between each part of the prayer as he held the jug of holy water he had taken from the font and poured it over Branna's head. She giggled as the old priest dabbed with a towel at the little rivulets of holy water ran down her neck. Clearly relieved she hadn't succeeded in dislodged the small pouring jug from his grasp, the priest smiled at her.

Sue picked up BB and prepared to move forward. As Bradley placed his right hand on BB's shoulder, Rayan felt her hands clasping and unclasping, willing BB not to cry out as the old priest repeated the words of baptism.

"Good boy," Father Donnell said smiling at him.

"Can I put my cowboy hat on now?" BB lisped.

To Rayan's relief, Father Donnell chuckled. "A gentleman never wears his hat in church," the priest chuckled smiling down at him.

There was utter silence in the chapel as the old priest solemnly prayed over each of the children in turn; before anointed both of them in turn on the crown of their heads with the oil of Chrism.

Tired of standing still, Branna fidgeted and then sat down on the carpeted raised dais that held the christening font and began to sing. As usual, following his sister's lead, BB joined in.

"Praise be to God—you are now children of Christ," Father Donnell said. "Perhaps the children have the right idea. We will all sing a hymn," he said, clapping his hands together in delight as he invited the congregation to join in.

To Rayan's amazement, the gathered parishioners stood up as one body and began to lustily sing, *this is the day the Lord has made for us,* as the priest placed a white garment on each child.

Rayan felt tears choke her throat. She had never witnessed anything like it.

"You have clothed yourself in Christ," Father Donnell was saying, blessing the small white piece of garment each child now wore.

Rayan felt a great leap of joy swell up in her as the priest indicated they should all gather around.

Reaching out, he brought the Easter Pascal Candle forward and instructed each of the godparents to light their own candle from the Easter candle flame.

Bradley guided Branna's hand as she placed it on the creamy wax candle and held it there. Then it was Sue and BB's turn to grasp the glowing candle "Walk always as a child of the Light," the old priest murmured softly. Gently, he placed his hands on BB's ears and eyes and then repeated the same on his sister. "May your ears receive His Word. And your mouth proclaim His Faith," he murmured.

Taking each child by the hand, he led them before the altar followed in a little procession by the godparents and Rayan and Isaac. Each carried their own lighted candle for the children.

"These children are now children of God," the priest announced addressing the body of the church. "We will now have the final prayers." Rayan felt peace steal over her as the voices of the congregation rose up again in prayer. It had all gone beautifully, she thought.

The christening is nearly over, now all you have to do is bring them up good Catholics, her inner voice reminded her. "I'll do my best," she murmured looking around at the statue of Mary, the Mother of God holding her son. "I'm sure you made mistakes in your day too," she mused.

Her heart overflowing, she smiled at her daughter and son's glowing faces. A corner of her heart was sad that Raphael hadn't been there to be part of it the ceremony. She glanced at Imelda who was dabbing at her eyes. She wondered if she was thinking the same thing.

"Let us pray the Lord's Prayer for family and friends who are far from home and couldn't make it to out celebration today," Father Donnell said, glancing in her direction leading the prayer.

Rayan stood up feeling slightly lightheaded. She had the strangest sensation that in having the twins christened, she had in some way earned forgiveness for planning to have them aborted. I'm not a believer, she told herself. It's just all this pomp and ceremony, she thought wistfully.

Father Donnell locked eyes with Isaac as he followed Rayan out of the seat his penetrating look willing Isaac to come into the sacristy and sign his name as father of the twins on the baptismal certificate.

That would make it official and really make Rayan's day, he thought.

Chapter Sixty-Seven

"It's magic," BB breathed. Tumbling out of the car, he turned round and round, his eyes wide in wonderment.

Clapping her hands, his twin shrieked with delight at the plethora of multicoloured decorative lights that glowed and twinkled from the trees and shrubbery in the grounds of the Manse. "Look, BB, look. It's a *swing*!" Branna squealed, starting to run towards the orchard.

"Not in that dress, honey. Your Mommy Vivian would have my guts for garters," Bill laughed, scooping her up into his arms. "Come inside," he coaxed as she began to wriggle free. "I have a very special present…"

"You have a special present just for *me*, Pappy Bill?"

"For your brother too," Bill smiled.

Inside, a festoon of streamers and halogen filled balloon decorated with pictures of the twins as infants and toddlers danced from the ceiling of the sunroom. In the centre of a large oval table stood an exquisitely decorated christening cake in pink and blue in the shape of twin babies.

"Thank you, Maddie, everything looks…amazing," Rayan said with a catch in her voice as she looked at the finger buffet specially prepared by the chef.

"The photographer from the paper is outside. He followed us home from the church hoping for some family shots," Imelda said.

"Son of a bitch," Bill bellowed, starting for the door.

"Maybe if he gets some decent shots, his editor will be kind in his write-up," Isaac said nonchalantly reaching out to take a glass of champagne from the drinks table.

His arm jerked as Granny Norah put it firmly back on the table. "Don't even think about it," she hissed. "Didn't your mother teach you anything? The first drink is a toast to wet the babies' heads."

Isaac stuck his shaking hands in his pockets. "They're not babies. They are three years old and even Father Donnell says OK to wet the bab—twins' heads," Isaac lamented.

Imelda looked across the room at her mother bending Isaac's ear. She wondered what Raphael was doing right now. She went into the kitchen and glanced at the clock that Rayan kept on Australian time. It was coming up to midnight in Perth. She hadn't heard from him in a while. She wasn't even sure if he was still in Australia.

She drew a deep breath and plastered a smile on her face as the photographer approached. "Donegal hasn't seen a christening like this before," he commented with a smile. "American style, would you say? Or, maybe it's Aussie fashion," he probed. Imelda smiled a noncommittal smile.

She watched him take a picture of Bill and BB, both wearing their Stetsons leading big placid Buddy around the kitchen as if he was a small pony.

"Yer man, the photographer, fishing with a long line," Mac Lochlainn said coming to stand beside her. "Ah hope ye told him nothing if ye did it will likely be front page news in next Friday's paper," he scowled putting a bottle of Guinness to his head and drinking deeply.

Imelda realised Mac was quite drunk. That startled her because for all his faults, Mac wasn't a boozer. He likes a drink but he wasn't one for coming home to his wife roaring drunk, she mused. She made a mental note to make sure he got home safely.

"How's the young fella?" Mac said now sitting down heavily on the small sofa in the kitchen.

"Raphael? I haven't heard from him in a while." What a shock that had been to find out her son was a member of the Provisional IRA. It made her sick every time something came on the news about it. "How's old Manus?"

"The oul bastard not dead yet, they have no place in hell's fire hot enough for him yet. He's still calling the shots," Mac said.

"I never really got to thank you properly for…saving Raphael…that day," Rayan said in a low voice giving him an indebted smile.

Mac shifted in his seat. "You've nothin' to thank me for, Imelda. It's that woman over there, your mother Norah, you should be thanking. If it hadn't been for her you'd have a grave to visit—if you could have found out what bog hole they'd buried his body in. Aye, it's her not me that needs thanking," Mac slurred.

Startled, Imelda turned to stare at him. "What do you mean?" She gave a brittle laugh. "Mac O Lochlainn, you know my mother. She had no time for my boys—never had. Oh, I know she has Isaac living with her now but that is only because she's afraid to end up in the one of those support living places they sent her to get over what happened. If my mother did something for one of my boys, it'll be the first time," she said contemptuously.

Mac looked to where Norah had Walter Aimes cornered between the buffet table and the dresser. Drunk as he was, his memory flashed back to the day the gang of armed and masked IRA men—his own comrades at one time—had jumped the boundary wall around Norah's house and put a gun to Raphael's head.

Norah, like a lioness protecting her cub, had pushed Raphael behind her. One of the men raised his handgun and ordered her to stand aside. "We're here for the fuckin' tout."

"Is that you behind that mask, young Laverty?" Norah had demanded to know. Before Mac could stop her, she had reached out and whipped the black balaclava with the cut-out eyes from his head. "It is you! Don't you dare come into my house!"

Shocked at his identity being revealed, the man shrank back. Then, recovering himself, he'd bellowed, "You've just signed your own death warrant, you interfering old bag."

As if in slow motion Mac saw in his mind's eye, the young paramilitary point the gun at Norah's head.

Mac's blood chilled remembering the sound of the click of the safety catch being released; the trigger finger moving into position. Then, the blood spurting from Norah as he pistol whipped her about the head. "You're not worth fuckin' wasting a bullet on," he'd bellowed, standing over her.

Mac jerked spilling his drink. "Did ye never wonder how Norah got that concussion that put her in Letterkenny Hospital?" Mac heard himself ask Imelda "She warned me—said what happened that day wasn't to be *never mentioned again*," Mac blurted out.

Imelda snorted. "She fell and hit her head on the radiator. At least that's what she told the doctors." Imelda looked at him quizzically. "Do you know something different? Did somebody break in and attack her? Whatever happened, it did her the world of good. She's a changed woman, almost. She has more time for the twins than I have," she admitted.

"Pay no heed to me rambling', Imelda," Mac said, attempting a smile. "It's time ah went home."

"Bill will take you," Imelda said.

Anxious to get away now, Mac wondered if Imelda would be so cordial if she knew it was him, big man Mac O Lochlainn, who had gotten her son involved in the IRA in the first place. He emptied his glass in one go. The drink was the only thing that dulled his memory, helped him sleep at night.

Young Laverty had been picked up by the Guards. And was lying in jail now. Mac shuddered. Oul Manus wasn't finished with the Wright family yet. One day, or night, Norah would be found dead, Mac was certain of it. No guns to use on her now, with the Good Friday Agreement in place in the North. But that wouldn't stop the oul dying bastard, he mused. Her sight was poor now. A speeding car could do the same job. He listened to the obituary notices every morning expecting to hear her name read out.

He stumbled to his feet. "Forget ah spoke. Arthur Guinness and John Powers have a lot to answer for loosening oul fools' tongues like mine." He looked around him. "Thank Rayan for me. It was a lovely christening. Raphael has a lot to thank Rayan for—and the rest o' you."

Concerned at his unsteady gait, Imelda made him sit down again. "Maddie is just about to cut the cake. Branna and BB are going to serve it to their guests…"

BB, his face wreathed in smiles beneath the cowboy hat, proffered a plate of cake. "A blue slice for you 'cos you're a boy and a pink slice for you, Granny 'Melda, 'cos you're a girl," he said triumphantly, handing them a wobbly paper plate each.

"Oh, thank you, darling," Imelda said.

"Pappy Bill says he want you, Granny 'Melda," he said an excited sparkle lighting up his eyes.

She looked to where Bill was standing with a big smile on his face. Imelda's heart lightened. "I must have done something right to have a man like Bill love me," she murmured under her breath.

"Maddie, charge everybody's glasses," Bill ordered. "Branna and BB, come to Pappy Bill. I have a wonderful surprise for you both."

Imelda smiled. Bill loved nothing more than have a roomful of people's full attention. "Isaac and Rayan—come, stand beside your children."

Rayan's heart fluttered as she wondered would Isaac come to stand beside her and publicly present himself as the twins' father.

"Good," Bill said. "We are all here. Drum roll, please," he called playfully. Reaching into his pocket, he withdrew two bunches of keys. "BB, this set is for you. Branna, these are for you," he said with a flourish handing each child a set of keys.

BB studied the keys. Branna jangled her set, a disappointed look on her face. "Is this *my* big surprise?" she said petulantly.

"Yes, this is your big surprise," Bill laughed swinging her up into his arms. Bending down again, he scooped BB up.

"Raise your glasses, you good folks, and drink a toast to the new owners of this fine old house," he said beaming from ear to ear. A stunned silence followed his announcement. And then a great buzz of voices and the clinking of glasses filled the room.

The photographer, who had been sitting unobtrusively at the kitchen table, reached for his camera and started snapping.

Branna, sensing something important had just happened, threw her arms around Bill's neck and gave him a big kiss. "Thank you, Pappy Bill," she cooed.

"You're welcome, little lady," he said putting her down and drawing both her and BB to him. "You were firstborn, Branna, so you must always make sure you take care of your brother. That's what your christening present is for. It's what your mum Rayan always wanted—a safe place for BB…and for you. To grow up surrounded by family who love you."

Imelda felt her heart jolt up into her throat. Bill was giving the Manse away to Rayan and her twins! She snapped her mouth shut, struggling to keep her composure. He hadn't discussed it with her! The Manse had been her and Isaac and Raphael's home. It was never theirs officially; of course, it had always belonged to Bill although she didn't know it then. But it had been *her twins' home* nevertheless. She gulped down her champagne. Bill's announcement—which he had not made her privy to—effectively made her boys, Isaac and Raphael, homeless!

Raphael was unlikely to return any time soon to Ireland. He didn't need a home. Isaac needed a home. Was he meant to live with her bloody mother Norah for the rest of his days?

Vivian tiptoed down the creaking stairs and into the kitchen. "Branna is finally asleep. I read her a story and brushed out her hair but she refused to take off the dress."

Rayan stretched out her hands. "Her dress and all her stuff were truly exquisite. I'm sorry Father Donnell didn't let you be a sponsor—"

Vivian shrugged. "He let Sue be the godmother…if he hadn't; I'd definitely would have had something to say to both him and the bishop."

"How was BB after all the cake and juices?" Rayan asked, changing the subject.

"Fell asleep as soon as his head hit the pillow—still wearing the cowboy hat," Sue laughed.

"He looked like a little movie star in his linen suit," Rayan said.

A shadow passed over Sue's face. "Do you think I am—we are—babying him too much?"

"He didn't cry today," Vivian reminded her.

She touched Sue's hand. "Don't worry about his baby ways. He'll grow up soon enough. A bit of loving never hurt anybody. It's when you're not loved that the problems start."

A look passed between Vivian and Sue. "Did your mother phone?" Vivian asked tartly.

Rayan shook her head. "It's OK. All the family I need are right here beside me," she said softly.

The phone rang as Rayan closed the door behind her friends. For a moment, she considered letting it ring. Isaac had left right after Bill had announced that her twins were now the owners of the Manse—once they came of age. He hadn't looked happy at the news.

"Hello Rayan," Raphael's voice said as clear as if he was in the next room. "How did the day go? Did old Father Donnell keep you long?"

"It was a wonderful, wonderful day. I missed you not being here," she said simply.

"Yeah, I missed being there too. But Kate and I are making our own life here. Maybe someday, we'll be back to Donegal," he said wistfully. "Isaac phoned—filled me in about the christening—and the house."

Rayan felt a tug at her heart remembering how he loved walking the Minors Trail on Muckish Mountain. Rayan told him about the letter from Children's Services.

"You could apply for their passports—maybe come back…"

"They are settled here now. Soon they'll be going to school. I have to think what's best for them now." She gulped. "Did Isaac tell you BB is officially called Bradley Isaac Raphael—he's named for both of you?"

"He forgot to tell me that," Raphael said, a pleased note in his voice. There was a pause. "Did you let them have your surname or ours?"

"I gave them my—my father's surname."

This came as a surprise to Raphael. "But I thought…you didn't want anything to do with—"

"I know. But I'm trying to let go of…my past. BB will carry on my family name. Someday he may want to know where he came from." She said after a pause, "Have you heard from Nathanial?"

"The last I hear he was working on his own home farm in the outback. You haven't heard from him, then?"

"Not for a while."

There was a pause on the line and for a moment Rayan thought they had been cut off. "Nathanial loves you, Rayan. You know that, don't you? You should have had his kids," Raphael said quietly. "You could have worked out your problems."

"Maybe I should. But then I wouldn't have BB and Branna," she said surprising herself.

There was another silence. "Have you seen Mac O Lochlainn lately?"

"He came into the party after the christening. He was very drunk."

Raphael frowned. "That's not like him. He'll lose his licence."

"I have to go now, Raff. I think I hear BB crying in his sleep," Rayan said, feeling her throat tighten with tears. She didn't want Raphael to guess how lonely she was or how much she missed him. "Keep in touch," she whispered, putting down the phone.

Feeling restless, she went outside. A light spring frost glittered on the lights strung between the trees in the orchard. She sat down on the swing, letting its gentle movement calm her.

A movement on the road caught her eye—two men walking towards the gate. Retracing her steps towards the kitchen door, remembering Raphael's warning when she had first come to live in the isolated Manse about keeping the lights dim and keeping her doors and windows locked at night she made for the kitchen door.

"It's me and Father Donnell," Isaac's voice called out.

Rayan hesitated. The old priest hadn't come for something to eat after the christening. Why was he here now, and with Isaac?

"Isaac has something to give you," the old priest said, stopping just short of the door.

Rayan swung her eyes in Isaac's direction. He'd had a few glasses of champagne but she knew that was enough to break his sobriety and his 12-step recovery programme. She hoped he didn't want to stay the night.

"This is for you," he said soberly. "It's copies of the twins' baptismal certificates." Wordlessly, Rayan withdrew the two single sheets of paper from the envelope. She stared at the small rectangular space that said 'father's name'.

She didn't realise she was crying until Father Donnell pushed a snow-white linen square into her hands.

"I think I knew all along they were mine. I just didn't have the sense to admit it," Isaac said.

"Go on, man, you have something else to ask her," the old priest prompted.

Isaac looked away from Rayan towards the illuminated orchard. "I'm finished with banking. Would my children," he said stumbling over the words, "let me put in a few tunnels in the orchard…start a garden centre?"

"Thank you for…doing this," Rayan said. "It means a lot to me that the twins know who their father is." She swung the door wide. "Come in. This will always be your home, Isaac. But only when you are sober." She hesitated. "Perhaps, in time," she said falteringly… "The idea of starting a gardening business could be considered."

Freshening up her glass of champagne after Isaac and Father Donnell left, Rayan open the kitchen drawer and took the photograph she kept of Nathanial. "Here's to you, Nat," she said, raising her glass. "Who knows; one day I might open the door and you'll be standing there."

The End